RICHMOND

NOW YOU!

CB135022

1 Introduction

2 Methodology

3 Teaching notes

4 Answer keys and Transcripts

Richmond

TEACHER'S BOOK 4

WELCOME TO NOW YOU!

Richmond NOW YOU! is a four-level English Secondary course which takes students from A1 to B1+ of the Common European Framework. The course features an eclectic approach which takes the best of the latest developments in ELT teaching methodology and carefully interweaves them within a communicative framework.

Learning threads

The course makes use of these **learning threads** to help streamline the learning and teaching experience and **increase learning efficiency** while also **motivating the students** to connect with the learning process.

Learner-centred approach

Personalisation exercises throughout the course make every student the focus of their own learning journey and help to consolidate language and skills. **Learning to learn tools** provide students with tips and tricks for more effective learning.

Vloggers

In every level of the course the student is accompanied by three vloggers who introduce the context of each unit in their **Vlogs**. The vloggers also narrate the **Culture videos**, creating a cultural link between the unit content and the wider world.

Flipped Learning

There are many tools at the teacher's disposal for implementing Flipped Learning with **NOW YOU!**, such as the fun **Grammar animations** which accompany every grammar point and table. The **Vlogs** with their worksheets also present a great opportunity for introducing the lesson content outside of the classroom.

Project-based Learning

Multi-student **Project tasks** are staged across two units and brought together in a **Final task**. Students recap on the tasks, prepare for a presentation and focus on **21st century skills**. Students are also asked to think carefully about the format of the project and to evaluate themselves and their peers, encouraging **Collaborative Learning**.

Attention to values

Reading content is further explored with speaking tasks, in which students focus on and discuss a specific **Core value**.

Mediation

Project tasks throughout the book and information gap **Pairwork** activities for each unit presented at the end of the book combine unit content with practice of **CEFR mediation** activities and strategies.

External exam preparation

The **Review** pages at the end of each book combine course content with **external exam practice questions**, ensuring students are familiar with the format and can apply their knowledge in an exam context.

For the Student

Student's Book

The **NOW YOU! Student's Book** is a dynamic, attractive course book with clear lesson objectives, a wide variety of interesting material for students to engage with and a strong focus on developing skills to help students become confident and competent users of English and well-rounded 21st century citizens. The **Student's Book** includes **integrated skills** practice, **Learning to learn** tools, **Core values, Projects, external exam practice Unit reviews,** information-gap **Pairwork activities,** a **Grammar reference** and **Wordlists**.

Workbook

The **NOW YOU! Workbook** is a **full-colour** resource with more engaging material to complement the **Student's Book**, handy **guided notes pages** for the Writing lessons and Projects, **extra practice for the Grammar reference and Wordlists** and a **Reflect on your learning section** to encourage learner autonomy. Access to **extra interactive practice** based on real-world situations is also available with the **Workbook**.

Workbook Audio

LISTEN ON Spotify

Also available to listen to and download on the **Richmond***Learning***Platform**.

All videos and worksheets available on the **Richmond***Learning***Platform**

For the Teacher

Teacher's Book

The **Teacher's Book** is your comprehensive guide to teaching **NOW YOU!** and the key methodologies on which the course is based. For each unit of the **Student's Book** there is an **overview** for fast lesson planning, plus complete **teaching notes**, audio **transcripts** and **answer keys** for the student's material.

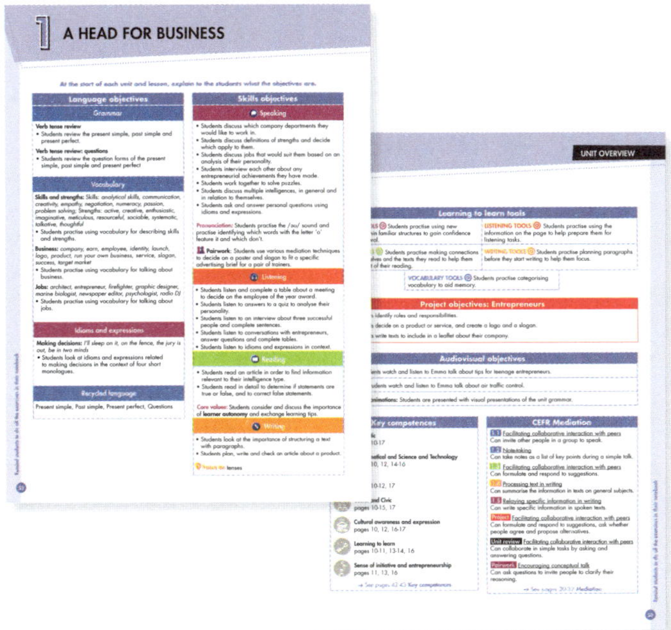

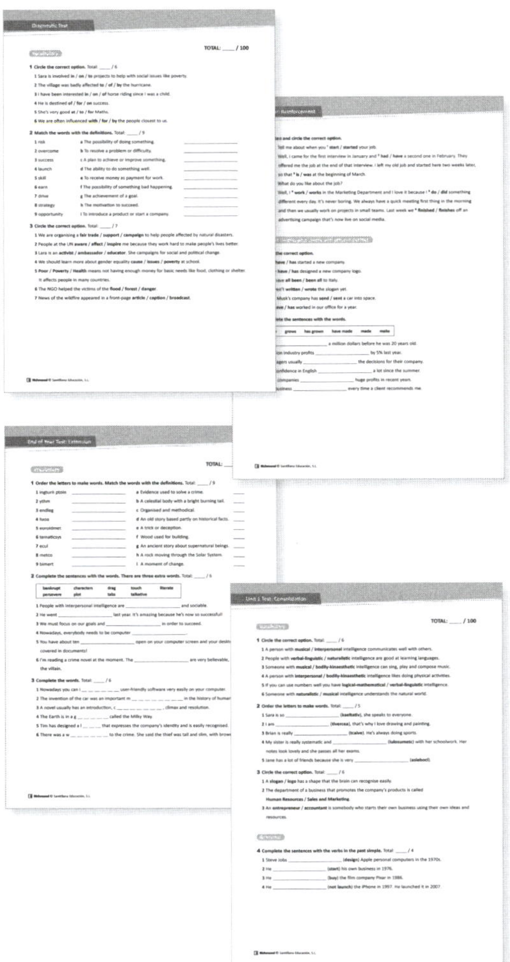

Teacher's Resources

Available on the Richmond*Learning*Platform

A wide range of ready-to-print and editable material is provided to complement and enhance your teaching.

- **Vocabulary worksheets** at 3 levels of difficulty
- **Grammar worksheets** at 3 levels of difficulty
- **Diagnostic**, **Unit**, **End-of-term** and **End-of-year tests** at 2 levels of difficulty
- **Vlog Flipped Learning worksheets**
- **Culture video worksheets**
- **Essential maps** for each unit

Teacher's Audio

Available on the Richmond*Learning*Platform

All audio for listening exercises used in the **Student's Book**, **Workbook** and **Teacher's Resources** is available to listen to and download.

All videos and worksheets available on the Richmond*Learning*Platform

NOW YOU! DIGITAL

Student's i-book

The **NOW YOU! Student's i-book** is an online multi-device version of the **Student's Book** to enable students to access the course material at home. It includes:

- All **videos**
- All **Student's Book audio**

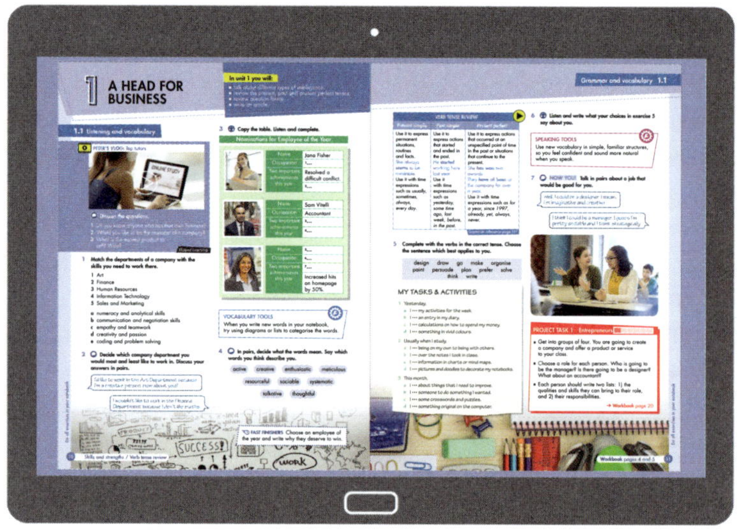

Videos

Three different types of videos (see **Video material** pages 18-19) help teenagers engage with the language in a way that is relevant to their lives outside the classroom.

Vlogs

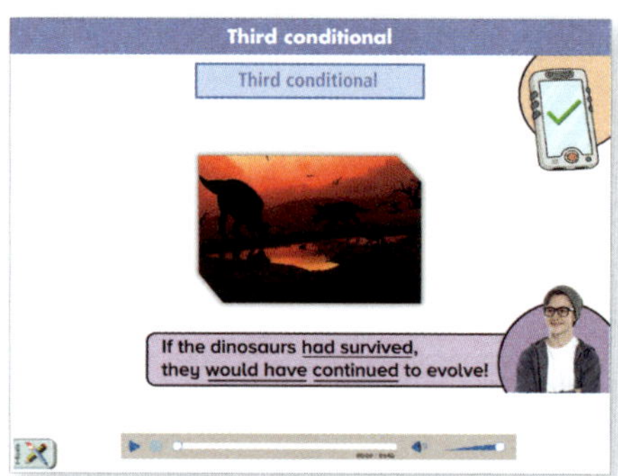

Grammar animations

Culture videos

Student's Interactive Practice

There is also additional interactive practice to consolidate the course content and to develop the concept of English for life. The activities are contextualised in real-world situations. This helps to make the acquisition of language more meaningful for the students.

The **Student's Interactive Practice** includes learning progress and it is ideal for fast finishers or for homework.

Also available to purchase
A fully interactive, **digital version of the Student's Book and Workbook** which provides a complete tracking of the students' progress.

Free App

RICHMOND NOW YOU!

Offline and online multi-device versions available

Teacher's i-solutions

The **NOW YOU! Teacher's i-solutions** for the classroom include the **Teacher's i-book**, as well as all the resources for the print version of the **Teacher's Book**.

In the **Teacher's i-book** every lesson in the course is presented in the form of a **Learning path**, a step-by step lesson plan that works as a quick lesson guide where the teaching sequence is clear at a glance. All the teaching and learning materials in the course are included and the **resources are colour-coded** to identify what is **core material** and what is **optional**. Teachers can therefore choose activities according to the time available and **tips** for all the material are available **at the click of a button**.

Richmond Test Manager

An online interactive tool to create and assign tests.

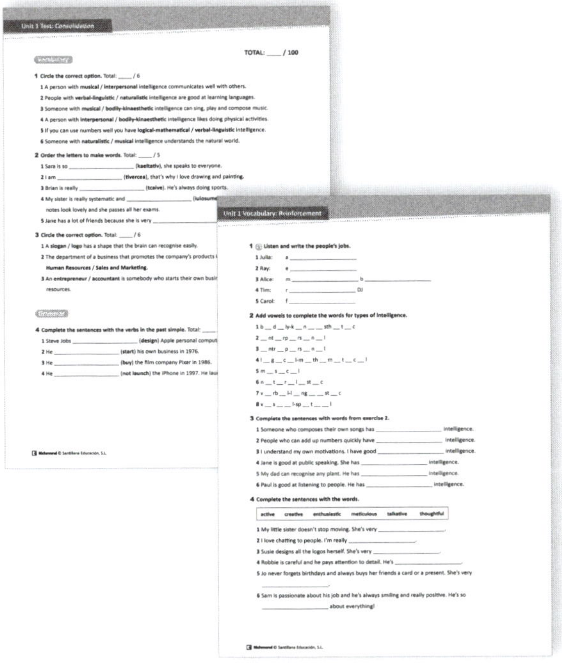

Downloadable material

Teacher's Resources available:

- **Vocabulary worksheets** at 3 levels of difficulty **(PDF and Word format)**
- **Grammar worksheets** at 3 levels of difficulty **(PDF and Word format)**
- **Diagnostic**, **Unit**, **End-of-term** and **End-of-year tests** at 2 levels of difficulty **(PDF and Word format)**
- **Vlog Flipped Learning worksheets**
- **Culture video worksheets**
- **Essential maps**

All videos and worksheets available on the **Richmond** *Learning* **Platform**

UNIT WALKTHROUGH

LESSON 1 Grammar, Vocabulary and Listening

1 The **unit menu** outlines the key learning aims of each unit. The four points outline the general communication goal, the central grammar points and the writing task genre. This provides both teacher and student with a clear learning map for the unit.

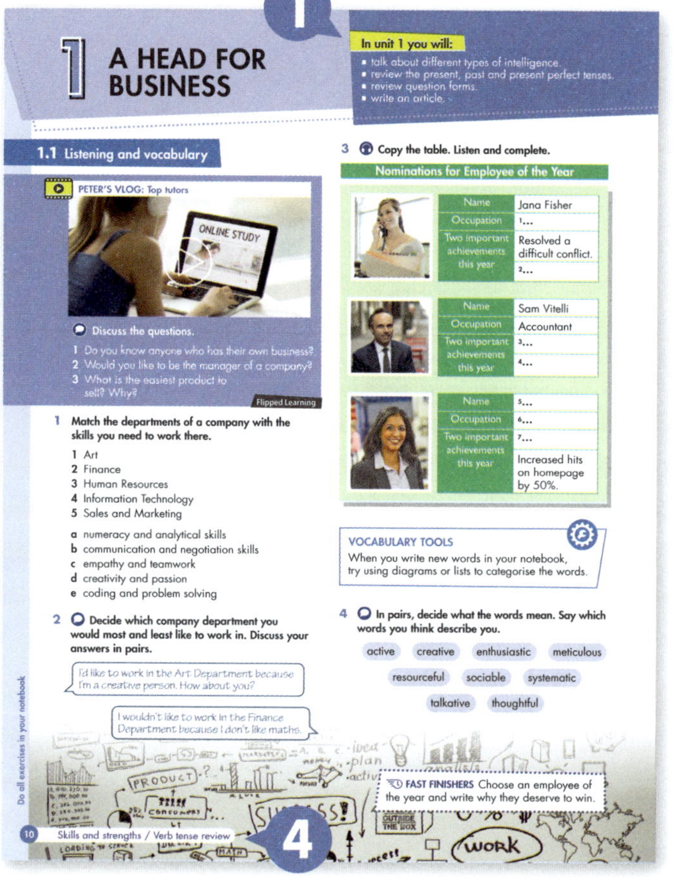

1 A HEAD FOR BUSINESS

In unit 1 you will:
- talk about different types of intelligence.
- review the present, past and present perfect tenses.
- review question forms.
- write an article.

1.1 Listening and vocabulary

PETER'S VLOG: Top tutors

Discuss the questions.
1 Do you know anyone who has their own business?
2 Would you like to be the manager of a company?
3 What is the easiest product to sell? Why?

Flipped Learning

1 **Match the departments of a company with the skills you need to work there.**
1 Art
2 Finance
3 Human Resources
4 Information Technology
5 Sales and Marketing

a numeracy and analytical skills
b communication and negotiation skills
c empathy and teamwork
d creativity and passion
e coding and problem solving

2 **Decide which company department you would most and least like to work in. Discuss your answers in pairs.**

I'd like to work in the Art Department because I'm a creative person. How about you?

I wouldn't like to work in the Finance Department because I don't like maths.

3 **Copy the table. Listen and complete.**

Nominations for Employee of the Year

Name	Jana Fisher
Occupation	1...
Two important achievements this year	Resolved a difficult conflict. 2...
Name	Sam Vitelli
Occupation	Accountant
Two important achievements this year	3... 4...
Name	5...
Occupation	6...
Two important achievements this year	7... Increased hits on homepage by 50%.

VOCABULARY TOOLS
When you write new words in your notebook, try using diagrams or lists to categorise the words.

4 **In pairs, decide what the words mean. Say which words you think describe you.**

active creative enthusiastic meticulous resourceful sociable systematic talkative thoughtful

FAST FINISHERS Choose an employee of the year and write why they deserve to win.

Do all exercises in your notebook

10 Skills and strengths / Verb tense review

2 The **lesson focus** tags highlight the main skills focus of each page.

Lessons 1 and 2 provide **grammar**, **vocabulary** and **listening** input. Speaking exercises throughout give students opportunities to practise the key grammar points and vocabulary sets.

Lesson 3 provides **reading** input with a focus on deepening the students' understanding of the unit language in an authentic context.

Lesson 4 guides **writing** output, putting the students' knowledge to practical use.

Lesson 5 is a **culture and communication** page where students are encouraged to recognise their place in global culture and interact with the world around them.

3 Three **vloggers** provide an engaging context for the unit content.
The optional **Flipped Learning** tasks encourage students to take control of their learning by beginning the learning process outside of the classroom. For information about Flipped Learning, see pages 20-23.

These **Vlogs** provide exposure to the unit language aims and can be re-watched in order to capitalise on the content, but students can answer the discussion questions and complete the unit without having watched them.

LESSON 1 Grammar, Vocabulary and Listening

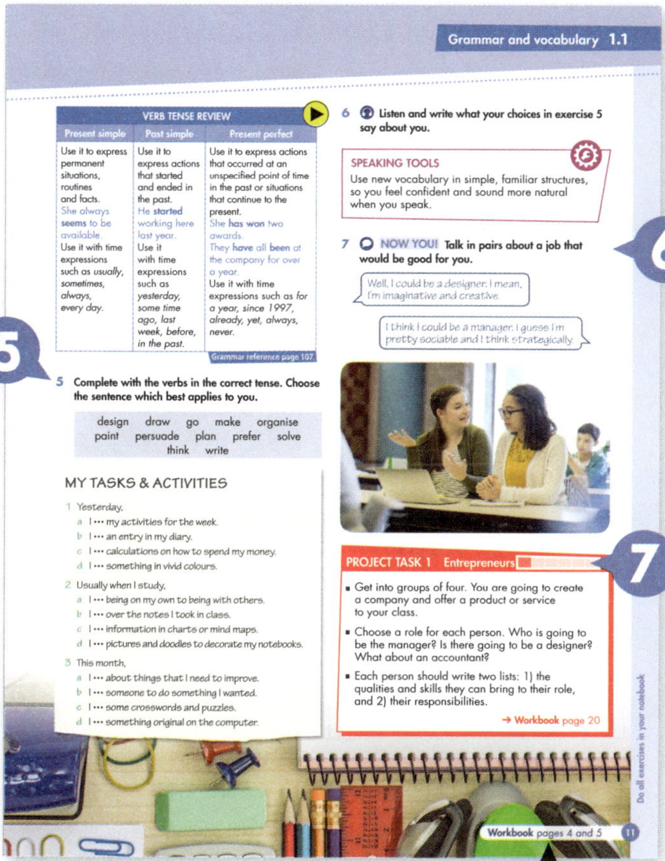

Grammar and vocabulary 1.1

VERB TENSE REVIEW		
Present simple	Past simple	Present perfect
Use it to express permanent situations, routines and facts. *She always seems to be available.* Use it with time expressions such as *usually, sometimes, always, every day.*	Use it to express actions that started and ended in the past. *He started working here last year.* Use it with time expressions such as *yesterday, some time ago, last week, before, in the past.*	Use it to express actions that occurred at an unspecified point of time in the past or situations that continue to the present. *She has won two awards. They have all been at the company for over a year.* Use it with time expressions such as *for a year, since 1997, already, yet, always, never.*

Grammar reference page 107

5 Complete with the verbs in the correct tense. Choose the sentence which best applies to you.

design draw go make organise paint persuade plan prefer solve think write

MY TASKS & ACTIVITIES

1 Yesterday,
a I ••• my activities for the week.
b I ••• an entry in my diary.
c I ••• calculations on how to spend my money.
d I ••• something in vivid colours.

2 Usually when I study,
a I ••• being on my own to being with others.
b I ••• over the notes I took in class.
c I ••• information in charts or mind maps.
d I ••• pictures and doodles to decorate my notebooks.

3 This month,
a I ••• about things that I need to improve.
b I ••• someone to do something I wanted.
c I ••• some crosswords and puzzles.
d I ••• something original on the computer.

6 Listen and write what your choices in exercise 5 say about you.

SPEAKING TOOLS
Use new vocabulary in simple, familiar structures, so you feel confident and sound more natural when you speak.

7 NOW YOU! Talk in pairs about a job that would be good for you.

Well, I could be a designer. I mean, I'm imaginative and creative.

I think I could be a manager. I guess I'm pretty sociable and I think strategically.

PROJECT TASK 1 Entrepreneurs

- Get into groups of four. You are going to create a company and offer a product or service to your class.
- Choose a role for each person. Who is going to be the manager? Is there going to be a designer? What about an accountant?
- Each person should write two lists: 1) the qualities and skills they can bring to their role, and 2) their responsibilities.

→ Workbook page 20

Do all exercises in your notebook

Workbook pages 4 and 5 11

6 The NOW YOU! exercises at the end of the lesson challenge students to put their knowledge to practical use in the form of personalised speaking or writing exercises.

7 Project tasks develop and build towards a final presentation over two units. These tasks draw on the content of the lesson and promote collaborative work. The bar helps students know how many tasks they have completed and have left to complete the project.

In unit 9 students are given Review tasks which encourage them to reflect on what they have learnt from units 1 to 9 and develop revision strategies.

8 At the end of each lesson students are directed to their **Workbook** for further practice of the unit content.

4 The lesson objective clarifies the grammar and vocabulary goals of each lesson. This provides an at-a-glance summary of the lesson for both the teacher and student.

5 The exercises give students a variety of ways to practise what they are learning.

Unit walkthrough

LESSON 2 Grammar, Vocabulary and Listening

1. Through the unit students are asked to complete a variety of exercises that build on growing knowledge of the unit aims. Special effort has been made to ensure that all the content is visually appealing to students.

2. Each grammar lesson contains a **Grammar table** that shows key structures. These tables show clear models which can be used as a quick reference to complete the accompanying exercises.

   The connected **Grammar reference** page at the back of the book includes more detailed explanations of both form and use.

1.2 Grammar and listening

1 Listen and make notes about why the people are famous. Compare your answers in pairs.

2 Complete the questions with the verb in the correct tense. Listen again and check. Then answer the questions.

1 What ··· Bill Gates ··· (**do**) now?
2 How long ··· he ··· (**have**) the charity?
3 How ··· Chanel's designs ··· (**change**) fashion?
4 What ··· the Nike slogan ··· (**represent**)?
5 ··· Wieden ··· (**create**) any other famous slogans?

VERB TENSE REVIEW: QUESTIONS	Present simple	Past simple	Present perfect
Yes/No questions	**Does** Gates own a company?	**Did** Chanel create the logo?	**Have** Wieden and his team **written** any other famous slogans?
Wh- questions	What **do** graphic designers do?	When **did** Chanel launch her company?	What **has** Gates **done** through his charity?

Grammar reference page 107

3 Complete the text with the correct form of the verbs.

be come earn get grow love make need realise see start work (x2) write

Adam: This week on *Bright Ideas* we're talking to Serena Tisdale. Serena's blog [1]··· her a millionaire at the age of 20. Serena, what's your secret?

Serena: Well, I [2]··· writing since I [3]··· a teenager. At school, I [4]··· for the school newsletter and then I [5]··· a job at a local newspaper. I think you [6]··· to be passionate about what you do.

Adam: And how did you [7]··· up with the idea of a blog?

Serena: I [8]··· that fewer and fewer people were reading printed newspapers, so I [9]··· a market for quality online news. When I [10]··· the blog, it was just me. Since then, the company [11]··· to over 30 employees.

Adam: It seems like you [12]··· really hard to get where you are.

Serena: You won't be successful if you don't [13]··· for it!

Adam: Well, you certainly [14]··· your success!

FAST FINISHERS Write about what type of job you would like to do in the future.

Do all exercises in your notebook

12 Business / Verb tense review: questions

3. The **Grammar animations** present the grammar in an appealing visual format to help to engage the students and consolidate their understanding of the grammatical structures.
   These animations also provide opportunities for **Flipped Learning**.

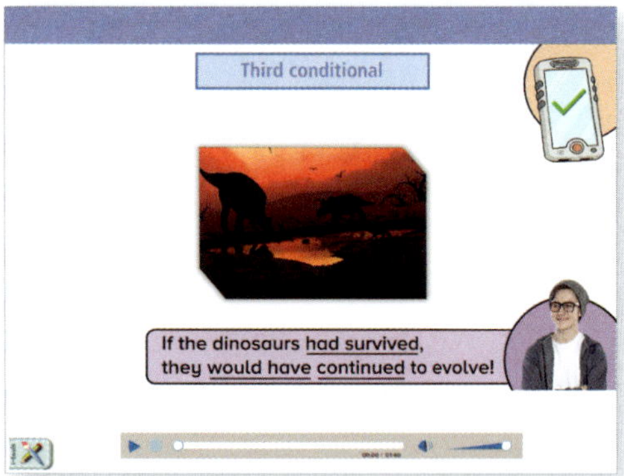

4. There is a **Fast finishers** exercise in lessons 1, 2, 3 and 5 to keep stronger students challenged and engaged if they finish the other exercises quickly. These are short, personalised writing exercises that students can complete alone and could keep as part of a language diary.

LESSON 2 Grammar, Vocabulary and Listening

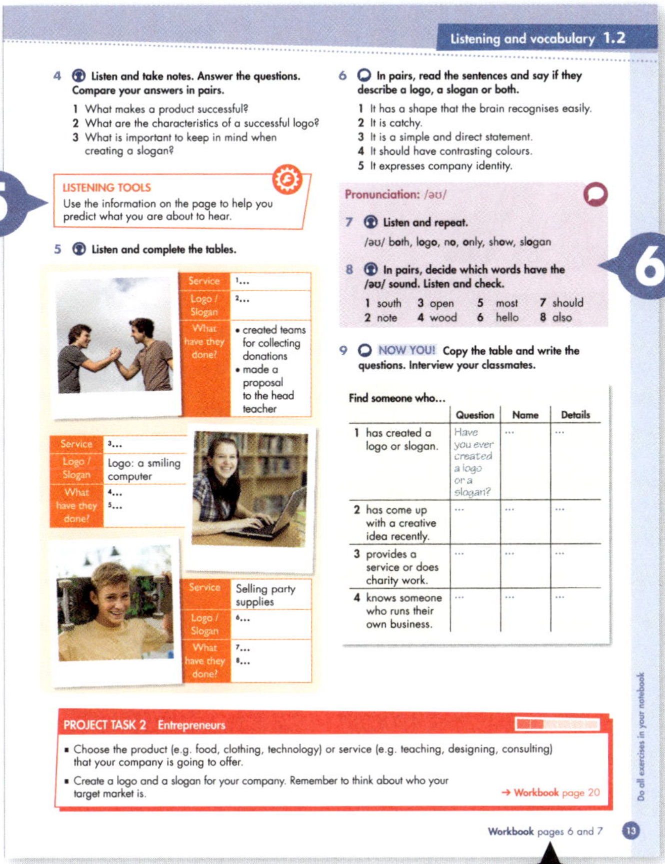
Listening and vocabulary 1.2

4 Listen and take notes. Answer the questions. Compare your answers in pairs.
1 What makes a product successful?
2 What are the characteristics of a successful logo?
3 What is important to keep in mind when creating a slogan?

LISTENING TOOLS
Use the information on the page to help you predict what you are about to hear.

5 Listen and complete the tables.

Service	1…
Logo / Slogan	2…
What have they done?	• created teams for collecting donations • made a proposal to the head teacher

Service	3…
Logo / Slogan	Logo: a smiling computer
What have they done?	4… 5…

Service	Selling party supplies
Logo / Slogan	6…
What have they done?	7… 8…

6 In pairs, read the sentences and say if they describe a logo, a slogan or both.
1 It has a shape that the brain recognises easily.
2 It is catchy.
3 It is a simple and direct statement.
4 It should have contrasting colours.
5 It expresses company identity.

Pronunciation: /əʊ/
7 Listen and repeat.
/əʊ/ both, logo, no, only, show, slogan
8 In pairs, decide which words have the /əʊ/ sound. Listen and check.
1 south 3 open 5 most 7 should
2 note 4 wood 6 hello 8 also

9 NOW YOU! Copy the table and write the questions. Interview your classmates.

Find someone who…

	Question	Name	Details
1 has created a logo or slogan.	Have you ever created a logo or a slogan?	…	…
2 has come up with a creative idea recently.	…	…	…
3 provides a service or does charity work.	…	…	…
4 knows someone who runs their own business.	…	…	…

PROJECT TASK 2 Entrepreneurs
• Choose the product (e.g. food, clothing, technology) or service (e.g. teaching, designing, consulting) that your company is going to offer.
• Create a logo and a slogan for your company. Remember to think about who your target market is.
→ Workbook page 20

Do all exercises in your notebook

Workbook pages 6 and 7 13

5 There is a **Learning to learn tool** for each skill across the unit which gives students strategies to help develop their listening, speaking, reading and writing skills, as well their ability to acquire, retain and use vocabulary.
The colour coding helps students identify the skills at a glance:

- Listening tools
- Reading tools
- Speaking tools
- Writing tools
- Vocabulary tools

6 There is a **pronunciation** exercise in each unit to develop students' ability to recognise and produce the different features of spoken English.

7

The **Teacher's Resources** provide students with worksheets for further practice of both **vocabulary** and **grammar** at their level — ideal for mixed-ability classes. Each worksheet comes at three levels of difficulty:

- Reinforcement — lower level
- Consolidation — course level
- Extension — higher level

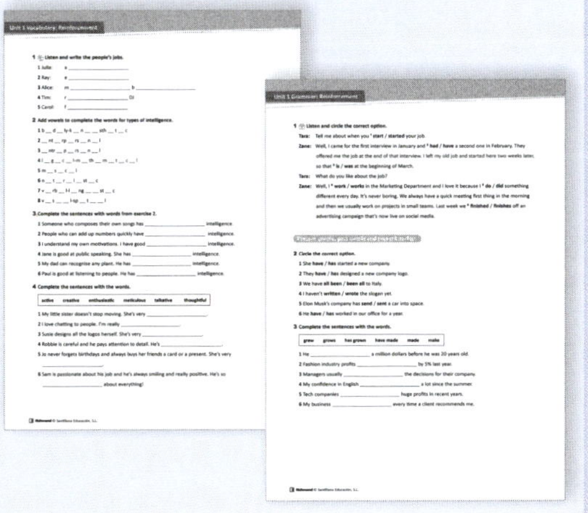

7 Further practice of the lesson content can be found in the **Workbook.**

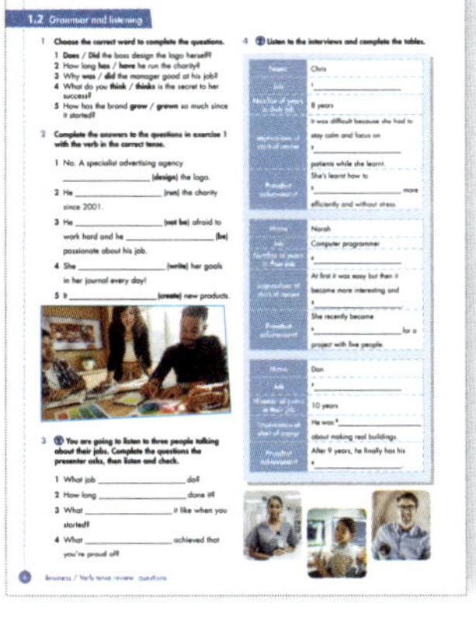

Unit walkthrough

LESSON 3 Reading

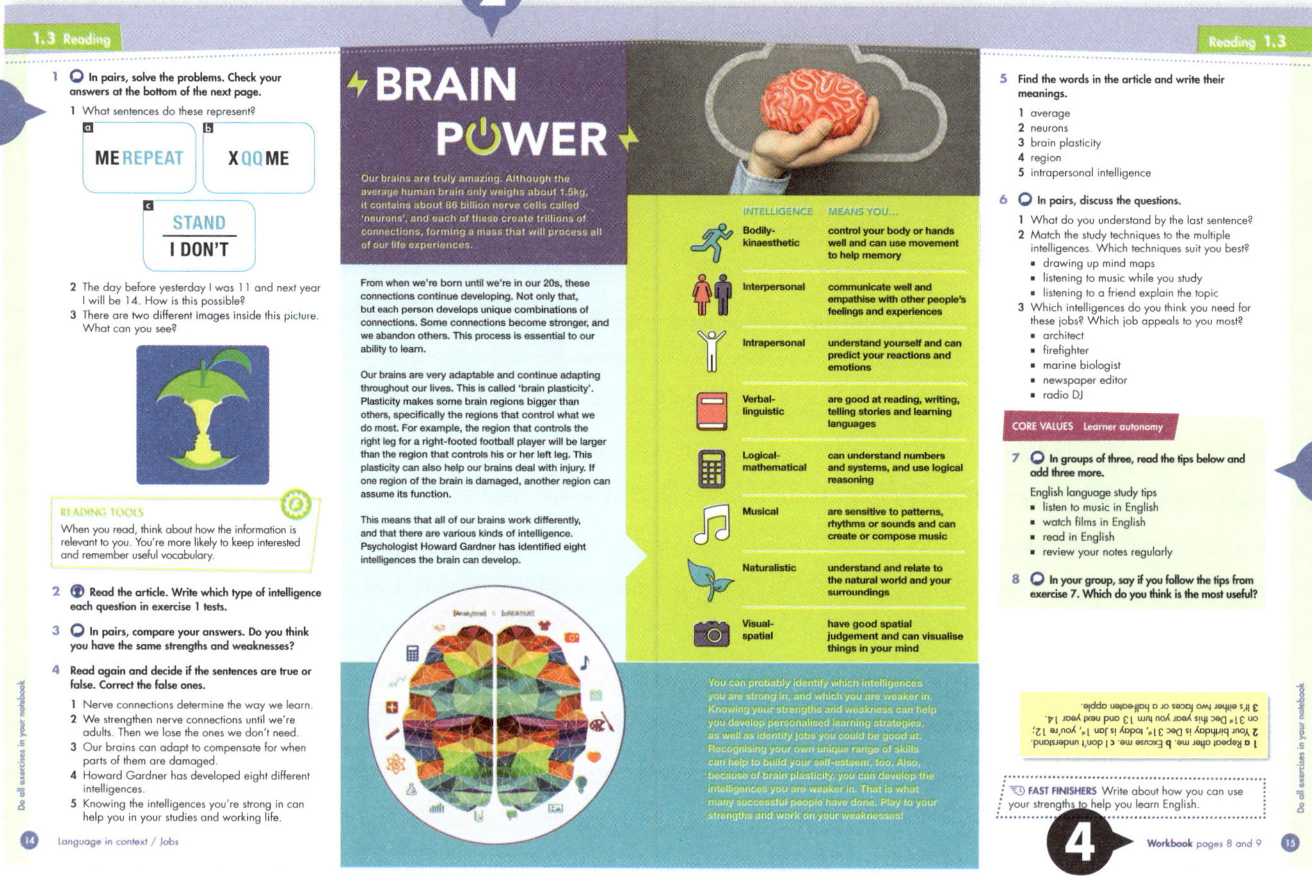

1.3 Reading

1 In pairs, solve the problems. Check your answers at the bottom of the next page.

1 What sentences do these represent?

a ME REPEAT b X QQ ME c STAND / I DON'T

2 The day before yesterday I was 11 and next year I will be 14. How is this possible?

3 There are two different images inside this picture. What can you see?

READING TOOLS
When you read, think about how the information is relevant to you. You're more likely to keep interested and remember useful vocabulary.

2 Read the article. Write which type of intelligence each question in exercise 1 tests.

3 In pairs, compare your answers. Do you think you have the same strengths and weaknesses?

4 Read again and decide if the sentences are true or false. Correct the false ones.

1 Nerve connections determine the way we learn.
2 We strengthen nerve connections until we're adults. Then we lose the ones we don't need.
3 Our brains can adapt to compensate for when parts of them are damaged.
4 Howard Gardner has developed eight different intelligences.
5 Knowing the intelligences you're strong in can help you in your studies and working life.

14 Language in context / Jobs

BRAIN POWER

Our brains are truly amazing. Although the average human brain only weighs about 1.5kg, it contains about 86 billion nerve cells called 'neurons', and each of these create trillions of connections, forming a mass that will process all of our life experiences.

From when we're born until we're in our 20s, these connections continue developing. Not only that, but each person develops unique combinations of connections. Some connections become stronger, and we abandon others. This process is essential to our ability to learn.

Our brains are very adaptable and continue adapting throughout our lives. This is called 'brain plasticity'. Plasticity makes some brain regions bigger than others, specifically the regions that control what we do most. For example, the region that controls the right leg for a right-footed football player will be larger than the region that controls his or her left leg. This plasticity can also help our brains deal with injury. If one region of the brain is damaged, another region can assume its function.

This means that all of our brains work differently, and that there are various kinds of intelligence. Psychologist Howard Gardner has identified eight intelligences the brain can develop.

INTELLIGENCE	MEANS YOU...
Bodily-kinaesthetic	control your body or hands well and can use movement to help memory
Interpersonal	communicate well and empathise with other people's feelings and experiences
Intrapersonal	understand yourself and can predict your reactions and emotions
Verbal-linguistic	are good at reading, writing, telling stories and learning languages
Logical-mathematical	can understand numbers and systems, and use logical reasoning
Musical	are sensitive to patterns, rhythms or sounds and can create or compose music
Naturalistic	understand and relate to the natural world and your surroundings
Visual-spatial	have good spatial judgement and can visualise things in your mind

You can probably identify which intelligences you are strong in, and which you are weaker in. Knowing your strengths and weakness can help you develop personalised learning strategies, as well as identify jobs you could be good at. Recognising your own unique range of skills can help to build your self-esteem, too. Also, because of brain plasticity, you can develop the intelligences you are weaker in. That is what many successful people have done. Play to your strengths and work on your weaknesses!

Reading 1.3

5 Find the words in the article and write their meanings.

1 average
2 neurons
3 brain plasticity
4 region
5 intrapersonal intelligence

6 In pairs, discuss the questions.

1 What do you understand by the last sentence?
2 Match the study techniques to the multiple intelligences. Which techniques suit you best?
- drawing up mind maps
- listening to music while you study
- listening to a friend explain the topic

3 Which intelligences do you think you need for these jobs? Which job appeals to you most?
- architect
- firefighter
- marine biologist
- newspaper editor
- radio DJ

CORE VALUES Learner autonomy

7 In groups of three, read the tips below and add three more.

English language study tips
- listen to music in English
- watch films in English
- read in English
- review your notes regularly

8 In your group, say if you follow the tips from exercise 7. Which do you think is the most useful?

1 a Repeat after me. b Excuse me. c I don't understand.
2 Your birthday is Dec 31st, today is Jan 1st, you're 12; on 31st Dec this year you turn 13 and next year 14.
3 It's either two faces or a half-eaten apple.

FAST FINISHERS Write about how you can use your strengths to help you learn English.

Workbook pages 8 and 9

15

1 The **reading** lesson contains exercises that guide students through the process of effective reading. They include pre-reading exercises, comprehension exercises and follow-up vocabulary and speaking exercises.

2 There are a range of **reading texts** that provide an accessible, authentic context and connect the content of the unit with the world outside the classroom.

3 The **Core values** section provides an opportunity for students to reflect on ideas and beliefs that are considered important in society and the effect these values have on how we behave. The emphasis is on understanding and respecting ourselves and others. This contextualisation of values helps to deepen the students' connection with the reading material and give a clear, communicative resolution to the lesson.

4 More reading practice can be found in the **Workbook**.

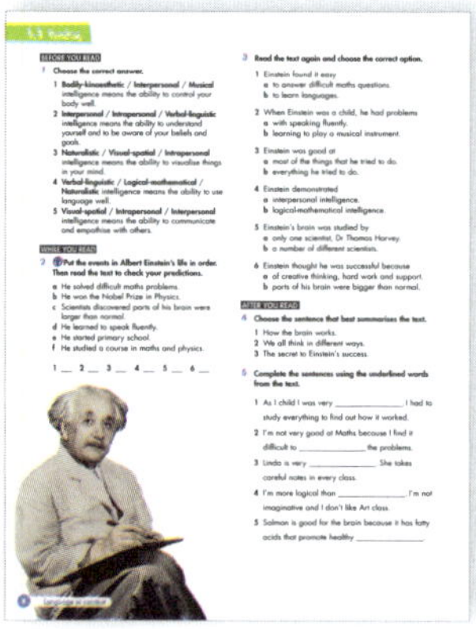

LESSON 4 Writing

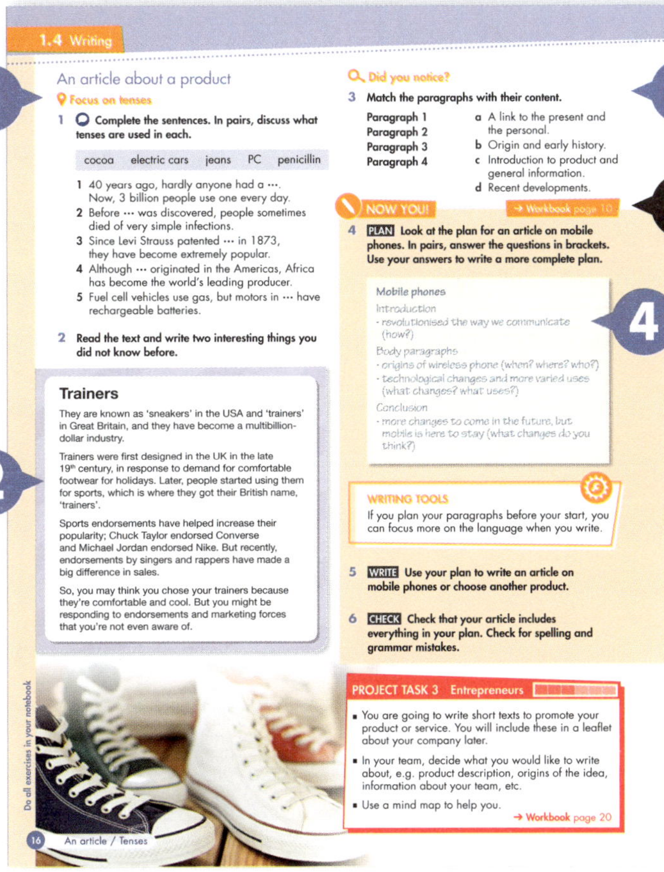
1.4 Writing

An article about a product

Focus on tenses

1 Complete the sentences. In pairs, discuss what tenses are used in each.

cocoa electric cars jeans PC penicillin

1 40 years ago, hardly anyone had a ⋯. Now, 3 billion people use one every day.
2 Before ⋯ was discovered, people sometimes died of very simple infections.
3 Since Levi Strauss patented ⋯ in 1873, they have become extremely popular.
4 Although ⋯ originated in the Americas, Africa has become the world's leading producer.
5 Fuel cell vehicles use gas, but motors in ⋯ have rechargeable batteries.

2 Read the text and write two interesting things you did not know before.

Trainers

They are known as 'sneakers' in the USA and 'trainers' in Great Britain, and they have become a multibillion-dollar industry.

Trainers were first designed in the UK in the late 19th century, in response to demand for comfortable footwear for holidays. Later, people started using them for sports, which is where they got their British name, 'trainers'.

Sports endorsements have helped increase their popularity; Chuck Taylor endorsed Converse and Michael Jordan endorsed Nike. But recently, endorsements by singers and rappers have made a big difference in sales.

So, you may think you chose your trainers because they're comfortable and cool. But you might be responding to endorsements and marketing forces that you're not even aware of.

Did you notice?

3 Match the paragraphs with their content.

Paragraph 1
Paragraph 2
Paragraph 3
Paragraph 4

a A link to the present and the personal.
b Origin and early history.
c Introduction to product and general information.
d Recent developments.

NOW YOU! → Workbook page 10

4 PLAN Look at the plan for an article on mobile phones. In pairs, answer the questions in brackets. Use your answers to write a more complete plan.

Mobile phones
Introduction
- revolutionised the way we communicate (how?)
Body paragraphs
- origins of wireless phone (when? where? who?)
- technological changes and more varied uses (what changes? what uses?)
Conclusion
- more changes to come in the future, but mobile is here to stay (what changes do you think?)

WRITING TOOLS
If you plan your paragraphs before your start, you can focus more on the language when you write.

5 WRITE Use your plan to write an article on mobile phones or choose another product.

6 CHECK Check that your article includes everything in your plan. Check for spelling and grammar mistakes.

PROJECT TASK 3 Entrepreneurs

- You are going to write short texts to promote your product or service. You will include these in a leaflet about your company later.
- In your team, decide what you would like to write about, e.g. product description, origins of the idea, information about your team, etc.
- Use a mind map to help you.

→ Workbook page 20

Do all exercises in your notebook

16 An article / Tenses

1 The **Focus on** section gives students an opportunity to revise language they have learnt that will be useful in completing the writing task.

2 A **model text** of the same type required in the writing task provides students with an appropriate scaffold of structure, style and language. The texts are of a range of genres and cover text types and linguistic conventions required in external exams.

3 The **Did you notice?** section highlights contextualised language, style and structural features of the model text for the students to include in their writing.

4 The **NOW YOU!** writing task has **Plan**, **Write** and **Check** exercises to give students a step-by-step guide to producing an appropriate written text, drawing on language they have learnt.

5 The **Workbook** contains a dedicated area per unit for students to complete the writing task. This allows students to build up their own portfolio of writing work.

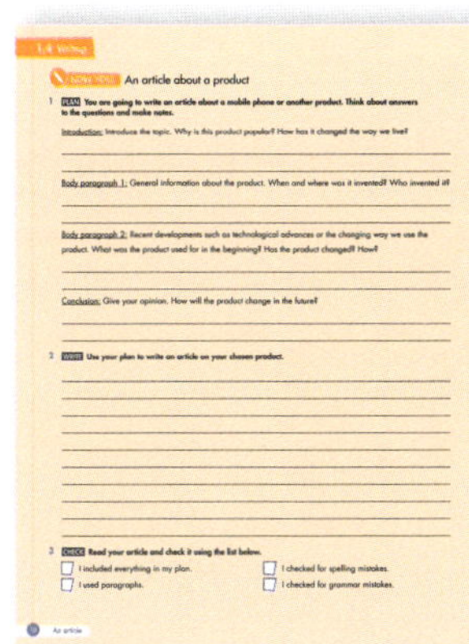

Unit walkthrough

LESSON 5 Culture and Communication

1 The lesson starts with a **Culture video** introduced by the unit vlogger that gives students a window on the world from a cultural perspective using natural language.

As with the **Vlog** at the beginning of the unit, students' responses to the discussion questions will be informed by the content of the video; however, the questions can also be answered by students who have not seen the video.

Understanding of the video is consolidated in the optional **Culture video worksheets** available in the **Teacher's Resources**.

2 Themed sets of **Idioms and expressions** highlight natural, everyday language and phrases. This increases students' confidence by deepening understanding of English as spoken by native speakers and developing fluency.

3 The **Pairwork** exercises provide communicative tasks which practise the target language in line with **CEFR mediation descriptors**. Students analyse, interpret and exchange information using key language from the unit.

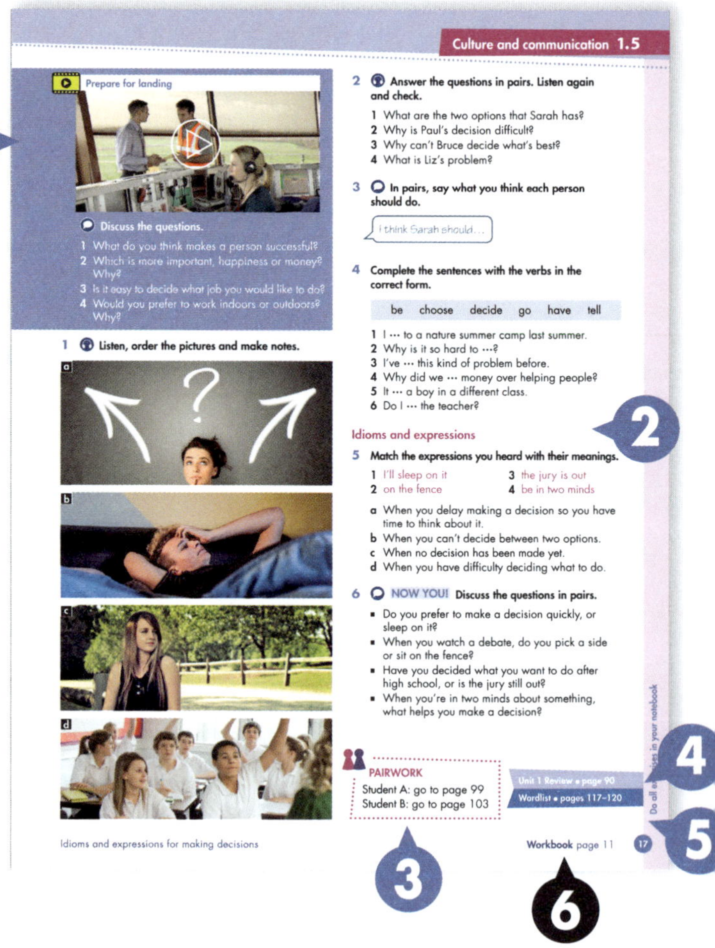

Culture and communication 1.5

Prepare for landing

Discuss the questions.

1 What do you think makes a person successful?
2 Which is more important, happiness or money? Why?
3 Is it easy to decide what job you would like to do?
4 Would you prefer to work indoors or outdoors? Why?

1 Listen, order the pictures and make notes.

2 Answer the questions in pairs. Listen again and check.

1 What are the two options that Sarah has?
2 Why is Paul's decision difficult?
3 Why can't Bruce decide what's best?
4 What is Liz's problem?

3 In pairs, say what you think each person should do.

I think Sarah should…

4 Complete the sentences with the verbs in the correct form.

be choose decide go have tell

1 I … to a nature summer camp last summer.
2 Why is it so hard to …?
3 I've … this kind of problem before.
4 Why did we … money over helping people?
5 It … a boy in a different class.
6 Do I … the teacher?

Idioms and expressions

5 Match the expressions you heard with their meanings.

1 I'll sleep on it
2 on the fence
3 the jury is out
4 be in two minds

a When you delay making a decision so you have time to think about it.
b When you can't decide between two options.
c When no decision has been made yet.
d When you have difficulty deciding what to do.

6 NOW YOU! Discuss the questions in pairs.

- Do you prefer to make a decision quickly, or sleep on it?
- When you watch a debate, do you pick a side or sit on the fence?
- Have you decided what you want to do after high school, or is the jury still out?
- When you're in two minds about something, what helps you make a decision?

PAIRWORK
Student A: go to page 99
Student B: go to page 103

Unit 1 Review • page 90
Wordlist • pages 117–120

Idioms and expressions for making decisions

Workbook page 11 17

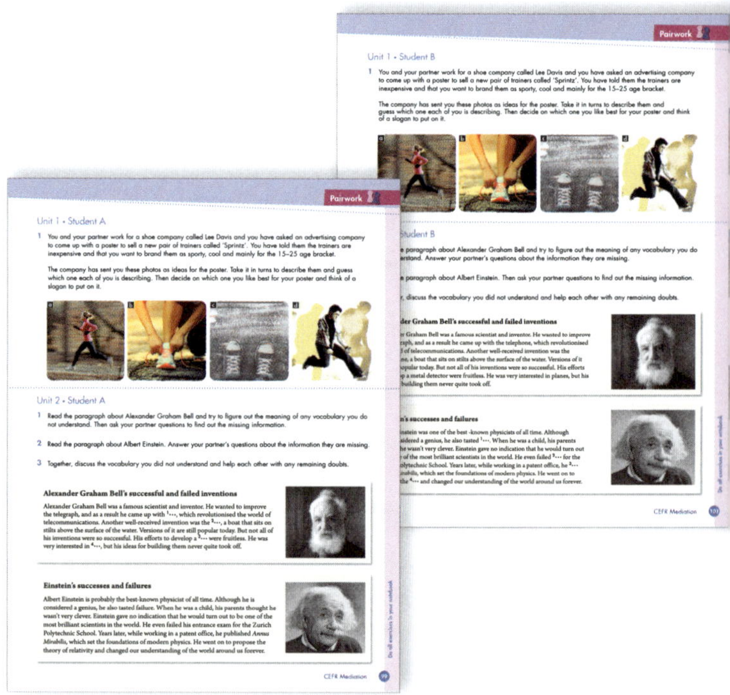

LESSON 5 Culture and Communication

4 The **Unit reviews** help students to revise the language from the unit and practise for external exams. The reading, writing, listening and speaking tasks mirror external exam format and provide comprehensive exam practice.

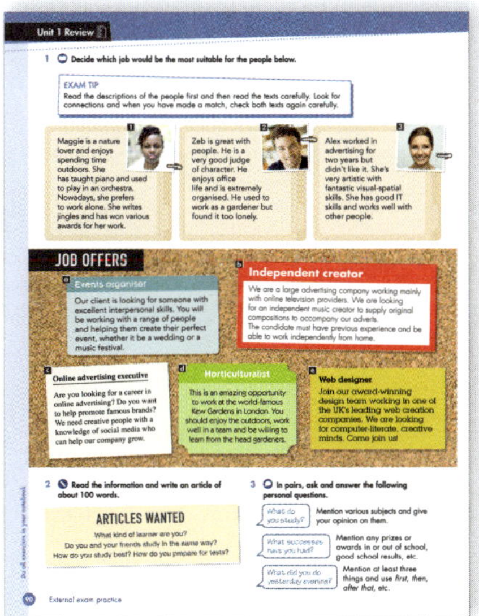

5 The **Wordlist** for each unit helps students to revise the main vocabulary from the unit. The wordlists include key and high frequency words from the unit. There is also an irregular verb list for reference.

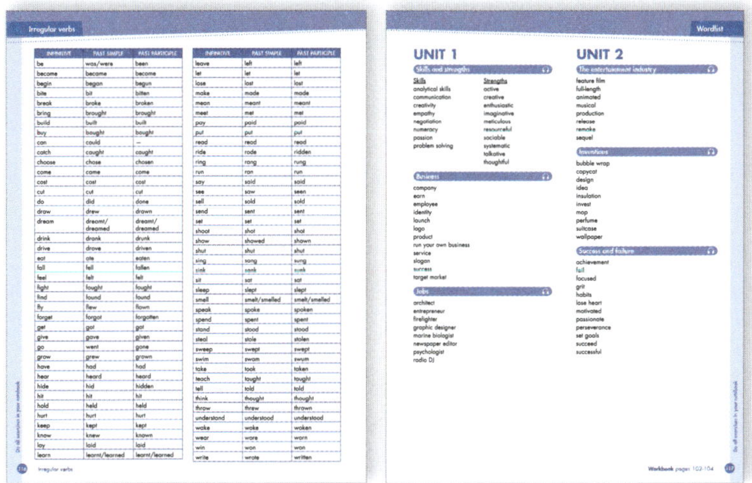

The **Teacher's Resources** contain **tests** which can be used at the end of every unit, term and year. Students can be tested on their knowledge of vocabulary and grammar along with their skills development at two levels of difficulty:

- Consolidation — course level
- Extension — higher level

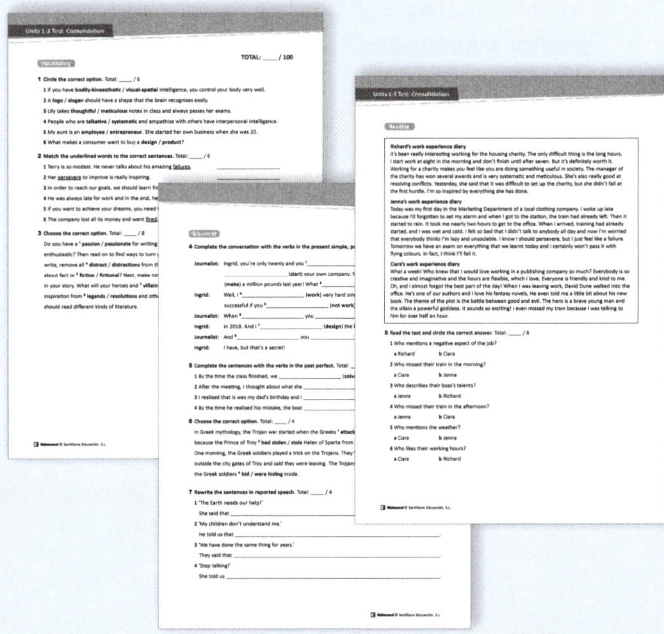

6 In the **Workbook** students will find further practice of the **Idioms and expressions** along with a **Reflect on your learning** table for them to assess their progress using 'I can' statements.

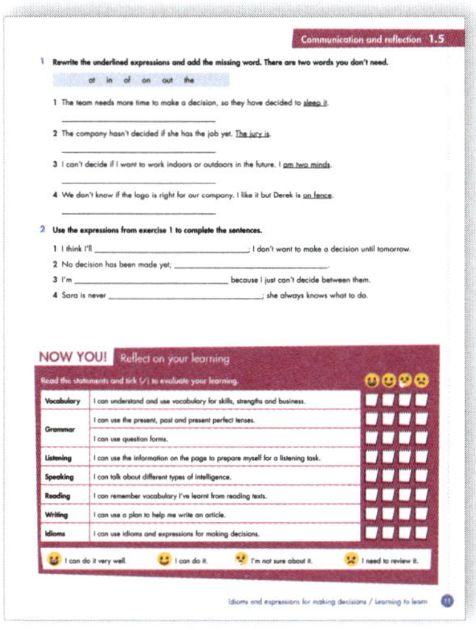

Unit walkthrough

PROJECT

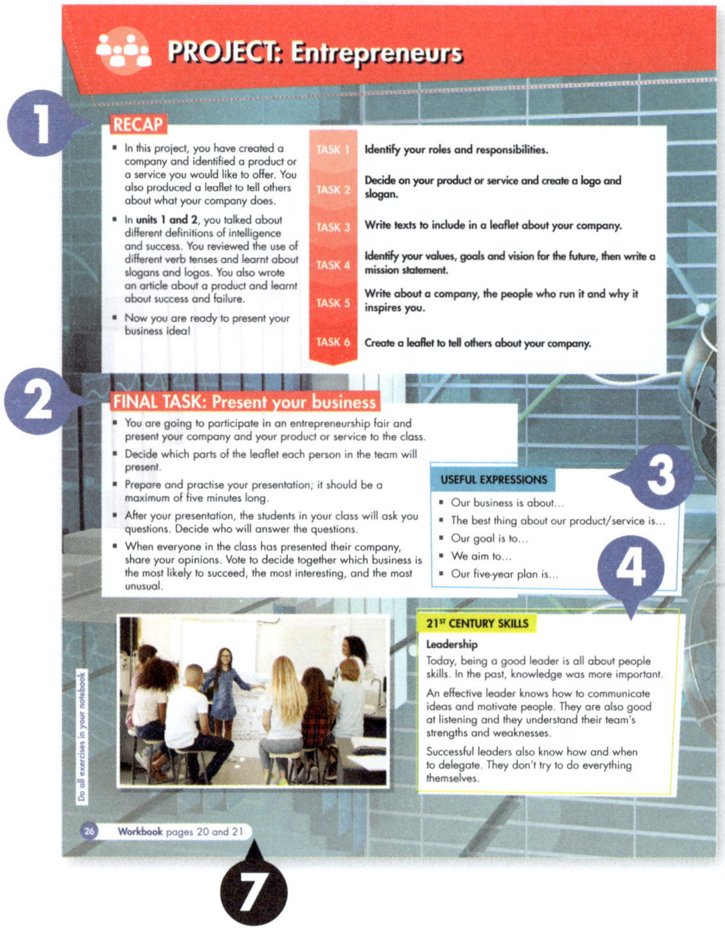

PROJECT: Entrepreneurs

RECAP

- In this project, you have created a company and identified a product or a service you would like to offer. You also produced a leaflet to tell others about what your company does.
- In **units 1 and 2**, you talked about different definitions of intelligence and success. You reviewed the use of different verb tenses and learnt about slogans and logos. You also wrote an article about a product and learnt about success and failure.
- Now you are ready to present your business idea!

TASK 1	**Identify your roles and responsibilities.**
TASK 2	**Decide on your product or service and create a logo and slogan.**
TASK 3	**Write texts to include in a leaflet about your company.**
TASK 4	**Identify your values, goals and vision for the future, then write a mission statement.**
TASK 5	**Write about a company, the people who run it and why it inspires you.**
TASK 6	**Create a leaflet to tell others about your company.**

FINAL TASK: Present your business

- You are going to participate in an entrepreneurship fair and present your company and your product or service to the class.
- Decide which parts of the leaflet each person in the team will present.
- Prepare and practise your presentation; it should be a maximum of five minutes long.
- After your presentation, the students in your class will ask you questions. Decide who will answer the questions.
- When everyone in the class has presented their company, share your opinions. Vote to decide together which business is the most likely to succeed, the most interesting, and the most unusual.

USEFUL EXPRESSIONS

- Our business is about…
- The best thing about our product/service is…
- Our goal is to…
- We aim to…
- Our five-year plan is…

21ST CENTURY SKILLS

Leadership

Today, being a good leader is all about people skills. In the past, knowledge was more important.

An effective leader knows how to communicate ideas and motivate people. They are also good at listening and they understand their team's strengths and weaknesses.

Successful leaders also know how and when to delegate. They don't try to do everything themselves.

Do all exercises in your notebook

26 **Workbook** pages 20 and 21

1 At the end of lessons 1, 2, and 4 of each unit students complete a project task. There are six tasks spread over two units. These tasks build towards a final project. The **Recap** section reflects on the six project tasks students have undertaken over the course of these units.
Each of these tasks requires students to apply the knowledge they have acquired in each lesson, which helps boost their motivation.

2 The **Final task** is where students come together to organise, refine and present their work. The projects are conceived as multi-skill activities that develop students' ability to collaborate and to express their knowledge, aptitudes, interests and feelings.

3 The **Useful expressions** are a list of phrases that students can incorporate into the final presentation.

4 The **21st century skills** box shows students how the soft skills they have developed during the project can be useful to them outside the classroom. This helps the students to see how they can apply broader skills they have developed in the classroom to the real world.

PROJECT

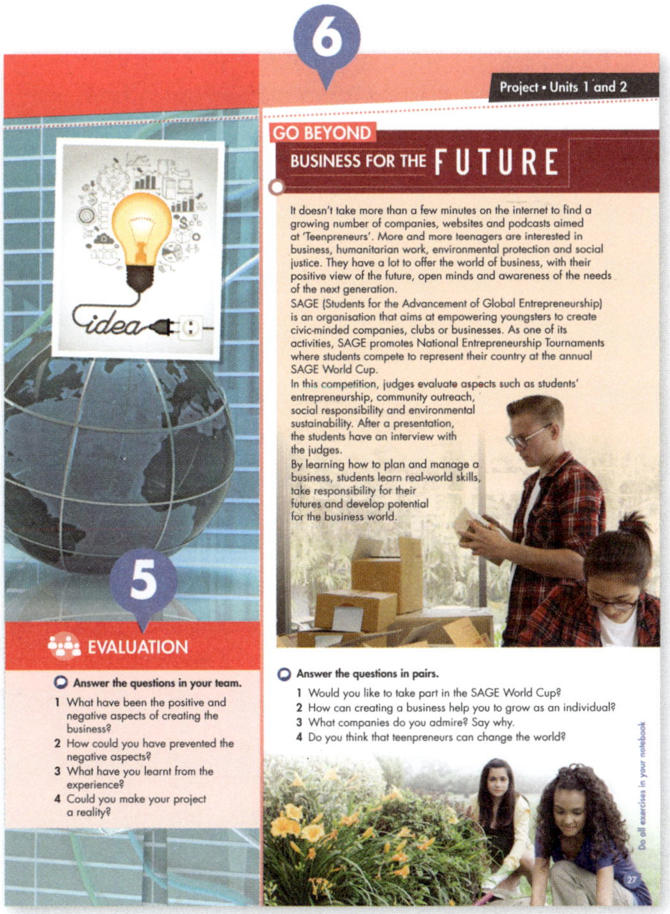
Project • Units 1 and 2

GO BEYOND
BUSINESS FOR THE FUTURE

It doesn't take more than a few minutes on the internet to find a growing number of companies, websites and podcasts aimed at 'Teenpreneurs'. More and more teenagers are interested in business, humanitarian work, environmental protection and social justice. They have a lot to offer the world of business, with their positive view of the future, open minds and awareness of the needs of the next generation.
SAGE (Students for the Advancement of Global Entrepreneurship) is an organisation that aims at empowering youngsters to create civic-minded companies, clubs or businesses. As one of its activities, SAGE promotes National Entrepreneurship Tournaments where students compete to represent their country at the annual SAGE World Cup.
In this competition, judges evaluate aspects such as students' entrepreneurship, community outreach, social responsibility and environmental sustainability. After a presentation, the students have an interview with the judges.
By learning how to plan and manage a business, students learn real-world skills, take responsibility for their futures and develop potential for the business world.

Answer the questions in pairs.
1 Would you like to take part in the SAGE World Cup?
2 How can creating a business help you to grow as an individual?
3 What companies do you admire? Say why.
4 Do you think that teenpreneurs can change the world?

EVALUATION

Answer the questions in your team.
1 What have been the positive and negative aspects of creating the business?
2 How could you have prevented the negative aspects?
3 What have you learnt from the experience?
4 Could you make your project a reality?

Do all exercises in your notebook

27

5 The **Evaluation** questions help students to evaluate individual and team performance from the context of the 21st century skills. This process of reflection promotes a thoughtful approach to the learning process.

6 The **Go beyond** section takes a closer look at an aspect of the project theme. This can be used as a vehicle for class discussion or as a fast finishers activity for students who complete the final task ahead of time.

7 In the **Workbook** the students are provided with a **project notes** organiser to complete each of the project tasks. This ensures that students have all the notes and ideas at hand, creating a portfolio of their work which they can look back on for evaluation purposes.

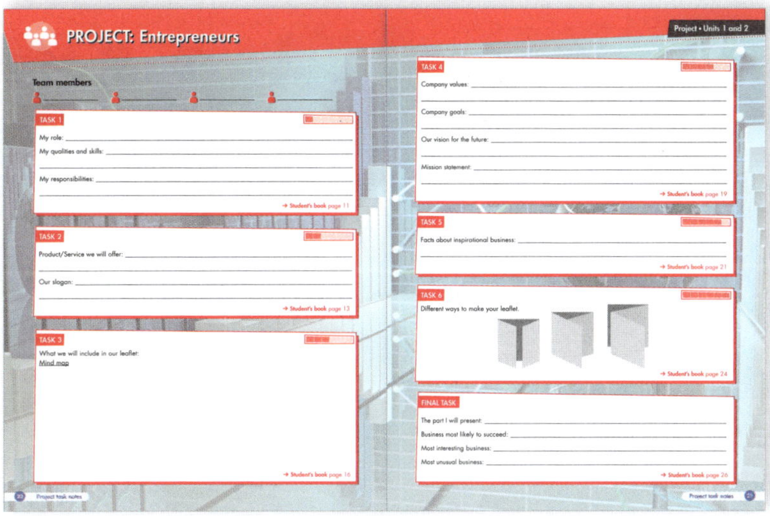
PROJECT: Entrepreneurs
Project • Units 1 and 2

Team members

TASK 1
My role:
My qualities and skills:
My responsibilities:

TASK 2
Product/Service we will offer:
Our slogan:

TASK 3
What we will include in our leaflet:
Mind map

TASK 4
Company values:
Company goals:
Our vision for the future:
Mission statement:

TASK 5
Facts about inspirational business:

TASK 6
Different ways to make your leaflet:

FINAL TASK
The part I will present:
Business most likely to succeed:
Most interesting business:
Most unusual business:

Project task notes

Video material

The benefits of learning through video

Video is an essential tool in today's ELT classroom and should be embraced as one of the most important resources for learning by both teachers and students alike. Not only does video offer many benefits for students, it is also the **preferred medium of content** for teenagers all over the world. Videos allow students to engage and **connect with English** in a way that written texts do not. This feeling of connection is one of the most **powerful motivational tools** available when learning a language.

Language input and review

Video is a useful tool **for introducing new language** – grammar, vocabulary and functional language. It provides a natural, more complete context for the language, which helps students develop a more **thorough understanding of how the language is used**. Videos give students information about register and pronunciation, as well as lots of audiovisual clues to aid understanding like tone of voice, gestures and facial expressions. This also helps **memory retention**, especially when language is reviewed in subsequent videos. Videos are a very **dynamic review tool**.

Video is also a vital resource for **Flipped Learning**, a dynamic educational model whereby students begin learning new structures by watching a video at home. This is particularly useful for mixed-ability classes because students can learn at their own pace. For more on **Flipped Learning**, see pages 20-23.

Key competences

Video material is also an excellent opportunity to instil **Key competences for lifelong learning**, which encourage students to become responsible citizens in 21st century communities (see **Key competences** pages 42-43). As well as **Linguistic competence**, video helps build these two competences:

- **Cultural awareness and expression:** videos show students how people live and express themselves around the world, thus promoting cultural empathy.
- **Digital competence:** students can gain confidence using digital technologies for learning. This is particularly relevant for students who may be at risk of digital exclusion.

The **videos in NOW YOU!** have **been specifically designed to appeal to teenage students** of English. They are presented in formats that teenagers enjoy and are familiar with. There are three types of video, as outlined below and explained in more detail on the next page.

NOW YOU! videos at a glance

- A **Vlog** about the daily life of the vlogger at the start of every unit.
- **Teacher's Resources** include a **Vlog worksheet** to be completed in class or at home (**Flipped Learning**).

- A **Culture video** narrated by the vlogger to extend the students' knowledge of the world.
- **Teacher's Resources** include a **Culture video worksheet** to be completed in class or for homework.

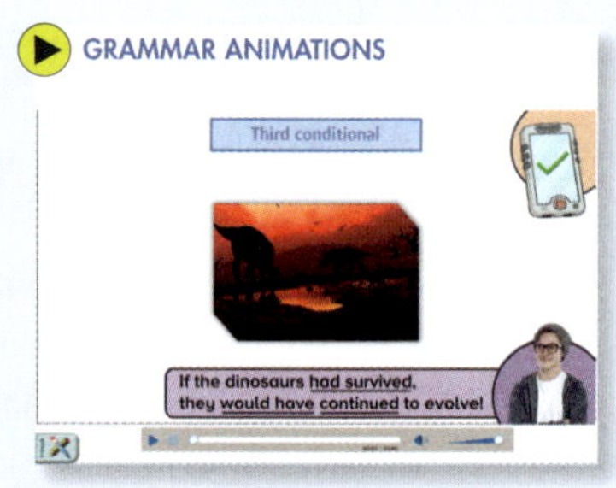

- A **Grammar animation** for every **Grammar table**.
- To be watched either in class or at home (**Flipped Learning**).

How the NOW YOU! videos work

Vlogs and Culture videos

The **Vlogs** and **Culture videos** are used to present and review unit themes and key language, and reflect the way teenagers engage with the world around them. Both videos revolve around **three age-appropriate teenage characters** who are dealing with **authentic, relevant topics** that students can easily identify with. Students hear the unit language being used naturally in context by a native speaker, with visual support from **gifs, emoticons, key words** on screen and, of course, **subtitles**.

The characters' stories evolve throughout the course, from the **Get started!** unit, where students meet the characters, to **Unit 9,** where they say goodbye to them for the summer break. This continuity creates anticipation for the next unit and serves as a memory aid for previous units. There are worksheets to help students get the most out of the videos in the **Teacher's Resources**. Both **Vlog** and **Culture video worksheets** can be used in class and both include exercises to prepare students to watch the videos, to guide them as they watch and to consolidate what they have watched in a way that is personal and accessible to students at all levels of competence. The **Vlog worksheets can also be flipped** (see **Flipped Learning** pages 20-23).

Grammar animations

The **Grammar animations** are a series of fun animations that bring grammar to life for young digital natives. They feature a character called Grammar Gadget, an enthusiastic smartphone in training. It interacts with a group of teenagers on a wide variety of **digital platforms** such as chats and apps. Through their interactions, Grammar Gadget **learns new grammar**, saving it onto its system and **building on it as the level progresses**. Grammar Gadget breaks down each grammar point on screen, so that **students learn along with it**. There are often **multiple grammar animations for each grammar point**. This allows students to focus on each grammar point individually before using them together in subsequent activities. **Like the Vlogs, the Grammar animations can be watched in class or flipped** (see **Flipped Learning** pages 20-23).

All videos and worksheets available on the Richmond Learning Platform

Flipped Learning

What is Flipped Learning?

Flipped Learning is an educational model originally developed by Aaron Sams and John Bergmann, two high school teachers in the US, as a strategy for meeting the needs of students who could not attend class. They started by sending them informative videos so that they did not fall behind in their studies. They realised that by providing such videos to all students before class, students could spend class time discussing content, experimenting with the material and receiving assistance from their teachers. Little by little, teachers discovered the benefits and possibilities offered by this model and it was perfected and extended over time.

In a traditional class, teachers first explain new material to their students in the classroom and students subsequently apply that information to class work or homework. In a **Flipped classroom**, this order is reversed or 'flipped'; students first engage with the new material at home and then apply their newly learnt knowledge in the classroom. This approach was born in the digital age and has become increasingly relevant to the challenges facing students preparing to become citizens of the of the 21st century and their teachers. Today, students can access educational content more easily than ever before, and because of this, the teacher's role is no longer merely to transmit content but to be a guide in the education process, awakening the students' curiosity for learning and helping them to develop the skills that will allow them to become more autonomous learners.

Flipped Learning benefits

The benefits of **Flipped Learning** can be divided into three main areas.

Competences and skills

- It develops the student's **Digital competence** and **audio-visual language**.
- It works as an **initial, autonomous evaluation of the student's understanding of vocabulary and grammar**.
- It promotes the development of the student's **Learning to learn competence**.
- It **promotes creativity**.

Methodological and pedagogical

- It allows the teacher to **save class time** and thus significantly increases opportunities to reinforce the key content and **complete tasks in the classroom**.
- It anticipates the context of the lesson and ensures that **each student can work at their own pace** to get ready for the class.
- It maximises the use of the course resources.
- It allows **multidimensional work** through video images and audio to encourage the student's **comprehension** and **memory**.
- It allows the teacher to include a **wider diversity of tasks** that promote different **thinking skills** and richer access to learning.

Emotional

- It helps **build confidence** by giving students a more active role in their own learning.
- It **motivates** students because it brings classroom work into their real lives. This allows students to **link what they are learning to their emotions, feelings and experiences**.
- It **personalises learning** so that each student can access the new content as often as needed without restriction.
- It provides a space for work on content and pronunciation **in a climate of safety and trust**.

Flipped Learning in NOW YOU!

NOW YOU! has two main resources that favour **Flipped Learning**. These resources can be used to promote change in the English classroom in order to **motivate students** to participate actively in their own learning process and take responsibility for it.

They can also be used to anticipate the content of the next lesson. This encourages **meta-learning** and helps the students to be aware of what will happen in the classroom later. This awareness promotes **security** and **confidence** in our students.

The **Vlog** at the start of every unit anticipates and facilitates the introduction of both the unit theme and the new vocabulary in an engaging context.

PETER'S VLOG: Top tutors

All the **Grammar animations** can be used to anticipate the presentation of the key grammar structure or structures of each unit. **Grammar Gadget** presents the grammar rules in a very **systematic and standardised** way to facilitate the understanding of each rule and improve the **student's long-term learning and memory**.

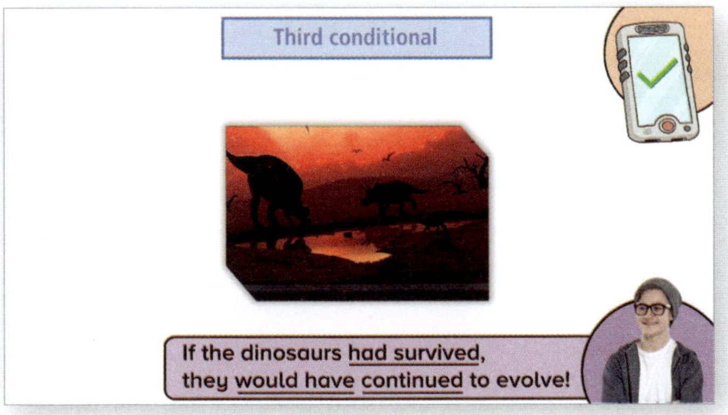

How to get started

Using **Flipped Learning** involves a **commitment on the part of both students and teachers**, each one accepting their role and responsibility. It is advisable that the **starting point** be to **inform the students about this approach** before beginning to use the dynamics of **Flipped Learning** in **NOW YOU!** It is very important that students understand **the benefits that Flipped Learning brings to their global learning process**.

In order to help teachers explain to students how the model works, the **Flipped Learning visual guide** below can be downloaded and printed from the **Richmond*Learning*Platform** to be given out to students during setup.

All the students need to have **access to a computer or mobile device, and internet connection at home**.

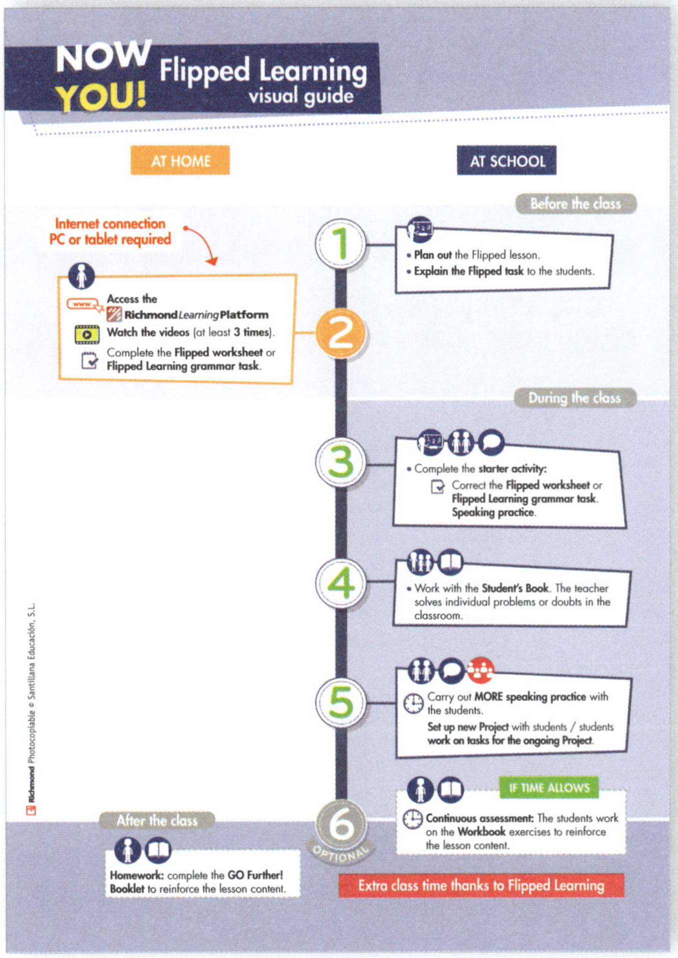

Flipped Learning

How to flip the Vlog

The unit theme is introduced by **watching the Vlog from Lesson 1 at home**. Not only is the content specifically tailored to the relevant age group, the videos are also based on popular formats the students are familiar with and will therefore easily hold their attention.

The videos are available for students on the **Richmond***Learning***Platform**, in a section called **Flipped Learning**. Explain to the students that they have to register on the platform using the **access code included in their Student's Book**. The videos can be viewed from any device, whether it be a computer, mobile or tablet.

PETER'S VLOG: Top tutors

Before the start of a new unit, the students take home a task that will promote participation and autonomous learning. **Explain the task** in advance in class as follows:

1 **Give a copy of the Flipped worksheet** to each student so they can complete it at home. Make sure it is clear what they have to do. The worksheets are available for teachers in **PDF** format in the **Teacher's Resources** on the **Richmond***Learning***Platform**.

AT HOME

2 The students read all the exercises to get an overall vision of the task and then **complete the** Before you watch section in the **Flipped worksheet** that was given out in the previous class. These worksheets are also available for the students on the **Richmond***Learning***Platform**.

3 The students watch the **Vlog** at least 3 times:

- **A first time** where the video is played all the way through.
- **A second time** stopping at moments of interest to answer the questions in the While you watch section in the **Flipped worksheet**.
- **A third time** to check that the content has been understood. This time it is also played without stopping and students should be encouraged to practise the pronunciation of key words while they watch it.

If there are students who need to watch the video more than 3 times, encourage them to do so. The important thing is that **each student can work at their own pace and come to the next class prepared.** This approach adapts to the learning process of each student.

4 The students complete the After you watch section in the **Flipped worksheet**. The worksheet must be returned to the classroom so the teacher can check that the initial work with the new unit has been done.

AT SCHOOL

5 Once in the classroom, the starter activity of the unit will be to check that the video has been watched, the **Flipped worksheet** completed, and the content understood. This starter activity practises speaking skills and the students use the completed **Flipped worksheets** to participate.

6 After this starter activity has been carried out, the new content is then used in more complex, communicative and active ways during the rest of the class. Some of the **Student's Book** exercises can then be skipped to save time for the **Project tasks**.

Flipped Learning

How to flip a grammar lesson

The **animated grammar presentations** in **NOW YOU!** provide **clear step-by-step explanations** for all the grammar rules covered in the course, ensuring **students can work autonomously**.

Any grammar lesson in the Student's Book can be flipped. However, if teachers have already used the Flipped Learning approach for the start of the unit, it is advisable to flip the grammar presentation in Lesson 2. Remember the videos are available for students on the **Richmond***Learning***Platform**, in a section called **Flipped Learning**.

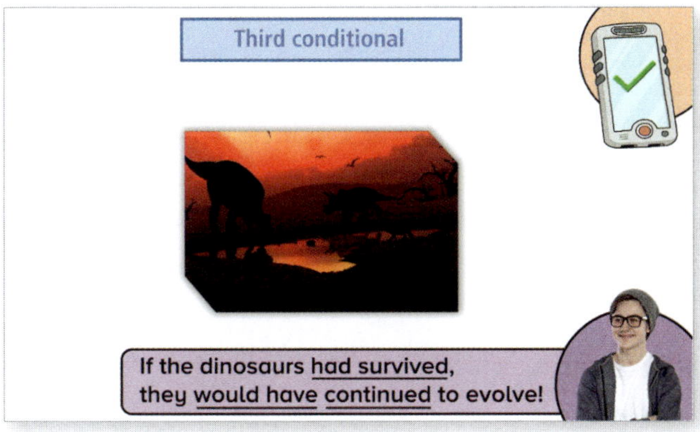

1 **Before the start of Lesson 2**, give students one of these **Flipped Learning grammar** tasks to complete at home:

- Write five true/false sentences using the grammar structure to be shared in class.
- Write five sentences with a word missing for a classmate to complete.
- Write a short dialogue to perform with a classmate in class.
- Write a short quiz of 5 questions and the answers to be shared in class.
- Write a short message for a classmate to reply to using the grammar structure.

AT HOME

2 The students watch the animated grammar presentations before the start of the grammar lesson. Note there may be more than one video for each key grammar structure in the **Student's Book**. The students should **watch each video at least 3 times**:

- **A first time** where they watch the presentation all the way through without stopping.
- **A second time** stopping the presentation several times in order to focus on the most important aspects and write down questions to take to class.
- **A third time** to check that the content has been understood. They watch without stopping while trying to practise the pronunciation and intonation of questions and statements.

If there are students who need to watch the video more than 3 times, encourage them to do so. The important thing is that **each student can work at their own pace and come to the class prepared**. This approach adapts to the learning process of each student.

3 The students **complete** the **Flipped task** that was explained by the teacher in the previous class. The **Flipped task** must be seen in the classroom so the teacher can check the student's understanding of the grammar rule shown in the video(s).

AT SCHOOL

4 When teaching the lesson where the grammar table appears, check that the grammar presentation(s) have been watched at home, the **Flipped task** completed and the content understood.

5 Resolve individual queries and help the students who still have problems with the grammar structures while the rest of their classmates focus on the **Student's Book** exercises individually or in pairs.

Projects

Project-based Learning

Project-based Learning is a method in which students learn through completing real-world projects. The project is completed over a period of time and is an opportunity for students to demonstrate their knowledge and skills and apply them in a practical context, as well as learning from each other.

During the project, the students also learn new skills through the vehicle of the project itself. These skills include not just linguistic skills, but also **higher-order thinking skills** such as **reasoning**, **problem solving** and **critical thinking**, and equally importantly **soft skills** such as **communication** and **collaboration**.

Collaborative Learning

Collaborative Learning is an approach in which groups of learners work together to complete a task, solve a problem or create a product. Collaborative tasks can be outlined and explained to the student; however, the responsibility for checking that tasks are understood and completed appropriately lies with them. Similarly, each participant in the group is responsible for not only their own actions, but the completion of the final product. This in turn encourages exploratory talk within the group into how the work will be completed.

Students are encouraged to **formulate and challenge ideas**, learn to manage and deliver **feedback** and develop **time management skills**. Group members work together to accomplish the shared learning goal, which encourages students to respect the abilities and contributions of their peers.

Unlike more dictated structures of team-based learning, consensus building in collaborative learning relies on cooperation by group members and their identification of the personality types in their group. This method empowers the students to take responsibility for their own learning process and develop their ability to communicate with others.

Project-based Learning and Collaborative Learning in NOW YOU!

Based on the principle that students learn best when engaged in meaningful tasks which involve knowledge, comprehension and production skills, **NOW YOU!** includes many activities which motivate students to use language meaningfully, communicatively and cooperatively.

Each **Project** in **NOW YOU!** is a natural space for **Project-based Learning** and **Collaborative Learning** skills. Students are asked to think carefully about the format of their project and to evaluate themselves and their peers, encouraging them to see the importance of effective collaboration. The tasks draw on the content of the lesson and in this way, students understand the purpose of the target language they are learning rather than understanding it as an isolated verbatim linguistic structure.

By drawing the students' attention to the accumulative nature of their work and the ways in which their own performance affects the members of their group, they also develop metacognitive skills. Students will become aware of their progress, and they will also be presented with concrete examples of how their new knowledge is useful to them.

Challenge-based Learning

Challenge-based Learning is a collaborative experience in which students identify and propose a solution, then implement and evaluate it, finally culminating in a public presentation of a final product. The holistic process encourages students to identify their approach to a problem, develop the material and then reflect on their learning process.

The framework for **Challenge-based Learning** was developed with a focus on real-world challenges. However, this specific skills process can be developed through any task which calls for students to reflect on the key steps involved in solving a problem. Students are called upon to identify an issue, ask appropriate questions to develop their understanding and then develop a method to complete the task. When faced with a challenge, successful groups are able to use their relevant experience, identify and employ available resources, develop a plan and find the best solution to the problem that is posed.

Challenge-based Learning in NOW YOU!

The **Projects** can be used as a vehicle for **developing Challenge-based Learning skills**. In order to do this, the teacher should invert the sequence of the presentation of the project tasks to the students as outlined below. In this way, students are encouraged to understand the importance of both the content and the method by which the final product is created. This will motivate the students' learning experience, help to develop their relevant soft skills and create learner autonomy. This method will also help the students to connect with the language they learn as they begin to understand the learning process as delivering them with useful building blocks for communication and not isolated linguistic content.

Using Challenge-based Learning skills to frame the Project experience

Before beginning each pair of units, direct the students to the **Recap** and **Final task** boxes on the **Project** pages (see the **Project** section of the **Unit walkthrough** on pages 16-17). Promote a discussion either as a class or in small groups about the **Final task** the students will be working towards. Encourage the students to think about the materials, knowledge and the types of personal qualities that will best help them to complete the task.

On page 26 you will find a list detailing ways in which the **Project tasks** can be adapted. This list can be shared with the students, and as a class they can decide the best way to complete the tasks for each particular project.

Once the students have engaged with the **Final task** and method in which they will complete the tasks, direct their attention back to the first lesson of the pair of units. Before you begin teaching each lesson, ask the students to read the contents of the **Project task** box. By framing their learning experience in this way, the students will come to understand their language learning in terms of its real-world application.

Projects

The benefits of projects

Encouraging students to work effectively in groups towards a final product has many benefits. The structured and practical tasks give students an immediate opportunity to practise the language and structures they have learnt during the lesson, which develops their **confidence** and **fluency**. These tasks also improve **motivation** due to the immediate, real world application of skills students have learnt on the page.

Projects provide a natural space for the development of **Mediation skills** (see pages 30-33). As students think together and work together in order to complete a project, they are given a space to grow their **social competence** and **self-esteem**. As students reflect on their contribution to the group's success or failure, they are also made aware of the need for **positive, supportive interactions**. Finally, the structure of the tasks themselves encourage **responsibility, learner independence** and **time management skills**.

How to use NOW YOU! Projects

The **Project tasks** that are woven through **NOW YOU!** can be found at the end of lessons 1, 2 and 5 of each unit. There are six tasks which are then brought together in a **Final task** which can be found on the **Project** pages at the end of the two units. Each **Project task** consolidates the material presented to the students during the lesson.

The instructions included in the task boxes outline the type of group the students will work in for the particular **Project**.Throughout the **Student's Book** there is a combination of group sizes, from pairs to groups of four. This is intended to encourage different group dynamics and avoid students working with the same classmates each time.

The **Projects** are themselves **optional, flexible, integrated** and **adaptable**. They are separated into these six, bitesize tasks so that the students are able to complete the **Project** in a controlled and efficient way, integrated into their class time. The tasks can, however, be used in various ways in class, as outlined in the following list.

Ways to use the Project tasks in class

- Students can complete each **Project task** as indicated in the **Student's Book**, consolidating the content of the lesson and building steadily towards the **Final task**.
- As above, but the teacher can choose to miss out or adapt **Project tasks** as dictated by available class time.
- Students can complete all three **Project tasks** together at the end of each unit as a method of reviewing the content, followed by the **Final task**.
- Students can complete all six **Project tasks** and the **Final task** together in one block of work after the two units.
- Teachers can use a discussion of the **Project tasks** as a vehicle for developing **Challenge-based Learning** skills; students will then complete them using their chosen method.
- All or some of the **Project tasks** can be completed by the groups outside of class time and later brought together or presented in the classroom.
- Alternatively, the **Project tasks** can be avoided altogether, in the case that students do not have available class time. This does not affect the progression of the material in the **Student's Book**.

The Final task

The culmination of the Project is the **Final task**, which consists of a **Recap** and **task summary**, instructions for the **Final Task**, a **Useful expressions** box, **21st century skills** and **Evaluation** boxes and a **Go beyond** section (see the **Project** section of the **Unit walkthrough** on pages 16-17).

The **Recap** section helps students understand the practical use of the grammar and vocabulary structures they have learnt. Similarly, the **task summary** in this initial section helps students to recall the material they have created. Teachers may wish to read this section with their students as they begin **Project task** 1 in order to motivate the students and help them understand their work in relation to the final product.

The **Final task** is the moment when students are encouraged to review, edit and refine the work they have completed over the previous two units. A **Useful expressions** box provides students with relevant language structures that will enable them to present their final product with confidence.

When students have all completed the **Final task**, they are provided with material which encourages them to reflect on their experience. This material can be found in the **21st century skills** and **Evaluation** boxes. For more information on how to use the **21st century skills box**, see pages 28-29. The rubric in the **Evaluation** box directs students to answer the questions included either in their groups after the **Final task** or during the presentations of their peers. This section encourages students to evaluate their individual or group performance and reflect on the learning process.

Finally, the **Go beyond** section includes a short text related to the material that the students have completed in order to bring a broader, real-world context to the content or form of the work they have created. This text can be used to stimulate further class discussion on the **Project** content.

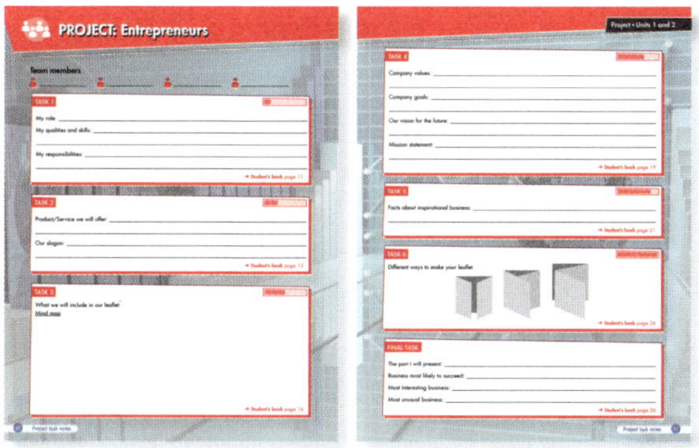

The **Project notes** pages in the **NOW YOU! Workbook** work as an organiser and provide students with a visual presentation of how their work culminates to create the final product. This gradual building of a portfolio of work means that students can also compare their progress over the school year by looking back over the **Projects** they have completed.

21st century skills

What are 21st century skills?

Our world is changing before our eyes. Technological advances, societal and economic developments and a hyper-connected globalisation mean that our students face an exciting yet unpredictable future. The new technologies and types of employment they will encounter are unknown both to them and to us – the adults that shape their education. This poses the question: how can we effectively prepare our students for success in a future we cannot predict?

In answer to this question, educators and academics have identified certain skills as **21st century skills**; that is, soft skills which we can teach our students in order to better prepare them for the future, whatever it may hold.

A quick online search will render multiple definitions of the key **21st century skills**. However, most commonly these are understood in terms of **the 7 Cs**.

The 7 Cs of 21st century skills

- **Collaboration:** Teamwork, adaptability, cooperation, etc.
- **Communication:** Information literacy, ability to share thoughts and ideas, etc.
- **Creativity:** Innovation, productivity, identifying solutions, etc.
- **Critical thinking:** Problem solving, analysis, linking learning across subjects, etc.
- **Career and learning self-reliance:** Responsibility, initiative, self-direction, etc.
- **Computing:** Digital literacy, effective use of electronic tools, etc.
- **Cross-cultural understanding:** Respect for diversity, effective social interaction, etc.

21st century skills in NOW YOU!

Natural spaces for the development of these seven skill sets exist throughout **NOW YOU!**, for example in the **Culture videos** (cross-cultural understanding), **Project tasks** (collaboration) and **NOW YOU! exercises** (communication).

However, a clearly identified **21st century skills box** can be found on the **Project** pages. Here, a specific **21st century skill** that the students have developed during the completion of the **Project tasks** is identified and presented to the student, and the student's attention is drawn to the ways in which it is useful to them outside the classroom. For example, in a **Project** where students are called upon to conduct online research into an individual for a biography, the 21st century skill focus is fact checking.

Teachers who choose not to use the **Project pages** can, however, use this box independently.

In both cases, the teacher should encourage students to read the **21st century skills box** together and discuss their reactions as a class or in small groups. Productive discussion of the themes will include the teacher asking the students to identify their own strengths and weaknesses with regards to the particular skill. Students could also identify ways in which they can develop or apply the skill more effectively in their own lives.

21st century skills from the previous levels are then addressed in the **Get started!** unit of each subsequent level of **NOW YOU!** in order to refresh the student's memory. The connection of the **21st century skill** to a new context also highlights its broader use.

Each skill has been named with the student's understanding in mind, but can also be mapped onto **the 7 Cs** as detailed in the table below.

The benefits of teaching 21st century skills

Aside from the obvious future benefits of teaching students these types of skills, there are also clear implications in terms of **learner motivation**. Encouraging students to recognise and value abilities that are not knowledge-based leads to greater **self-esteem** and **acceptance of diversity**. Furthermore, these skills are intended to promote **learner independence**, develop **positive lifelong learning habits** and place value on **higher-order thinking skills**.

Project	21st century skill	From the 7 Cs
Units 1 & 2: Entrepreneurs	Leadership	Career and learning self-reliance
Units 3 & 4: Comic strip	Problem solving	Creativity
Units 5 & 6: A mystery	Critical thinking	Critical thinking
Units 7 & 8: Campaign	Online security	Computing

CEFR mediation

What is Mediation?

The **Common European Framework of Reference for Languages** (CEFR) in 2001 defined mediation as facilitating cross-linguistic communication; they saw the language learner as a social agent acting between individuals with no common language.

The updated 2018 CEFR, however, gives the skill greater importance and takes a broader interpretation. It sees mediation as those key soft skills required for competent communication, the ability to **reformulate language to facilitate understanding**.

Rather than simply referring to the interpretation or translation of language, mediation is understood as a more meaningful act within the language learning experience. It is an act of interaction that **bridges reception and production**; that interaction can be **between individuals**, **between languages** or **language registers** or in a personal **act of processing language**.

In this way, mediation skills can be developed in a **monolingual learning environment** where use of L1 is not encouraged in the classroom.

The diagram on the next page shows all of the aspects of mediation recognised by the CEFR. There are three main categories of **mediation activities: mediating communication, mediating a text** and **mediating concepts**. Then there are **mediation strategies**, grouped separately because they can be used while doing the mediation activities. As with other skills, there is a range of **CEFR Mediation descriptors** for different levels. For example, in relaying information in speech a language user at B1 level 'can relay specific information given in straightforward informational texts'.

CEFR Mediation in NOW YOU!

NOW YOU! provides opportunities in every lesson for mediation activities and strategies to be developed and has a strong focus on mediation in the **Projects** and **Pairwork** sections.The **overviews** at the beginning of each unit in the **Teaching notes** indicate which **CEFR Mediation descriptors** apply to each lesson (see examples on pages 32-33).

Mediation activities and strategies

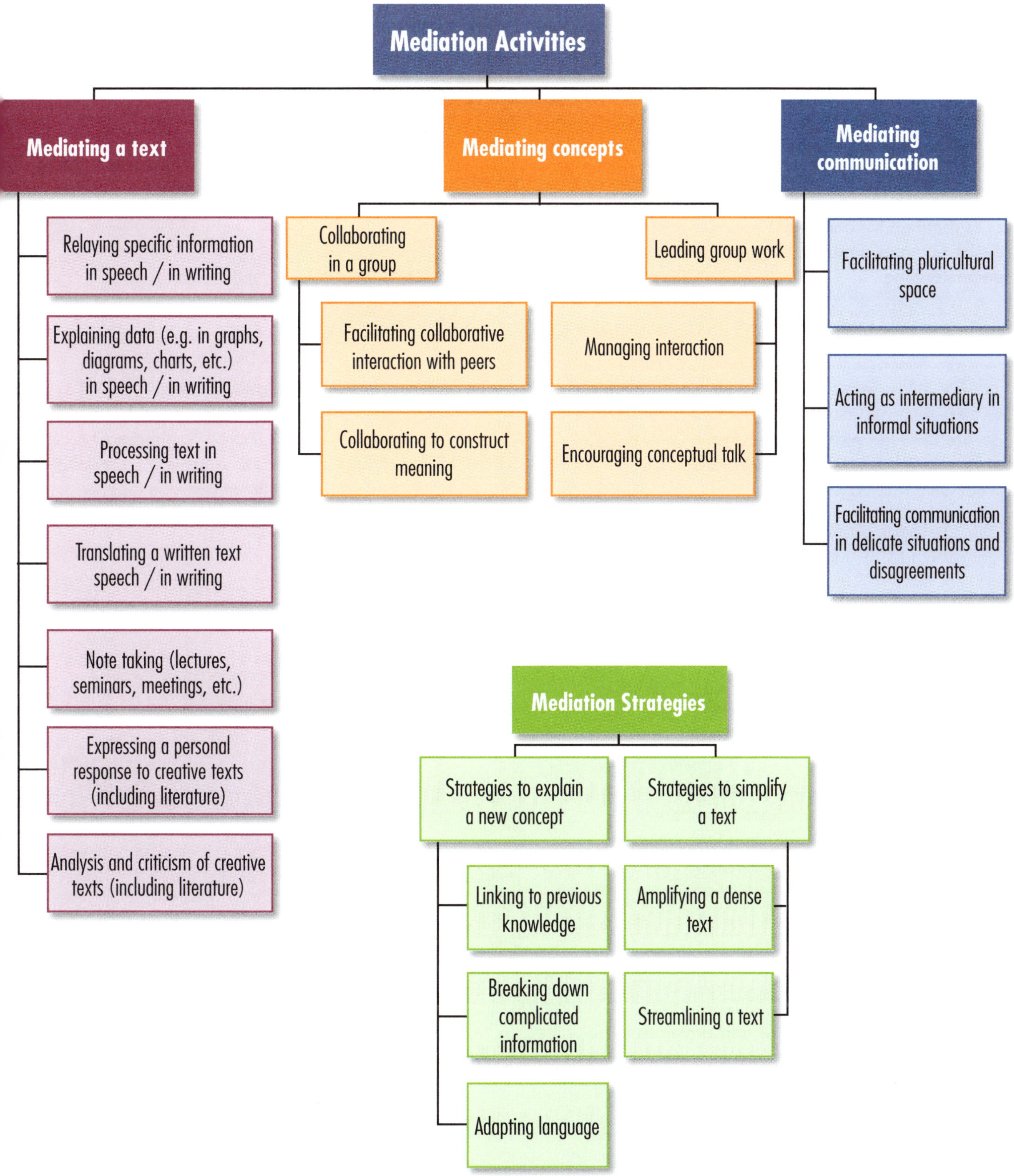

Taken from: Common European Framework of Reference for languages; learning, teaching, assessment Companion volume with new descriptors 2018

CEFR mediation

Main units

All the lessons in the main units of **NOW YOU!** offer students concrete opportunities to develop the **important transferable skills** defined in the **mediation descriptors** in order to become competent, confident communicators, as outlined in the descriptions and examples below.

Lessons 1 & 2 • Grammar, vocabulary & listening

NOW YOU! exercises provide practice for a wide range of mediation skills:
Note-taking
Can make simple notes about familiar subject matter.

Lesson 3 • Reading

Reading lessons develop skills for **mediating a text**:
Expressing a personal response to creative texts
Can describe a character's feelings and explain the reasons for them.
The **Core values** section provides further opportunities:
Facilitating communication in delicate situations and disagreements
Can recognise when difficulties occur in interaction and adapt simple phrases to seek compromise.

Lesson 4 • Writing

Exercises in the **Focus on** and **Did you notice?** sections also develop skills for **mediating a text**:
Processing text in writing
Can pick out and reproduce key words and phrases or short sentences from a short text.

Lesson 5 • Culture and communication

The **Culture video** and **Idioms and expressions** sections provide a space for students to develop skills for **mediating communication**:
Facilitating pluricultural space
Can help to develop a shared communication culture by exchanging information in a simple way about values and attitudes to language and culture.

Projects

The **Project tasks** and the **Final project** are a natural vehicle for Mediation skills concerned with **mediating concepts**; these are further divided into **collaborating in a group** and **leading group work**.

The below tables illustrate the integration of these and other **mediation skills** into the **NOW YOU! Projects**.

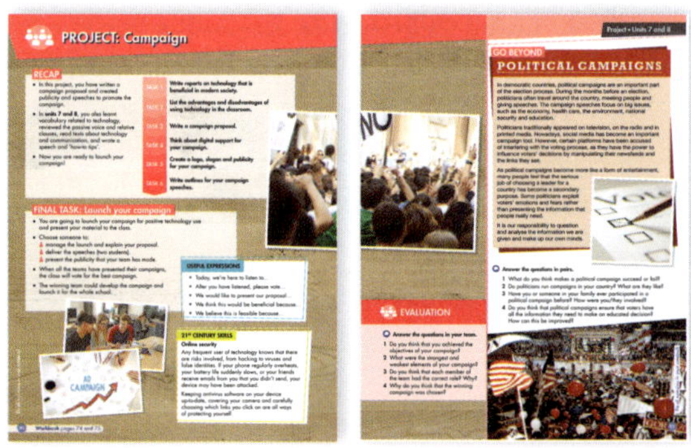

Projects • Student's Book 4	
Project	**B1 / B2 CEFR Mediation descriptors**
Units 1 & 2 Entrepreneurs	Collaborating to construct meaning Can present their ideas in a group and post questions that invite reactions from other group members' perspectives.
Units 3 & 4 Comic book	Analysis and criticism of creative texts Can describe the way in which different works differ in their treatment of the same theme.
Units 5 & 6 A mystery	Encouraging conceptual talk Can ask why someone thinks something, or how they think something would work.
Units 7 & 8 Campaign	Facilitating collaborative interaction with peers Can collaborate on a shared task, for example formulating and responding to suggestions, asking whether people agree, and proposing alternative approaches.

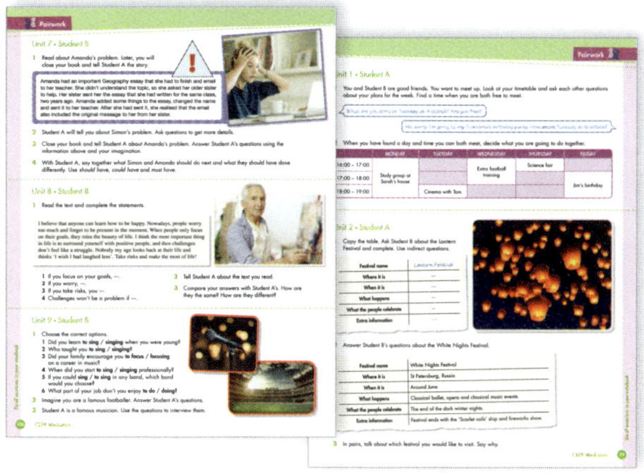

Pairwork

The communicative, interactive nature of the **Pairwork section** creates a natural space for the development of **Mediation skills**.

Pairwork • Student's Book 4	
Unit	**B1 / B2 CEFR Mediation descriptors**
Unit 1 Discussing images	Collaborating to construct meaning Can present their ideas in a group and pose questions that invite reactions from other group members' perspectives.
Unit 2 Exchanging information	Facilitating collaborative interaction with peers Can collaborate in simple, shared tasks and work towards a common goal in a group by asking and answering straightforward questions.
Unit 3 Requesting information	Adapting language Can paraphrase short written passages in a simple fashion, using the original order of the text.
Unit 4 Completing information	Relaying specific information in speech Can relay specificinformation given in straightforward informational texts.
Unit 5 Refuting a story	Collaborating to construct meaning Can consider two different sides of an issue, giving arguments for and against, and propose a solution or compromise.
Unit 6 Interpreting clues	Encouraging conceptual talk Can ask questions to invite people to clarify their reasoning.
Unit 7 Requesting information	Processingtextin speech Cansummarisesimply the main information content of straightforward texts on familiar subjects.
Unit 8 Discovering information	Facilitating collaborative interaction with peers Can collaborate in simple, shared tasks and work towards a common goal in a group by asking and answering straightforward questions.
Unit 9 Defending ideas	Adapting language Can paraphrase more simply the main points made in short, straightforward spoken or written texts on familiar subjects.

Plurilingualism

What is plurilingualism?

The **Common European Framework of Reference for Languages** defines plurilingualism as the ability of an individual to call flexibly upon an inter-related repertoire of linguistic experience and strategies to resolve a communicative situation in a given cultural context.

Because it is called on in a given cultural context, the CEFR points out that 'Plurilingualism has itself to be seen in the context of pluriculturalism. Language is not only a major aspect of culture, but also a means of access to cultural manifestations.'

Consequently, an individual will be competent in plurilingualism when he/she develops the ability to use all his/her linguistic knowledge and experience to achieve effective communication with an interlocutor that takes into account their cultural and linguistic background.

Plurilingualism at secondary level

Because of the transversal nature of plurilingualism, it is not considered necessary to define assessable competences at the level of compulsory secondary education, but it is important to **highlight plurilingual strategies** alongside other linguistic competences.

On the basis of the above, in compulsory secondary school we should focus on the development of plurilingualism in two areas:

1 a **knowledge of culture and traditions** in English-speaking regions (mealtimes, customs, habits, etc.)

2 **experience of communicative success** when an individual overcomes his/her fear of oral and written comprehension and expression

Plurilingualism with NOW YOU!

There are several features of **NOW YOU!** that offer students the opportunity to work on developing their plurilingual competences.

Culture and communication

These lessons offer students an opportunity to develop their plurilingual competences by **watching and responding to videos** about various different aspects, features and events of English-speaking cultures throughout the world, including Irish dancing, the Edinburgh Fringe Festival and the American barbecue. The lessons also include listening exercises involving **short talks and conversations** using frequent English **idioms** and a chance to practise the idioms in short **personalised speaking exercises**. Thus both aspects of plurilingualism as outlined above are developed in these lessons.

NOW YOU! exercises and Pairwork

The **NOW YOU! exercises** throughout each unit and the **Pairwork** activities at the end are designed to develop students' ability to communicate effectively in spoken and sometimes written English. In these exercises, students do activities like comparing what they do in their free time, describing other people, using newly acquired expressions in a conversation and writing a description of someone they admire, among others.

Point out to students that these are not just exercises for putting their linguistic knowledge into practice, but also for **building confidence** in and developing their ability to **communicate and interact** with each other using all their linguistic and communicative resources. In the spoken activities, encourage them to participate **without fear of embarrassment** and using whatever language and communicative strategies they have, including **paralinguistic strategies** like gestures and facial expressions, and asking a speaker to slow down to give them the chance to check that they have understood what the speaker is saying.

Projects

The **Projects** require students to collaborate to prepare and then present a final product. Providing students with this challenge **facilitates the transferral of communication strategies** learnt in their own language (and any other languages they speak) over to their English language competence and vice versa. These strategies, which are necessary for effective completion of the project, help build students' ability to communicate more effectively and confidently **in a range of real-life contexts** involving any language.

Other activities you can do in class to develop your students' plurilingual competence include:

- Showing them **TV programmes**, **films** or **plays** with a strong cultural element.
- **Extending speaking activities** in class to include longer class discussions and **other types of discourse** not already featured in the course: role-plays, formal interviews and debates, etc.
- Asking students to **identify similarities in grammar and vocabulary** between English and their own language (and indeed other languages) to help their linguistic ability and confidence.
- Using **digital communications resources** (like Skype, Zoom, Microsoft Teams, etc.) to help develop communication with students from other countries.
- Encouraging students to get involved in **collaborative projects with students or NGOs in other countries** to put the strategies they have learnt into practice in real-life situations.

Literature

What do we mean by literature?

Literature can be defined as the creative production and comprehension of written, spoken and audiovisual texts in an attempt to produce an emotional and/or intellectual reaction in the reader, listener or viewer.

Written literature at secondary level includes novels, short stories, written plays and essays, as well as comics, articles and blog entries.

Oral literature includes all recited or interpreted texts, such as poems, songs, dramatizations (sketches and short plays), and even tongue-twisters, rhymes, sayings and jokes.

Audiovisual literature refers to works that combine images and spoken or written text, such as cartoons, films, series, advertisements, videoclips, trailers, etc.

The benefits of teaching literature at secondary level

Literature provides us all with a **sense of community** and our place within it, and gives us tools to **express ourselves effectively** to other members of the community to **strengthen bonds** between us and help build our **sense of identity**, both individual and communal. Living in a global and multi-lingual community makes this more of a challenge but also more rewarding.

Focusing on English-language literature at secondary school helps students develop this sense of community and their **understanding of the world**, their **own culture** and their **own identity**.

It also helps develop their **skills** in and **enjoyment** of **reading**, **writing** and other forms of communication, as well as stimulating **creativity** and developing **critical thinking**.

At secondary level, students need to learn to **understand** and **assess** a variety of **literary texts** both adapted and authentic, and to be able to **orally reproduce literary texts** (oral literature) both adapted and authentic. They also need to be able to **express themselves** in ways that show an **awareness of literary culture** as defined above.

Literature in NOW YOU!

There are several features of **NOW YOU!** that offer students the opportunity to develop a healthy relationship with literature and to build on their literary skills.

Reading and Writing lessons

In the **Reading** and the **Writing** lessons, students encounter various **different text types**, including articles, stories, blog entries and descriptions of people and artworks, throughout the course. Both lessons provide students with the opportunity to **offer personal responses** to the texts. To help develop their literary skills, use this opportunity to **highlight literary devices and features** of the text, starting with those they found effective and pointing out any that you think worth remarking on. The **Writing lesson** has a specific **Did you notice?** section to help them **develop literary awareness** and to guide them in using relevant features of the model text to produce their own effective writing.

Vlogs and Culture videos

The **Vlogs** and the **Culture videos** are both typical examples of **21st century audiovisual literature**. They also include personal and cultural anecdotes, jokes and sayings to help students develop their knowledge of global literary culture, and the accompanying material gives them the opportunity to share their responses.

To **further exploit** the literary element of these videos videos, prepare extra questions that encourage students to respond to the content with reference to their own experience and cultural and literary knowledge, with a view to **preparing their own videos**, based on the content they have just seen and heard. Give them time to write scripts, prepare questions for other students to answer and then record themselves. Encourage them to include some literary content (even a joke or an anecdote) and to ask questions that require comprehension and interpretation of that content, as well as giving them the chance to express their opinions, feelings and thoughts in response to the videos.

You could also get students to **find a simple literary text** that is related to one of the videos and get them to **recite** or **dramatize** it. This could be a short poem or rap involving rhyme and metre, which help develop good word stress and pronunciation. Encourage supportive and constructive class feedback.

Graded readers

Richmond offers **a wide range of graded readers**, including adaptations of **classic literature** and **original short novels**, each with **audio CD, glossary** and **activities** designed to help comprehension and generate meaningful and informed responses to the content.

You could have your **class choose a reader** for everyone to read and dedicate some class time to do the related activities and discuss the story. We recommend that you encourage them to **discuss excerpts** that they have read or listened to, offering them whatever support they need to do this effectively. Provide them with valid models of literary assessment so that you can help them **develop literary assessment skills**. You could also get students to do **rewriting activities** to help build confidence and as basic training for more **independent writing**. Such tasks could include varying words or phrases, rewriting an excerpt as a different text type (e.g. a play or a speech), writing part of the story from a different character's perspective or writing an alternative ending.

The learning and interest acquired from lessons based around the one reader you chose as a class could then be used as a springboard for students to **each choose a reader or another literary text** to share with the class as a whole or in smaller groups. They could simply **give an assessment** of the work to share and discuss in order to see if it generates interest among their classmates, or perhaps **recite or interpret** it and prepare activities for their classmates to do in response. Encourage them to find something of particular interest to them individually and in any format and using whatever platforms they want, as long as it doesn't make it impractical for them to share their assessment in class.

Mixed-ability classes

The basics of Mixed-ability classes

To some extent, all classes are of mixed ability. Students have different levels of **knowledge** as well as **ability** and learn at **different speeds** and in **different ways**. It can be a challenge to manage a class where these differences are pronounced, a challenge that many teachers have to face. Some students may become stressed and demotivated because they find the class difficult while others in the same class are bored or frustrated because they find it easy and perhaps finish exercises very quickly. However, with a bit of planning, a few helpful strategies and judicious use of resources, teaching a mixed-ability group can be very rewarding for teachers and students alike.

Mixed-ability in NOW YOU!

The Student's Book

Collaborative Learning

With its strong focus on **Collaborative Learning**, **NOW YOU!** helps highlight the idea of language as a tool for communication, and communication as a collaborative activity with **all parties taking responsibility** for its success. With this methodology as the basis, the **Student's Book** provides a range of tools to develop students' skills across various levels and abilities.

The **The Projects**, **Pairwork** activities and **NOW YOU! speaking exercises** all help emphasise broader **communicative criteria** rather than just language accuracy as a way to grade speaking performance (see **Assessment** pages 40-41 for ideas on assessment criteria). They also **help identify students' strengths and weaknesses** and to help them recognise them **without fear of judgement**. For these activities, giving confident and strong students roles that enable them to share their knowledge and understanding with others gives students the **opportunity to help each other**. Students who are less confident can be encouraged to ask questions to check their understanding. Additionally, students who are confident in their knowledge are not always right and if other students are **encouraged to question their knowledge** it can help check accuracy, and develop critical thinking skills **and reinforce what students have learnt**.

Make students aware **all roles are important** in any group activity, for example timekeeper, materials distributor, note-taker, spokesperson, a nominated person to keep the group on task, etc. **Let them assign roles** within their groups where possible. This can be based on their strengths at first, but then encourage students to **swap** roles regularly so that all students can **learn a variety of skills** by practising them themselves and by observing their classmates demonstrating them. Offer and encourage support to all members of a group as much as possible.

Independent Learning

The **Student's Book** also contains tools to allow students to help themselves and to take ownership of their own learning journey.

For students at a lower level, the **Grammar tables** and **animations** provide a reference point when unsure or underconfident against which to check their learning. Similarly, the **Learning to learn tools** offer students strategies for developing their weaker skills. Make sure to always draw students' attention to these tools and encourage independent learning outside of the classroom. For students at a higher level, the **Fast finishers** exercises in lessons 1, 2, 3 and 5 of every unit give further personalised practice for students who finish exercises before the rest of the class. Check the work students produce in these exercises to make sure they are making the most of them and consider asking them to share their work if it could be of interest or use to rest of the class.

Flipped Learning

The integration of the **Flipped Learning** methodology throughout **NOW YOU!** provides students with further opportunities to **take control of their learning**, and to assimilate knowledge **at their own pace** and in their **own way** (see pages 20-23).

The Workbook

The **Workbook** contains lots of extra practice to help students **consolidate their knowledge**, including **more personalised NOW YOU! exercises** for students to write sentences at their own level of complexity to consolidate language points, and specific sections with **extra practice** for the **Grammar reference** and **Wordlist** at each level, which is ideal for mixed-ability classes. It also includes a **Reflect on your learning** section at the end of each unit so that students can **identify their own strengths and weaknesses** and know when and where to ask for guidance.

Teacher's Resources

The **Teacher's Resources** include **Grammar** and **Vocabulary** worksheets for each unit at **three levels**: Revision, Consolidation and Extension, from lowest to highest. There is also a series of tests including a **Diagnostic test** and then **tests at two levels** after each unit, each group of three units and at the end of the year (see **Assessment** pages 40-41). Thus a teacher can **determine their students' levels** at the start of the year and give them **level-appropriate tests** to monitor them throughout the year in a way that gives students a **sense of confidence and progress**. The worksheets are all also **editable** so they can be tailored to the needs of specific students or groups of students.

Assessment

The basics of assessment

In the context of secondary level English language learning, students can be assessed on their performance and progress by **regular tests and exams**, **continuous teacher assessment** and **self-assessment**. In the 21st century language classroom, students should be assessed not only on their language skills, but also on their **ability to use their language skills** in a wider context and on their capacity for **independent learning**, i.e. their ability to learn how to learn.

Assessment in NOW YOU!

Regular tests

The **Richmond Test Manager** offers a comprehensive battery of tests. There is a **Diagnostic test** you can use at the start of the year to assess students' knowledge and use of vocabulary and grammar before they start the course. Then there are **Unit tests**, **End-of-term tests** and an **End-of-year test** to assess students' vocabulary and grammar, as well as their listening, reading and writing skills. These exist at two levels (Consolidation and Extension) and each have a marking scheme that gives a total of 100. There are also **Speaking tests** at the same intervals. These have no marking scheme so as to allow flexibility in using them, but the following criteria could be used to give a mark: overall task completion, fluency, interaction and language (range, appropriacy and accuracy of vocabulary and grammar).

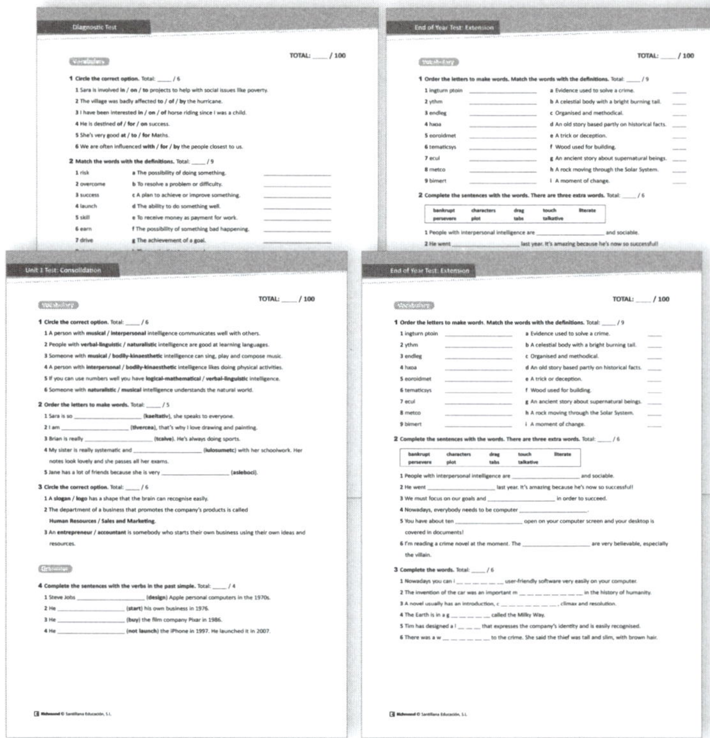

Diagnostic Test

TOTAL: ___ / 100

1 Circle the correct option. Total: ___ / 6

1 Sara is involved **in / on / to** projects to help with social issues like poverty.
2 The village was badly affected **to / of / by** the hurricane.
3 I have been interested **in / on / of** horse riding since I was a child.
4 He is destined **of / for / on** success.
5 She's very good **at / to / for** Maths.
6 We are often influenced **with / for / by** the people closest to us.

2 Match the words with the definitions. Total: ___ / 9

1 risk — a The possibility of doing something. ___
2 overcome — b To resolve a problem or difficulty. ___
3 success — c A plan to achieve or improve something. ___
4 launch — d The ability to do something well. ___
5 skill — e To receive money as payment for work. ___
6 earn — f The possibility of something bad happening. ___
7 drive — g The achievement of a goal. ___

Unit 1 Test: Consolidation

TOTAL: ___ / 100

1 Circle the correct option. Total: ___ / 6

1 A person with **musical / interpersonal** intelligence communicates well with others.
2 People with **verbal-linguistic / naturalistic** intelligence are good at learning languages.
3 Someone with **musical / bodily-kinaesthetic** intelligence can sing, play and compose music.
4 A person with **interpersonal / bodily-kinaesthetic** intelligence likes doing physical activities.
5 If you can use numbers well you have **logical-mathematical / verbal-linguistic** intelligence.
6 Someone with **naturalistic / musical** intelligence understands the natural world.

2 Order the letters to make words. Total: ___ / 5

1 Sara is so ___ (**kaeltativ**), she speaks to everyone.
2 I am ___ (**tivercea**), that's why I love drawing and painting.
3 Brian is really ___ (**tcaive**). He's always doing sports.
4 My sister is really systematic and ___ (**iulosumetc**) with her schoolwork. Her notes look lovely and she passes all her exams.
5 Jane has a lot of friends because she is very ___ (**asleboci**).

3 Circle the correct option. Total: ___ / 6

1 A **slogan / logo** has a shape that the brain can recognise easily.
2 The department of a business that promotes the company's products is called **Human Resources / Sales and Marketing**.
3 An **entrepreneur / accountant** is somebody who starts their own business using their own ideas and resources.

4 Complete the sentences with the verbs in the past simple. Total: ___ / 4

1 Steve Jobs ___ (**design**) Apple personal computers in the 1970s.
2 He ___ (**start**) his own business in 1976.
3 He ___ (**buy**) the film company Pixar in 1986.
4 He ___ (**not launch**) the iPhone in 1997. He launched it in 2007.

Richmond © Santillana Educación, S.L.

End of Year Test: Extension

TOTAL: ___ / 100

1 Order the letters to make words. Match the words with the definitions. Total: ___ / 9

1 ingturn ptoin ___ — a Evidence used to solve a crime. ___
2 ythm ___ — b A celestial body with a bright burning tail. ___
3 endleg ___ — c Organised and methodical. ___
4 hxoa ___ — d An old story based partly on historical facts. ___
5 eoroidmet ___ — e A trick or deception. ___
6 tematicsys ___ — f Wood used for building. ___
7 ecul ___ — g An ancient story about supernatural beings. ___
8 metco ___ — h A rock moving through the Solar System. ___
9 bimert ___ — i A moment of change. ___

2 Complete the sentences with the words. There are three extra words. Total: ___ / 6

bankrupt	**characters**	**drag**	**touch**	**literate**
persevere	**plot**	**tabs**	**talkative**	

1 People with interpersonal intelligence are ___ and sociable.
2 He went ___ last year. It's amazing because he's now so successful!
3 We must focus on our goals and ___ in order to succeed.
4 Nowadays, everybody needs to be computer ___.
5 You have about ten ___ open on your computer screen and your desktop is covered in documents!
6 I'm reading a crime novel at the moment. The ___ are very believable, especially the villain.

3 Complete the words. Total: ___ / 6

1 Nowadays you can i _ _ _ _ _ _ user-friendly software very easily on your computer.
2 The invention of the car was an important m _ _ _ _ _ _ _ _ in the history of humanity.
3 A novel usually has an introduction, c _ _ _ _ _ _ _, climax and resolution.
4 The Earth is in a g _ _ _ _ _ called the Milky Way.
5 Tim has designed a l _ _ _ that expresses the company's identity and is easily recognised.
6 There was a w _ _ _ _ _ _ to the crime. She said the thief was tall and slim, with brown hair.

Richmond © Santillana Educación, S.L.

At the end of the main units in the **Student's Book**, there is also a **Review** for every unit. These offer further assessment of the language content of the unit in the **format of external exams** at the appropriate level.

Continuous assessment

For every lesson there is a **Continuous assessment** footer in the **Teacher's book** for the teacher to be mindful of as students go through the lesson. These are connected to the language and skills objectives of the lesson as outlined in the **overviews** at the start of each unit in the **Teaching notes**. It is a good idea to observe and keep records of all of the students' performances as best you can and offer support to those who need it. The **Writing** lessons require students to produce texts that can also be assessed more formally, perhaps using criteria you set specifically for each writing task or more general criteria you apply throughout, such as task completion, structure/linking, style, language range and language accuracy.

Self-assessment

At the end of every unit in the **Workbook**, there is a **Reflect on your learning** section in the **Communication and reflection** lesson. It offers students an opportunity to **assess their own abilities** in the relevant language points and skills areas. Make sure they understand that the purpose of this is to **build their confidence** in their knowledge and use of English and to **help improve** any areas of weakness. Use their assessments to offer material to help them in these areas. The **Teacher's Resources** offer such material at different levels to suit different students' support needs.

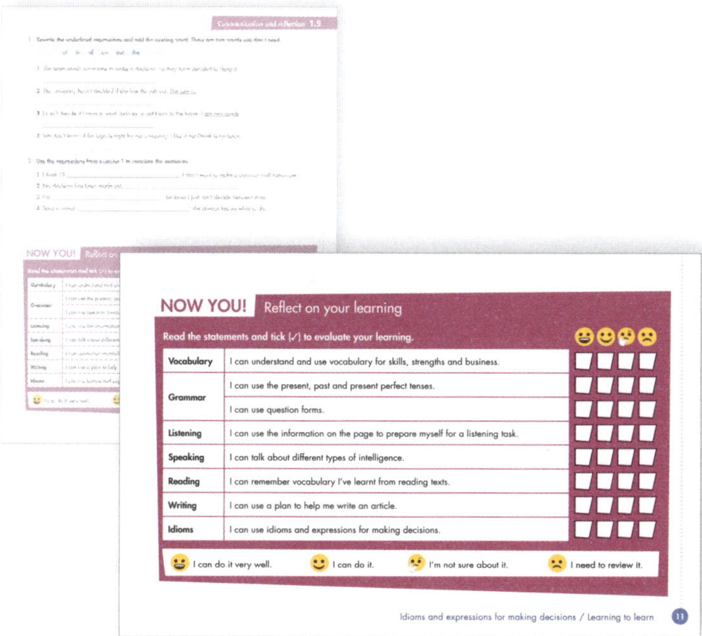

NOW YOU! Reflect on your learning

Read the statements and tick (✓) to evaluate your learning.

		😀	🙂	🤔	😟
Vocabulary	I can understand and use vocabulary for skills, strengths and business.				
Grammar	I can use the present, past and present perfect tenses.				
	I can use question forms.				
Listening	I can use the information on the page to prepare myself for a listening task.				
Speaking	I can talk about different types of intelligence.				
Reading	I can remember vocabulary I've learnt from reading texts.				
Writing	I can use a plan to help me write an article.				
Idioms	I can use idioms and expressions for making decisions.				

😀 I can do it very well. 🙂 I can do it. 🤔 I'm not sure about it. 😟 I need to review it.

Idioms and expressions for making decisions / Learning to learn 11

There is also an opportunity for students to self-assess more informally in the **Evaluation** section of the **Project**. These activities allow students to **assess individual and team performance**, as well as their personal experience of bringing the project to completion.

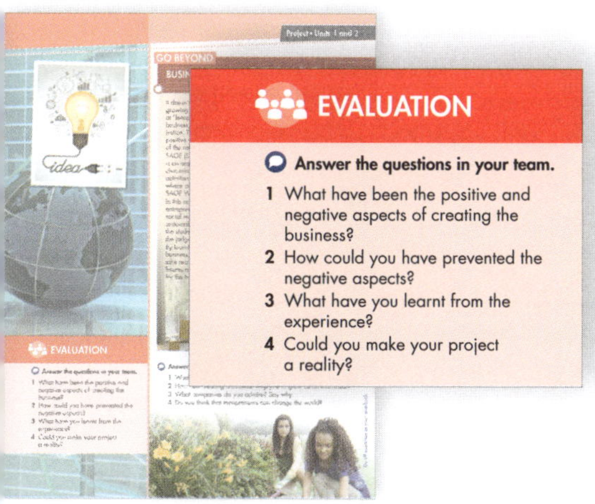

EVALUATION

Answer the questions in your team.

1 What have been the positive and negative aspects of creating the business?
2 How could you have prevented the negative aspects?
3 What have you learnt from the experience?
4 Could you make your project a reality?

It is a good idea to get students to keep a **self-assessment diary**, and their discussions in the **Project Evaluation** could be an opportune moment for them to start and continue the diary.

This diary could include a range of criteria on which students could assess themselves, including linguistic skills as well as other broader skills that **NOW YOU!** helps teach students.

These include the **21st century skills** on the **Project pages**, **the Core values** in the **Reading lessons**, **Learning to learn tools** throughout the book and **mediation skills** from the unit overviews in the **Teacher's Book**. You could make a list of these and get students to write what knowledge and skills they have acquired and developed, and which they want to work on. Encourage them to write how they feel about their learning and progress too. Collect these diaries at intervals to monitor students' awareness of their abilities, performance and development, as well as their morale and motivation.

Key competences

What are the Key competences?

Key competences combine the **knowledge**, **skills** and **attitudes** necessary to develop and achieve success as well being active **in all areas of social and civic life**. Each of the competences is equally important, and for that reason there are many shared goals which support and underpin one another. The basic skills of language, literacy, numeracy and information and communication technologies provide the foundation blocks for critical thinking, creativity, taking initiative, problem-solving, decision-making and management of feelings.

NOW YOU! works on these **Key competences** as set out by the European Commission.

LC

Linguistic competence

This competence develops the use of language as a tool for communication. It involves understanding and producing oral and written messages and requires knowledge of vocabulary and grammar. The focus here is on understanding, expressing and interpreting a range of facts, opinions, thoughts and feelings in a variety of different contexts. Language skills students learn when studying a foreign language can be transferred to their native language and use of other languages, which enhances their plurilingual abilities.

MST

Mathematical competence and basic competences in Science and Technology

The use of mathematical thinking to solve problems in everyday situations, scientific knowledge to explain the natural world and an understanding of technological principles are the focus of this competence. An awareness of the world around us and the effect we have on it are at the core. Introducing these competences into the language learning environment enriches the students' learning experience.

DC

Digital competence

Digital competence involves the use of information technology as a way of researching, presenting and exchanging information. Students use computers, the internet, the interactive whiteboard, audiovisual material and other multimedia resources to enhance their own learning experience. They also learn to critically evaluate different information technologies and the content they provide access to.

SCC

Social and Civic competences

These competences equip students with the necessary skills to participate fully in social and civic life on both a personal and interpersonal level. On a personal level, students focus on those skills needed to function effectively and constructively in everyday life, skills such as being able to know, express and assert themselves. Students also focus on values such as diversity, tolerance and understanding, which will help them become an active part of the local and wider community.

CAE

Cultural awareness and expression

Studying a foreign language involves an awareness of the culture of the people that speak it, including their art, their food, their festivals and their customs, as well as a general sense of global culture. By learning about other cultures through reading texts, videos and discussions to share different cultural experiences, students also become more aware of their own culture and learn to express themselves creatively in a way that shows awareness of their cultural context, reinforcing their sense of the world and their place in it.

LL

Learning to learn

Students need to develop effective strategies to improve their ability to learn independently. This means trying a variety of strategies to find ones which suit them and their learning styles, evaluating their own progress and thinking of ways to improve their ability to gain new knowledge and skills. Many of these strategies can be transferred to other subjects and learning contexts.

IE

Sense of initiative and entrepreneurship

Creativity, innovation, risk-taking and the ability to plan and manage projects in order to achieve objectives form the core of this competence. Collaborative projects give students a range of contexts in which to demonstrate and develop these abilities. Success in this competence gives students skills that are transferable from the classroom directly to the workplace.

Key competences in the Student's Book

Linguistic competence	
Every page of the **Student's Book** is dedicated to this competence.	
Mathematical competence and basic competences in Science and Technology	
Unit 1 pages 10, 12, 14-16 **Unit 2** pages 21-23, 25 **Unit 3** pages 30-33 **Unit 4** pages 36-43	**Unit 5** pages 46-51, 53 **Unit 6** pages 54, 55, 57, 60 **Unit 7** pages 64-71 **Unit 8** pages 72-74, 76, 77, 79 **Unit 9** pages 82, 83, 86-87
Digital competence	
Get started page 6 **Unit 1** pages 10-12, 17 **Unit 2** pages 18, 19, 21, 25 **Unit 3** pages 28, 29, 31, 35 **Unit 4** pages 36, 37, 39, 43	**Unit 5** pages 46, 47, 49, 52, 53 **Unit 6** pages 54, 55, 57, 61 **Unit 7** pages 64-71 **Unit 8** pages 72-75, 79 **Unit 9** pages 82-85, 89
Social and Civic competences	
Get started pages 6-9 **Unit 1** pages 10-15, 17 **Unit 2** pages 18, 20-25 **Unit 3** pages 28, 30-33, 35 **Unit 4** pages 39-43	**Unit 5** pages 48-53 **Unit 6** pages 54-58, 61 **Unit 7** pages 65-71 **Unit 8** pages 72-79 **Unit 9** pages 82-85
Cultural awareness and expression	
Get started pages 6-9 **Unit 1** pages 10, 12, 16, 17 **Unit 2** pages 18, 19, 24, 25 **Unit 3** pages 28-35 **Unit 4** pages 38-41, 43	**Unit 5** pages 46-48, 52, 53 **Unit 6** pages 54, 56, 57, 61 **Unit 7** pages 64, 67, 71 **Unit 8** pages 72, 75-77, 79 **Unit 9** pages 82-85, 89
Learning to learn	
Get started page 7 **Unit 1** pages 10, 11, 13, 14, 16 **Unit 2** pages 19, 20, 22, 24 **Unit 3** pages 32-35 **Unit 4** pages 37, 39, 42	**Unit 5** pages 47, 48, 50, 52, 53 **Unit 6** pages 54, 56, 58, 60 **Unit 7** pages 64, 66, 68, 70 **Unit 8** pages 72, 75, 76, 77, 79 **Unit 9** pages 82, 85, 86, 88
Sense of initiative and entrepreneurship	
Get started pages 6, 8, 9 **Unit 1** pages 11, 13, 16 **Unit 2** pages 19, 21, 24 **Unit 3** pages 29, 31, 34 **Unit 4** pages 37, 39, 42	**Unit 5** pages 47, 49, 52 **Unit 6** pages 55, 57, 60 **Unit 7** pages 65, 67, 90 **Unit 8** pages 73, 75, 78 **Unit 9** pages 83, 85, 88

CONTENTS NOW YOU! 4

- *Wish* and *If only* with past perfect
- Indirect questions
- Verb patterns

GET STARTED!

At the start of each unit and lesson, explain to the students what the objectives are.

Language objectives

Grammar

Present perfect and past simple
- Students review and practise the present perfect and past simple.

Adjective and preposition pairs
- Students review and practise adjectives and their prepositions in combination.

***Wish* and *If only* with past perfect**
- Students review and practise *Wish* and *If only* for wishes and past regrets.

Indirect questions
- Students review and practise asking indirect questions.

Verb patterns
- Students review and practise verbs and the set grammatical patterns that follow them.

Vocabulary

Goals and personal development: *achieve, challenge, confidence, determination, overcome, strategy, struggle, target, volunteer*
- Students review and practise vocabulary for goals and personal development.

Activism: *campaign, climate change, fundraising, gender equality, get involved, manage, poverty, raise awareness, social issues, task*
- Students review and practise vocabulary related to activism.

Career steps: *get a job, go to university, manage a team, pass an exam, pass your driving test, retire*
- Students review and practise vocabulary for career steps.

21st Century skills objectives

Challenging stereotypes
- Students discuss and reflect on stereotypes and different ways to challenge them.

Time management
- Students discuss and reflect on the importance of good time management.

Decision-making
- Students discuss and reflect on effective decision-making strategies.

Audiovisual objectives

The vloggers are back: Students watch and listen to Robert, Holly and Peter talk about the summer holidays and their thoughts about the year ahead.

Key competences

LC **Linguistic**
pages 6 - 9

DC **Digital**
page 6

SCC **Social and Civic**
pages 6-9

CAE **Cultural awareness and expression**
pages 6-9

LL **Learning to learn**
page 7

IE **Sense of initiative and entrepreneurship**
pages 6, 8-9

→ See pages 42-43 **Key competences**

CEFR Mediation

Facilitating collaborative interaction with peers
Can make and respond to suggestions and ask if people agree.
Can help work towards a common goal by asking and answering questions.

Relaying information in writing
Can relay specific information contained in spoken texts on familiar subjects.

Collaborating to construct meaning
Can make simple remarks and pose occasional questions to show that he/she is following.
Can make suggestions in a simple way to move the discussion forward.

Encouraging conceptual talk
Can ask what somebody thinks of an idea.

→ See pages 30-33 **Mediation**

Remind students to do all the exercises in their notebook

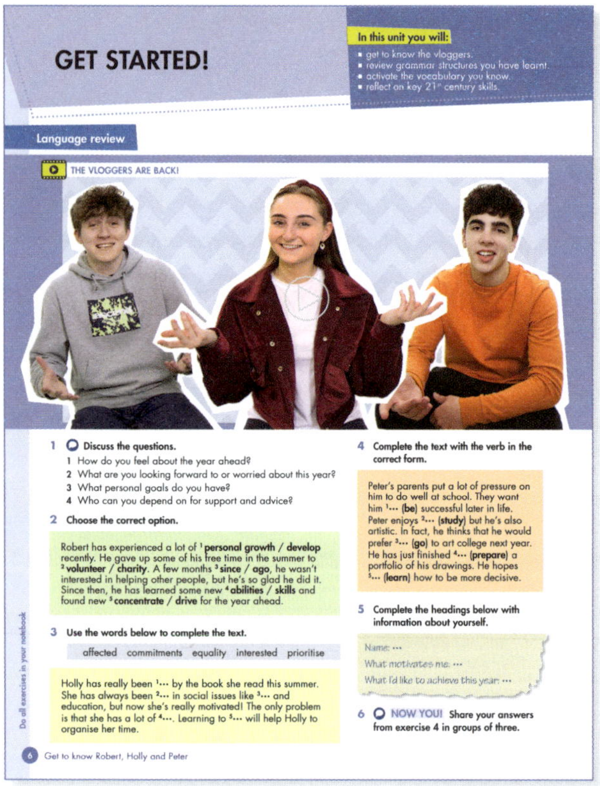

GET STARTED!

In this unit you will:
- get to know the vloggers.
- review grammar structures you have learnt.
- activate the vocabulary you know.
- reflect on key 21st century skills.

Language review

THE VLOGGERS ARE BACK!

1 Discuss the questions.
1 How do you feel about the year ahead?
2 What are you looking forward to or worried about this year?
3 What personal goals do you have?
4 Who can you depend on for support and advice?

2 Choose the correct option.

Robert has experienced a lot of [1] **personal growth / develop** recently. He gave up some of his free time in the summer to [2] **volunteer / charity**. A few months [3] **since / ago**, he wasn't interested in helping other people, but he's so glad he did it. Since then, he has learned some new [4] **abilities / skills** and found new [5] **concentrate / drive** for the year ahead.

3 Use the words below to complete the text.

affected commitments equality interested prioritise

Holly has really been [1]… by the book she read this summer. She has always been [2]… in social issues like [3]… and education, but now she's really motivated! The only problem is that she has a lot of [4]…. Learning to [5]… will help Holly to organise her time.

4 Complete the text with the verb in the correct form.

Peter's parents put a lot of pressure on him to do well at school. They want him [1]… (**be**) successful later in life. Peter enjoys [2]… (**study**) but he's also artistic. In fact, he thinks that he would prefer [3]… (**go**) to art college next year. He has just finished [4]… (**prepare**) a portfolio of his drawings. He hopes [5]… (**learn**) how to be more decisive.

5 Complete the headings below with information about yourself.

Name: …
What motivates me: …
What I'd like to achieve this year: …

6 NOW YOU! Share your answers from exercise 4 in groups of three.

Do all exercises in your notebook

6 Get to know Robert, Holly and Peter

ANSWER KEY

Page 6

1 *Student's own answers*

2
1 personal growth
2 volunteer
3 ago
4 skills
5 drive

3
1 affected
2 interested
3 equality
4 commitments
5 prioritise

4
1 to be
2 studying
3 to go
4 preparing
5 to learn

5 *Student's own answers*

6 *Student's own answers*

LESSON FOCUS

Grammar Present perfect and past simple
Vocabulary Goals and personal development
Speaking Comparing goals and motivation

Resources
Teacher's i-solutions, Vlog and worksheets

THE VLOGGERS ARE BACK!

Video and worksheet available on the RichmondLearningPlatform

- In pairs, ask students to complete the *Before you watch…* exercises on the vlog worksheet.
- Show students the vlog and ask them to complete the *While you watch…* exercises on the worksheet.
- In pairs, students compare answers.
- In small groups, tell students to complete the *After you watch…* exercises on the worksheet.

Warmer

Tell students that you are going to tell them 3 simple things about yourself but that one of them is not true, and they have to guess which one it is. Put the students in pairs or small groups to repeat the activity.

1 Get students to leave their books closed and dictate the questions to them. Then get them to open their books and ask and answer the questions in pairs.

2, 3 and 4 You may like to put students in groups of three for exercises 2, 3 and 4. When they have finished, write the answers to all three exercises on the board and ask them to write them in their notebooks. Then each group of three could test how much they remember about the text with their books closed.

5 Encourage students to write as much as they can for the last part of the fact file and help them with any vocabulary they need.

6 **NOW YOU!** After students compare their answers, ask the groups what answers they had in common.

Remind students to do all the exercises in their notebook

 CONTINUOUS ASSSESMENT Students can understand people writing about their summer holidays and the year ahead.

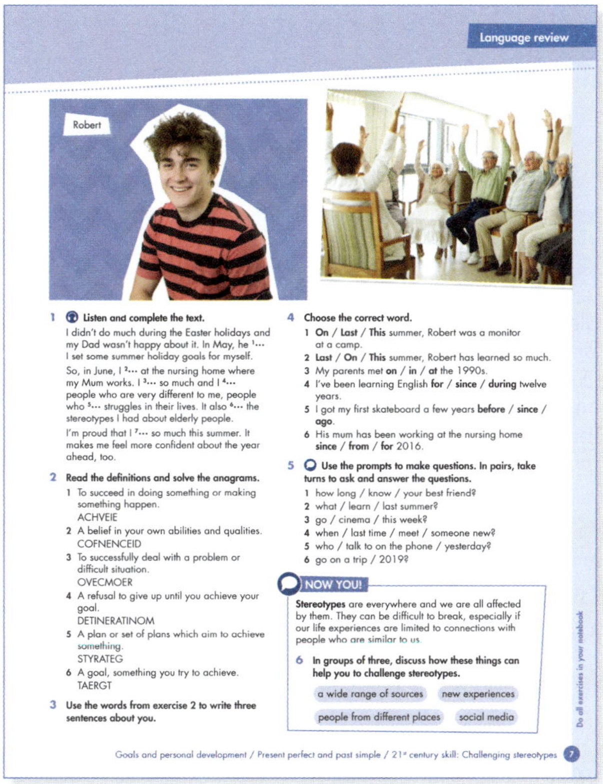

Language review

Robert

1 Listen and complete the text.

I didn't do much during the Easter holidays and my Dad wasn't happy about it. In May, he [1]… I set some summer holiday goals for myself.

So, in June, I [2]… at the nursing home where my Mum works. I [3]… so much and I [4]… people who are very different to me, people who [5]… struggles in their lives. It also [6]… the stereotypes I had about elderly people.

I'm proud that I [7]… so much this summer. It makes me feel more confident about the year ahead, too.

2 Read the definitions and solve the anagrams.

1 To succeed in doing something or making something happen.
ACHVEIE
2 A belief in your own abilities and qualities.
COFNENCEID
3 To successfully deal with a problem or difficult situation.
OVECMOER
4 A refusal to give up until you achieve your goal.
DETINERATINOM
5 A plan or set of plans which aim to achieve something.
STYRATEG
6 A goal, something you try to achieve.
TAERGT

3 Use the words from exercise 2 to write three sentences about you.

4 Choose the correct word.

1 **On / Last / This** summer, Robert was a monitor at a camp.
2 **Last / On / This** summer, Robert has learned so much.
3 My parents met **on / in / at** the 1990s.
4 I've been learning English **for / since / during** twelve years.
5 I got my first skateboard a few years **before / since / ago**.
6 His mum has been working at the nursing home **since / from / for** 2016.

5 Use the prompts to make questions. In pairs, take turns to ask and answer the questions.

1 how long / know / your best friend?
2 what / learn / last summer?
3 go / cinema / this week?
4 when / last time / meet / someone new?
5 who / talk to on the phone / yesterday?
6 go on a trip / 2019?

NOW YOU!

Stereotypes are everywhere and we are all affected by them. They can be difficult to break, especially if our life experiences are limited to connections with people who are similar to us.

6 In groups of three, discuss how these things can help you to challenge stereotypes.

a wide range of sources | new experiences | people from different places | social media

Do all exercises in your notebook

Goals and personal development / Present perfect and past simple / 21st century skill: Challenging stereotypes 7

LESSON FOCUS

Grammar Present perfect and past simple
Vocabulary Goals and personal development
Listening Completing a text
Speaking Asking and answering personal questions; A discussion about stereotypes
21st century skill Students reflect on stereotypes and what can help us challenge them

Resources
Teacher's i-solutions, Student's Book audio

Warmer

Put students in pairs and ask them to guess what their partner did over the summer using past simple questions. See who can come up with the most correct guesses.

1 1.1 (See page 168 for transcripts) Tell students that they will hear Robert talk about his summer goals and achievements. Ask them to read the text quickly before they listen and tell them there are 1-2 words per gap. Ask them if they have ever done something similar.

2 Tell students that all the words are related to goals and personal development and that the first letter of the anagram is also the first letter of the word.

3 Check that students understand the words and their definitions and get them to compare their sentences in pairs or small groups.

4 Elicit which tenses are being used in the exercise (past simple, present perfect continuous and present perfect) and get students to do the exercise.

5 Tell students that the exercise will continue the practice of the same two tenses. Encourage them to give extended answers. Remind them that when asking about details of a past event, they should use the past simple.

6 **NOW YOU!** Read through the paragraph on stereotypes together and ask what stereotypes students can think of (e.g. gender, age, nationality, etc.). When students have finished, ask volunteers for the ideas their groups came up with.

ANSWER KEY

Page 7

1
1 suggested
2 volunteered
3 learned
4 met
5 have overcome
6 challenged
7 have achieved

2
1 achieve
2 confidence
3 overcome
4 determination
5 strategy
6 target

3 *Student's own answers*

4
1 Last
2 This
3 in
4 for
5 ago
6 since

5
1 How long have you known your best friend?
Student's own answers
2 What did you learn last summer?
Student's own answers
3 Have you gone to the cinema this week?
Student's own answers
4 When was the last time you met someone new?
Student's own answers
5 Who did you talk to on the phone yesterday?
Student's own answers
6 Did you go on a trip in 2019?
Student's own answers

6 *Student's own answers*

Remind students to do all the exercises in their notebook

CONTINUOUS ASSESSMENT Students can use the present perfect and past simple, and vocabulary for goals and personal development.

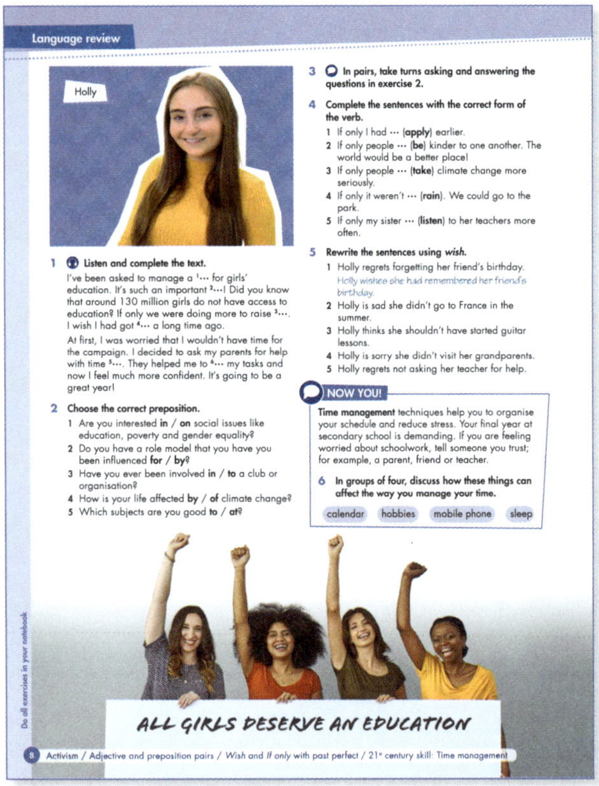
Language review

Holly

1 Listen and complete the text.

I've been asked to manage a [1]··· for girls' education. It's such an important [2]···! Did you know that around 130 million girls do not have access to education? If only we were doing more to raise [3]···. I wish I had got [4]··· a long time ago.

At first, I was worried that I wouldn't have time for the campaign. I decided to ask my parents for help with time [5]···. They helped me to [6]··· my tasks and now I feel much more confident. It's going to be a great year!

2 Choose the correct preposition.
1 Are you interested **in** / **on** social issues like education, poverty and gender equality?
2 Do you have a role model that you have you been influenced **for** / **by**?
3 Have you ever been involved **in** / **to** a club or organisation?
4 How is your life affected **by** / **of** climate change?
5 Which subjects are you good **to** / **at**?

3 In pairs, take turns asking and answering the questions in exercise 2.

4 Complete the sentences with the correct form of the verb.
1 If only I had ··· (**apply**) earlier.
2 If only people ··· (**be**) kinder to one another. The world would be a better place!
3 If only people ··· (**take**) climate change more seriously.
4 If only it weren't ··· (**rain**). We could go to the park.
5 If only my sister ··· (**listen**) to her teachers more often.

5 Rewrite the sentences using *wish*.
1 Holly regrets forgetting her friend's birthday.
Holly wishes she had remembered her friend's birthday.
2 Holly is sad she didn't go to France in the summer.
3 Holly thinks she shouldn't have started guitar lessons.
4 Holly is sorry she didn't visit her grandparents.
5 Holly regrets not asking her teacher for help.

NOW YOU!

Time management techniques help you to organise your schedule and reduce stress. Your final year at secondary school is demanding. If you are feeling worried about schoolwork, tell someone you trust; for example, a parent, friend or teacher.

6 In groups of four, discuss how these things can affect the way you manage your time.

calendar hobbies mobile phone sleep

ALL GIRLS DESERVE AN EDUCATION

Do all exercises in your notebook

8 Activism / Adjective and preposition pairs / *Wish* and *If only* with past perfect / 21st century skill: Time management

ANSWER KEY

Page 8

1
1 fundraising campaign
2 issue
3 awareness
4 involved
5 management
6 prioritise

2 **1** in **2** by **3** in **4** by **5** at

3 *Student's own answers*

4
1 applied
2 were
3 took
4 raining
5 listened

5
1 Holly wishes she had remembered her friend's birthday.
2 Holly wishes she had gone to France in the summer.
3 Holly wishes she hadn't started guitar lessons.
4 Holly wishes she had visited her grandparents.
5 Holly wishes she had asked her teacher for help.

6 *Student's own answers*

LESSON FOCUS

Grammar Adjective and preposition pairs; *Wish* and *If only* with past perfect
Vocabulary Activism
Listening Completing a text
Speaking Asking and answering questions about social issues
21st century skill Students discuss and reflect on time management

Resources

Teacher's i-solutions, Student's Book audio

Warmer

Write some social issues on the board (e.g. the environment, healthcare, education, poverty, gender equality, employment, etc.) and, in pairs, ask students to say which they think are the most important.

1 1.2 (See page 168 for transcripts) Tell students that they will hear Holly talking about one particular social issue and ask them to scan the text to find the issue and her connection to it (girls' education – she is involved in a campaign). Give them time to read though the text properly and predict the answers before playing the audio.

2 Answer the questions for yourself in a random order using the correct preposition. Ask students to tell you which question you are answering and the preposition.

3 Monitor students' use of prepositions and ask for volunteers to tell you some of their partner's answers.

4 Ask students which tenses they need to use for the exercise (past simple, past continuous and past perfect).

5 Ask students which tense we use with *Wish* and past regrets (past perfect).

6 NOW YOU! Read through the paragraph on time management together and ask students to do the exercise. Ask volunteers for recommendations for the rest of the class on what time management techniques they find effective.

Remind students to do all the exercises in their notebook

CONTINUOUS ASSESSMENT Students can use adjective and preposition pairs, *Wish* and *If only* with past perfect and vocabulary for activ

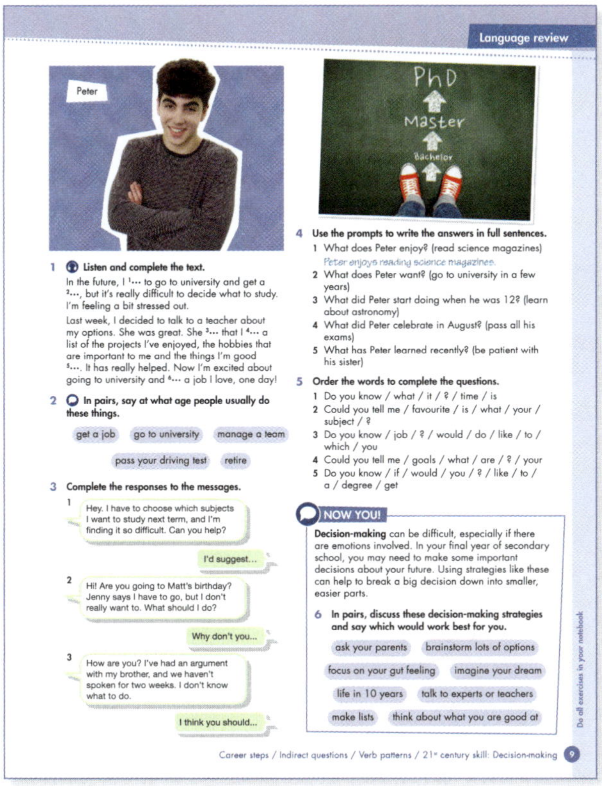

Language review

1 Listen and complete the text.

In the future, I [1]… to go to university and get a [2]…, but it's really difficult to decide what to study. I'm feeling a bit stressed out.

Last week, I decided to talk to a teacher about my options. She was great. She [3]… that I [4]… a list of the projects I've enjoyed, the hobbies that are important to me and the things I'm good [5]…. It has really helped. Now I'm excited about going to university and [6]… a job I love, one day!

2 In pairs, say at what age people usually do these things.

get a job / go to university / manage a team / pass your driving test / retire

3 Complete the responses to the messages.

1 Hey. I have to choose which subjects I want to study next term, and I'm finding it so difficult. Can you help?
I'd suggest…

2 Hi! Are you going to Matt's birthday? Jenny says I have to go, but I don't really want to. What should I do?
Why don't you…

3 How are you? I've had an argument with my brother, and we haven't spoken for two weeks. I don't know what to do.
I think you should…

4 Use the prompts to write the answers in full sentences.

1 What does Peter enjoy? (read science magazines)
Peter enjoys reading science magazines.
2 What does Peter want? (go to university in a few years)
3 What did Peter start doing when he was 12? (learn about astronomy)
4 What did Peter celebrate in August? (pass all his exams)
5 What has Peter learned recently? (be patient with his sister)

5 Order the words to complete the questions.

1 Do you know / what / it / ? / time / is
2 Could you tell me / favourite / is / what / your / subject / ?
3 Do you know / job / ? / would / do / like / to / which / you
4 Could you tell me / goals / what / are / ? / your
5 Do you know / if / would / you / ? / like / to / a / degree / get

NOW YOU!

Decision-making can be difficult, especially if there are emotions involved. In your final year of secondary school, you may need to make some important decisions about your future. Using strategies like these can help to break a big decision down into smaller, easier parts.

6 In pairs, discuss these decision-making strategies and say which would work best for you.

ask your parents / brainstorm lots of options / focus on your gut feeling / imagine your dream life in 10 years / talk to experts or teachers / make lists / think about what you are good at

Do all exercises in your notebook

Career steps / Indirect questions / Verb patterns / 21st century skill: Decision-making 9

ANSWER KEY

Page 9

1
1 hope
2 degree
3 suggested
4 make
5 at
6 getting

2 *Student's own answers*

3 *Student's own answers*

4
1 Peter enjoys reading science magazines.
2 Peter wants to go to university in a few years.
3 Peter started learning about astronomy when he was 12 years old.
4 Peter celebrated passing all his exams in August.
5 Peter has recently learned to be patient with his sister.

5
1 Do you know what time it is?
2 Could you tell me what your favourite subject is?
3 Do you know which job you would like to do?
4 Could you tell me what your goals are?
5 Do you know if you would like to get a degree?

6 *Student's own answers*

LESSON FOCUS

Grammar Indirect questions; Verb patterns
Vocabulary Career steps
Listening Listening and completing a text
Speaking Asking and answering questions about life goals.
21st century skill Students discuss and reflect on effective decision-making strategies

Resources
Teacher's i-solutions, Student's Book audio

Warmer

Put students in pairs or small groups and ask them to discuss what they think they might like to do when they finish school. Encourage them to elaborate, giving possible options if they are not sure, on what they think is involved in achieving their goals.

1 1.3 (See page 168 for transcripts) Tell students that they will hear Peter talk about meeting a teacher to discuss what subjects to study in his last year at school. Ask them to read the text and guess the answers before listening.

2 After students complete the exercise, ask if they know any people who did these things at an unusual age.

3 Compare students' answers and ask which advice the class thinks is the best.

4 Elicit which verb in each sentence needs which verb form after it. Extend the exercise by asking students similar questions with the same verbs and verb forms.

5 Point out that the first words are always at the beginning of the sentence and ask what kind of questions they will be forming (indirect questions) and if they remember how to form them.

6 **NOW YOU!** Read through the paragraph on decision-making together and ask what Peter did to help him make his decision. After students complete the exercise, do a quick class survey to find out which strategies were the most popular.

Remind students to do all the exercises in their notebook

CONTINUOUS ASSESSMENT Students can use indirect questions, verb patterns and vocabulary for career steps.

1 A HEAD FOR BUSINESS

At the start of each unit and lesson, explain to the students what the objectives are.

Language objectives

Grammar

Verb tense review

- Students review the present simple, past simple and present perfect.

Verb tense review: questions

- Students review the question forms of the present simple, past simple and present perfect

Vocabulary

Skills and strengths: Skills: *analytical skills, communication, creativity, empathy, negotiation, numeracy, passion, problem solving;* Strengths: *active, creative, enthusiastic, imaginative, meticulous, resourceful, sociable, systematic, talkative, thoughtful*

- Students practise using vocabulary for describing skills and strengths.

Business: *company, earn, employee, identity, launch, logo, product, run your own business, service, slogan, success, target market*

- Students practise using vocabulary for talking about business.

Jobs: *architect, entrepreneur, firefighter, graphic designer, marine biologist, newspaper editor, psychologist, radio DJ*

- Students practise using vocabulary for talking about jobs.

Idioms and expressions

Making decisions: *I'll sleep on it, on the fence, the jury is out, be in two minds*

- Students look at idioms and expressions related to making decisions in the context of four short monologues.

Recycled language

Present simple, Past simple, Present perfect, Questions

Skills objectives

Speaking

- Students discuss which company departments they would like to work in.
- Students discuss definitions of strengths and decide which apply to them.
- Students discuss jobs that would suit them based on an analysis of their personality.
- Students interview each other about any entrepreneurial achievements they have made.
- Students work together to solve puzzles.
- Students discuss multiple intelligences, in general and in relation to themselves.
- Students ask and answer personal questions using idioms and expressions.

Pronunciation: Students practise the /əʊ/ sound and practise identifying which words with the letter 'o' feature it and which don't.

Pairwork: Students use various mediation techniques to decide on a poster and slogan to fit a specific advertising brief for a pair of trainers.

Listening

- Students listen and complete a table about a meeting to decide on the employee of the year award.
- Students listen to answers to a quiz to analyse their personality.
- Students listen to an interview about three successful people and complete sentences.
- Students listen to conversations with entrepreneurs, answer questions and complete tables.
- Students listen to idioms and expressions in context.

Reading

- Students read an article in order to find information relevant to their intelligence type.
- Students read in detail to determine if statements are true or false, and to correct false statements.

Core values: Students consider and discuss the importance of **learner autonomy** and exchange learning tips.

Writing

- Students look at the importance of structuring a text with paragraphs.
- Students plan, write and check an article about a product.

Focus on tenses

Remind students to do all the exercises in their notebook

Learning to learn tools

SPEAKING TOOLS Students practise using new vocabulary within familiar structures to gain confidence and sound natural.	**LISTENING TOOLS** Students practise using the information on the page to help prepare them for listening tasks.
READING TOOLS Students practise making connections between themselves and the texts they read to help them get the most out of their reading.	**WRITING TOOLS** Students practise planning paragraphs before they start writing to help them focus.

VOCABULARY TOOLS Students practise categorising vocabulary to aid memory.

Project objectives: Entrepreneurs

Task 1 Students identify roles and responsibilities.

Task 2 Students decide on a product or service, and create a logo and a slogan.

Task 3 Students write texts to include in a leaflet about their company.

Audiovisual objectives

Vlog: Students watch and listen to Emma talk about tips for teenage entrepreneurs.

Culture: Students watch and listen to Emma talk about air traffic control.

Grammar animations: Students are presented with visual presentations of the unit grammar.

Key competences

LC **Linguistic**
pages 10-17

MST **Mathematical and Science and Technology**
pages 10, 12, 14-16

DC **Digital**
pages 10-12, 17

SCC **Social and Civic**
pages 10-15, 17

CAE **Cultural awareness and expression**
pages 10, 12, 16-17

LL **Learning to learn**
pages 10-11, 13-14, 16

IE **Sense of initiative and entrepreneurship**
pages 11, 13, 16

→ See pages 42-43 **Key competences**

CEFR Mediation

1.1 Facilitating collaborative interaction with peers
Can invite other people in a group to speak.

1.2 Note-taking
Can take notes as a list of key points during a simple talk.

1.3 Facilitating collaborative interaction with peers
Can formulate and respond to suggestions.

1.4 Processing text in writing
Can summarise the information in texts on general subjects.

1.5 Relaying specific information in writing
Can write specific information in spoken texts.

Project Facilitating collaborative interaction with peers
Can formulate and respond to suggestions, ask whether people agree and propose alternatives.

Unit review Facilitating collaborative interaction with peers
Can collaborate in simple tasks by asking and answering questions.

Pairwork Encouraging conceptual talk
Can ask questions to invite people to clarify their reasoning.

→ See pages 30-33 **Mediation**

Remind students to do all the exercises in their notebook

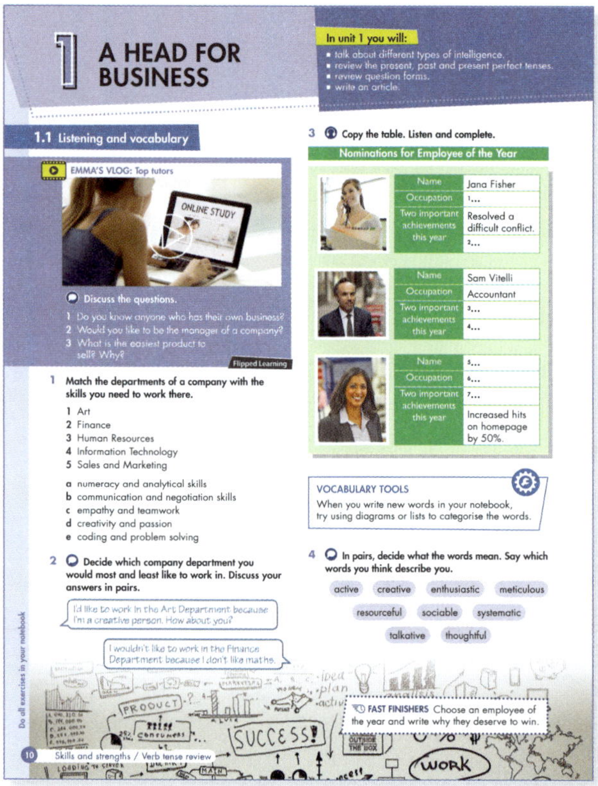

1 A HEAD FOR BUSINESS

In unit 1 you will:
- talk about different types of intelligence.
- review the present, past and present perfect tenses.
- review question forms.
- write an article.

1.1 Listening and vocabulary

EMMA'S VLOG: Top tutors

Discuss the questions.
1 Do you know anyone who has their own business?
2 Would you like to be the manager of a company?
3 What is the easiest product to sell? Why?

Flipped Learning

1 Match the departments of a company with the skills you need to work there.
1 Art
2 Finance
3 Human Resources
4 Information Technology
5 Sales and Marketing

a numeracy and analytical skills
b communication and negotiation skills
c empathy and teamwork
d creativity and passion
e coding and problem solving

2 Decide which company department you would most and least like to work in. Discuss your answers in pairs.

I'd like to work in the Art Department because I'm a creative person. How about you?

I wouldn't like to work in the Finance Department because I don't like maths.

3 Copy the table. Listen and complete.

Nominations for Employee of the Year

Name	Jana Fisher
Occupation	1...
Two important achievements this year	Resolved a difficult conflict. 2...
Name	Sam Vitelli
Occupation	Accountant
Two important achievements this year	3... 4...
Name	5...
Occupation	6...
Two important achievements this year	7... Increased hits on homepage by 50%.

VOCABULARY TOOLS
When you write new words in your notebook, try using diagrams or lists to categorise the words.

4 In pairs, decide what the words mean. Say which words you think describe you.

active creative enthusiastic meticulous resourceful sociable systematic talkative thoughtful

FAST FINISHERS Choose an employee of the year and write why they deserve to win.

10 Skills and strengths / Verb tense review

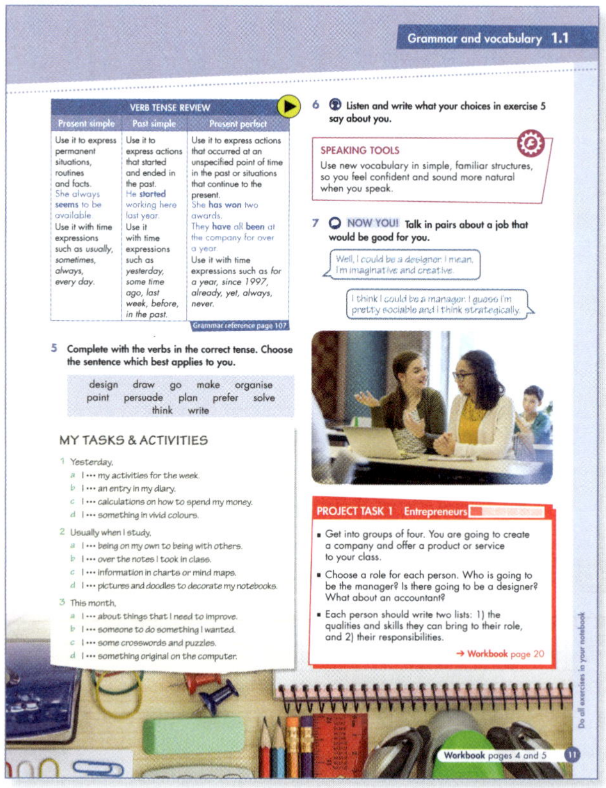

Grammar and vocabulary 1.1

VERB TENSE REVIEW

Present simple	Past simple	Present perfect
Use it to express permanent situations, routines and facts. She always seems to be available. Use it with time expressions such as usually, sometimes, always, every day.	Use it to express actions that started and ended in the past. He started working here last year. Use it with time expressions such as yesterday, some time ago, last week, before, in the past.	Use it to express actions that occurred at an unspecified point of time in the past or situations that continue to the present. She has won two awards. They have all been at the company for over a year. Use it with time expressions such as for a year, since 1997, already, yet, always, never.

Grammar reference page 107

5 Complete with the verbs in the correct tense. Choose the sentence which best applies to you.

design draw go make organise paint persuade plan prefer solve think write

MY TASKS & ACTIVITIES

1 Yesterday,
a I ··· my activities for the week.
b I ··· an entry in my diary.
c I ··· calculations on how to spend my money.
d I ··· something in vivid colours.

2 Usually when I study,
a I ··· being on my own to being with others.
b I ··· over the notes I took in class.
c I ··· information in charts or mind maps.
d I ··· pictures and doodles to decorate my notebooks.

3 This month,
a I ··· about things that I need to improve.
b I ··· someone to do something I wanted.
c I ··· some crosswords and puzzles.
d I ··· something original on the computer.

6 Listen and write what your choices in exercise 5 say about you.

SPEAKING TOOLS
Use new vocabulary in simple, familiar structures, so you feel confident and sound more natural when you speak.

7 NOW YOU! Talk in pairs about a job that would be good for you.

Well, I could be a designer. I mean, I'm imaginative and creative.

I think I could be a manager. I guess I'm pretty sociable and I think strategically.

PROJECT TASK 1 Entrepreneurs
- Get into groups of four. You are going to create a company and offer a product or service to your class.
- Choose a role for each person. Who is going to be the manager? Is there going to be a designer? What about an accountant?
- Each person should write two lists: 1) the qualities and skills they can bring to their role, and 2) their responsibilities.

→ Workbook page 20

Workbook pages 4 and 5 11

ANSWER KEY

Pages 10-11

1 **1** d
2 a
3 c
4 e
5 b

2 *Student's own answers*

3 **1** Human resources officer
2 Set up a social programme to improve staff relations
3 Made sure all the financial records are accurate and up to date
4 Helped save over ten thousand pounds in unnecessary expenses
5 Christina Brent
6 Web designer
7 Won two awards for the design of the web page

4 *Suggested answers:*
active: energetic
creative: artistic/imaginative
enthusiastic: interested/passionate
meticulous: perfectionist/careful
resourceful: capable/intelligent
sociable: friendly/good-natured
systematic: organised/analytical
talkative: communicative
thoughtful: attentive/careful

5 **1** **a** planned
b wrote
c made
d painted

2 **a** prefer
b go
c organise
d draw

3 **a** have thought
b have persuaded
c have solved
d have designed

6 *Student's own answers*

7 *Student's own answers*

Remind students to do all the exercises in their notebook

LESSON FOCUS

Grammar Verb tense review
Vocabulary Skills and strengths
Listening Completing a table about a meeting; Answers to a quiz to analyse personality types
Speaking Discussing company departments students would like to work in; Discussing words to describe strengths; Discussing suitable jobs based on personalities
Project task 1 Identify roles and responsibilities

Resources

Teacher's i-solutions, Student's Book audio, Vlog and worksheet

Flipped Learning

EMMA'S VLOG: Top tutors

- Make sure to set up the **Flipped Learning** work with the students beforehand. **See pages 20-23 for complete Flipped Learning guidelines**.
- Ask students to put the **Flipped Learning worksheets** on their desks and walk around to check how many have completed the Flipped task.
- In pairs or small groups, ask students to compare and check the *Before you watch...* and *While you watch...* exercises on the worksheet.
- Show students **Emma's Vlog** and ask volunteers to provide correct answers and clarify any doubts other students may have.
- Choose three or four students to read aloud their answers to the *After you watch...* exercises on the worksheet and encourage some class discussion.
- Move straight to exercise 1 on page 10.

Warmer

Watch Emma's Vlog and discuss the questions with the whole class. If you don't have video facilities, simply discuss the questions.

1 Get students to call out different job titles and write them on the board. Ask the class what skills they think are needed to do each of the jobs. Students can then complete the exercise alone or in pairs.

2 Encourage students to give each other constructive feedback on each other's preferences.

3 1.4 (See page 168 for transcripts) Tell students they are going to listen in on a company meeting to decide the employee of the month and draw their attention to the table. Let them check their answers in pairs and then let them decide who they think should be the employee of the month.

VOCABULARY TOOLS

Get students to read the **Vocabulary tool**. Draw their attention to the **Wordlist** at the back of the book and ask what diagrams they could use to record vocabulary (mind maps, for example).

4 Point out that students have already seen these words in some form in the **Student's Book** and get them to try to remember the context, but also let them use dictionaries. Encourage them to give reasons for their choices about which words describe them.

FAST FINISHERS Students can complete this exercise alone or in pairs.

Flipped Learning

VERB TENSE REVIEW

Draw students' attention to the **Grammar table**. Remind students that they can use this as a quick reference while completing the exercises.

Show students the **Grammar animation** and/or refer students to the **Grammar reference** on page 107 for further information on form and use.

→ See page 23 for how to flip the **grammar lesson**

5 You could help students by eliciting which tense they think goes with each number (1 - past simple, 2 - present simple, 3 - present perfect) before they start.

6 1.5 (See page 168 for transcripts) You could ask around the class to see who answered 2 or 3 of the same letter. Tell students they are going to listen to an assessment of their personality based on the quiz. Ask how much they agree with their assessments.

SPEAKING TOOLS

Get students to read the **Speaking tool** and tell them to put it into practice in the next exercise.

7 NOW YOU! Ask students to draw on what they heard in exercise 6 and their discussions in exercises 2 and 4 to give each other feedback. Ask students what answers their partners gave.

PROJECT TASK 1 Entrepreneurs

Organise students into groups of four and read through the first task of the project together. Tell them they can start thinking about what their company will do, but they will make a final decision on that in the next task. Next they should choose roles based on the skills and qualities they bring to the responsibilities they will have to fulfil. Remind students that they need to keep their project notes together in their **Workbook** (page 20) or in their own notebook.

→ See pages 24-27 **Projects**

FURTHER PRACTICE

Workbook pages 4-5
- **Grammar reference and practice** pages 84 and 93
- **Wordlist and exercises** pages 98 and 102

Remind students to do all the exercises in their notebook

CONTINUOUS ASSESSMENT Students can talk about skills and strengths, and use a range of verb tenses.

1.2 Grammar and listening

1 Listen and make notes about why the people are famous. Compare your answers in pairs.

VERB TENSE REVIEW: QUESTIONS

	Present simple	Past simple	Present perfect
Yes/No questions	Does Gates own a company?	Did Chanel create the logo?	Have Wieden and his team written any other famous slogans?
Wh- questions	What do graphic designers do?	When did Chanel launch her company?	What has Gates done through his charity?

Grammar reference page 107

2 Complete the questions with the verb in the correct tense. Listen again and check. Then answer the questions.

1 What ··· Bill Gates ··· (do) now?
2 How long ··· he ··· (have) the charity?
3 How ··· Chanel's designs ··· (change) fashion?
4 What ··· the Nike slogan ··· (represent)?
5 ··· Wieden ··· (create) any other famous slogans?

3 Complete the text with the correct form of the verbs.

be come earn get grow love make need realise see start work (x2) write

Adam: This week on *Bright Ideas* we're talking to Serena Tisdale. Serena's blog [1]··· her a millionaire at the age of 20. Serena, what's your secret?
Serena: Well, I [2]··· writing since I [3]··· a teenager. At school, I [4]··· for the school newsletter and then I [5]··· a job at a local newspaper. I think you [6]··· to be passionate about what you do.
Adam: And how did you [7]··· up with the idea of a blog?
Serena: I [8]··· that fewer and fewer people were reading printed newspapers, so I [9]··· a market for quality online news. When I [10]··· the blog, it was just me. Since then, the company [11]··· to over 30 employees.
Adam: It seems like you [12]··· really hard to get where you are.
Serena: You won't be successful if you don't [13]··· for it!
Adam: Well, you certainly [14]··· your success!

FAST FINISHERS Write about what type of job you would like to do in the future.

Do all exercises in your notebook

12 Business / Verb tense review: questions

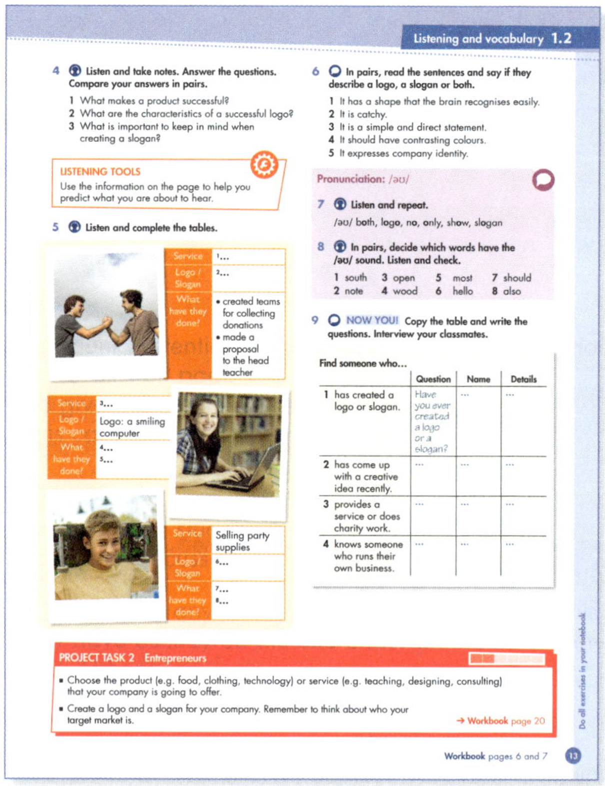
Listening and vocabulary 1.2

4 Listen and take notes. Answer the questions. Compare your answers in pairs.
1 What makes a product successful?
2 What are the characteristics of a successful logo?
3 What is important to keep in mind when creating a slogan?

LISTENING TOOLS
Use the information on the page to help you predict what you are about to hear.

5 Listen and complete the tables.

Service	[1]...
Logo / Slogan	[2]...
What have they done?	• created teams for collecting donations • made a proposal to the head teacher

Service	[3]...
Logo / Slogan	Logo: a smiling computer
What have they done?	[4]... [5]...

Service	Selling party supplies
Logo / Slogan	[6]...
What have they done?	[7]... [8]...

6 In pairs, read the sentences and say if they describe a logo, a slogan or both.
1 It has a shape that the brain recognises easily.
2 It is catchy.
3 It is a simple and direct statement.
4 It should have contrasting colours.
5 It expresses company identity.

Pronunciation: /əʊ/

7 Listen and repeat.
/əʊ/ both, logo, no, only, show, slogan

8 In pairs, decide which words have the /əʊ/ sound. Listen and check.
1 south 2 note 3 open 4 wood 5 most 6 hello 7 should 8 also

9 NOW YOU! Copy the table and write the questions. Interview your classmates.

Find someone who...	Question	Name	Details
1 has created a logo or slogan.	Have you ever created a logo or a slogan?	...	...
2 has come up with a creative idea recently.	...	...	...
3 provides a service or does charity work.	...	...	...
4 knows someone who runs their own business.	...	...	...

PROJECT TASK 2 Entrepreneurs
▪ Choose the product (e.g. food, clothing, technology) or service (e.g. teaching, designing, consulting) that your company is going to offer.
▪ Create a logo and a slogan for your company. Remember to think about who your target market is.
→ Workbook page 20

Do all exercises in your notebook

Workbook pages 6 and 7 13

ANSWER KEY

Pages 12-13

1 *Student's own answers*

2
1 does; do; Bill Gates runs a charity focused on healthcare, education and ending poverty.
2 has; had; he has had it for 20 years. He started it in the year 2000.
3 did; change; Chanel's designs changed fashion by making women's clothes more practical and comfortable.
4 does; represent; the slogan represents the 'can do' attitude of the company.
5 Has; created; yes, he has created lots more.

3
1 made
2 have loved
3 was
4 wrote
5 got
6 need
7 come
8 realised
9 saw
10 started
11 has grown
12 have worked
13 work
14 have earned

4 *Suggested answers:*
1 It must meet some need in the market.
2 It must be simple and original.
3 You have only a couple of seconds to catch your audience's attention.

5
1 a charity that provides students with books and food
2 'Together we're better'
3 computer repair business
4 made a list of the most common problems computers have
5 paid friends who know about computers to work for her
6 'There's no party better'
7 helped his friends to plan their parties
8 hired friends and family to host parties

6
1 a logo
2 a slogan
3 a slogan
4 a logo
5 both

7 *Student's own answers*

8 note, open, most, hello, also

9 *Student's own answers*

Remind students to do all the exercises in their notebook

LESSON FOCUS

Listening Taking notes and completing sentences; Answering questions and completing a table

Speaking Interviews about entrepreneurial achievements

Project task 2 Decide on a product or service and create a logo and a slogan

Resources

Teacher's i-solutions, Student's Book audio

Preparation Pictures of famous entrepreneurs the students might know, and a bit of basic research about their achievements

Warmer

Put the pictures of the entrepreneurs on the board and ask students if they recognise them. Get students to speculate about what they might have done and then confirm or correct their speculations for each.

1 1.6 (See page 168 for transcripts) Ask if students know who the entrepreneurs are. Tell them they are going to hear a radio programme about them and that they must take notes while listening.

2 1.7 (See page 169 for transcripts) Get students to try and do this exercise from memory (from their knowledge of grammar and from the previous exercise). You could then play up to the question, pause and check, and pause at the end of the answer for them to have time to complete their notes before playing the next question, and so on. At the end, students compare the notes they wrote about the answers to the questions.

Flipped Learning

VERB TENSE REVIEW: QUESTIONS

Draw students' attention to the **Grammar table**. Remind students that they can use this as a quick reference while completing the exercises.

Show students the **Grammar animation** and/or refer students to the **Grammar reference** on page 107 for further information on form and use.

→ See page 23 for how to flip the **grammar lesson**

3 Let students look at the picture and the beginning of the text and ask who the woman is and what she does (Serena Tisdale, young millionaire blogger). Tell them to use the tenses reviewed in the unit and refer them to the **Grammar table** if necessary. For extra question practice, get students in pairs to write another couple of questions to ask Serena and to write imaginary answers to the questions.

FAST FINISHERS Students can complete this exercise alone or in pairs.

4 1.8 (See page 169 for transcripts) Tell students they are going to hear an interview with a successful entrepreneur giving advice that will be useful for the **Project task**. Check that they understand the definitions of 'logo' and 'slogan'. Play the audio and have them compare their notes.

LISTENING TOOLS

Get students to read the **Listening tool** and ask them what information on the page in exercise 5 might help them (the photos, the table headings and the parts already filled in).

5 1.9 (See page 169 for transcripts) Give students time to look at the tables and encourage them to guess what the first two services might be without confirming or denying. After playing the audio, ask them if any of their guesses were correct before you check the answers.

6 To extend this exercise, ask students to think of logos and slogans that they think fulfil the criteria in the exercise.

Pronunciation

7 1.10 (See page 169 for transcripts) Show students how your lips move when you make the sound and check that they are making the diphthong sound correctly.

8 1.11 (See page 169 for transcripts) Tell students that this sound is almost always produced by the letter 'o' but that the letter 'o' doesn't always produce this sound. Let them read through the words first to see if they remember how they're pronounced before they listen and check.

9 NOW YOU! Elicit the questions students will need as a class first and maybe elicit another related question or two for them to ask to extend the exercise. After they've finished, ask students to tell you the most interesting information they found out about people in the class.

PROJECT TASK 2 Entrepreneurs

Put students back in their teams, remind them of the roles they chose for each other and get them to discuss their product or service, their slogan and their logo. Remind students that they need to keep their project notes together in their **Workbook** (page 20) or in their own notebook.

→ See pages 24-27 **Projects**

FURTHER PRACTICE

Workbook pages 6-7

- **Grammar reference and practice** pages 84 and 93
- **Wordlist and exercises** pages 98 and 102

Vocabulary and Grammar worksheets available to download and edit from the **Richmond** *Learning* **Platform**

→ See pages 38-39 **Mixed-ability classes**

Remind students to do all the exercises in their notebook

CONTINUOUS ASSESSMENT Students can talk about business and ask questions in a range of verb tenses.

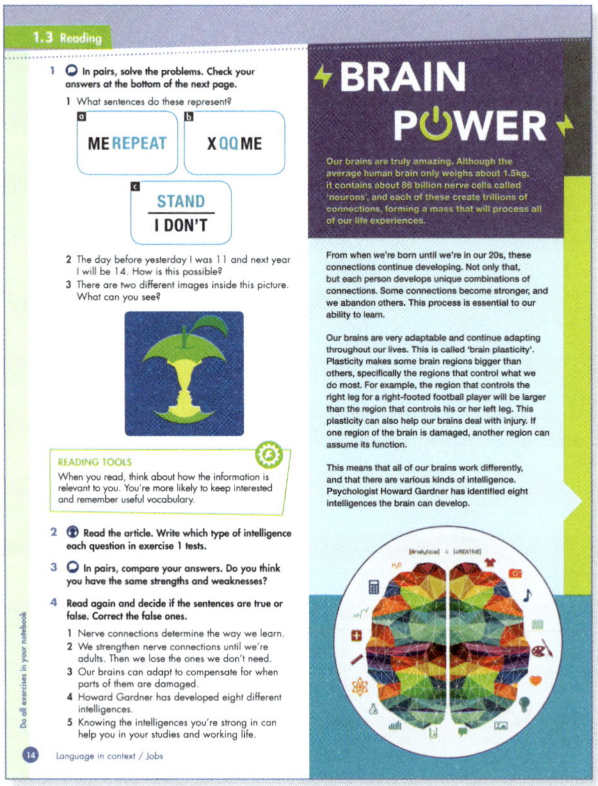

1.3 Reading

1 In pairs, solve the problems. Check your answers at the bottom of the next page.

1 What sentences do these represent?

a ME REPEAT

b X QQ ME

c STAND / I DON'T

2 The day before yesterday I was 11 and next year I will be 14. How is this possible?

3 There are two different images inside this picture. What can you see?

READING TOOLS
When you read, think about how the information is relevant to you. You're more likely to keep interested and remember useful vocabulary.

2 Read the article. Write which type of intelligence each question in exercise 1 tests.

3 In pairs, compare your answers. Do you think you have the same strengths and weaknesses?

4 Read again and decide if the sentences are true or false. Correct the false ones.

1 Nerve connections determine the way we learn.
2 We strengthen nerve connections until we're adults. Then we lose the ones we don't need.
3 Our brains can adapt to compensate for when parts of them are damaged.
4 Howard Gardner has developed eight different intelligences.
5 Knowing the intelligences you're strong in can help you in your studies and working life.

Do all exercises in your notebook

14 Language in context / Jobs

BRAIN POWER

Our brains are truly amazing. Although the average human brain only weighs about 1.5kg, it contains about 86 billion nerve cells called 'neurons', and each of these create trillions of connections, forming a mass that will process all of our life experiences.

From when we're born until we're in our 20s, these connections continue developing. Not only that, but each person develops unique combinations of connections. Some connections become stronger, and we abandon others. This process is essential to our ability to learn.

Our brains are very adaptable and continue adapting throughout our lives. This is called 'brain plasticity'. Plasticity makes some brain regions bigger than others, specifically the regions that control what we do most. For example, the region that controls the right leg for a right-footed football player will be larger than the region that controls his or her left leg. This plasticity can also help our brains deal with injury. If one region of the brain is damaged, another region can assume its function.

This means that all of our brains work differently, and that there are various kinds of intelligence. Psychologist Howard Gardner has identified eight intelligences the brain can develop.

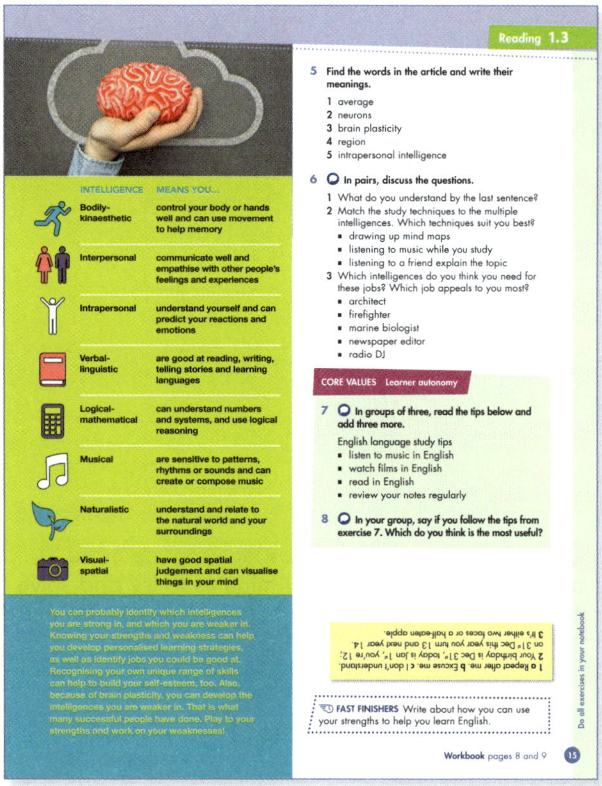

INTELLIGENCE	MEANS YOU...
Bodily-kinaesthetic	control your body or hands well and can use movement to help memory
Interpersonal	communicate well and empathise with other people's feelings and experiences
Intrapersonal	understand yourself and can predict your reactions and emotions
Verbal-linguistic	are good at reading, writing, telling stories and learning languages
Logical-mathematical	can understand numbers and systems, and use logical reasoning
Musical	are sensitive to patterns, rhythms or sounds and can create or compose music
Naturalistic	understand and relate to the natural world and your surroundings
Visual-spatial	have good spatial judgement and can visualise things in your mind

You can probably identify which intelligences you are strong in, and which you are weaker in. Knowing your strengths and weakness can help you develop personalised learning strategies, as well as identify jobs you could be good at. Recognising your own unique range of skills can help to build your self-esteem, too. Also, because of brain plasticity, you can develop the intelligences you are weaker in. That is what many successful people have done. Play to your strengths and work on your weaknesses!

Reading 1.3

5 Find the words in the article and write their meanings.

1 average
2 neurons
3 brain plasticity
4 region
5 intrapersonal intelligence

6 In pairs, discuss the questions.

1 What do you understand by the last sentence?
2 Match the study techniques to the multiple intelligences. Which techniques suit you best?
- drawing up mind maps
- listening to music while you study
- listening to a friend explain the topic
3 Which intelligences do you think you need for these jobs? Which job appeals to you most?
- architect
- firefighter
- marine biologist
- newspaper editor
- radio DJ

CORE VALUES Learner autonomy

7 In groups of three, read the tips below and add three more.

English language study tips
- listen to music in English
- watch films in English
- read in English
- review your notes regularly

8 In your group, say if you follow the tips from exercise 7. Which do you think is the most useful?

1 a Repeat after me. b Excuse me. c I don't understand.
2 Your birthday is Dec 31st, today is Jan 1st, you're 12; on 31st Dec this year you turn 13 and next year 14.
3 It's either two faces or a half-eaten apple.

FAST FINISHERS Write about how you can use your strengths to help you learn English.

Do all exercises in your notebook

Workbook pages 8 and 9 15

ANSWER KEY

Pages 14-15

1 *Answers given at bottom of page 15*

2 **1** verbal-linguistic and visual-spatial
2 logical-mathematical
3 visual-spatial

3 *Student's own answers*

4 **1** True
2 False. We strengthen and abandon nerve connections from when we are born until we're in our 20s.
3 True
4 False. He has identified eight intelligences.
5 True

5 **1** normal or typical
2 nerve cells
3 the ability of our brains to adapt
4 area
5 the ability to understand yourself

6 *Suggested answers:*
1 It means you should make the most of your strengths and also try to improve any areas of weakness.
2 drawing up mind maps – visual-spatial; listening to music while you study – musical; listening to a friend explain the topic – interpersonal, verbal-linguistic
Student's own answers
3 architect: visual-spatial; firefighter: bodily-kinaesthetic; marine biologist: naturalistic; newspaper editor: verbal-linguistic; radio DJ: musical
Student's own answers

7 *Student's own answers*

8 *Student's own answers*

Remind students to do all the exercises in their notebook

LESSON FOCUS

Language in context Jobs

Core values Learner autonomy

Resources

Teacher's i-solutions, Student's Book audio

→ See pages 36-37 **Literature**

Warmer

Tell the class this riddle (or any other that you know) and get them to ask you questions in order to find the answer. A boy and his father are in an accident and they're taken to hospital, where they doctor says, 'I can't operate on this boy – he's my son.' How is this possible? (The doctor is the boy's mother.)

1 Tell students they will now solve some more problems. Give them a few minutes to try and solve the problems, but they shouldn't spend too long on this.

READING TOOLS

Get students to read the **Reading tool** and tell them to apply it in the next exercise.

2 1.12 (See page 169 for transcripts) Ask students to look at the different intelligence types on page 15 and then scan the text on page 14 to see what they refer to (the eight different intelligences that psychologist Howard Gardiner identified). Ask them what information is most interesting to them and then ask them to quickly identify which type they most strongly identify with before they continue the exercise.

3 Refer students to their answers from exercise 2 and get them to compare their strengths and weaknesses, reflecting on the text and their ability to solve the problems in exercise 1.

4 Give students time to read in more detail and let them answer in pairs, making sure they use the text to justify their answers.

5 Let students guess meanings from context but help them with their definitions.

6 Tell students there are no right or wrong answers to these questions, but that they should give their reasons in the discussion.

CORE VALUES Learner autonomy

7 Point out that the **Learning to learn** tools in the **Student's Book** are learning tips and ask which of them they have found most helpful.

8 Remind students that different people have different learner styles and so the tips that will be of use will differ from student to student.

FAST FINISHERS Students can complete this exercise alone or in pairs.

FURTHER PRACTICE

Workbook pages 8-9

Remind students to do all the exercises in their notebook

CONTINUOUS ASSESSMENT Students can understand a text about the brain and talk about jobs.

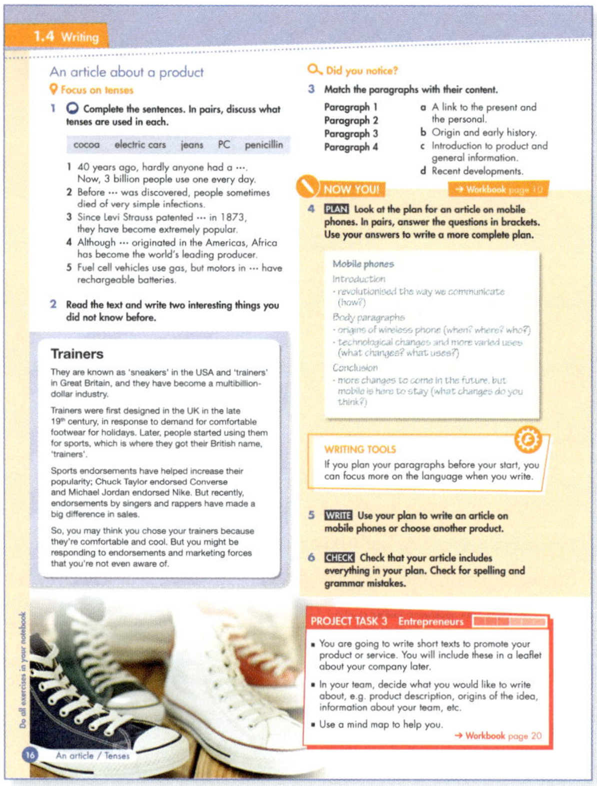

1.4 Writing

An article about a product

Focus on tenses

1 Complete the sentences. In pairs, discuss what tenses are used in each.

cocoa electric cars jeans PC penicillin

1 40 years ago, hardly anyone had a ···. Now, 3 billion people use one every day.
2 Before ··· was discovered, people sometimes died of very simple infections.
3 Since Levi Strauss patented ··· in 1873, they have become extremely popular.
4 Although ··· originated in the Americas, Africa has become the world's leading producer.
5 Fuel cell vehicles use gas, but motors in ··· have rechargeable batteries.

2 Read the text and write two interesting things you did not know before.

Trainers

They are known as 'sneakers' in the USA and 'trainers' in Great Britain, and they have become a multibillion-dollar industry.

Trainers were first designed in the UK in the late 19th century, in response to demand for comfortable footwear for holidays. Later, people started using them for sports, which is where they got their British name, 'trainers'.

Sports endorsements have helped increase their popularity; Chuck Taylor endorsed Converse and Michael Jordan endorsed Nike. But recently, endorsements by singers and rappers have made a big difference in sales.

So, you may think you chose your trainers because they're comfortable and cool. But you might be responding to endorsements and marketing forces that you're not even aware of.

Did you notice?

3 Match the paragraphs with their content.

Paragraph 1
Paragraph 2
Paragraph 3
Paragraph 4

a A link to the present and the personal.
b Origin and early history.
c Introduction to product and general information.
d Recent developments.

NOW YOU! → Workbook page 10

4 PLAN Look at the plan for an article on mobile phones. In pairs, answer the questions in brackets. Use your answers to write a more complete plan.

Mobile phones
Introduction
- revolutionised the way we communicate (how?)
Body paragraphs
- origins of wireless phone (when? where? who?)
- technological changes and more varied uses (what changes? what uses?)
Conclusion
- more changes to come in the future, but mobile is here to stay (what changes do you think?)

WRITING TOOLS
If you plan your paragraphs before your start, you can focus more on the language when you write.

5 WRITE Use your plan to write an article on mobile phones or choose another product.

6 CHECK Check that your article includes everything in your plan. Check for spelling and grammar mistakes.

PROJECT TASK 3 Entrepreneurs

- You are going to write short texts to promote your product or service. You will include these in a leaflet about your company later.
- In your team, decide what you would like to write about, e.g. product description, origins of the idea, information about your team, etc.
- Use a mind map to help you.

→ Workbook page 20

Do all exercises in your notebook

16 An article / Tenses

LESSON FOCUS

Focus on Tenses

Writing An article about a product

Project task 3 Compose information to include in a leaflet about the company

Resources

Teacher's i-solutions

Warmer

Think of a product (one that's not mentioned in exercise 1) and tell the class they have 20 *yes/no* questions to guess what it is. Give them clues if they need them. Students can then continue the activity in pairs or small groups.

Focus on tenses

1 After students complete the exercise, see if they can give you reasons why the tenses are used in each case.

2 In pairs, get students to compare the things they found interesting to make the exercise more personalised.

Did you notice?

3 Tell students that they will have to write a similar article to that of the model and so they should use the model to copy its style and structure. Remind them that good paragraph structure makes a big difference in effective writing.

4 PLAN Students should do this planning exercise in pairs so that you can monitor them and react to the planning process. Tell them they must do the writing on their own, but they can check each other's work when they're finished to see how much their writing has benefited from planning.

WRITING TOOLS

Get students to read the **Writing tool** and remind them to check their language as they write.

5 WRITE Before students start writing, make a checklist on the board of any elements related to content, structure, language and style that they should bear in mind.

6 CHECK Once students have checked their own articles, they can swap with a partner and check theirs.

PROJECT TASK 3 Entrepreneurs

Put students back in their teams to plan and start writing the texts for their leaflets. Draw an example mind map on the board if they don't know what one is. Remind students that they need to keep their project notes together in their **Workbook** (page 20) or in their own notebook.

→ See pages 24-27 **Projects**

ANSWER KEY

Page 16

1
1 PC
2 penicillin
3 jeans
4 cocoa
5 electric cars

2 *Student's own answers*

3
Paragraph 1 c
Paragraph 2 b
Paragraph 3 d
Paragraph 4 a

4 *Student's own answers*

5 *Student's own answers*

6 *Student's own answers*

FURTHER PRACTICE

Workbook page 10

Remind students to do all the exercises in their notebook

CONTINUOUS ASSESSMENT Students can use appropriate tenses to write an article about a product.

Culture and communication 1.5

Prepare for landing

Discuss the questions.

1 What do you think makes a person successful?
2 Which is more important, happiness or money? Why?
3 Is it easy to decide what job you would like to do?
4 Would you prefer to work indoors or outdoors? Why?

1 Listen, order the pictures and make notes.

a b c d

2 Answer the questions in pairs. Listen again and check.

1 What are the two options that Sarah has?
2 Why is Paul's decision difficult?
3 Why can't Bruce decide what's best?
4 What is Liz's problem?

3 In pairs, say what you think each person should do.

I think Sarah should…

4 Complete the sentences with the verbs in the correct form.

be choose decide go have tell

1 I ··· to a nature summer camp last summer.
2 Why is it so hard to ···?
3 I've ··· this kind of problem before.
4 Why did we ··· money over helping people?
5 It ··· a boy in a different class.
6 Do I ··· the teacher?

Idioms and expressions

5 Match the expressions you heard with their meanings.

1 I'll sleep on it 3 the jury is out
2 on the fence 4 be in two minds

a When you delay making a decision so you have time to think about it.
b When you can't decide between two options.
c When no decision has been made yet.
d When you have difficulty deciding what to do.

6 NOW YOU! Discuss the questions in pairs.

- Do you prefer to make a decision quickly, or sleep on it?
- When you watch a debate, do you pick a side or sit on the fence?
- Have you decided what you want to do after high school, or is the jury still out?
- When you're in two minds about something, what helps you make a decision?

PAIRWORK
Student A: go to page 99
Student B: go to page 103

Unit 1 Review • page 90
Wordlist • pages 117–120

Do all exercises in your notebook

Idioms and expressions for making decisions

Workbook page 11

17

ANSWER KEY

Page 71

1 c, d, b, a

2 **1** To study for a career she thinks she'll love in forestry or for something more serious, like law, which is what her mother wants her to do.
2 If he does what he would like to do and changes groups to work on the charity project, he thinks his teammates will be annoyed.
3 Because although they have always written the truth in the school blog, this time it doesn't feel good.
4 She can't decide whether or not to tell the teacher that her classmates aren't doing their share of the work because they might get angry.

3 *Student's own answers*

4 **1** went **2** decide **3** had **4** choose **5** was **6** tell

5 **1** a **2** d **3** c **4** b

6 *Student's own answers*

FURTHER PRACTICE AND UNIT ASSESSSMENT

Unit 1 Review Student's Book page 90

Workbook page 11

- **Reflect on your learning** page 11
- **Grammar reference and practice** pages 84 and 93
- **Wordlist and exercises** pages 98 and 102

Tests available to download and edit from the **Richmond** *Learning* **Platform**

→ See pages 40-41 **Assessment**

LESSON FOCUS

Idioms and expressions Making decisions

Listening Taking notes about four short monologues

Speaking Asking and answering personal questions using idioms and expressions

Resources

Teacher's i-solutions, Student's Book audio, Culture video and worksheet

Prepare for landing

Video and worksheet available on the Richmond *Learning* **Platform**

- In pairs, ask students to complete the *What I know…* exercises on the **Culture video worksheet**.
- Show students the **Culture video** and ask them to complete the *What I learned…* exercises on the worksheet.
- In pairs, students compare answers.
- In small groups, tell students to complete the *What I wonder…* exercises on the worksheet.

Warmer

Watch the **Culture video** and discuss the questions with the whole class. If you don't have video facilities, simply discuss the questions.

1 1.13 (See page 170 for transcripts) Tell students they will hear four people talking about difficult decisions. Play the audio for students to complete the exercise.

2 1.14 (See page 170 for transcripts) Get students to use their notes to answer the questions as best they can before playing the audio again.

3 Get students to refer to their notes and answers to question 2 to discuss their advice.

4 Point out that these sentences all come from the monologues and revise the tenses they have looked at in the unit. Play the audio again if it helps.

Idioms and expressions

5 Ask students if they remember the context for the idioms and expressions in the monologues. Write or read out the sentences to help them guess their meanings.

6 NOW YOU! Where appropriate, encourage students to use the idioms and expressions in their answers. Ask individuals to tell you what they and their partners answered for some of the questions.

PAIRWORK Student's Book pages 99 and 103
See **Teacher's Book** page 62 for more information.
→ See pages 30-33 **Mediation**

Remind students to do all the exercises in their notebook

Unit 1 Review

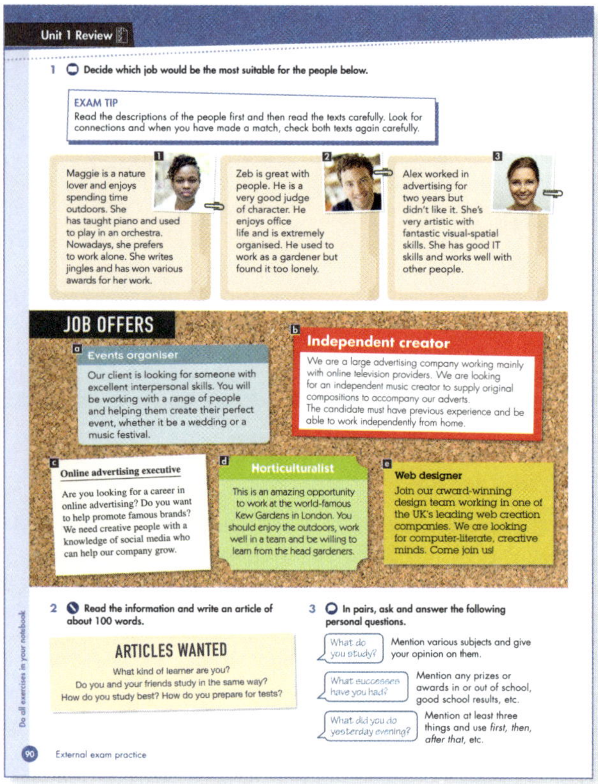

Unit 1 Review

1 Decide which job would be the most suitable for the people below.

EXAM TIP
Read the descriptions of the people first and then read the texts carefully. Look for connections and when you have made a match, check both texts again carefully.

1 Maggie is a nature lover and enjoys spending time outdoors. She has taught piano and used to play in an orchestra. Nowadays, she prefers to work alone. She writes jingles and has won various awards for her work.

2 Zeb is great with people. He is a very good judge of character. He enjoys office life and is extremely organised. He used to work as a gardener but found it too lonely.

3 Alex worked in advertising for two years but didn't like it. She's very artistic with fantastic visual-spatial skills. She has good IT skills and works well with other people.

JOB OFFERS

a Events organiser
Our client is looking for someone with excellent interpersonal skills. You will be working with a range of people and helping them create their perfect event, whether it be a wedding or a music festival.

b Independent creator
We are a large advertising company working mainly with online television providers. We are looking for an independent music creator to supply original compositions to accompany our adverts. The candidate must have previous experience and be able to work independently from home.

c Online advertising executive
Are you looking for a career in online advertising? Do you want to help promote famous brands? We need creative people with a knowledge of social media who can help our company grow.

d Horticulturalist
This is an amazing opportunity to work at the world-famous Kew Gardens in London. You should enjoy the outdoors, work well in a team and be willing to learn from the head gardeners.

e Web designer
Join our award-winning design team working in one of the UK's leading web creation companies. We are looking for computer-literate, creative minds. Come join us!

2 Read the information and write an article of about 100 words.

ARTICLES WANTED
What kind of learner are you?
Do you and your friends study in the same way?
How do you study best? How do you prepare for tests?

3 In pairs, ask and answer the following personal questions.

What do you study? – Mention various subjects and give your opinion on them.
What successes have you had? – Mention any prizes or awards in or out of school, good school results, etc.
What did you do yesterday evening? – Mention at least three things and use *first, then, after that*, etc.

Do all exercises in your notebook

90 External exam practice

Student's Book page 90

ANSWER KEY

1 **1** b
2 a
3 e

2 *Student's own answers*

3 *Student's own answers*

Pairwork

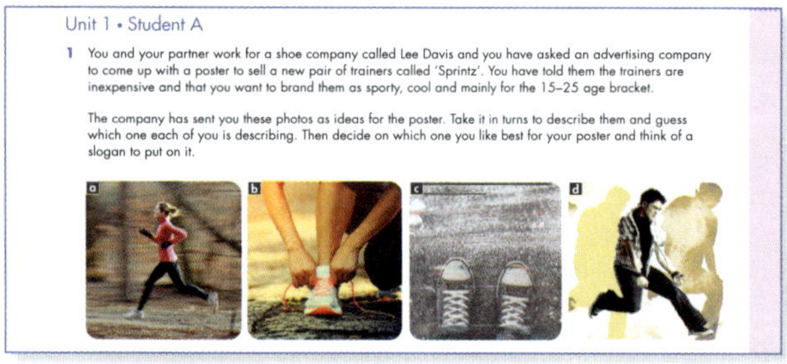

Unit 1 • Student A

1 You and your partner work for a shoe company called Lee Davis and you have asked an advertising company to come up with a poster to sell a new pair of trainers called 'Sprintz'. You have told them the trainers are inexpensive and that you want to brand them as sporty, cool and mainly for the 15–25 age bracket.

The company has sent you these photos as ideas for the poster. Take it in turns to describe them and guess which one each of you is describing. Then decide on which one you like best for your poster and think of a slogan to put on it.

a b c d

Student's Book page 99

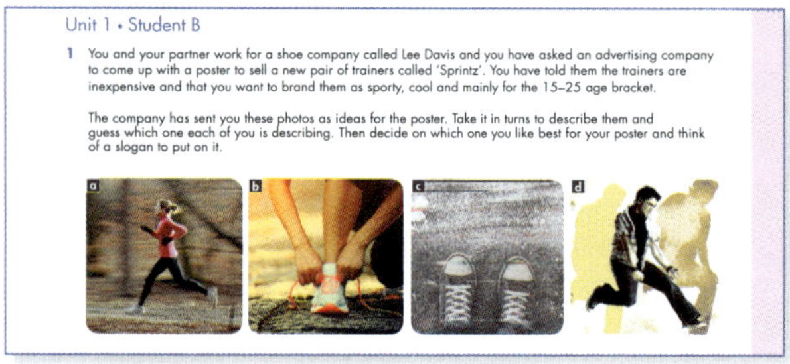

Unit 1 • Student B

1 You and your partner work for a shoe company called Lee Davis and you have asked an advertising company to come up with a poster to sell a new pair of trainers called 'Sprintz'. You have told them the trainers are inexpensive and that you want to brand them as sporty, cool and mainly for the 15–25 age bracket.

The company has sent you these photos as ideas for the poster. Take it in turns to describe them and guess which one each of you is describing. Then decide on which one you like best for your poster and think of a slogan to put on it.

a b c d

Student's Book page 103

CEFR MEDIATION DESCRIPTOR

- **Collaborating to construct meaning**
  Students can present their ideas in a group and pose questions that invite reactions from other group members' perspectives.

- **Discussing images**
  Put students in pairs, decide who is A and who is B and direct them to their corresponding pages. Tell them that they have the same information for this exercise and ask a few key questions from the instructions: *Who do you work do for and what do they produce? Who is your target market for the product? What do you have to do?* Elicit answers and let them continue the exercise in their pairs.

Remind students to do all the exercises in their notebook

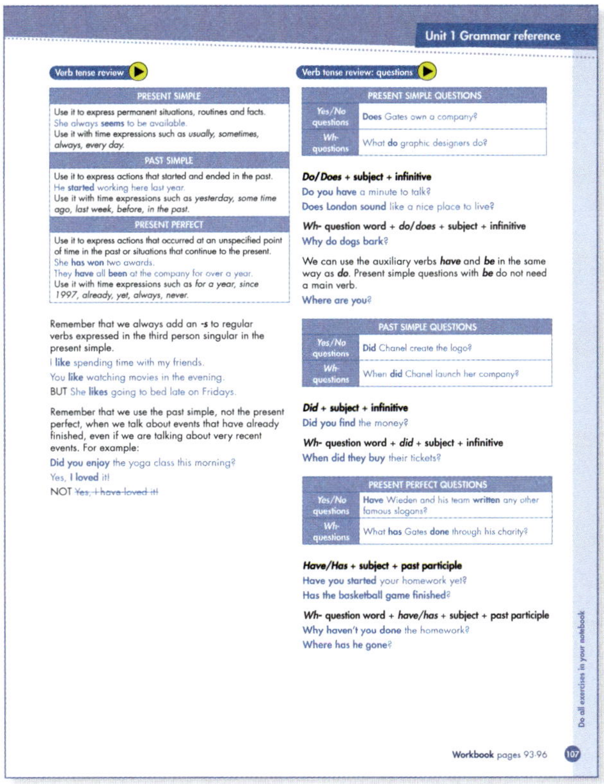

Unit 1 Grammar reference

Verb tense review

PRESENT SIMPLE
Use it to express permanent situations, routines and facts. She always **seems** to be available. Use it with time expressions such as *usually, sometimes, always, every day.*
PAST SIMPLE
Use it to express actions that started and ended in the past. He **started** working here last year. Use it with time expressions such as *yesterday, some time ago, last week, before, in the past.*
PRESENT PERFECT
Use it to express actions that occurred at an unspecified point of time in the past or situations that continue to the present. She **has won** two awards. They **have** all **been** at the company for over a year. Use it with time expressions such as *for a year, since 1997, already, yet, always, never.*

Remember that we always add an **-s** to regular verbs expressed in the third person singular in the present simple.

I **like** spending time with my friends.

You **like** watching movies in the evening.

BUT She **likes** going to bed late on Fridays.

Remember that we use the past simple, not the present perfect, when we talk about events that have already finished, even if we are talking about very recent events. For example:

Did you enjoy the yoga class this morning?

Yes, **I loved** it!

NOT ~~Yes, I have loved it!~~

Verb tense review: questions

PRESENT SIMPLE QUESTIONS	
Yes/No questions	**Does** Gates own a company?
Wh- questions	What **do** graphic designers do?

***Do/Does* + subject + infinitive**

Do you have a minute to talk?

Does London sound like a nice place to live?

***Wh-* question word + *do/does* + subject + infinitive**

Why do dogs bark?

We can use the auxiliary verbs ***have*** and ***be*** in the same way as ***do***. Present simple questions with ***be*** do not need a main verb.

Where are you?

PAST SIMPLE QUESTIONS	
Yes/No questions	**Did** Chanel create the logo?
Wh- questions	When **did** Chanel launch her company?

***Did* + subject + infinitive**

Did you find the money?

***Wh-* question word + *did* + subject + infinitive**

When did they buy their tickets?

PRESENT PERFECT QUESTIONS	
Yes/No questions	**Have** Wieden and his team **written** any other famous slogans?
Wh- questions	What **has** Gates **done** through his charity?

***Have/Has* + subject + past participle**

Have you started your homework yet?

Has the basketball game finished?

***Wh-* question word + *have/has* + subject + past participle**

Why haven't you done the homework?

Where has he gone?

Do all exercises in your notebook

Workbook pages 93-96 107

Student's Book page 107

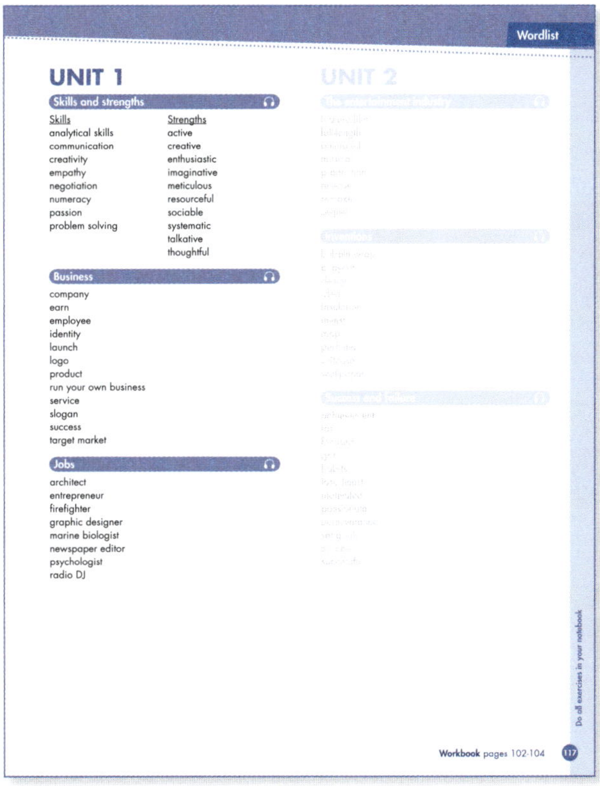

Wordlist

UNIT 1

Skills and strengths

Skills	Strengths
analytical skills	active
communication	creative
creativity	enthusiastic
empathy	imaginative
negotiation	meticulous
numeracy	resourceful
passion	sociable
problem solving	systematic
	talkative
	thoughtful

Business

company
earn
employee
identity
launch
logo
product
run your own business
service
slogan
success
target market

Jobs

architect
entrepreneur
firefighter
graphic designer
marine biologist
newspaper editor
psychologist
radio DJ

UNIT 2

Do all exercises in your notebook

Workbook pages 102-104 117

Student's Book page 117

2.41 2.42 2.43

Remind students to do all the exercises in their notebook

2 THE BIG TIME

At the start of each unit and lesson, explain to the students what the objectives are.

Language objectives

Grammar

Past perfect: affirmative
- Students are introduced to the form and use of the past perfect.

Past simple and past perfect
- Students practise using the past perfect alongside the past simple to show the order of events in the past.

Vocabulary

The entertainment industry: *animated, feature film, full-length, musical, production, release, remake, sequel*
- Students practise vocabulary related to entertainment.

Inventions: *bubble wrap, copycat, design, idea, insulation, invest, mop, perfume, suitcase, wallpaper*
- Students use vocabulary related to inventions.

Success and failure: *achievement, fail, focused, grit, habits, lose heart, motivated, passionate, perseverance, set goals, succeed, successful*
- Students use vocabulary connected to success and failure.

Idioms and expressions

Success: *be in the bag, pass with flying colours, go to the dogs, fall at the first hurdle*
- Students look at idioms and expressions in the context of success and failure.

Recycled language

Past simple, Time expressions, Linking language, Word formation

Skills objectives

Speaking

- Students create sentences about *The Lion King* using a timeline.
- Students discuss which successful people they admire.
- Students discuss two stories about successful businesses.
- Students discuss the characteristics of a successful person.
- Students ask and answer questions about their habits and experiences using idioms and expressions.

Pronunciation: Students practise the /ɒ/ sound with different letters.

Pairwork: Students use various mediation techniques in order to complete texts about two successful people from history.

Listening

- Students listen and complete a text about Walt Disney.
- Students listen to a talk about successful people and answer questions.
- Students listen and complete a text about an invention.
- Students listen to idioms and expressions in context.

Reading

- Students skim a text to compare ideas about success.
- Students read a text to match headings and paragraphs.
- Students read in detail to answer specific questions.
- Students scan a text for words to help complete a word formation table.

Core values: Students help develop their **perseverance** by drafting a step-by-step plan to achieve a goal.

Writing

- Students focus on using a model to help them build a set of useful expressions for formal writing.
- Students plan, write and check an email to a career counsellor

Focus on vocabulary for success: *achieve, effective, failure, focused, goals, improvement, plan*

Remind students to do all the exercises in their notebook

Learning to learn tools

SPEAKING TOOLS Students practise using new grammatical structures with different vocabulary to help consolidate learning.	LISTENING TOOLS Students practise predicting key words in an audio to help them listen more effectively.
READING TOOLS Students practise matching headings with paragraphs to help them gain a better understanding of a text.	WRITING TOOLS Students make a list of useful set expressions for formal writing.

Project objectives: Entrepreneurs

Task 4 Students identify their values, goals and vision for the future, then write a mission statement.

Task 5 Students write about a company, the people who run it and why it inspires them.

Task 6 Students create a leaflet to tell others about their company.

Audiovisual objectives

Vlog: Students watch and listen to Robert talk about a way to break bad habits.

Culture: Students watch and listen to Robert talk about the story of Thomas Edison.

Grammar animations: Students are presented with visual presentations of the unit grammar.

Key competences

LC **Linguistic**
pages 18-25

MST **Mathematical and Science and Technology**
pages 21-23, 25

DC **Digital**
pages 18-19, 21, 25

SCC **Social and Civic**
pages 18, 20-25

CAE **Cultural awareness and expression**
pages 18-19, 24-25

LL **Learning to learn**
pages 19-20, 22, 24

IE **Sense of initiative and entrepreneurship**
pages 19, 21, 24

→ See pages 42-43 **Key competences**

CEFR Mediation

2.1 Explaining data in speech
Can interpret and describe information in diagrams.

2.2 Relaying specific information in writing
Can write specific information from spoken texts.

2.3 Processing text in writing
Can paraphrase short written passages.

2.4 Processing text in writing
Can pick out and reproduce key words and phrases from a short text.

2.5 Note-taking
Can take notes in point form on a familiar topic.

Project Facilitating collaborative interaction with peers
Can formulate and respond to suggestions, ask whether people agree and propose alternatives.

Unit review Encouraging conceptual talk
Can ask questions to invite people to clarify their reasoning.

Pairwork Facilitating collaborative interaction with peers
Can collaborate in simple, shared tasks by asking and answering simple questions.

→ See pages 30-33 **Mediation**

Remind students to do all the exercises in their notebook

2 THE BIG TIME

In unit 2 you will:

- talk about different types of success.
- review the past perfect tense.
- practise using the past perfect and past simple tenses.
- write an email.

2.1 Vocabulary and listening

ROBERT'S VLOG: The 20-second rule

Discuss the questions.

1 What does success mean to you?
2 Do successful people waste less time than other people?
3 Think of someone who is very successful. What are they like?

Flipped Learning

1 **In pairs, say what you know about the Walt Disney Company.**

2 **Use the words to complete the text. Listen and check.**

achievements amusement bankrupt business empire fired imaginative successful

DREAMS CAN COME TRUE

Walt Disney had 1… ideas from a very young age. By the time he died in 1966, he had created a multimillion-dollar business 2…, made countless films, and built the world's most 3… theme park.

Disney's success didn't come easily. He experienced lots of failure. He was 4… from his job at a Kansas newspaper in 1919; they said that he wasn't 5… enough! In 1922, he started Laugh-O-gram Studio; it went 6… in one year.

His failures are not well known, but we all know about Walt Disney's 7…. He created Mickey Mouse in 1928. Before he produced *Snow White and the Seven Dwarfs* in 1937, there had never been a full-length, hand-drawn animated feature film.

A friend remembered him standing outside an 8… park in Kansas as a child and saying, 'I'm going to have a park like this one day'. Disneyland opened in 1955 and after two months, it had already received over one million visitors! In 1971, some years after Walt died, his brother Roy opened the Magic Kingdom.

FAST FINISHERS Write a paragraph about your favourite Disney film or character.

Do all exercises in your notebook

18 The entertainment industry / Past perfect: affirmative

Grammar and vocabulary 2.1

PAST PERFECT: AFFIRMATIVE

Use the **past perfect** to show that an action happened before another action in the past.

Walt Disney **had built** a multimillion-dollar business empire before his death in 1966.

- He built the empire. Then he died.

By the time he opened Disneyland, many people **had seen** his films.

- People saw the films. Then he opened Disneyland.

Use time expressions like *by then, by the time, before that, already*.

Grammar reference page 108

3 **Order the events from Walt Disney's life.**

a Produced *Snow White and the Seven Dwarfs*.
b Fired from Kansas newspaper.
c Died.
d Laugh-O-Gram Studio went bankrupt.
e Created Mickey Mouse.
f Opened Disneyland.

4 **Read the text again and complete the sentences.**

1 By the time he opened Disneyland, ….
2 Before he created Mickey Mouse, ….
3 By 1966, ….
4 Before he opened the Laugh-O-Gram Studio, ….

SPEAKING TOOLS

To help memorise grammar structures, repeat the same structure with different vocabulary.

5 **NOW YOU! In pairs, use the information about *The Lion King* to make sentences.**

Production had begun by 1991.

THE LION KING

1988 Development started
1991 Production began
1994 Film released (Disney's 32nd animated feature film)
1995 Won two Oscars
1997 Musical released
1998 Sequel released: The Lion King II – Simba's Pride
2019 Film remake released

PROJECT TASK 4 Entrepreneurs

- Together, decide on your company values, goals and vision for the future.
- Think about existing companies that are similar to yours. Research their mission statements and write one for your own company. You will include this in your leaflet later.

→ Workbook page 21

Workbook pages 12 and 13 19

Do all exercises in your notebook

ANSWER KEY

Pages 18-19

1 *Student's own answers*

2 **1** business
2 empire
3 successful
4 fired
5 imaginative
6 bankrupt
7 achievements
8 amusement

3 **1** b
2 d
3 e
4 a
5 f
6 c

4 **1** he had been successful in film and television
2 he had had many failures; he had started Laugh-O-Gram Studio and it had gone bankrupt
3 he had created a multimillion-dollar business empire
4 he had been fired from his job at a Kansas newspaper

5 *Student's own answers*

Remind students to do all the exercises in their notebook

LESSON FOCUS

Grammar Past perfect: affirmative
Vocabulary The entertainment industry
Listening Completing a text about Walt Disney
Speaking Creating sentences about *The Lion King* using a timeline
Project task 4 Write a mission statement

Resources

Teacher's i-solutions, Student's Book audio, Vlog and worksheets

Flipped Learning

ROBERT'S VLOG: The 20-second rule

- Make sure to set up the **Flipped Learning** work with the students beforehand. **See pages 22-23 for complete Flipped Learning guidelines**.
- Ask students to put the **Flipped Learning worksheets** on their desks and walk around to check how many have completed the Flipped task.
- In pairs or small groups, ask students to compare and check the *Before you watch...* and *While you watch...* exercises on the worksheet.
- Show students **Robert's Vlog** and ask volunteers to provide correct answers and clarify any doubts other students may have.
- Choose three or four students to read aloud their answers to the *After you watch...* exercises on the worksheet and encourage some class discussion.
- Move straight to exercise 1 on page 18.

Warmer

Watch Robert's Vlog and discuss the questions with the whole class. If you don't have video facilities, simply discuss the questions.

1 Elicit what students came up with and tell them that they are going to read about the man behind the company.

2 1.15 (See page 170 for transcripts) Discuss any words students don't know. Let them complete the text as best they can before you play the audio for them to check. Extend the exercise by getting students to test each other on the relevance of the words in the Wordpool.

FAST FINISHERS Students can complete this exercise alone or in pairs.

Flipped Learning

PAST PERFECT: AFFIRMATIVE

Draw students' attention to the **Grammar table**. Remind students that they can use this as a quick reference while completing the exercises.

Show students the **Grammar animation** and/or refer students to the **Grammar reference** on page 108 for further information on form and use.

→ See page 23 for how to flip the **grammar lesson**

3 Find the first event together and let the students complete the rest.

4 Draw students' attention to the time expressions and the **Grammar table** and ask which tense they will use (past perfect), and whether the events they are looking for happened before or after the event already in each sentence (before).

SPEAKING TOOLS

Get students to read the **Speaking tool** and point out that they will use the past perfect in the next exercise with different verbs.

5 NOW YOU! Encourage students to make meaningful sentences in which the past perfect is interesting. You could model a sentence for them like: *By the time the film was released, Walt Disney had already made 31 animated feature films!* Alternatively, prompt them with sentence stems like in exercise 4.

PROJECT TASK 4 Entrepreneurs

Put students in their groups again and tell them to think more broadly about their company. Explain what a mission statement is and let them discuss their company's values, goals and vision, and decide how to proceed. Remind students that they need to keep their project notes together in their **Workbook** (page 21) or in their own notebook.

→ See pages 24-27 **Projects**

FURTHER PRACTICE

Workbook pages 12-13
- **Grammar reference and practice** pages 85 and 93
- **Wordlist and exercises** pages 98 and 102

Remind students to do all the exercises in their notebook

CONTINUOUS ASSESSMENT Students can talk about the entertainment industry and use the past perfect affirmative.

2.2 Listening and grammar

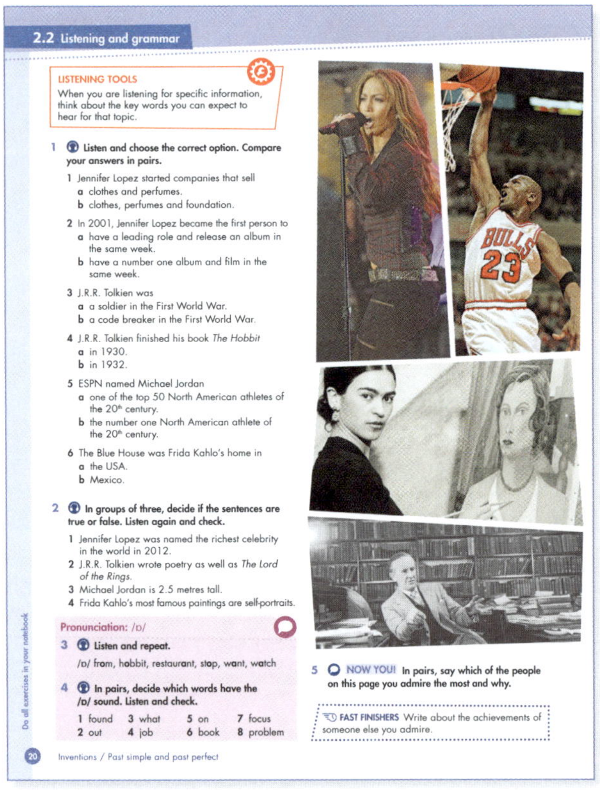

2.2 Listening and grammar

LISTENING TOOLS
When you are listening for specific information, think about the key words you can expect to hear for that topic.

1 **Listen and choose the correct option. Compare your answers in pairs.**

1 Jennifer Lopez started companies that sell
   a clothes and perfumes.
   b clothes, perfumes and foundation.
2 In 2001, Jennifer Lopez became the first person to
   a have a leading role and release an album in the same week.
   b have a number one album and film in the same week.
3 J.R.R. Tolkien was
   a a soldier in the First World War.
   b a code breaker in the First World War.
4 J.R.R. Tolkien finished his book *The Hobbit*
   a in 1930.
   b in 1932.
5 ESPN named Michael Jordan
   a one of the top 50 North American athletes of the 20th century.
   b the number one North American athlete of the 20th century.
6 The Blue House was Frida Kahlo's home in
   a the USA.
   b Mexico.

2 **In groups of three, decide if the sentences are true or false. Listen again and check.**

1 Jennifer Lopez was named the richest celebrity in the world in 2012.
2 J.R.R. Tolkien wrote poetry as well as *The Lord of the Rings*.
3 Michael Jordan is 2.5 metres tall.
4 Frida Kahlo's most famous paintings are self-portraits.

Pronunciation: /ɒ/

3 **Listen and repeat.**

/ɒ/ from, hobbit, restaurant, stop, want, watch

4 **In pairs, decide which words have the /ɒ/ sound. Listen and check.**

1 found	3 what	5 on	7 focus
2 out	4 job	6 book	8 problem

5 **NOW YOU! In pairs, say which of the people on this page you admire the most and why.**

FAST FINISHERS Write about the achievements of someone else you admire.

20 Inventions / Past simple and past perfect

Grammar and vocabulary 2.2

PAST SIMPLE AND PAST PERFECT

Use the **past simple** to talk about an event or a chain of events that finished in the past.	Use the **past perfect** with the **past simple** to show that an action happened before another action in the past.
Bubble wrap **didn't become** successful until IBM **used** it to package a computer.	Manuel Jalón Corominas **had already** invented the mop but Joy Mangano **improved** the design.

Grammar reference page 108

6 **Read and choose the correct option. Listen and check.**

Marc Chavannes and Al Fielding [1] **created / had created** bubble wrap in 1957. They [2] **designed / had designed** it as a new style of textured wallpaper, but it was a complete commercial disaster. Following that, they [3] **tried / had tried** to sell the bubble wrap as insulation for homes. But that was as unpopular as the wallpaper idea [4] **was / had been**. In 1960, IBM [5] **decided / had decided** to use it to package their new computers for transport. Finally, after three years and several business failures, bubble wrap [6] **became / had become** a hit!

7 **Read and connect the sentences with the words in brackets. Use the past simple and the past perfect.**

Dragon's Den is a reality TV programme in which people present business ideas to successful entrepreneurs and ask them to invest money. In 2006, Rob Law presented a product he had designed: a suitcase that small children can sit on called the 'Trunki'. The entrepreneurs told him that his idea wasn't good – but they had made a huge mistake! By 2016, Law's company had sold millions of pounds' worth of Trunkis. Recently, however, he discovered that a copycat company had made a very similar product to his.

1 He presented the product on TV. He designed the product. (before)
   He had designed the product before he presented it on TV.
2 He became successful.
   The investors made a mistake. (so it was clear)
3 By 2016 he was rich.
   He sold a lot of Trunkis. (because)
4 He found out.
   A company copied his idea. (that)

8 **NOW YOU! In pairs, say which of the two stories on this page interested you the most and why.**

PROJECT TASK 5 Entrepreneurs
- Research a business that inspires you. Find information about the people who run the company and work there.
- Write about the people who run the business and why it inspires you. You will include this information in the leaflet about your company later.

→ **Workbook** page 21

Workbook pages 14 and 15 21

ANSWER KEY

Pages 20-21

1
1 a
2 b
3 a
4 b
5 b
6 b

2
1 False. She was named the most powerful celebrity.
2 True
3 False. He is 1.98 metres tall.
4 True

3 *Student's own answers*

4 what, job, on, problem

5 *Student's own answers*

6
1 created
2 had designed
3 tried
4 had been
5 decided
6 had become

7
1 He had designed the product before he presented it on television.
2 He became successful, so it was clear the investors had made a mistake.
3 By 2016 he was rich because he had sold a lot of Trunkis.
4 He found out that a company had copied his idea.

8 *Student's own answers*

LESSON FOCUS

Grammar Past simple and past perfect
Vocabulary Inventions
Listening A talk about successful people in different fields; A text about an invention
Speaking Discussions of successful people; Two stories of business successes
Project task 5 Research an inspiring company

Resources
Teacher's i-solutions, Student's Book audio

Warmer

Play a game of 20 questions. Think of a famous person in any field and tell students that they have 20 *yes/no* questions to guess who it is.

LISTENING TOOLS

Get students to read the **Listening tool** and tell them they will get to apply it in the next exercise.

1 1.16 (See page 170 for transcripts) Ask students to identify the four people in the photos. In pairs, ask them to come up with two words they think they might apply to each person. After playing the audios, get them to compare answers and see if any of their words appeared in the talk.

2 1.17 (See page 170 for transcripts) Ask students to discuss their answers before playing the audio again. You could stop after the part of the audio that contains each answer and get them to compare again before confirming the answers.

Pronunciation

3 1.18 (See page 170 for transcripts) Point out that the sounds are not always produced by the letter 'o'.

4 1.19 (See page 170 for transcripts) Let students try saying the words aloud in pairs before playing the audio for them to check and repeat.

5 NOW YOU! To focus on grammar again, and to give students ideas for the discussion, write these prompts on the board: *By the time she released her first single, Jennifer Lopez had...; When J.R.R. Tolkien wrote* The Hobbit, *he had already...; By 1995, Michael Jordan had...; Before living in the Blue House, Frida Kahlo had... .*

FAST FINISHERS Students can complete this exercise alone or in pairs.

PAST SIMPLE AND PAST PERFECT

Flipped Learning

Draw students' attention to the **Grammar table**. Remind students that they can use this as a quick reference while completing the exercises.

Show students the **Grammar animation** and/or refer students to the **Grammar reference** on page 108 for further information on form and use.

→ See page 23 for how to flip the **grammar lesson**

6 1.20 (See page 170 for transcripts) Ask students to scan the text for the name of what is depicted in the photo (bubble wrap). Yovu could do the first two questions together to help contrast the tenses, asking which they think came first: the designing or the actual creating.

7 Again, ask students to scan the text to find the name of the product (The 'Trunki'). Get students to try to retell the story to each other from memory before doing the connecting exercise.

8 NOW YOU! After discussing, ask students to report on their and their partner's choices.

PROJECT TASK 5 Entrepreneurs

Put students in their groups again to get them to decide how to proceed with the research. They need to decide on a business that inspires them and find out more information about the company. Remind students that they need to keep their project notes together in their **Workbook** (page 21) or in their own notebook.

→ See pages 24-27 **Projects**

FURTHER PRACTICE

Workbook pages 14-15
- **Grammar reference and practice** pages 85 and 93
- **Wordlist and exercises** pages 98 and 102

Vocabulary and Grammar worksheets available to download and edit from the **Richmond***Learning***Platform**

→ See pages 38-39 **Mixed-ability classes**

Remind students to do all the exercises in their notebook

CONTINUOUS ASSESSMENT Students can talk about inventions, and use the past simple and past perfect.

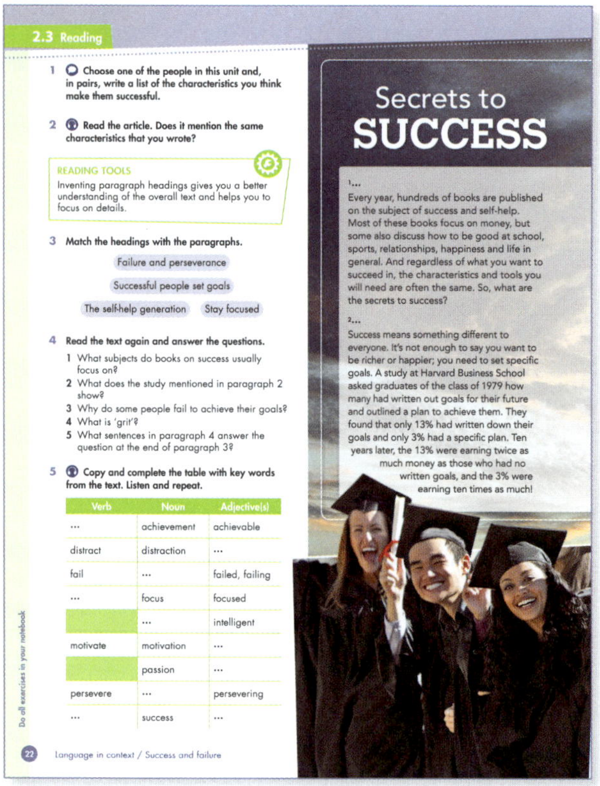

1 Choose one of the people in this unit and, in pairs, write a list of the characteristics you think make them successful.

2 Read the article. Does it mention the same characteristics that you wrote?

READING TOOLS
Inventing paragraph headings gives you a better understanding of the overall text and helps you to focus on details.

3 Match the headings with the paragraphs.

Failure and perseverance
Successful people set goals
The self-help generation
Stay focused

4 Read the text again and answer the questions.
1 What subjects do books on success usually focus on?
2 What does the study mentioned in paragraph 2 show?
3 Why do some people fail to achieve their goals?
4 What is 'grit'?
5 What sentences in paragraph 4 answer the question at the end of paragraph 3?

5 Copy and complete the table with key words from the text. Listen and repeat.

Verb	Noun	Adjective(s)
...	achievement	achievable
distract	distraction	...
fail	...	failed, failing
...	focus	focused
	...	intelligent
motivate	motivation	...
	passion	...
persevere	...	persevering
...	success	...

Secrets to SUCCESS

1...
Every year, hundreds of books are published on the subject of success and self-help. Most of these books focus on money, but some also discuss how to be good at school, sports, relationships, happiness and life in general. And regardless of what you want to succeed in, the characteristics and tools you will need are often the same. So, what are the secrets to success?

2...
Success means something different to everyone. It's not enough to say you want to be richer or happier; you need to set specific goals. A study at Harvard Business School asked graduates of the class of 1979 how many had written out goals for their future and outlined a plan to achieve them. They found that only 13% had written down their goals and only 3% had a specific plan. Ten years later, the 13% were earning twice as much money as those who had no written goals, and the 3% were earning ten times as much!

Do all exercises in your notebook

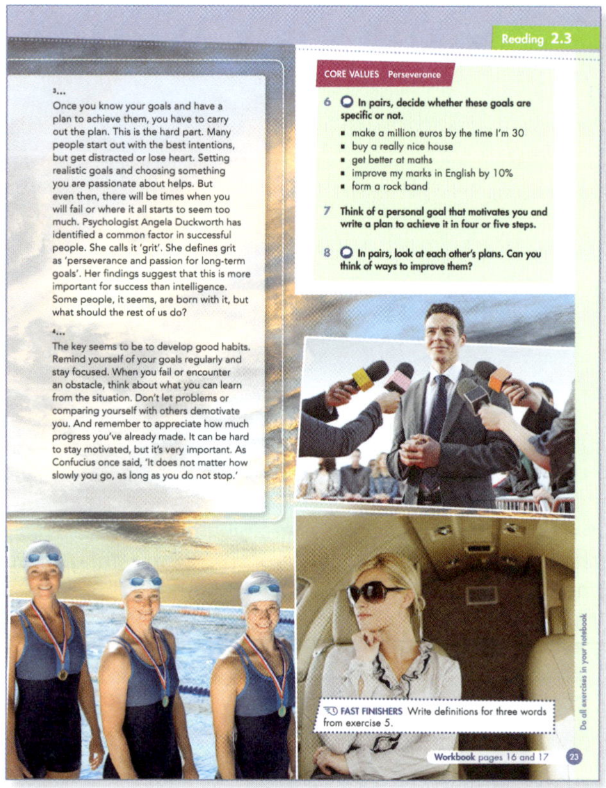

3...
Once you know your goals and have a plan to achieve them, you have to carry out the plan. This is the hard part. Many people start out with the best intentions, but get distracted or lose heart. Setting realistic goals and choosing something you are passionate about helps. But even then, there will be times when you will fail or where it all starts to seem too much. Psychologist Angela Duckworth has identified a common factor in successful people. She calls it 'grit'. She defines grit as 'perseverance and passion for long-term goals'. Her findings suggest that this is more important for success than intelligence. Some people, it seems, are born with it, but what should the rest of us do?

4...
The key seems to be to develop good habits. Remind yourself of your goals regularly and stay focused. When you fail or encounter an obstacle, think about what you can learn from the situation. Don't let problems or comparing yourself with others demotivate you. And remember to appreciate how much progress you've already made. It can be hard to stay motivated, but it's very important. As Confucius once said, 'It does not matter how slowly you go, as long as you do not stop.'

CORE VALUES Perseverance

6 In pairs, decide whether these goals are specific or not.
- make a million euros by the time I'm 30
- buy a really nice house
- get better at maths
- improve my marks in English by 10%
- form a rock band

7 Think of a personal goal that motivates you and write a plan to achieve it in four or five steps.

8 In pairs, look at each other's plans. Can you think of ways to improve them?

FAST FINISHERS Write definitions for three words from exercise 5.

Do all exercises in your notebook

ANSWER KEY

Pages 22-23

1 *Student's own answers*

2 *Student's own answers*

3
1 The self-help generation
2 Successful people set goals
3 Failure and perseverance
4 Stay focused

4
1 They usually focus on money.
2 People who write down their goals and a plan of how to achieve them earn more money.
3 They get distracted or lose heart.
4 Perseverance and passion for long-term goals.
5 Develop good habits, remind yourself of your goals regularly and stay focused.

5

Verb	Noun	Adjective(s)
achieve	achievement	achievable
distract	distraction	distracted
fail	failure	failed, failing
focus	focus	focused
	intelligence	intelligent
motivate	motivation	motivated
	passion	passionate
persevere	perseverance	persevering
succeed	success	successful

6 *Student's own answers*

7 *Student's own answers*

8 *Student's own answers*

Remind students to do all the exercises in their notebook

LESSON FOCUS
Language in context Success and failure
Core values Perseverance

Resources
Teacher's i-solutions, Student's Book audio

→ See pages 36-37 **Literature**

Warmer

Write on the board: *By the time I was 5…* and say things you had already done, for example: *I had learnt to read and ride a bike and I had lived in two different cities.* Then erase the number 5 from the board and replace it with the number 12. Get students to complete the sentence with as many things as they can think of that they had done. Put them in pairs to compare how many things they have in common and then ask the class for interesting things their partners had done.

1 Broaden the discussion to include anyone successful that students can think of and elicit some common characteristics to write on the board.

2 1.21 (see page 171 for transcripts) Give students time to read, but make sure they know that they are only comparing the characteristics mentioned with the ones they wrote. Compare the answers with the ones you wrote on the board.

READING TOOLS

Ask students to read the **Reading tool** and point out that headings act as a summary of the content of a paragraph, and make it easy to find information before a first reading.

3 Discuss any vocabulary from the headings that students are unfamiliar with. Give them time and assistance where necessary.

4 Let students compare their answers in pairs so you can check that they are finding specific answers in the text.

5 1.22 (See page 171 for transcripts) Point out that verbs from *intelligent* (e.g. intellectualise) and *passion* (e.g. impassion) are not used as frequently as the other words here.

CORE VALUES Perseverance

6 Remind students of the text's advice on specific goals and ask them which of the more vague goals could be made more specific.

7 Encourage students to think of something important to them that is also realistic. Cut the number of steps if you think that it will make the task more achievable in class.

8 Encourage students to be positive in their feedback but also to make gentle suggestions for improvement.

FAST FINISHERS Students can complete this exercise alone or in pairs.

FURTHER PRACTICE

Workbook pages 16-17

Remind students to do all the exercises in their notebook

CONTINUOUS ASSESSMENT Students can understand vocabulary related to success and failure in a text about how to achieve success.

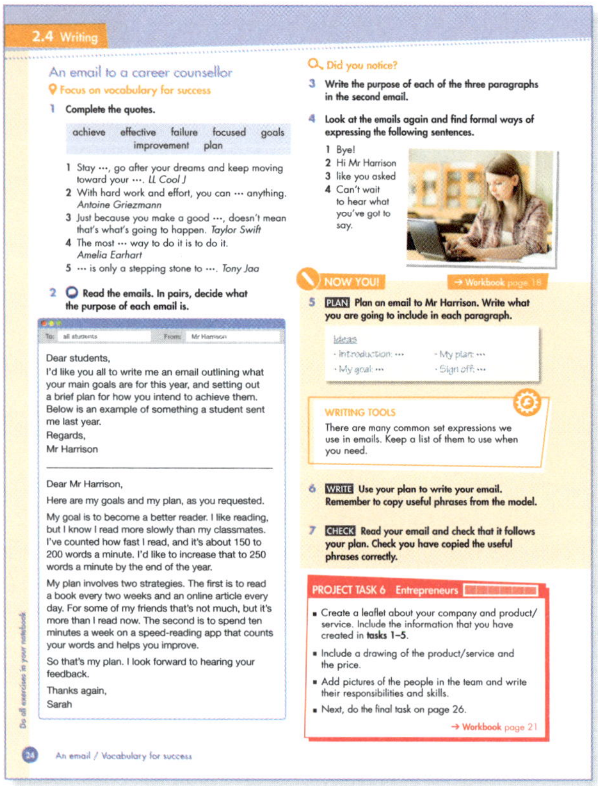

2.4 Writing

An email to a career counsellor

Focus on vocabulary for success

1 Complete the quotes.

achieve effective failure focused goals improvement plan

1 Stay ···, go after your dreams and keep moving toward your ···. *LL Cool J*
2 With hard work and effort, you can ··· anything. *Antoine Griezmann*
3 Just because you make a good ···, doesn't mean that's what's going to happen. *Taylor Swift*
4 The most ··· way to do it is to do it. *Amelia Earhart*
5 ··· is only a stepping stone to ···. *Tony Jaa*

2 Read the emails. In pairs, decide what the purpose of each email is.

To: all students From: Mr Harrison

Dear students,
I'd like you all to write me an email outlining what your main goals are for this year, and setting out a brief plan for how you intend to achieve them. Below is an example of something a student sent me last year.
Regards,
Mr Harrison

Dear Mr Harrison,
Here are my goals and my plan, as you requested.
My goal is to become a better reader. I like reading, but I know I read more slowly than my classmates. I've counted how fast I read, and it's about 150 to 200 words a minute. I'd like to increase that to 250 words a minute by the end of the year.
My plan involves two strategies. The first is to read a book every two weeks and an online article every day. For some of my friends that's not much, but it's more than I read now. The second is to spend ten minutes a week on a speed-reading app that counts your words and helps you improve.
So that's my plan. I look forward to hearing your feedback.
Thanks again,
Sarah

Did you notice?

3 Write the purpose of each of the three paragraphs in the second email.

4 Look at the emails again and find formal ways of expressing the following sentences.

1 Bye!
2 Hi Mr Harrison
3 like you asked
4 Can't wait to hear what you've got to say.

NOW YOU! → Workbook page 18

5 PLAN Plan an email to Mr Harrison. Write what you are going to include in each paragraph.

Ideas
- Introduction: ···
- My goal: ···
- My plan: ···
- Sign off: ···

WRITING TOOLS
There are many common set expressions we use in emails. Keep a list of them to use when you need.

6 WRITE Use your plan to write your email. Remember to copy useful phrases from the model.

7 CHECK Read your email and check that it follows your plan. Check you have copied the useful phrases correctly.

PROJECT TASK 6 Entrepreneurs
- Create a leaflet about your company and product/service. Include the information that you have created in **tasks 1–5**.
- Include a drawing of the product/service and the price.
- Add pictures of the people in the team and write their responsibilities and skills.
- Next, do the final task on page 26.

→ Workbook page 21

Do all exercises in your notebook

24 An email / Vocabulary for success

ANSWER KEY

Page 24

1 **1** focused; goals
2 achieve
3 plan
4 effective
5 Failure, improvement

2 **Email 1:** to ask all students to email Mr Harrison with their goals for the year and a plan to achieve them.
Email 2: a student outlining her goals for the year and how she plans to achieve them.

3 **Paragraph 1:** Set her goals
Paragraph 2: Outline her strategies
Paragraph 3: Close the email and say goodbye

4 **1** Regards,
2 Dear Mr Harrison,
3 as you requested
4 I look forward to hearing your feedback.

5 *Student's own answers*

6 *Student's own answers*

7 *Student's own answers*

FURTHER PRACTICE

Workbook page 18

LESSON FOCUS

Focus on Vocabulary for success

Writing An email to a career counsellor

Project task 6 Create a leaflet

Resources

Teacher's i-solutions

Warmer

Draw students' attention to the Success and failure section of the Wordlist on page 117. Choose a word from the list and give a definition for students to guess the word. Students can continue in pairs or small groups.

Focus on vocabulary for success

1 You could get students to compare their answers in pairs and discuss what the quotes mean to them.

2 Help with any vocabulary questions that students may have as they do the exercise. Ask them what they think of her plan.

Did you notice?

3 Ask students if they think the email is clear and, if so, what makes it clear. Remind them of the importance of clear paragraphing from the writing task in unit 1.

4 Point out that apart from *Bye!*, the words and phrases are in the order in which they can be found in the emails.

5 PLAN Tell students that they can use what they wrote for exercise 7 on page 23 of the **Student's Book** as the basis for their email if they want. Get them to compare plans with a partner.

WRITING TOOLS

Get students to read the **Writing tool** and encourage them to keep a list in their notebooks. Remind them that they will find many other useful phrases in examples of correspondence online.

6 WRITE Before students start writing, make a checklist on the board of any elements related to content, structure, language and style that they should bear in mind.

7 CHECK Once students have checked their own emails, they can swap with a partner and check theirs.

PROJECT TASK 6 Entrepreneurs

Put students in their groups to collate the information they have so far and carry out the final step for this task this task. Tell students that they need to keep their project notes together in their **Workbook** (page 21) or in their own notebook.

→ See pages 24-27 **Projects**

Remind students to do all the exercises in their notebook

CONTINUOUS ASSESSMENT Students can use vocabulary for success to write an email to a career counsellor.

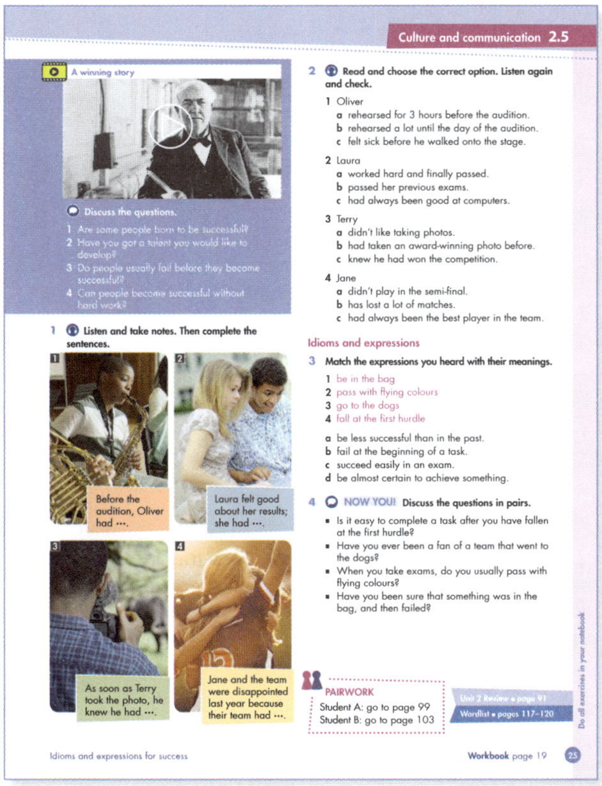
Culture and communication 2.5

A winning story

Discuss the questions.

1 Are some people born to be successful?
2 Have you got a talent you would like to develop?
3 Do people usually fail before they become successful?
4 Can people become successful without hard work?

1 Listen and take notes. Then complete the sentences.

1 Before the audition, Oliver had ···.
2 Laura felt good about her results; she had ···.
3 As soon as Terry took the photo, he knew he had ···.
4 Jane and the team were disappointed last year because their team had ···.

2 Read and choose the correct option. Listen again and check.

1 Oliver
a rehearsed for 3 hours before the audition.
b rehearsed a lot until the day of the audition.
c felt sick before he walked onto the stage.

2 Laura
a worked hard and finally passed.
b passed her previous exams.
c had always been good at computers.

3 Terry
a didn't like taking photos.
b had taken an award-winning photo before.
c knew he had won the competition.

4 Jane
a didn't play in the semi-final.
b has lost a lot of matches.
c had always been the best player in the team.

Idioms and expressions

3 Match the expressions you heard with their meanings.

1 be in the bag
2 pass with flying colours
3 go to the dogs
4 fall at the first hurdle

a be less successful than in the past.
b fail at the beginning of a task.
c succeed easily in an exam.
d be almost certain to achieve something.

4 NOW YOU! Discuss the questions in pairs.

- Is it easy to complete a task after you have fallen at the first hurdle?
- Have you ever been a fan of a team that went to the dogs?
- When you take exams, do you usually pass with flying colours?
- Have you been sure that something was in the bag, and then failed?

PAIRWORK
Student A: go to page 99
Student B: go to page 103

Unit 2 Review • page 91
Wordlist • pages 117–120

Do all exercises in your notebook

Idioms and expressions for success

Workbook page 19

25

LESSON FOCUS

Idioms and expressions Success

Listening Asking and answering questions about habits and experiences

Speaking Taking notes and answering questions

Resources

Teacher's i-solutions, Student's Book audio, Culture video and worksheet

A winning story

Video and worksheet available on the Richmond*Learning*Platform

- In pairs, ask students to complete the *What I know...* exercises on the **Culture video worksheet**.
- Show students the **Culture video** and ask them to complete the *What I learned...* exercises on the worksheet.
- In pairs, students compare answers.
- In small groups, tell students to complete the *What I wonder...* exercises on the worksheet.

Warmer

Watch the **Culture video** and discuss the questions with the whole class. If you don't have video facilities, simply discuss the questions.

1 1.23 (See page 171 for transcripts) With their books closed, tell students they are going to hear four different stories of people succeeding in or failing at something, and ask them to take notes as they listen. Let them compare their notes and then open their books to see if they can complete the sentences together.

2 1.24 (See page 171 for transcripts) Let students read the options and try to answer from memory before you play the audio again.

Idioms and expressions

3 Ask students if they remember who said the expressions and write the sentences on the board or read them aloud to help them guess from context if necessary. Check that they know what the subjects for each sentence normally are (1 and 3 something, 2 and 4 someone).

4 NOW YOU! To extend the exercise, ask students to choose an answer to give to the class for the class to guess what the question was.

ANSWER KEY

Page 25

1
1 fallen at the first hurdle
2 passed with flying colours
3 it in the bag
4 gone to the dogs

2
1 b
2 a
3 c
4 b

3
1 d
2 c
3 a
4 b

4 *Student's own answers*

FURTHER PRACTICE AND UNIT ASSESSSMENT

Unit 2 Review Student's Book page 91

Workbook page 19

- **Reflect on your learning** page 19
- **Grammar reference and practice** pages 85 and 93
- **Wordlist and exercises** pages 98 and 102

Tests available to download and edit from the **Richmond*Learning*Platform**

→ See pages 40-41 **Assessment**

PAIRWORK Student's Book pages 99 and 103

See **Teacher's Book** page 74 for more information.

→ See page 30-33 **Mediation**

Remind students to do all the exercises in their notebook

CONTINUOUS ASSESSMENT Students can use idioms and expressions for success.

Unit 2 Review

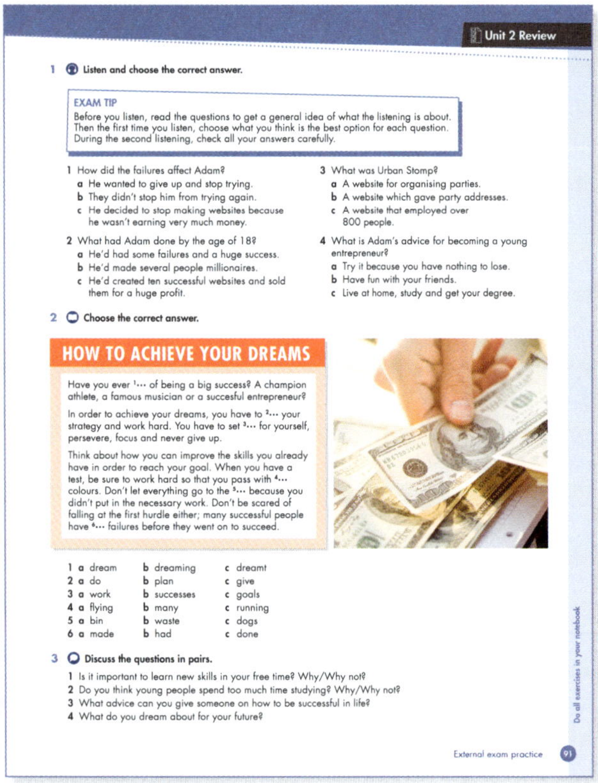
Unit 2 Review

1 Listen and choose the correct answer.

EXAM TIP
Before you listen, read the questions to get a general idea of what the listening is about. Then the first time you listen, choose what you think is the best option for each question. During the second listening, check all your answers carefully.

1 How did the failures affect Adam?
a He wanted to give up and stop trying.
b They didn't stop him from trying again.
c He decided to stop making websites because he wasn't earning very much money.

2 What had Adam done by the age of 18?
a He'd had some failures and a huge success.
b He'd made several people millionaires.
c He'd created ten successful websites and sold them for a huge profit.

3 What was Urban Stomp?
a A website for organising parties.
b A website which gave party addresses.
c A website that employed over 800 people.

4 What is Adam's advice for becoming a young entrepreneur?
a Try it because you have nothing to lose.
b Have fun with your friends.
c Live at home, study and get your degree.

2 Choose the correct answer.

HOW TO ACHIEVE YOUR DREAMS

Have you ever [1]··· of being a big success? A champion athlete, a famous musician or a succesful entrepreneur?

In order to achieve your dreams, you have to [2]··· your strategy and work hard. You have to set [3]··· for yourself, persevere, focus and never give up.

Think about how you can improve the skills you already have in order to reach your goal. When you have a test, be sure to work hard so that you pass with [4]··· colours. Don't let everything go to the [5]··· because you didn't put in the necessary work. Don't be scared of falling at the first hurdle either; many successful people have [6]··· failures before they went on to succeed.

1 a dream b dreaming c dreamt
2 a do b plan c give
3 a work b successes c goals
4 a flying b many c running
5 a bin b waste c dogs
6 a made b had c done

3 Discuss the questions in pairs.
1 Is it important to learn new skills in your free time? Why/Why not?
2 Do you think young people spend too much time studying? Why/Why not?
3 What advice can you give someone on how to be successful in life?
4 What do you dream about for your future?

Do all exercises in your notebook

External exam practice 91

Student's Book page 91

ANSWER KEY

See page 182 for transcripts

1 2.33
1 b
2 a
3 b
4 a

2 1 c
2 b
3 c
4 a
5 c
6 b

3 *Student's own answers*

Pairwork

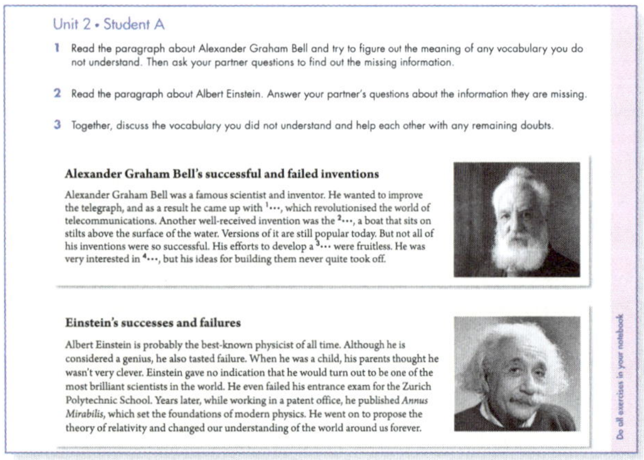
Unit 2 • Student A

1 Read the paragraph about Alexander Graham Bell and try to figure out the meaning of any vocabulary you do not understand. Then ask your partner questions to find out the missing information.

2 Read the paragraph about Albert Einstein. Answer your partner's questions about the information they are missing.

3 Together, discuss the vocabulary you did not understand and help each other with any remaining doubts.

Alexander Graham Bell's successful and failed inventions

Alexander Graham Bell was a famous scientist and inventor. He wanted to improve the telegraph, and as a result he came up with [1]···, which revolutionised the world of telecommunications. Another well-received invention was the [2]···, a boat that sits on stilts above the surface of the water. Versions of it are still popular today. But not all of his inventions were so successful. His efforts to develop a [3]··· were fruitless. He was very interested in [4]···, but his ideas for building them never quite took off.

Einstein's successes and failures

Albert Einstein is probably the best-known physicist of all time. Although he is considered a genius, he also tasted failure. When he was a child, his parents thought he wasn't very clever. Einstein gave no indication that he would turn out to be one of the most brilliant scientists in the world. He even failed his entrance exam for the Zurich Polytechnic School. Years later, while working in a patent office, he published *Annus Mirabilis*, which set the foundations of modern physics. He went on to propose the theory of relativity and changed our understanding of the world around us forever.

Do all exercises in your notebook

Student's Book page 99

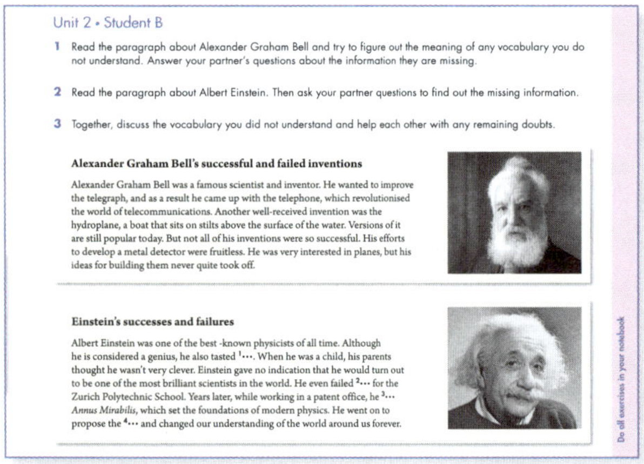
Unit 2 • Student B

1 Read the paragraph about Alexander Graham Bell and try to figure out the meaning of any vocabulary you do not understand. Answer your partner's questions about the information they are missing.

2 Read the paragraph about Albert Einstein. Then ask your partner questions to find out the missing information.

3 Together, discuss the vocabulary you did not understand and help each other with any remaining doubts.

Alexander Graham Bell's successful and failed inventions

Alexander Graham Bell was a famous scientist and inventor. He wanted to improve the telegraph, and as a result he came up with the telephone, which revolutionised the world of telecommunications. Another well-received invention was the hydroplane, a boat that sits on stilts above the surface of the water. Versions of it are still popular today. But not all of his inventions were so successful. His efforts to develop a metal detector were fruitless. He was very interested in planes, but his ideas for building them never quite took off.

Einstein's successes and failures

Albert Einstein was one of the best -known physicists of all time. Although he is considered a genius, he also tasted [1]···. When he was a child, his parents thought he wasn't very clever. Einstein gave no indication that he would turn out to be one of the most brilliant scientists in the world. He even failed [2]··· for the Zurich Polytechnic School. Years later, while working in a patent office, he [3]··· *Annus Mirabilis*, which set the foundations of modern physics. He went on to propose the [4]··· and changed our understanding of the world around us forever.

Do all exercises in your notebook

Student's Book page 103

CEFR MEDIATION DESCRIPTOR

- **Facilitating collaborative interaction with peers**
  Students can collaborate in simple, shared tasks and work towards a common goal in a group by asking and answering straightforward questions.

- **Exchanging information**
  Put students in pairs and get them to turn to their corresponding page. Tell them that they have information on the same two important historical figures, but that one of them has gaps in one text and the complete version of the other text, so they must ask each other questions in order to have a complete version of the texts.

Remind students to do all the exercises in their notebook

Unit 2 Grammar reference

Past perfect: affirmative

Use the **past perfect** to show that an action happened before another action in the past.

Walt Disney **had built** a multimillion-dollar business empire before his death in 1966.

- He built the empire. Then he died.

By the time he opened Disneyland, many people **had seen** his films.

- People saw the films. Then he opened Disneyland.

Use time expressions like *by then, by the time, before that, already*.

We use the past perfect when we talk about two things that happened at different times in the past. We use the past perfect to make clear which action happened first.

He went home because **he had injured** himself.

injured himself → went home

The school had been open for a year when the new head teacher arrived.

school opened → new head teacher arrived

We use ***before***, ***after*** and ***already*** with the past perfect.

I **hadn't seen** giraffes **before** I went on a safari in Africa.

After we'd said goodnight, I went upstairs and brushed my teeth.

I**'d already arrived** home when it started to rain.

We form the past perfect with ***had*** + **past participle**. We use the same form, ***had***, for all subjects. For irregular past participles, see the Irregular Verbs List on page 116.

Past simple and past perfect

Use the **past simple** to talk about an event or a chain of events that finished in the past.	Use the **past perfect** with the **past simple** to show that an action happened before another action in the past.
Bubble wrap **didn't become** successful until IBM **used** it to package a computer.	Manuel Jalón Corominas **had already** invented the mop but Joy Mangano **improved** the design.

We often use the past simple and the past perfect when the order of verbs in a story is not the same as the order of events.

We **arrived** in London and **realised** we **had left** our cameras at home.

left cameras → arrived → realised

We use the past perfect to add information when we talk about an event that happened in the past.

Past simple	Past simple & past perfect
Joy Mangano **improved** the design of the mop in 1990.	Manuel Jalón Corominas **had already invented** the mop but Joy Mangano **improved** the design in 1990.
My sister **moved** to England in 2014.	My sister **had never spoken** English before she **moved** to England in 2014.
The athlete **won** three races in July.	The athlete **had lost** every race that year until she **won** three in July.

Do all exercises in your notebook

108 **Workbook** pages 93-96

Student's Book page 108

Wordlist

Wordlist

UNIT 2

The entertainment industry

feature film
full-length
animated
musical
production
release
remake
sequel

Inventions

bubble wrap
copycat
design
idea
insulation
invest
mop
perfume
suitcase
wallpaper

Success and failure

achievement
fail
focused
grit
habits
lose heart
motivated
passionate
perseverance
set goals
succeed
successful

Do all exercises in your notebook

Workbook pages 102-104 117

Student's Book page 117

2.42 2.43 2.44

Remind students to do all the exercises in their notebook

PROJECT: Entrepreneurs

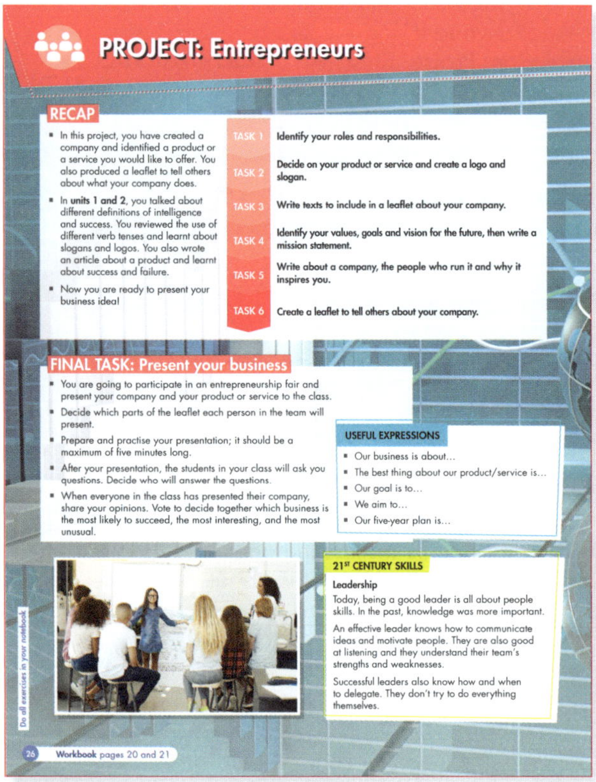

PROJECT: Entrepreneurs

RECAP

- In this project, you have created a company and identified a product or a service you would like to offer. You also produced a leaflet to tell others about what your company does.
- In **units 1 and 2**, you talked about different definitions of intelligence and success. You reviewed the use of different verb tenses and learnt about slogans and logos. You also wrote an article about a product and learnt about success and failure.
- Now you are ready to present your business idea!

TASK 1	**Identify your roles and responsibilities.**
TASK 2	**Decide on your product or service and create a logo and slogan.**
TASK 3	**Write texts to include in a leaflet about your company.**
TASK 4	**Identify your values, goals and vision for the future, then write a mission statement.**
TASK 5	**Write about a company, the people who run it and why it inspires you.**
TASK 6	**Create a leaflet to tell others about your company.**

FINAL TASK: Present your business

- You are going to participate in an entrepreneurship fair and present your company and your product or service to the class.
- Decide which parts of the leaflet each person in the team will present.
- Prepare and practise your presentation; it should be a maximum of five minutes long.
- After your presentation, the students in your class will ask you questions. Decide who will answer the questions.
- When everyone in the class has presented their company, share your opinions. Vote to decide together which business is the most likely to succeed, the most interesting, and the most unusual.

USEFUL EXPRESSIONS

- Our business is about…
- The best thing about our product/service is…
- Our goal is to…
- We aim to…
- Our five-year plan is…

21ST CENTURY SKILLS

Leadership

Today, being a good leader is all about people skills. In the past, knowledge was more important.

An effective leader knows how to communicate ideas and motivate people. They are also good at listening and they understand their team's strengths and weaknesses.

Successful leaders also know how and when to delegate. They don't try to do everything themselves.

Do all exercises in your notebook

26 **Workbook** pages 20 and 21

Project • Units 1 and 2

GO BEYOND
BUSINESS FOR THE FUTURE

It doesn't take more than a few minutes on the internet to find a growing number of companies, websites and podcasts aimed at 'Teenpreneurs'. More and more teenagers are interested in business, humanitarian work, environmental protection and social justice. They have a lot to offer the world of business, with their positive view of the future, open minds and awareness of the needs of the next generation.

SAGE (Students for the Advancement of Global Entrepreneurship) is an organisation that aims at empowering youngsters to create civic-minded companies, clubs or businesses. As one of its activities, SAGE promotes National Entrepreneurship Tournaments where students compete to represent their country at the annual SAGE World Cup.

In this competition, judges evaluate aspects such as students' entrepreneurship, community outreach, social responsibility and environmental sustainability. After a presentation, the students have an interview with the judges.

By learning how to plan and manage a business, students learn real-world skills, take responsibility for their futures and develop potential for the business world.

Answer the questions in pairs.

1 Would you like to take part in the SAGE World Cup?
2 How can creating a business help you to grow as an individual?
3 What companies do you admire? Say why.
4 Do you think that teenpreneurs can change the world?

EVALUATION

Answer the questions in your team.

1 What have been the positive and negative aspects of creating the business?
2 How could you have prevented the negative aspects?
3 What have you learnt from the experience?
4 Could you make your project a reality?

Do all exercises in your notebook

27

Workbook project task notes

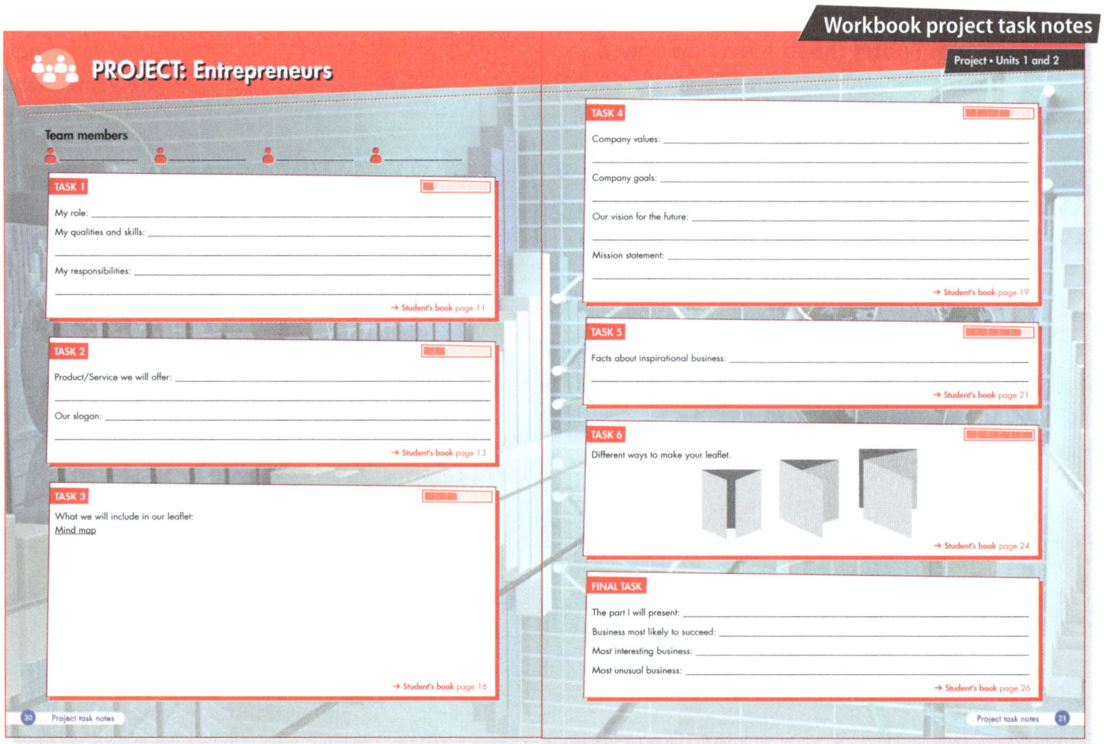

PROJECT: Entrepreneurs

Team members

TASK 1

My role: ____

My qualities and skills: ____

My responsibilities: ____

→ Student's book page 11

TASK 2

Product/Service we will offer: ____

Our slogan: ____

→ Student's book page 13

TASK 3

What we will include in our leaflet:

Mind map

→ Student's book page 16

20 Project task notes

Project • Units 1 and 2

TASK 4

Company values: ____

Company goals: ____

Our vision for the future: ____

Mission statement: ____

→ Student's book page 19

TASK 5

Facts about inspirational business: ____

→ Student's book page 21

TASK 6

Different ways to make your leaflet.

→ Student's book page 24

FINAL TASK

The part I will present: ____

Business most likely to succeed: ____

Most interesting business: ____

Most unusual business: ____

→ Student's book page 26

Project task notes 21

Remind students to do all the exercises in their notebook

PROJECT FOCUS

→ See pages 24-27 **Projects**

Skills

- Collaborate to develop and present a leaflet for a business idea
- Discuss and assign roles
- Write a list of skills, qualities and responsibilities for a designated role
- Reach consensus on a product or service
- Create a logo and write a slogan for a target market
- Write texts for a leaflet about the company
- Research mission statements and write one
- Research and write about an inspiring business
- Discuss evaluations of the project
- Read and discuss a text related to the project

CEFR mediation

Facilitating collaborative interaction with peers
Can collaborate on a shared task, for example formulating and responding to suggestions, asking whether people agree and proposing alternative approaches.

→ See pages 30-33 **Mediation**

Preparation Remind students to bring their work from tasks 1-6 and their notes from the **Workbook** project task notes (pages 20-21) or their own notebook. Bring cue cards if needed for the presentation. Have students bring in their self-assessment diaries if you decided that you wanted them to keep one.

RECAP

Put students in their teams and read through the **Recap** as a class. Draw their attention to the project tasks and the unit objectives and ask which task helped achieve which objectives. Make sure they have all the materials and notes that they need (see **Preparation**) for the **Final task**.

FINAL TASK: Present your business

Tell students they are now going to use their leaflets to present their companies and the product or service at an entrepreneurship fair. Direct their attention to the **21st Century skill** (see next column). Read through the first four steps, encourage them to use the **Useful expressions** and give them a time limit for the preparation and practice to make sure they can all finish their presentations and the rest of the project lesson. Monitor their preparation to make sure everyone is collaborating effectively. You could also check if teams have a leader and how good a job the others think they are doing, giving praise or some gentle advice as you think appropriate.

Before each presentation, give each team a round of applause to build confidence and generate enthusiasm. After each, lead with a question of your own if other students don't already have them. You could give some feedback immediately after each presentation while they have them fresh in their memories, as they may be more receptive to it and it could help students in the next presentation. Praise effort and be constructive. They will have a chance to assess themselves and each other in more detail in the **Evaluation** section.

21ST CENTURY SKILLS

Read through the **21st Century skill** with the students. Ask them if their company had a manager or leader or if they all led at different stages. How effective was the leadership? Tell them to bear in mind the leadership skills mentioned in the Final task.

→ See pages 28-29 **21st century skills**

EVALUATION

Before students discuss the questions as a group, give them time to prepare notes about their experience in the project. Remind students to be supportive and give constructive criticism if necessary, with ideas on how to do things better next time. Monitor discussions, adding your own feedback where appropriate and noting common observations to then convey to the class as a whole. Have a class discussion about what students have learnt from the project, reminding them of the unit objectives, the **Core values** and the **Learning tools** sections of units 1 and 2, as well as the **21st Century skills** section of the **Project** pages.

As is suggested in the introductory notes on assessment, the evaluation section of the project could be an opportunity for students to write a diary of self-assessment, with short comments on the knowledge and skills they have acquired and developed, which they want to work on and their feelings about their learning and progress. Encourage them to use the Evaluation discussion as a base and to refer to the **Reflect on your learning** section of the **Workbook** if they have one.

→ See pages 40-41 **Assessment**

GO BEYOND

Ask students if they know of any young entrepreneurs and what their business is. Tell them the text is about something called SAGE and ask them to scan the text to find what it is (see the second paragraph). Then give them time to read in detail and discuss answers to the questions below the text. Open up to a class discussion if there's time.

Remind students to do all the exercises in their notebook

3 MYTHS AND LEGENDS

At the start of each unit and lesson, explain to the students what the objectives are.

Language objectives

Grammar

Past simple and past continuous
- Students practise these two tenses in contrast.

Direct speech and reported speech
- Students practise transforming direct speech into reported speech and vice versa.

Vocabulary

Storytelling: *biography, character, climax, comic strip, conflict, fairy tale, fictional, hero, introduction, novel, play, plot, poem, resolution, setting, theme*
- Students use vocabulary for talking about stories.

The natural world: *burn, harmony, human, land, light, sky, the Earth, the Universe, water, wood*
- Students use vocabulary for describing the natural world.

Myths: *battle, death, evil, fight, giant, gift, god, goddess, Greek, humanity, king, knowledge, Norse*
- Students encounter vocabulary related to myths.

Idioms and expressions

Myths and legends: *a round-table discussion, Pandora's box, the Midas touch, an Achilles heel*

- Students look at idioms and expressions related to myths and legends in the context of a radio show.

Recycled language

Past simple, Present simple, continuous and perfect, Imperatives

Skills objectives

Speaking

- Students use pictures to retell the story of the Trojan War.
- Students retell the plot of their favourite story.
- Students discuss what they can learn from myths.
- Students write and perform a conversation using idioms and expressions.

Pronunciation: Students practise making the /k/ and /ks/ sounds.

Pairwork: Students use various mediation techniques in order to complete a comic strip about a Greek myth.

Listening

- Students listen and complete a table about the legend of William Tell.
- Students listen and choose the correct grammatical options in a conversation about the Trojan War.
- Students listen and complete a Mayan creation myth with verb tenses.
- Students listen and answer questions about a Chinese myth.
- Students listen and answer questions about an old English legend.

Reading

- Students skim a text to compare its content with their knowledge about two myths.
- Students read and complete a table about the structure of a myth.
- Students scan a text to match words with their synonyms.

Core values: Students discuss what we can learn from different myths and reflect on the value of **respect for other cultures**.

Writing

- Students look at structure, style and tense use in a legend.
- Students plan, write and check their own legend.

Focus on Narrative tenses

Remind students to do all the exercises in their notebook

Learning to learn tools

SPEAKING TOOLS Students practise repeating new expressions quickly so that when they say them at normal speed they feel more confident.

READING TOOLS Students use their knowledge of narrative structure to help them understand a story.

WRITING TOOLS Students practise planning elements of a story before writing to avoid 'writer's block'.

Project objectives: Comic strip

Task 1 Students decide on setting, characters and general plot of their chosen myth.

Task 2 Students write versions of the story, with dialogue.

Task 3 Students choose the best parts from each story and combine them.

Audiovisual objectives

Vlog: Students watch and listen to Holly tell a Cherokee legend.

Culture: Students watch and listen to Holly talk about books and libraries.

Grammar animations: Students are presented with visual presentations of the unit grammar.

Key competences

LC **Linguistic**
pages 28-35

MST **Mathematical and Science and Technology**
pages 30-33

DC **Digital**
pages 28-29, 31, 35

SCC **Social and Civic**
pages 28, 30-33, 35

CAE **Cultural awareness and expression**
pages 28-35

LL **Learning to learn**
pages 32-35

IE **Sense of initiative and entrepreneurship**
pages 29, 31, 34

→ See pages 42-43 **Key competences**

CEFR Mediation

3.1 Note-taking
Can take notes in point form on a familiar topic.

3.2 Processing text in writing
Can summarise the main points in simple spoken texts.

3.3 Expressing a personal response to creative texts
Can relate events in a story, film or play to similar events he/she has experienced or heard about.

3.4 Analysis and criticism of creative texts
Can describe the key themes and characters in short narratives.

3.5 Relaying specific information in speech
Can relay the content of spoken texts at normal speed.

Project Processing text in writing
Can summarise the information in texts on subjects of personal interest.

Unit review Relaying specific information in writing
Can write specific information in simple informational texts.

Pairwork Relaying specific information in speech
Can relay specific information in short, simple texts on familiar subjects.

→ See pages 30-33 **Mediation**

Remind students to do all the exercises in their notebook

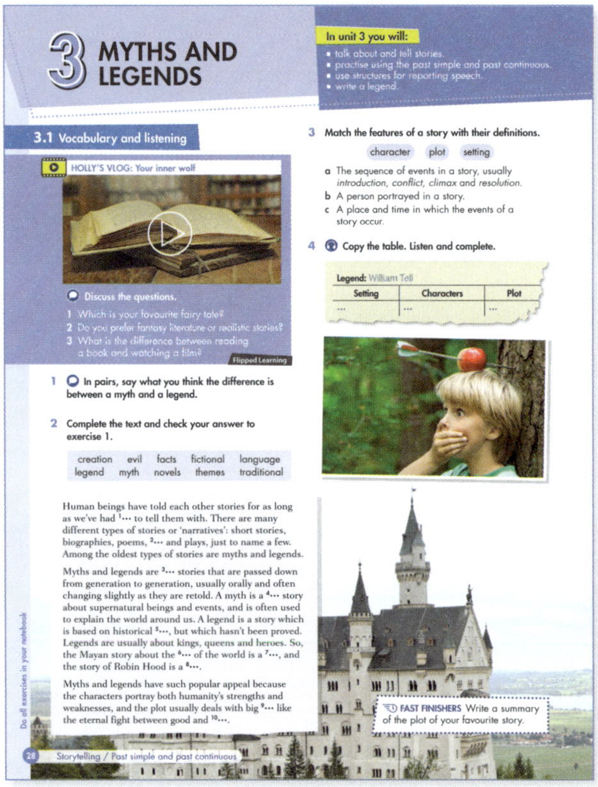

3 MYTHS AND LEGENDS

In unit 3 you will:
- talk about and tell stories.
- practise using the past simple and past continuous.
- use structures for reporting speech.
- write a legend.

3.1 Vocabulary and listening

HOLLY'S VLOG: Your inner wolf

Discuss the questions.
1 Which is your favourite fairy tale?
2 Do you prefer fantasy literature or realistic stories?
3 What is the difference between reading a book and watching a film?

Flipped Learning

1 **In pairs, say what you think the difference is between a myth and a legend.**

2 **Complete the text and check your answer to exercise 1.**

creation evil facts fictional language legend myth novels themes traditional

Human beings have told each other stories for as long as we've had [1]··· to tell them with. There are many different types of stories or 'narratives': short stories, biographies, poems, [2]··· and plays, just to name a few. Among the oldest types of stories are myths and legends.

Myths and legends are [3]··· stories that are passed down from generation to generation, usually orally and often changing slightly as they are retold. A myth is a [4]··· story about supernatural beings and events, and is often used to explain the world around us. A legend is a story which is based on historical [5]···, but which hasn't been proved. Legends are usually about kings, queens and heroes. So, the Mayan story about the [6]··· of the world is a [7]···, and the story of Robin Hood is a [8]···.

Myths and legends have such popular appeal because the characters portray both humanity's strengths and weaknesses, and the plot usually deals with big [9]··· like the eternal fight between good and [10]···.

3 **Match the features of a story with their definitions.**

character plot setting

a The sequence of events in a story, usually *introduction, conflict, climax* and *resolution*.
b A person portrayed in a story.
c A place and time in which the events of a story occur.

4 **Copy the table. Listen and complete.**

Legend: William Tell

Setting	Characters	Plot
···	···	···

FAST FINISHERS Write a summary of the plot of your favourite story.

Do all exercises in your notebook

28 Storytelling / Past simple and past continuous

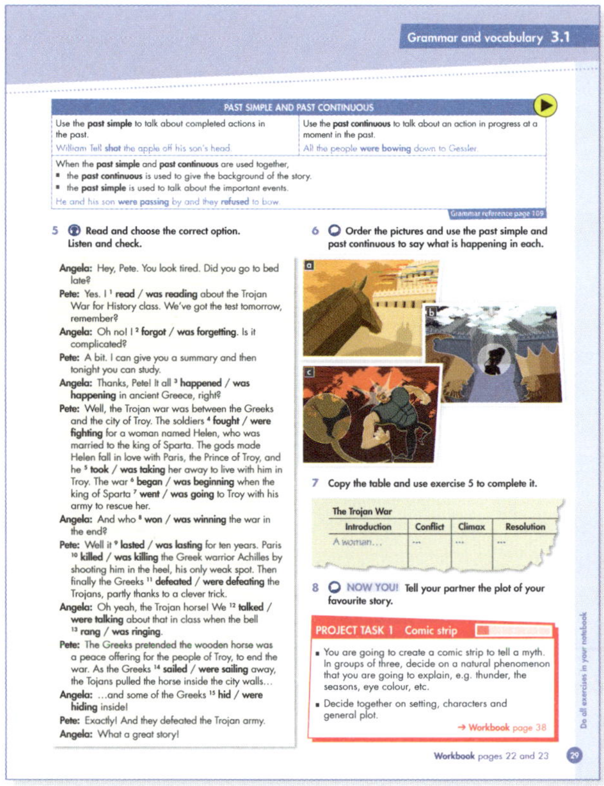

Grammar and vocabulary 3.1

PAST SIMPLE AND PAST CONTINUOUS

Use the **past simple** to talk about completed actions in the past. William Tell **shot** the apple off his son's head.	Use the **past continuous** to talk about an action in progress at a moment in the past. All the people **were bowing** down to Gessler.

When the **past simple** and **past continuous** are used together,
- the **past continuous** is used to give the background of the story.
- the **past simple** is used to talk about the important events.

He and his son **were passing** by and they **refused** to bow.

Grammar reference page 109

5 **Read and choose the correct option. Listen and check.**

Angela: Hey, Pete. You look tired. Did you go to bed late?
Pete: Yes. I [1] **read / was reading** about the Trojan War for History class. We've got the test tomorrow, remember?
Angela: Oh no! I [2] **forgot / was forgetting**. Is it complicated?
Pete: A bit. I can give you a summary and then tonight you can study.
Angela: Thanks, Pete! It all [3] **happened / was happening** in ancient Greece, right?
Pete: Well, the Trojan war was between the Greeks and the city of Troy. The soldiers [4] **fought / were fighting** for a woman named Helen, who was married to the king of Sparta. The gods made Helen fall in love with Paris, the Prince of Troy, and he [5] **took / was taking** her away to live with him in Troy. The war [6] **began / was beginning** when the king of Sparta [7] **went / was going** to Troy with his army to rescue her.
Angela: And who [8] **won / was winning** the war in the end?
Pete: Well it [9] **lasted / was lasting** for ten years. Paris [10] **killed / was killing** the Greek warrior Achilles by shooting him in the heel, his only weak spot. Then finally the Greeks [11] **defeated / were defeating** the Trojans, partly thanks to a clever trick.
Angela: Oh yeah, the Trojan horse! We [12] **talked / were talking** about that in class when the bell [13] **rang / was ringing**.
Pete: The Greeks pretended the wooden horse was a peace offering for the people of Troy, to end the war. As the Greeks [14] **sailed / were sailing** away, the Tojans pulled the horse inside the city walls…
Angela: …and some of the Greeks [15] **hid / were hiding** inside!
Pete: Exactly! And they defeated the Trojan army.
Angela: What a great story!

6 **Order the pictures and use the past simple and past continuous to say what is happening in each.**

a b c

7 **Copy the table and use exercise 5 to complete it.**

The Trojan War

Introduction	Conflict	Climax	Resolution
A woman…	···	···	···

8 NOW YOU! **Tell your partner the plot of your favourite story.**

PROJECT TASK 1 Comic strip
- You are going to create a comic strip to tell a myth. In groups of three, decide on a natural phenomenon that you are going to explain, e.g. thunder, the seasons, eye colour, etc.
- Decide together on setting, characters and general plot.

→ Workbook page 38

Do all exercises in your notebook

Workbook pages 22 and 23 29

ANSWER KEY

Pages 28-29

1 *Student's own answers*

2 **1** language **2** novels **3** traditional **4** fictional **5** facts **6** creation **7** myth **8** legend **9** themes **10** evil

3 **a** plot **b** character **c** setting

4 **Legend**: William Tell

Setting	Characters	Plot
Small town in Switzerland	William Tell Gessler (the tyrannical ruler of the town) William Tell's son	A tyrannical ruler called Gessler makes everyone in the town bow down to him. Tell and his son refuse. Gessler tells them he will kill them both unless Tell can shoot an apple off his son's head with his bow and arrow. Tell does this and saves their lives. Then he kills Gessler and sets the town people free.

5 **1** was reading **2** forgot **3** happened **4** were fighting **5** took **6** began **7** went **8** won **9** lasted **10** killed **11** defeated **12** were talking **13** rang **14** were sailing **15** were hiding

6 b, c, a

7 **The Trojan War**

Introduction	Conflict	Climax	Resolution
A woman called Helen was the wife of the King of Sparta. The gods made Helen fall in love with Paris, the Prince of Troy. Paris took her to live with him in Troy.	The King of Sparta went to Troy to rescue her. Paris killed the Greek warrior Achilles by shooting him in his only weak spot: his heel.	Greek soldiers entered Troy hidden inside a wooden horse they had pretended to give the people of Sparta as a peace offering.	The Greeks defeated the Trojans.

8 *Student's own answers*

Remind students to do all the exercises in their notebook

LESSON FOCUS

Grammar Past simple and past continuous
Vocabulary Storytelling
Listening Completing a table about the legend of William Tell; Choosing the correct grammatical options in a conversation about the Trojan War
Speaking Retelling the story of the Trojan War from illustrations; Retelling the plot of a favourite story
Project task 1 Decide on setting, characters and general plot for students' chosen myth

Resources

Teacher's i-solutions, Student's Book audio, Vlog and worksheets

Flipped Learning

HOLLY'S VLOG: Your inner wolf

- Make sure to set up the **Flipped Learning** work with the students beforehand. **See pages 20-23 for complete Flipped Learning guidelines**.
- Ask students to put the **Flipped Learning worksheets** on their desks and walk around to check how many have completed the Flipped task.
- In pairs or small groups, ask students to compare and check the *Before you watch…* and *While you watch…* exercises on the worksheet.
- Show students **Holly's Vlog** and ask volunteers to provide correct answers and clarify any doubts other students may have.
- Choose three or four students to read aloud their answers to the *After you watch…* exercises on the worksheet and encourage some class discussion.
- Move straight to exercise 1 on page 28.

Warmer

Watch Holly's Vlog and discuss the questions with the whole class. If you don't have video facilities, simply discuss the questions.

1 Ask students what other types of folk tales they know of. Tell them that myths and legends will be the focus of the unit, get them to do the exercise and elicit ideas.

2 Tell students that the text outlines some differences between myths and legends. Ask them to do the exercise and compare their ideas from exercise 1.

3 This exercise might be best done as a class. Get students to guess the meaning of the words and then complete the exercise.

4 1.25 (See page 171 for transcripts) Tell students they are going to hear a brief version of the legend of William Tell before playing the audio. Get students to compare their answers in pairs and listen again if necessary.

FAST FINISHERS Students can complete this exercise alone or in pairs.

Flipped Learning

PAST SIMPLE AND PAST CONTINUOUS

Draw students' attention to the **Grammar table**. Remind students that they can use this as a quick reference while completing the exercises.

Show students the **Grammar animation** and/or refer students to the **Grammar reference** on page 109 for further information on form and use.

→ See page 23 for how to flip the **grammar lesson**

5 1.26 (See page 171 for transcripts) Ask students what story the two people in the dialogue are talking about (the Trojan War). You could point out that it has elements of both myth and legend in that there are gods involved, but that some scholars believe the war was a real historical event. Do the first two items together to get them started and refer them to the **Grammar table**.

6 Let students refer to the text but encourage them not to read from it too much. To extend the exercise, first ask them to use the present continuous to say what is happening in each picture and then get them to use the past simple and past continuous to retell the story from memory.

7 Draw students' attention to the table and check that they understand the headings. Let them compare their answers in pairs.

8 NOW YOU! Before students start, ask them to take notes about their stories using the headings in exercise 7. Then encourage them to consult their notes to retell the story. You could ask their partners to check with them what the different parts of the story were.

PROJECT TASK 1 Comic strip

Organise students into teams of 3 and read through the task. Give them time to decide on the basic plot. Remind students that they need to keep their project notes together in their **Workbook** (page 38) or in their own notebook.

→ See pages 24-27 **Projects**

FURTHER PRACTICE

Workbook pages 22-23
- **Grammar reference and practice** pages 86 and 93-94
- **Wordlist and exercises** pages 99 and 102-103

Remind students to do all the exercises in their notebook

CONTINUOUS ASSESSMENT Students can talk about storytelling, and use the past simple and past continuous.

3.2 Listening and vocabulary

1 In pairs, find the words in the Mayan creation myth below and write definitions for them.

carve clay dissolve good-hearted mindless mould nutritious souls

Pronunciation: /k/ and /ks/

2 Listen and repeat.

/k/ carve, check, clay, folk, kind, queen

/ks/ box, climax, exercise, ox, six, text

3 In pairs, complete the Mayan creation myth with the correct tense of the verbs. Listen and check.

4 NOW YOU! Write a summary of the plot in your own words. Use the words from exercise 1.

FAST FINISHERS Write the present simple, past simple and past participle forms of the verbs you used to complete the Mayan creation myth.

Do all exercises in your notebook

30 The natural world / Direct speech and reported speech

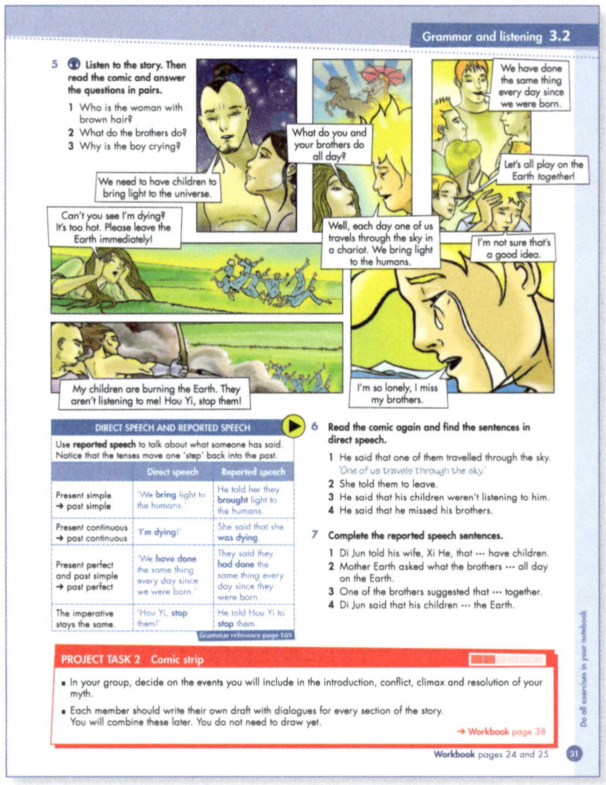
Grammar and listening 3.2

5 Listen to the story. Then read the comic and answer the questions in pairs.

1 Who is the woman with brown hair?
2 What do the brothers do?
3 Why is the boy crying?

DIRECT SPEECH AND REPORTED SPEECH

Use **reported speech** to talk about what someone has said. Notice that the tenses move one 'step' back into the past.

	Direct speech	Reported speech
Present simple → past simple	'We **bring** light to the humans.'	He told her they **brought** light to the humans.
Present continuous → past continuous	'I'm **dying**!'	She said that she **was dying**.
Present perfect and past simple → past perfect	'We **have done** the same thing every day since we were born.'	They said they **had done** the same thing every day since they were born.
The imperative stays the same.	'Hou Yi, **stop** them!'	He told Hou Yi to **stop** them.

Grammar reference page 109

6 Read the comic again and find the sentences in direct speech.

1 He said that one of them travelled through the sky. *'One of us travels through the sky.'*
2 She told them to leave.
3 He said that his children weren't listening to him.
4 He said that he missed his brothers.

7 Complete the reported speech sentences.

1 Di Jun told his wife, Xi He, that ··· have children.
2 Mother Earth asked what the brothers ··· all day on the Earth.
3 One of the brothers suggested that ··· together.
4 Di Jun said that his children ··· the Earth.

PROJECT TASK 2 Comic strip

- In your group, decide on the events you will include in the introduction, conflict, climax and resolution of your myth.
- Each member should write their own draft with dialogues for every section of the story. You will combine these later. You do not need to draw yet.

→ Workbook page 38

Workbook pages 24 and 25 31

Do all exercises in your notebook

ANSWER KEY

Pages 30-31

1 *Suggested answers:*

carve: to make something out of wood by cutting it
clay: a material that comes from the earth
dissolve: mix with a liquid and disappear
good-hearted: kind and generous
mindless: without intelligence
mould: change the shape of something
nutritious: healthy
souls: where our feelings or emotions come from

2 *Student's own answers*

3
1 decided
2 have made
3 are dissolving
4 was walking
5 carve
6 are
7 were

4 *Student's own answers*

5
1 Mother Earth
2 Every day, a different brother travels through the sky in a chariot to bring light to the humans on Earth.
3 Because he misses his brothers.

6
1 'One of us travels through the sky.'
2 'Please leave!'
3 'They aren't listening to me.'
4 'I miss my brothers.'

7
1 they needed to
2 did
3 they played
4 were burning

Remind students to do all the exercises in their notebook

LESSON FOCUS

Grammar Direct speech and reported speech
Vocabulary The natural world
Listening Completing a Mayan creation myth with verb tenses; Answering questions about a Chinese myth
Project task 2 Write versions of the story with dialogue

Resources
Teacher's i-solutions, Student's Book audio
Preparation Have another creation story ready to tell the students

Warmer

Write the word 'creation' on the board and tell students that most cultures have stories of how the world was created. Tell them your example story. Put students in small groups to discuss any creation stories they know. Encourage them to invent one together if they don't know any.

1 Tell students they are going to read and listen to a creation myth from the Mesoamerican Mayan culture in comic strip format. Get them to read the story and guess the vocabulary from the context before checking in a dictionary.

Pronunciation

2 1.27 (See page 172 for transcripts) Get students to pronounce the individual sounds before repeating the words.

3 1.28 (See page 172 for transcripts) Refer students to the **Grammar table** on page 109 to help them complete the exercise.

4 NOW YOU! You could get students to do the exercise in pairs. Make sure they are using their own words where possible.

FAST FINISHERS Students can complete this exercise alone or in pairs.

5 1.29 (See page 172 for transcripts) Get the students to close their books and tell them that they will hear a Chinese creation myth. Write the names of the characters on the board (Di Jun, Xi He, Mother Earth and Hou Yi) and ask them to take notes about the story as they listen. Then let them open their books to read along with the comic as they listen again, before checking their answers.

DIRECT SPEECH AND REPORTED SPEECH

Flipped Learning

Draw students' attention to the **Grammar table**. Remind students that they can use this as a quick reference while completing the exercises.

Show students the **Grammar animation** and/or refer students to the **Grammar reference** on page 109 for further information on form and use.

→ See page 23 for how to flip the **grammar lesson**

6 Point out that the story students heard contained the sentences in indirect speech. Refer them to the **Grammar table** and ask them to find the words that change (tenses and pronouns).

7 These sentences appear in a slightly different form in the audio. Play the audio again to help consolidate knowledge.

PROJECT TASK 2 Comic strip

Put students back in their groups. Point out that they will work together for the first part of this task. Then they will work alone and compare and combine work later. Remind students that they need to keep their project notes together in their **Workbook** (page 38) or in their own notebook.

→ See pages 24-27 **Projects**

FURTHER PRACTICE

Workbook pages 24-25
- **Grammar reference and practice** pages 86 and 93-94
- **Wordlist and exercises** pages 99 and 102-103

Vocabulary and Grammar worksheets available to download from the **Richmond***Learning***Platform**

→ See pages 38-39 **Mixed-ability classes**

Remind students to do all the exercises in their notebook

CONTINUOUS ASSESSMENT Students can talk about the natural world, and use direct speech and reported speech.

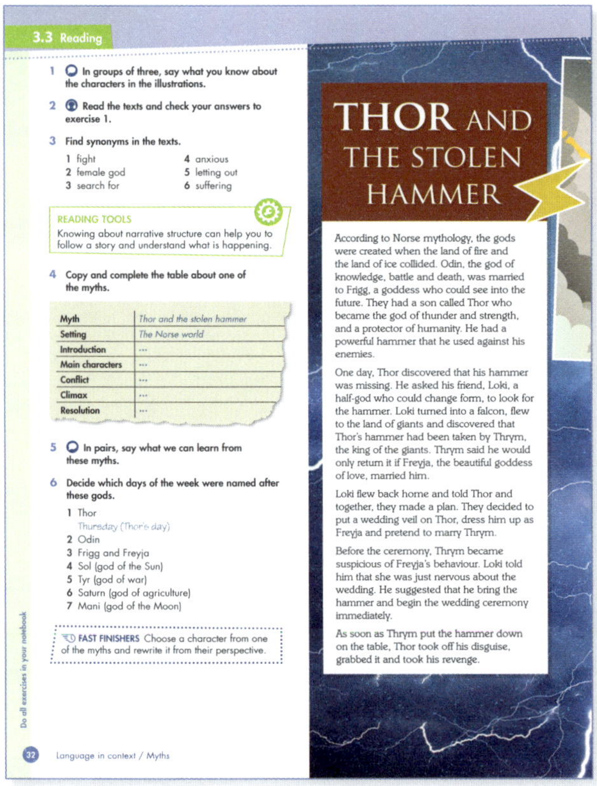

3.3 Reading

1 In groups of three, say what you know about the characters in the illustrations.

2 Read the texts and check your answers to exercise 1.

3 Find synonyms in the texts.

1 fight
2 female god
3 search for
4 anxious
5 letting out
6 suffering

READING TOOLS
Knowing about narrative structure can help you to follow a story and understand what is happening.

4 Copy and complete the table about one of the myths.

Myth	*Thor and the stolen hammer*
Setting	*The Norse world*
Introduction	···
Main characters	···
Conflict	···
Climax	···
Resolution	···

5 In pairs, say what we can learn from these myths.

6 Decide which days of the week were named after these gods.

1 Thor
Thursday (Thor's day)
2 Odin
3 Frigg and Freyja
4 Sol (god of the Sun)
5 Tyr (god of war)
6 Saturn (god of agriculture)
7 Mani (god of the Moon)

FAST FINISHERS Choose a character from one of the myths and rewrite it from their perspective.

Do all exercises in your notebook

32 Language in context / Myths

THOR AND THE STOLEN HAMMER

According to Norse mythology, the gods were created when the land of fire and the land of ice collided. Odin, the god of knowledge, battle and death, was married to Frigg, a goddess who could see into the future. They had a son called Thor who became the god of thunder and strength, and a protector of humanity. He had a powerful hammer that he used against his enemies.

One day, Thor discovered that his hammer was missing. He asked his friend, Loki, a half-god who could change form, to look for the hammer. Loki turned into a falcon, flew to the land of giants and discovered that Thor's hammer had been taken by Thrym, the king of the giants. Thrym said he would only return it if Freyja, the beautiful goddess of love, married him.

Loki flew back home and told Thor and together, they made a plan. They decided to put a wedding veil on Thor, dress him up as Freyja and pretend to marry Thrym.

Before the ceremony, Thrym became suspicious of Freyja's behaviour. Loki told him that she was just nervous about the wedding. He suggested that he bring the hammer and begin the wedding ceremony immediately.

As soon as Thrym put the hammer down on the table, Thor took off his disguise, grabbed it and took his revenge.

Reading 3.3

PANDORA'S BOX

According to Greek mythology, Zeus, the god of the sky, lightning, thunder and justice, told two Titans, the brothers Prometheus and Epimetheus, to go down to Earth and create humans and animals. Prometheus created man in the image of the gods, and Epimetheus created the animals.

Epimetheus gave each animal he created a gift. But by the time Prometheus finished creating humans, there weren't any gifts left. So, he decided to steal fire from the gods and give it to the humans. When Zeus found out, he was angry and decided to punish both Prometheus and Epimetheus.

He chained Prometheus to a mountain and tormented him. But Epimetheus' punishment was worse. First, he created the first human woman, Pandora, and made her curious and beautiful. Epimetheus fell in love with her and they got married. As a wedding present, Zeus gave the couple a box but told them not to open it.

One day, curiosity got the better of Pandora and she opened the box, releasing evil, pain and disease into the world.

To make matters worse, the only thing that did not escape from the box was hope. It remained trapped inside and could not provide any remedy for mankind's pain.

CORE VALUES Respect for other cultures

7 Discuss the questions in groups of three.

1 What similarities do you see in the myths of Pandora's box and Thor and the stolen hammer?
2 What other myths and legends can you think of that are cautionary tales?
3 What lessons do you think we can learn from other cultures?
4 Have you learnt anything from foreign films, books or meeting people from other countries?

Do all exercises in your notebook

Workbook pages 26 and 27 33

ANSWER KEY

Pages 32-33

1 *Student's own answers*

2 *Student's own answers*

3 **1** battle **2** goddess **3** look for **4** nervous **5** releasing **6** pain

4

Myth	Thor and the stolen hammer	Pandora's box
Setting	The Norse world	Ancient Greece
Introduction	Gods were created when the land of fire and land of ice collided.	Zeus tells two Titans to create humans and animals on earth.
Main characters	Odin, Frigg, Thor, Freyja, Loki, Thrym	Zeus, Prometheus, Epimetheus, Pandora
Conflict	Thrym the king of the giants steals Thor's powerful hammer. Thor sends his friend Loki to look for it. Thrym says he will only return the hammer if Freyja, the beautiful goddess of love, marries him.	Prometheus steals fire from Zeus to give humans. Zeus is angry and punishes them. He chains Prometheus to a mountain and punishes Epimetheus by creating a beautiful curious woman called Pandora. Epimetheus falls in love with her and they get married. Zeus gives them a box as a wedding present and tells them not to open it.
Climax	Thor dresses up as Freyja and Loki suggests that Thrym should bring the hammer to the ceremony. Thor removes his veil.	Pandora opens the box.
Resolution	Thor takes back his hammer.	Evil, pain and disease escape from the box. The only thing that doesn't escape is hope.

5 *Student's own answers*

6 **1** Thursday **2** Wednesday **3** Friday **4** Sunday **5** Tuesday **6** Saturday **7** Monday

7 *Student's own answers*

Remind students to do all the exercises in their notebook

LESSON FOCUS
Language in context Myths
Core values Respect for other cultures

Resources
Teacher's i-solutions, Student's Book audio

→ See pages 36-37 **Literature**

Warmer

Write 'Greek and Norse mythology' on the board and, in small groups, ask students to write down as many characters from the two myths as they can remember from the previous lesson and discuss who they were. Compare as a class afterwards.

1 Keeping students in the same groups, ask if the characters from this exercise came up in their discussions. Don't confirm or deny any of their ideas until the next exercise.

2 1.30 (See page 172 for transcripts) Give students time to read for interest and to compare their ideas and the vocabulary against the texts. Let them compare ideas in the same groups after reading.

3 You could do this exercise as a class to give more time for the next exercise. Point out that the words and phrases are in the same grammatical form as their synonyms.

READING TOOLS

Get students to read the **Reading tool** and tell them they will apply it to the next exercise.

4 You could put students in pairs and give each pair a different myth. Get them to compare at the end.

5 Remind students that myths were often told to explain the world as people at the time saw it, but they could also have moral or social lessons. Myths and legends can also teach us about the culture of the people who created them.

6 Point out that English is considered a Germanic language (and so connected to old Norse) with a lot of Latin influence. See if they can guess the names and etymologies of the months and the planets to extend the discussion.

FAST FINISHERS Students can complete this exercise alone or in pairs.

CORE VALUES Respect for other cultures

7 Ask students to draw on their answers to question 3 in order to develop their answer to the broader question 4. If they have difficulty answering the last two questions, you could ask them to compare US films and films and TV programmes from the rest of the world and ask what they think the stories in US films try to teach us and how that differs from the lessons of films from other countries.

FURTHER PRACTICE

Workbook pages 26-27

Remind students to do all the exercises in their notebook

CONTINUOUS ASSESSMENT Students can understand two myths.

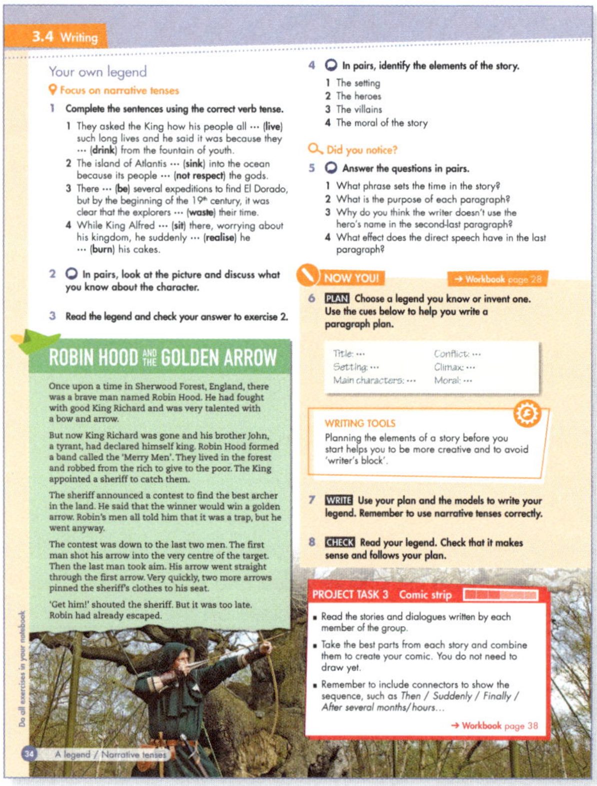

3.4 Writing

Your own legend

Focus on narrative tenses

1 **Complete the sentences using the correct verb tense.**

1 They asked the King how his people all ··· (**live**) such long lives and he said it was because they ··· (**drink**) from the fountain of youth.
2 The island of Atlantis ··· (**sink**) into the ocean because its people ··· (**not respect**) the gods.
3 There ··· (**be**) several expeditions to find El Dorado, but by the beginning of the 19th century, it was clear that the explorers ··· (**waste**) their time.
4 While King Alfred ··· (**sit**) there, worrying about his kingdom, he suddenly ··· (**realise**) he ··· (**burn**) his cakes.

2 **In pairs, look at the picture and discuss what you know about the character.**

3 **Read the legend and check your answer to exercise 2.**

ROBIN HOOD AND THE GOLDEN ARROW

Once upon a time in Sherwood Forest, England, there was a brave man named Robin Hood. He had fought with good King Richard and was very talented with a bow and arrow.

But now King Richard was gone and his brother John, a tyrant, had declared himself king. Robin Hood formed a band called the 'Merry Men'. They lived in the forest and robbed from the rich to give to the poor. The King appointed a sheriff to catch them.

The sheriff announced a contest to find the best archer in the land. He said that the winner would win a golden arrow. Robin's men all told him that it was a trap, but he went anyway.

The contest was down to the last two men. The first man shot his arrow into the very centre of the target. Then the last man took aim. His arrow went straight through the first arrow. Very quickly, two more arrows pinned the sheriff's clothes to his seat.

'Get him!' shouted the sheriff. But it was too late. Robin had already escaped.

4 **In pairs, identify the elements of the story.**

1 The setting
2 The heroes
3 The villains
4 The moral of the story

Did you notice?

5 **Answer the questions in pairs.**

1 What phrase sets the time in the story?
2 What is the purpose of each paragraph?
3 Why do you think the writer doesn't use the hero's name in the second-last paragraph?
4 What effect does the direct speech have in the last paragraph?

NOW YOU! → Workbook page 28

6 **PLAN Choose a legend you know or invent one. Use the cues below to help you write a paragraph plan.**

Title: ··· Conflict: ···
Setting: ··· Climax: ···
Main characters: ··· Moral: ···

WRITING TOOLS

Planning the elements of a story before you start helps you to be more creative and to avoid 'writer's block'.

7 **WRITE Use your plan and the models to write your legend. Remember to use narrative tenses correctly.**

8 **CHECK Read your legend. Check that it makes sense and follows your plan.**

PROJECT TASK 3 Comic strip

- Read the stories and dialogues written by each member of the group.
- Take the best parts from each story and combine them to create your comic. You do not need to draw yet.
- Remember to include connectors to show the sequence, such as *Then / Suddenly / Finally / After several months/hours…*

→ Workbook page 38

Do all exercises in your notebook

34 A legend / Narrative tenses

ANSWER KEY

Page 34

1 **1** lived; had drunk
2 sank; hadn't respected
3 were; were wasting
4 was sitting; realised; had burnt

2 *Student's own answers*

3 *Student's own answers*

4 **1** Sherwood Forest (England)
2 Robin Hood and the Merry Men
3 King John and the sheriff
4 A group of people can unite to fight against a tyrant and defeat them

5 **1** Once upon a time
2 To introduce the story, present the conflict, the climax and resolution
3 It increases the suspense because we don't know who the two men are
4 It makes the action more immediate and dramatic

6 *Student's own answers*

7 *Student's own answers*

8 *Student's own answers*

FURTHER PRACTICE

Workbook page 28

LESSON FOCUS

Focus on Narrative tenses

Writing Students write their own legend

Project task 3 Students choose the best parts from each story and combine them

Resources

Teacher's i-solutions, Student's Book audio

Preparation Prepare a series of sentences that follow the pattern: *You were doing X when Y happened;* A large illustration of Robin Hood

Warmer

Choose one of the sentences you prepared and mime it for the class to guess. Get a volunteer to mime the next sentence you have prepared.

Focus on narrative tenses

1 Ask students what tenses they used in the **Warmer** (past simple and past continuous) and ask them what tense they saw in unit 2 that showed an event that happened before another (past perfect). Tell them they will need these narrative tenses for this exercise.

2 If you have brought in an illustration of Robin Hood, show it to the students with their books closed for this discussion.

3 Give students time to read, check their answers and discuss briefly what they thought of the story in pairs.

4 Encourage students to discuss the answers but not to write them.

Did you notice?

5 Encourage students to write the example of direct speech to use as reference for how to punctuate direct speech.

6 **PLAN** Let students start in pairs if it helps them come up with ideas. Point out that while such stories have a moral, the moral isn't usually stated in the story.

WRITING TOOLS

Get students to read the **Writing tool** and point out that part of the process of planning involves brainstorming different ideas before you choose one that you like.

7 **WRITE** Before students start writing, make a checklist on the board of any elements related to content, structure, language and style that they should bear in mind.

8 **CHECK** Once students have checked their own legends, they can swap with a partner and check theirs.

PROJECT TASK 3 Comic strip

Put students in their groups to read and give feedback on each other's stories. Encourage them to include something from everyone's story. Tell students that they need to keep their project notes together in their **Workbook** (page 38) or in their own notebook.

→ See pages 24-27 **Projects**

Remind students to do all the exercises in their notebook

CONTINUOUS ASSESSMENT Students can use appropriate narrative tenses to write their own legend.

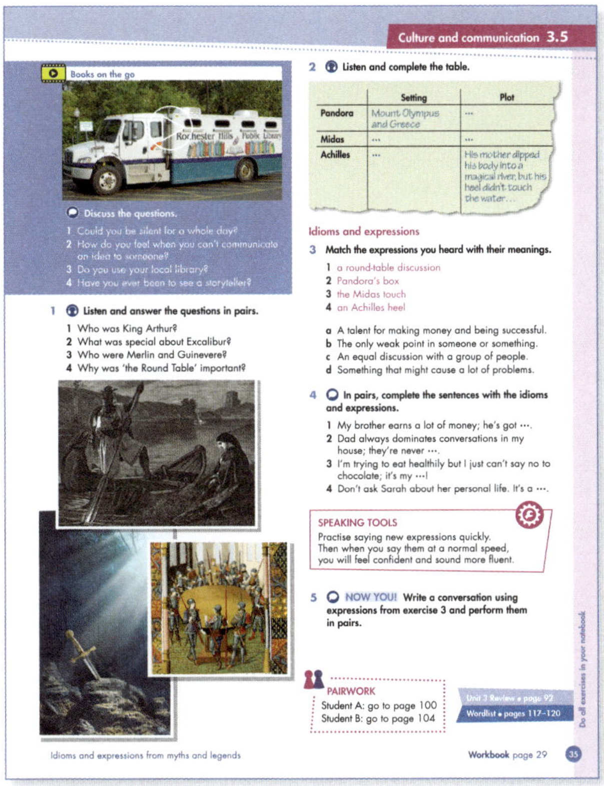
Culture and communication 3.5

Books on the go

Discuss the questions.

1 Could you be silent for a whole day?
2 How do you feel when you can't communicate an idea to someone?
3 Do you use your local library?
4 Have you ever been to see a storyteller?

1 Listen and answer the questions in pairs.

1 Who was King Arthur?
2 What was special about Excalibur?
3 Who were Merlin and Guinevere?
4 Why was 'the Round Table' important?

2 Listen and complete the table.

	Setting	Plot
Pandora	Mount Olympus and Greece	...
Midas	...	...
Achilles	...	His mother dipped his body into a magical river, but his heel didn't touch the water...

Idioms and expressions

3 Match the expressions you heard with their meanings.

1 a round-table discussion
2 Pandora's box
3 the Midas touch
4 an Achilles heel

a A talent for making money and being successful.
b The only weak point in someone or something.
c An equal discussion with a group of people.
d Something that might cause a lot of problems.

4 In pairs, complete the sentences with the idioms and expressions.

1 My brother earns a lot of money; he's got ···.
2 Dad always dominates conversations in my house; they're never ···.
3 I'm trying to eat healthily but I just can't say no to chocolate; it's my ···!
4 Don't ask Sarah about her personal life. It's a ···.

SPEAKING TOOLS
Practise saying new expressions quickly. Then when you say them at a normal speed, you will feel confident and sound more fluent.

5 NOW YOU! Write a conversation using expressions from exercise 3 and perform them in pairs.

PAIRWORK
Student A: go to page 100
Student B: go to page 104

Unit 3 Review • page 92
Wordlist • pages 117-120

Do all exercises in your notebook

Idioms and expressions from myths and legends

Workbook page 29

35

LESSON FOCUS

Idioms and expressions Myths and legends

Listening Answering questions about an old English legend

Speaking Writing and performing a conversation

Resources

Teacher's i-solutions, Student's Book audio, Culture video and worksheets

School uniforms

Video and worksheet available on the

Richmond*Learning***Platform**

- In pairs, ask students to complete the *What I know...* exercises on the **Culture video worksheet**.
- Show students the **Culture video** and ask them to complete the *What I learned...* exercises on the worksheet.
- In pairs, students compare answers.
- In small groups, tell students to complete the *What I wonder...* exercises on the worksheet.

ANSWER KEY

Page 35

1 **1** A legendary king of England who may not have existed.
2 It was a magical sword stuck in a stone that only the 'true King of England' could pull out.
3 Merlin was a wizard who helped King Arthur throughout his life and Guinevere was King Arthur's wife.
4 It showed that there was equality between all of King Arthur's knights.

2 Refer to page 192 of the **Teacher's Book**.

3 **1** c **2** d **3** a **4** b

4 **1** the Midas touch **2** a round-table discussion **3** Achilles heel **4** Pandora's box

5 *Student's own answers*

FURTHER PRACTICE AND UNIT ASSESSSMENT

Unit 3 Review **Student's Book** page 92
Workbook page 29
- **Reflect on your learning** page 29
- **Grammar reference and practice** pages 86 and 93-94
- **Wordlist and exercises** pages 99 and 102-103

Tests available to download and edit from the **Richmond***Learning***Platform**

→ See pages 40-41 **Assessment**

Warmer

Watch the **Culture video** and discuss the questions with the whole class. If you don't have video facilities, simply discuss the questions.

1 1.31 (See page 172 for transcripts) Tell students they are going to hear a programme about King Arthur. Get them to look at the pictures and answer what they can before playing the audio and comparing answers in pairs.

2 1.32 (See page 173 for transcripts) Tell students they are going to listen to more myths and expressions. Ask them to note the expressions they hear. Let them compare answers in pairs.

Idioms and expressions

3 Ask students what they remember the interviewer and professor said about the expressions before they complete the exercise.

4 Extend this exercise by asking students to write their own gapped sentences for others to complete.

SPEAKING TOOLS

Get students to read the **Speaking tool** and give them some practice by saying the idioms and expressions in exercise 3.

5 NOW YOU! Choose volunteers to perform their conversations in class. They could pause when they get to the expressions, for the class to shout them out.

PAIRWORK **Student's Book** pages 100 and 104
See **Teacher's Book** page 88 for more information.
→ See pages 30-33 for more on **Mediation**

Remind students to do all the exercises in their notebook

CONTINUOUS ASSESSMENT Students can use idioms and expressions from myths and legends.

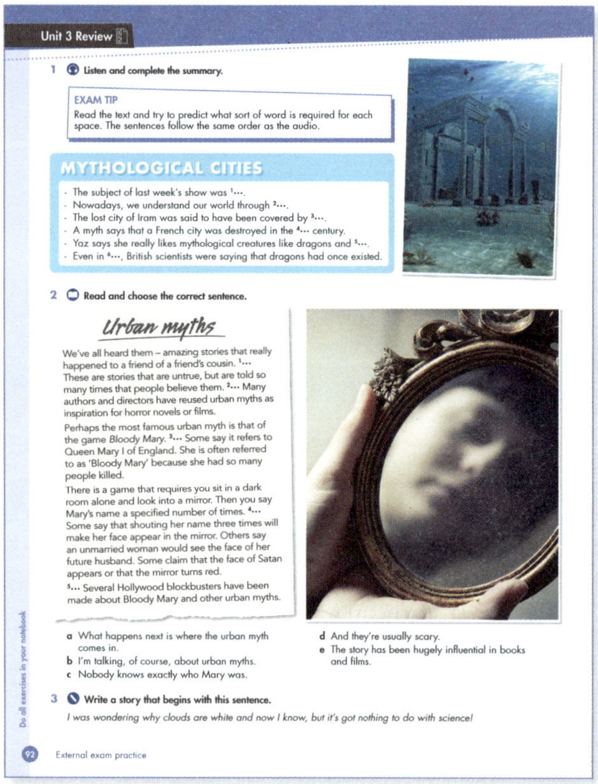
Unit 3 Review

1 Listen and complete the summary.

EXAM TIP
Read the text and try to predict what sort of word is required for each space. The sentences follow the same order as the audio.

MYTHOLOGICAL CITIES
- The subject of last week's show was ¹… .
- Nowadays, we understand our world through ²… .
- The lost city of Iram was said to have been covered by ³… .
- A myth says that a French city was destroyed in the ⁴… century.
- Yaz says she really likes mythological creatures like dragons and ⁵… .
- Even in ⁶…, British scientists were saying that dragons had once existed.

2 Read and choose the correct sentence.

Urban myths

We've all heard them – amazing stories that really happened to a friend of a friend's cousin. ¹… These are stories that are untrue, but are told so many times that people believe them. ²… Many authors and directors have reused urban myths as inspiration for horror novels or films.

Perhaps the most famous urban myth is that of the game Bloody Mary. ³… Some say it refers to Queen Mary I of England. She is often referred to as 'Bloody Mary' because she had so many people killed.

There is a game that requires you sit in a dark room alone and look into a mirror. Then you say Mary's name a specified number of times. ⁴… Some say that shouting her name three times will make her face appear in the mirror. Others say an unmarried woman would see the face of her future husband. Some claim that the face of Satan appears or that the mirror turns red.

⁵… Several Hollywood blockbusters have been made about Bloody Mary and other urban myths.

a What happens next is where the urban myth comes in.
b I'm talking, of course, about urban myths.
c Nobody knows exactly who Mary was.
d And they're usually scary.
e The story has been hugely influential in books and films.

3 Write a story that begins with this sentence.
I was wondering why clouds are white and now I know, but it's got nothing to do with science!

Do all exercises in your notebook

92 External exam practice

Student's Book page 92

ANSWER KEY

See page 182 for transcripts

1 2.34
1 ghost stories
2 modern science
3 a flood of sand
4 5th
5 unicorns
6 1886

2 **1** b
2 d
3 c
4 a
5 e

3 *Student's own answers*

Pairwork

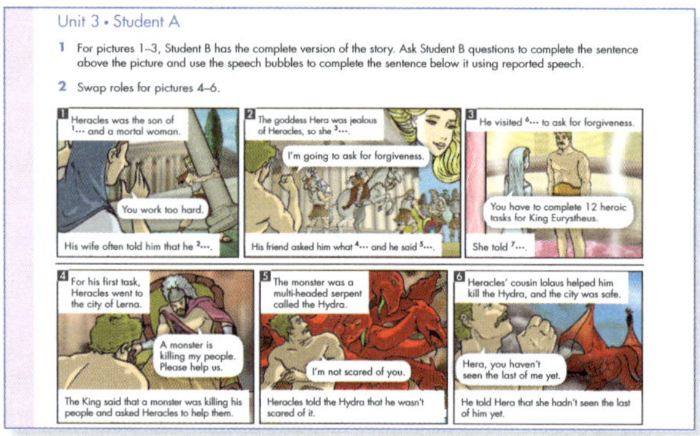
Unit 3 • Student A

1 For pictures 1–3, Student B has the complete version of the story. Ask Student B questions to complete the sentence above the picture and use the speech bubbles to complete the sentence below it using reported speech.

2 Swap roles for pictures 4–6.

Student's Book page 100

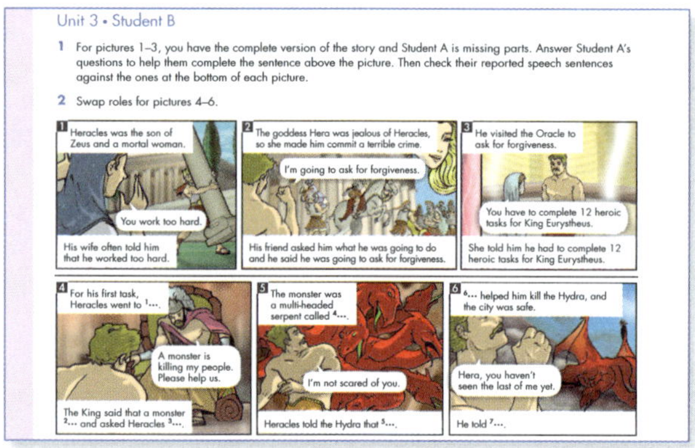
Unit 3 • Student B

1 For pictures 1–3, you have the complete version of the story and Student A is missing parts. Answer Student A's questions to help them complete the sentence above the picture. Then check their reported speech sentences against the ones at the bottom of each picture.

2 Swap roles for pictures 4–6.

Student's Book page 104

CEFR MEDIATION DESCRIPTOR

- **Adapting language**
  Students can paraphrase short written passages in a simple fashion, using the original order of the text.

- **Requesting information**
  Tell students they each have a comic strip version of the story of Heracles, with different parts missing. They must ask questions and use their knowledge of reported speech to complete their versions.

Remind students to do all the exercises in their notebook

Unit 3 Grammar reference

Past simple and past continuous

Use the **past simple** to talk about completed actions in the past. William Tell **shot** the apple off his son's head.
Use the **past continuous** to talk about an action in progress at a moment in the past. All the people **were bowing** down to Gessler.
When the **past simple** and **past continuous** are used together, ▪ the **past continuous** is used to give the background of the story. ▪ the **past simple** is used to talk about the important events. He and his son **were passing** by and they **refused** to bow.

We use the past simple to talk about finished actions and situations in the past.

They **lived** in a village in India.

His family **had** a farm.

What **did you do** after school yesterday?

We use the past continuous to talk about activities in progress, or activities which occurred over a period of time, in the past.

She **was staying** with her sister last week.

They **were cleaning** the shop for hours.

Where **were you living** at the time?

We can connect past actions with ***when*** and ***while***. We usually use ***when*** before the past simple, and ***when*** or ***while*** before the past continuous.

They were putting up the tent **when it started** to rain.

I got a text message **while I was watching** the film.

I saw something strange **when I was walking** home last night.

Direct speech and reported speech

Use **reported speech** to talk about what someone has said. Notice that the tenses move one 'step' back into the past.

	Direct speech	Reported speech
Present simple → past simple	'We **bring** light to the humans.'	He told her they **brought** light to the humans.
Present continuous → past continuous	'**I'm dying**!'	She said that she **was dying**.
Present perfect and past simple → past perfect	'We **have done** the same thing every day since we were born.'	They said they **had done** the same thing every day since they were born.
The imperative stays the same.	'Hou Yi, **stop** them!'	He told Hou Yi to **stop** them.

Reported speech is used to tell someone about what another person has said. We can include the word ***that*** or omit it; the meaning is the same.

Martin: 'I was really scared.' Martin told me (that) he had been really scared.

The verb moves one 'step' back in the past. This also happens with modal verbs.

Will → would

'I **will** be back soon.' He said (that) he **would** be back soon.

Can → could

'I **can** speak German.' She said she **could** speak German.

Must/have to → had to

'You **must** leave.'
'You **have to** leave.' She said that I **had to** leave.

May → might

'It **may** snow later.' He said it **might** snow later.

Said and ***told*** are the most common reporting verbs.

If we use ***told***, we must follow it with a person or an object pronoun.

The nurse **told me** to wait outside.

NOT ~~The nurse told to wait outside.~~

However, ***said*** must never be followed by a person or an object pronoun.

The nurse **said** to wait outside.

NOT ~~The nurse said me to wait outside.~~

Do all exercises in your notebook

Workbook pages 93-96

109

Student's Book page 109

Wordlist

UNIT 4

The Earth

algae
birds
dinosaurs
extinct
fern
homo sapiens
hospitable
life
ocean
oxygen
planet
revolve
swamp

The Universe

The planets
Mercury
Venus
Earth
Mars
Jupiter
Saturn
Uranus
Neptune

Celestial bodies
asteroid
comet
float
gravity
meteor
meteorite
meteoroid
Moon
orbit
star
Sun

Space exploration

astronaut
discovery
experiment
ISS (International Space Station)
mission
NASA
remote
research laboratory
satellite
science
Space Age
spaceflight
technology
telescope

Do all exercises in your notebook

118 **Workbook** pages 102-104

Student's Book page 118

2.45 2.46 2.47

Remind students to do all the exercises in their notebook

4 OUR UNIVERSE

At the start of each unit and lesson, explain to the students what the objectives are.

Language objectives

Grammar

Past perfect: negative and questions
- Students further develop their use of the past perfect.

Zero, first and second conditionals
- Students practise a range of conditional sentences.

Vocabulary

The Earth: *algae, birds, dinosaurs, extinct, fern, homo sapiens, hospitable, life, ocean, oxygen, planet, revolve, swamp*
- Students use vocabulary related to the history of life on Earth.

The Universe: The planets: *Mercury, Venus, Earth, Mars, Jupiter, Saturn, Uranus, Neptune;* Celestial bodies: *asteroid, comet, float, gravity, meteor, meteorite, meteoroid, Moon, orbit, star, Sun*
- Students use vocabulary related to the Solar System and celestial bodies.

Space exploration: *astronaut, discovery, experiment, ISS (International Space Station), mission, NASA, remote, research laboratory, satellite, science, Space Age, spaceflight, technology, telescope*
- Students encounter vocabulary related to the exploration of space.

Idioms and expressions

Planets and stars: *written in the stars, move heaven and earth; on top of the world, thank your lucky stars*
- Students look at idioms and expressions related to planets and stars in the context of three short talks from astronauts.

Recycled language

Past perfect, Past simple, *Will*, *Would*, Linking language

Skills objectives

Speaking

- Students quiz each other on vocabulary related to astronomy.
- Students ask and answer questions about natural history.
- Students ask and answer hypothetical questions related to space.
- Students discuss space exploration.
- Students discuss personal experiences using idioms and expressions.

Pronunciation: Students practise distinguishing between the /uː/ and /ʊ/ sounds.

Pairwork: Students use various mediation techniques in order to complete two texts about astronauts using questions in the past perfect.

Listening

- Students listen and choose the correct option in a text about basic astronomy.
- Students listen and identify the differences between asteroids, meteors, meteorites and meteoroids.
- Students listen and complete a table about the planets.
- Students listen and complete fact files about astronauts.

Reading

- Students skim a text and answer the question posed by the title.
- Students read in detail and answer multiple-choice questions.
- Students read and match vocabulary and definitions.

Core values: Students discuss **humility**, the effects of being too shy or too arrogant and how to deal with arrogance.

Writing

- Students practise writing questions in the past perfect using a timeline.
- Students plan, write and check a discursive essay about science and technology.

Focus on noun phrases

Remind students to do all the exercises in their notebook

Learning to learn tools

SPEAKING TOOLS Students practise using their imagination to develop their spoken English.	**LISTENING TOOLS** Students practise taking notes with key words to help remember content.
READING TOOLS Students practise recognising synonymous but paraphrased information.	**WRITING TOOLS** Students develop their ability to structure and link their writing.

VOCABULARY TOOLS Students practise using Latin and Greek roots to guess the meaning of words.

Project objectives: Comic strip

Task 4 Students draw the comic they have created.

Task 5 Students research the scientific explanation for the phenomenon featured in their myth.

Task 6 Students write a paragraph about each of their comics.

Audiovisual objectives

Vlog: Students watch and listen to Emma talk about space and the possible existence of alien life.

Culture: Students watch and listen to Emma talk about seeing Earth from space.

Grammar animations: Students are presented with visual presentations of the unit grammar.

Key competences

LC **Linguistic**
pages 36-43

MST **Mathematical and Science and Technology**
pages 36-43

DC **Digital**
pages 36-37, 39, 43

SCC **Social and Civic**
pages 39-43

CAE **Cultural awareness and expression**
pages 38-41, 43

LL **Learning to learn**
pages 37, 39, 42

IE **Sense of initiative and entrepreneurship**
pages 37, 39, 42

→ See pages 42-43 **Key competences**

CEFR Mediation

4.1 Explaining data in speech
Can interpret and describe detailed information in diagrams.

4.2 Note-taking
Can take notes in point form on a familiar topic.

4.3 Processing text in writing
Can summarise arguments in texts of general interest.

4.4 Processing text in writing
Can pick out and reproduce key words and phrases from a short text.

4.5 Relaying specific information in writing
Can write specific information in spoken texts.

Project Processing text in writing
Can summarise the information in texts on subjects of personal interest.

Unit review Facilitating collaborative interaction with peers
Can collaborate in shared tasks and work towards a common goal.

Pairwork Facilitating collaborative interaction with peers
Can collaborate in simple, shared tasks by asking and answering simple questions.

→ See pages 30-33 **Mediation**

Remind students to do all the exercises in their notebook

4 OUR UNIVERSE

In unit 4 you will:
- talk about the Universe.
- practise using the past perfect in questions.
- review the first, second and zero conditionals.
- write an essay.

4.1 Vocabulary and listening

PETER'S VLOG: Are we alone?

Discuss the questions.
1 Have you ever visited a planetarium?
2 Would you like to be an astronaut?
3 Do you think there could be life on other planets?

Flipped Learning

1 Choose the correct option. Listen and check.

For thousands of years, humanity has tried to make sense of what we see in the night sky. The study of this is called [1] **astronomy / galaxy**, and it has taught us a lot about the [2] **the Universe / astronomy**. We live in a [3] **Sun / galaxy** that is called the Milky Way. There are billions of [4] **stars / planets** here and one of the brightest is our [5] **Sun / Moon**.

We call everything that revolves around the Sun the [6] **Solar System / asteroid belt**. It includes our Earth and our [7] **Universe / Moon**, along with seven other [8] **planets / comets** and their moons. It also includes a collection of rocks between Mars and Jupiter called the [9] **Solar System / asteroid belt**, as well as objects made of ice and dust with bright burning tails that we call [10] **planets / comets**.

VOCABULARY TOOLS
Understanding the root of a word can help you guess the meaning:
uni (one) – uniform, unicycle
geo (earth) – geographic, geometry
astro (space) – astrology, astronaut

2 Label the pictures using the words in bold from exercise 1.

3 NOW YOU! Quiz your partner about the definitions of the key words from the page.

What is the Solar System?

It's everything that revolves around the Sun.

FAST FINISHERS Write definitions for three of the words from exercise 2.

Do all exercises in your notebook

36 The Earth / Past perfect: negative and questions

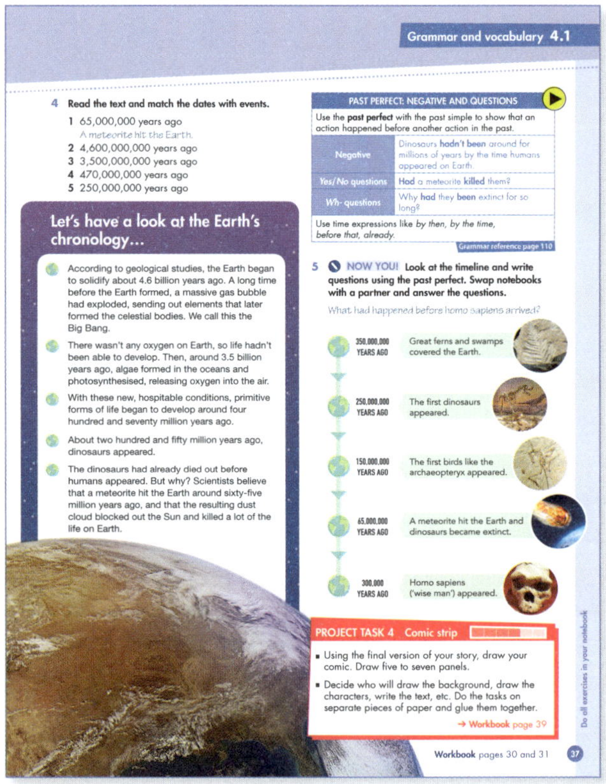
Grammar and vocabulary 4.1

4 Read the text and match the dates with events.
1 65,000,000 years ago
A meteorite hit the Earth.
2 4,600,000,000 years ago
3 3,500,000,000 years ago
4 470,000,000 years ago
5 250,000,000 years ago

Let's have a look at the Earth's chronology...

According to geological studies, the Earth began to solidify about 4.6 billion years ago. A long time before the Earth formed, a massive gas bubble had exploded, sending out elements that later formed the celestial bodies. We call this the Big Bang.

There wasn't any oxygen on Earth, so life hadn't been able to develop. Then, around 3.5 billion years ago, algae formed in the oceans and photosynthesised, releasing oxygen into the air.

With these new, hospitable conditions, primitive forms of life began to develop around four hundred and seventy million years ago.

About two hundred and fifty million years ago, dinosaurs appeared.

The dinosaurs had already died out before humans appeared. But why? Scientists believe that a meteorite hit the Earth around sixty-five million years ago, and that the resulting dust cloud blocked out the Sun and killed a lot of the life on Earth.

PAST PERFECT: NEGATIVE AND QUESTIONS

Use the **past perfect** with the past simple to show that an action happened before another action in the past.

Negative	Dinosaurs **hadn't been** around for millions of years by the time humans appeared on Earth.
Yes/No questions	**Had** a meteorite **killed** them?
Wh- questions	Why **had** they **been** extinct for so long?

Use time expressions like *by then, by the time, before that, already.*

Grammar reference page 110

5 NOW YOU! Look at the timeline and write questions using the past perfect. Swap notebooks with a partner and answer the questions.

What had happened before homo sapiens arrived?

350,000,000 YEARS AGO – Great ferns and swamps covered the Earth.
250,000,000 YEARS AGO – The first dinosaurs appeared.
150,000,000 YEARS AGO – The first birds like the archaeopteryx appeared.
65,000,000 YEARS AGO – A meteorite hit the Earth and dinosaurs became extinct.
300,000 YEARS AGO – Homo sapiens ('wise man') appeared.

PROJECT TASK 4 Comic strip
- Using the final version of your story, draw your comic. Draw five to seven panels.
- Decide who will draw the background, draw the characters, write the text, etc. Do the tasks on separate pieces of paper and glue them together.

→ Workbook page 39

Do all exercises in your notebook

Workbook pages 30 and 31 37

ANSWER KEY

Pages 36-37

1 **1** astronomy
2 the Universe
3 galaxy
4 stars
5 Sun
6 Solar System
7 Moon
8 planets
9 asteroid belt
10 comets

2 **1** The Moon
2 Stars
3 a galaxy
4 a planet
5 a comet
6 the asteroid belt

3 *Student's own answers*

4 **1** A meteorite hit the Earth.
2 The Earth began to solidify.
3 Algae formed in the oceans.
4 Primitive forms of life began to develop.
5 Dinosaurs appeared.

5 *Student's own answers*

Remind students to do all the exercises in their notebook

LESSON FOCUS

Grammar Past perfect: negative and questions
Vocabulary The Earth
Listening Choosing the correct option in a text about astronomy
Speaking Using vocabulary related to astronomy; Asking and answering questions about a natural history timeline
Project task 4 Create and draw the comic

Resources

Teacher's i-solutions, Student's Book audio, Vlog and worksheet

Flipped Learning

EMMA'S VLOG: Are we alone?

- Make sure to set up the **Flipped Learning** work with the students beforehand. **See pages 20-23 for complete Flipped Learning guidelines**.
- Ask students to put the **Flipped Learning worksheets** on their desks and walk around to check how many have completed the Flipped task.
- In pairs or small groups, ask students to compare and check the *Before you watch...* and *While you watch...* exercises on the worksheet.
- Show students **Emma's Vlog** and ask volunteers to provide correct answers and clarify any doubts other students may have.
- Choose three or four students to read aloud their answers to the *After you watch...* exercises on the worksheet and encourage some class discussion.
- Move straight to exercise 1 on page 36.

Warmer

Watch Emma's Vlog and discuss the questions with the whole class. If you don't have video facilities, simply discuss the questions.

1 1.33 (See page 173 for transcripts) Ask what words students know that begin with *astro-* (e.g. astronomy, astronaut, astrology, plus combinations with other sciences and those who study them like astrophysics/astrophysicist). Tell them they are going to read a short text about astronomy. Help them confirm the meaning of any unfamiliar vocabulary as they complete the exercise.

VOCABULARY TOOLS

Get students to read the **Vocabulary tool** and remind them of the words they came up with in the **Warmer**.

2 Give clues where necessary.

3 NOW YOU! Give students as much time as they need to consolidate new vocabulary and practise giving effective definitions, clearing up any doubts as they arise.

FAST FINISHERS Students can complete this exercise alone or in pairs.

4 Ask if students know where the prefix *chron-* comes from and what it means (ancient Greek, *chronos* – time). Tell them to complete the notes of the chronology by matching dates with events in the text.

Flipped Learning

PAST PERFECT: NEGATIVE AND QUESTIONS

Draw students' attention to the **Grammar table**. Remind students that they can use this as a quick reference while completing the exercises.

Show students the **Grammar animation** and/or refer students to the **Grammar reference** on page 110 for further information on form and use.

→ See page 23 for how to flip the **grammar lesson**

5 NOW YOU! Tell students to consult their notes and the **Grammar table** in order to write the questions, and then to try answering them with their books closed.

PROJECT TASK 4 Comic strip

Put students in their groups and get them to delegate as indicated so that each member knows which part they are doing. Remind students that they need to keep their project notes together in their **Workbook** (page 39) or in their own notebook.

→ See pages 24-27 **Projects**

FURTHER PRACTICE

Workbook pages 30-31
- **Grammar reference and practice** pages 87 and 94
- **Wordlist and exercises** pages 99 and 103

Remind students to do all the exercises in their notebook

CONTINUOUS ASSESSMENT Students can talk about the Earth and use the past perfect in the negative and with questions.

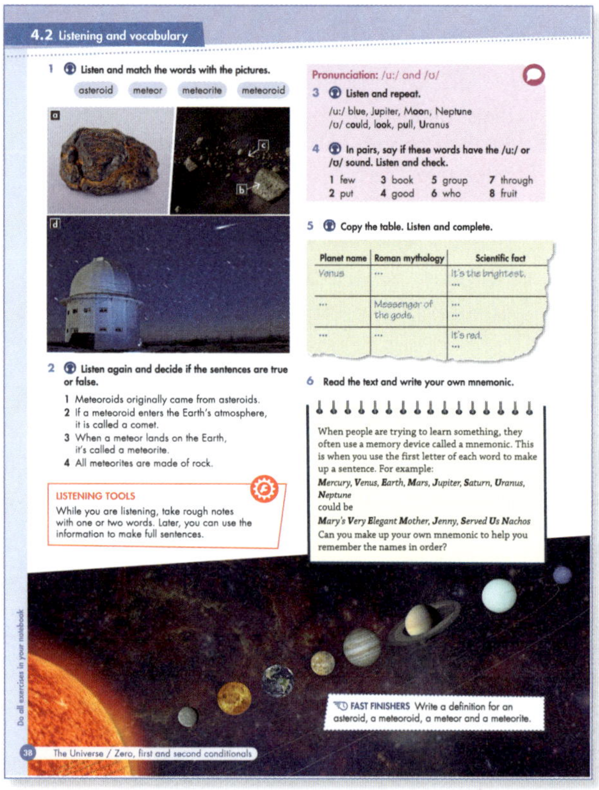

4.2 Listening and vocabulary

1 Listen and match the words with the pictures.

asteroid meteor meteorite meteoroid

a b c d

2 Listen again and decide if the sentences are true or false.

1 Meteoroids originally came from asteroids.
2 If a meteoroid enters the Earth's atmosphere, it is called a comet.
3 When a meteor lands on the Earth, it's called a meteorite.
4 All meteorites are made of rock.

LISTENING TOOLS
While you are listening, take rough notes with one or two words. Later, you can use the information to make full sentences.

Pronunciation: /uː/ and /ʊ/

3 Listen and repeat.

/uː/ blue, Jupiter, Moon, Neptune
/ʊ/ could, look, pull, Uranus

4 In pairs, say if these words have the /uː/ or /ʊ/ sound. Listen and check.

1 few 2 put 3 book 4 good 5 group 6 who 7 through 8 fruit

5 Copy the table. Listen and complete.

Planet name	Roman mythology	Scientific fact
Venus	···	It's the brightest. ···
···	Messenger of the gods.	··· ···
···	···	It's red. ···

6 Read the text and write your own mnemonic.

When people are trying to learn something, they often use a memory device called a mnemonic. This is when you use the first letter of each word to make up a sentence. For example:
Mercury, Venus, Earth, Mars, Jupiter, Saturn, Uranus, Neptune
could be
Mary's Very Elegant Mother, Jenny, Served Us Nachos
Can you make up your own mnemonic to help you remember the names in order?

FAST FINISHERS Write a definition for an asteroid, a meteoroid, a meteor and a meteorite.

Do all exercises in your notebook

38 The Universe / Zero, first and second conditionals

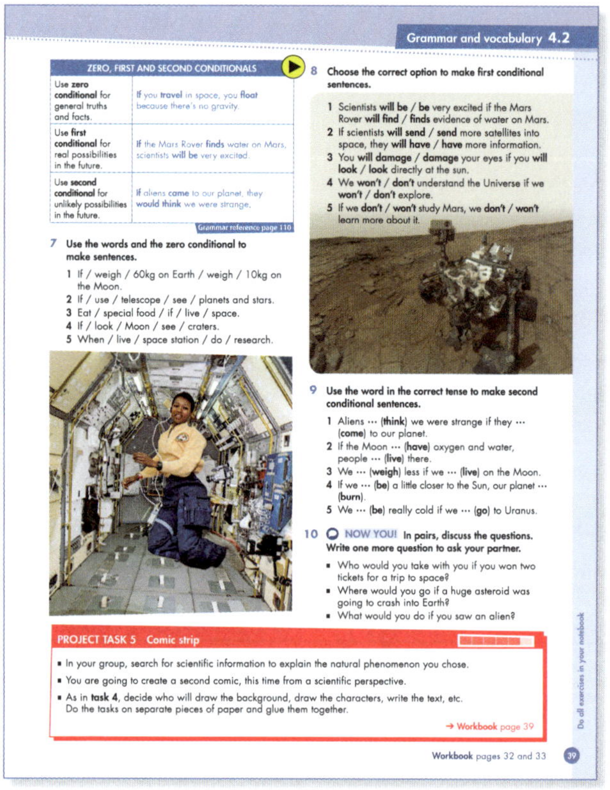

Grammar and vocabulary 4.2

ZERO, FIRST AND SECOND CONDITIONALS	
Use **zero conditional** for general truths and facts.	If you **travel** in space, you **float** because there's no gravity.
Use **first conditional** for real possibilities in the future.	If the Mars Rover **finds** water on Mars, scientists **will be** very excited.
Use **second conditional** for unlikely possibilities in the future.	If aliens **came** to our planet, they **would think** we were strange.

Grammar reference page 110

7 Use the words and the zero conditional to make sentences.

1 If / weigh / 60kg on Earth / weigh / 10kg on the Moon.
2 If / use / telescope / see / planets and stars.
3 Eat / special food / if / live / space.
4 If / look / Moon / see / craters.
5 When / live / space station / do / research.

8 Choose the correct option to make first conditional sentences.

1 Scientists **will be** / **be** very excited if the Mars Rover **will find** / **finds** evidence of water on Mars.
2 If scientists **will send** / **send** more satellites into space, they **will have** / **have** more information.
3 You **will damage** / **damage** your eyes if you **will look** / **look** directly at the sun.
4 We **won't** / **don't** understand the Universe if we **won't** / **don't** explore.
5 If we **don't** / **won't** study Mars, we **don't** / **won't** learn more about it.

9 Use the word in the correct tense to make second conditional sentences.

1 Aliens ··· (**think**) we were strange if they ··· (**come**) to our planet.
2 If the Moon ··· (**have**) oxygen and water, people ··· (**live**) there.
3 We ··· (**weigh**) less if we ··· (**live**) on the Moon.
4 If we ··· (**be**) a little closer to the Sun, our planet ··· (**burn**).
5 We ··· (**be**) really cold if we ··· (**go**) to Uranus.

10 NOW YOU! In pairs, discuss the questions. Write one more question to ask your partner.

- Who would you take with you if you won two tickets for a trip to space?
- Where would you go if a huge asteroid was going to crash into Earth?
- What would you do if you saw an alien?

PROJECT TASK 5 Comic strip

- In your group, search for scientific information to explain the natural phenomenon you chose.
- You are going to create a second comic, this time from a scientific perspective.
- As in **task 4**, decide who will draw the background, draw the characters, write the text, etc. Do the tasks on separate pieces of paper and glue them together.

→ **Workbook** page 39

Workbook pages 32 and 33 39

Do all exercises in your notebook

ANSWER KEY

Pages 38-39

1 **a** Meteorite **b** Asteroid **c** Meteoroid **d** Meteor

2
1 True
2 False. If a meteoroid enters the Earth's atmosphere it is called a meteor.
3 True
4 False. 90% are made of rock, but some are made of metal.

3 *Student's own answers*

4 *Student's own answers*

5

Planet name	Roman mythology	Scientific facts
Venus	Goddess of love and beauty	It's the brightest. It has almost the same gravity as Earth.
Mercury	Messenger of the gods	It's the fastest. It's the smallest.
Mars	God of war	It's red. It has thousands of craters.

6 *Student's own answers*

7
1 If you weigh 60kg on Earth, you weigh 10kg on the Moon.
2 If you use a telescope, you can see planets and stars.
3 You have to eat special food if you live in space.
4 If you look at the Moon, you can see craters.
5 When astronauts live on a space station, they do research.

8
1 will be; finds
2 send; will have
3 will damage; look
4 won't; don't
5 don't; won't

9
1 would think; came
2 had; would live
3 would weigh; lived
4 were; would burn.
5 would be; went

10 *Student's own answers*

Remind students to do all the exercises in their notebook

LESSON FOCUS

Grammar Zero, first and second conditionals
Vocabulary The Universe
Listening A talk about asteroids, meteors, meteorites and meteoroids; Completing a table about the planets
Speaking Asking and answering hypothetical questions related to space
Project task 5 Research the scientific explanation for the phenomenon featured in their myth

Resources
Teacher's i-solutions, Student's Book audio

Warmer

Choose a word from exercise 1 on page 36, and give a definition so that the class can guess the word. Students continue the exercise in pairs or small groups.

1 1.34 (See page 173 for transcripts) Ask students if they remember what an asteroid is and tell them that they will listen to a talk that explains the differences between the words in the lozenges. You could do exercises 1 and 2 to give them a chance to be sure of the distinctions before you check their answers. Get them to read ahead to the **Listening tool** and encourage them to follow it.

2 1.35 (See page 173 for transcripts) Let students read the sentences and try to do the exercise from memory before playing the audio again to check. Get them to define the words in exercise 1 in their own words to consolidate.

LISTENING TOOLS

Ask students if the **Listening tool** helped them in exercises 1 and 2.

Pronunciation

3 1.36 (See page 173 for transcripts) Point out that the /uː/ sound is longer than the /ʊ/ sound and check that students can make the distinction before saying the words.

4 1.37 (See page 173 for transcripts) Encourage students to say the words aloud to each other to see which sound they think each word contains before you play the audio. Drill especially the words they got wrong or were unsure about.

5 1.38 (See page 174 for transcripts) Tell students that they will hear a short talk about three planets. Let them look at the table and guess the answers before playing the audio for them to complete it.

6 Ask students what a *mnemonic* is (a 'memory device') and put them in pairs to say if they like the one in the text and to try and think up another one.

FAST FINISHERS Students can complete this exercise alone or in pairs.

ZERO, FIRST AND SECOND CONDITIONALS

Flipped Learning

Draw students' attention to the **Grammar table**. Remind students that they can use this as a quick reference while completing the exercises.

Show students the **Grammar animation** and/or refer students to the **Grammar reference** on page 110 for further information on form and use.

→ See page 23 for how to flip the **grammar lesson**

7 Refer students to the first row of the **Grammar table** to help them form the sentences. Ask them what the photo shows (a woman in a space station).

8 Refer students to the second row of the **Grammar table** to help them choose the correct option. Point out that not all the sentences start with the *If* clause like in the example.

9 Refer students to the third row of the **Grammar table** to help them complete the sentences.

10 NOW YOU! Ask which conditional the questions are in (second) and encourage students to give extended replies by offering further conditions (for example: *It depends. If my best friend didn't want to come, I'd invite my brother.)*

PROJECT TASK 5 Comic strip

Put students in their groups again to do the research or to decide how to go about the research and to decide roles for the second comic. Remind students that they need to keep their project notes together in their **Workbook** (page 39) or in their own notebook.

→ See page 24-27 **Projects**

FURTHER PRACTICE

Workbook pages 32-33
- **Grammar reference and practice** pages 87 and 94
- **Wordlist and exercises** pages 99 and 103

Vocabulary and Grammar worksheets available to download from the **Richmond*Learning*Platform**

→ See pages 38-39 **Mixed-ability classes**

Remind students to do all the exercises in their notebook

CONTINUOUS ASSESSMENT Students can talk about the Universe and use zero, first and second conditionals.

4.3 Reading

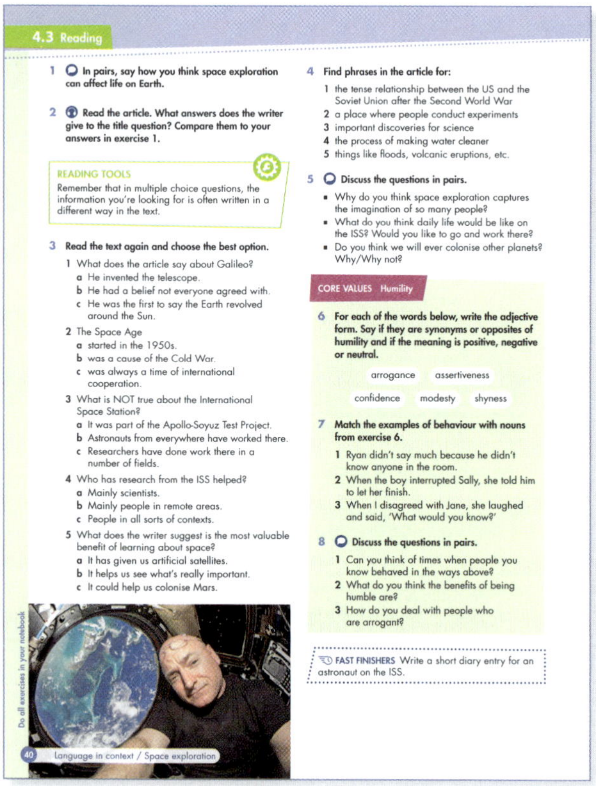
4.3 Reading

1 In pairs, say how you think space exploration can affect life on Earth.

2 Read the article. What answers does the writer give to the title question? Compare them to your answers in exercise 1.

READING TOOLS
Remember that in multiple choice questions, the information you're looking for is often written in a different way in the text.

3 Read the text again and choose the best option.
1 What does the article say about Galileo?
a He invented the telescope.
b He had a belief not everyone agreed with.
c He was the first to say the Earth revolved around the Sun.
2 The Space Age
a started in the 1950s.
b was a cause of the Cold War.
c was always a time of international cooperation.
3 What is NOT true about the International Space Station?
a It was part of the Apollo-Soyuz Test Project.
b Astronauts from everywhere have worked there.
c Researchers have done work there in a number of fields.
4 Who has research from the ISS helped?
a Mainly scientists.
b Mainly people in remote areas.
c People in all sorts of contexts.
5 What does the writer suggest is the most valuable benefit of learning about space?
a It has given us artificial satellites.
b It helps us see what's really important.
c It could help us colonise Mars.

4 Find phrases in the article for:
1 the tense relationship between the US and the Soviet Union after the Second World War
2 a place where people conduct experiments
3 important discoveries for science
4 the process of making water cleaner
5 things like floods, volcanic eruptions, etc.

5 Discuss the questions in pairs.
- Why do you think space exploration captures the imagination of so many people?
- What do you think daily life would be like on the ISS? Would you like to go and work there?
- Do you think we will ever colonise other planets? Why/Why not?

CORE VALUES Humility

6 For each of the words below, write the adjective form. Say if they are synonyms or opposites of humility and if the meaning is positive, negative or neutral.
arrogance assertiveness confidence modesty shyness

7 Match the examples of behaviour with nouns from exercise 6.
1 Ryan didn't say much because he didn't know anyone in the room.
2 When the boy interrupted Sally, she told him to let her finish.
3 When I disagreed with Jane, she laughed and said, 'What would you know?'

8 Discuss the questions in pairs.
1 Can you think of times when people you know behaved in the ways above?
2 What do you think the benefits of being humble are?
3 How do you deal with people who are arrogant?

FAST FINISHERS Write a short diary entry for an astronaut on the ISS.

Do all exercises in your notebook

40 Language in context / Space exploration

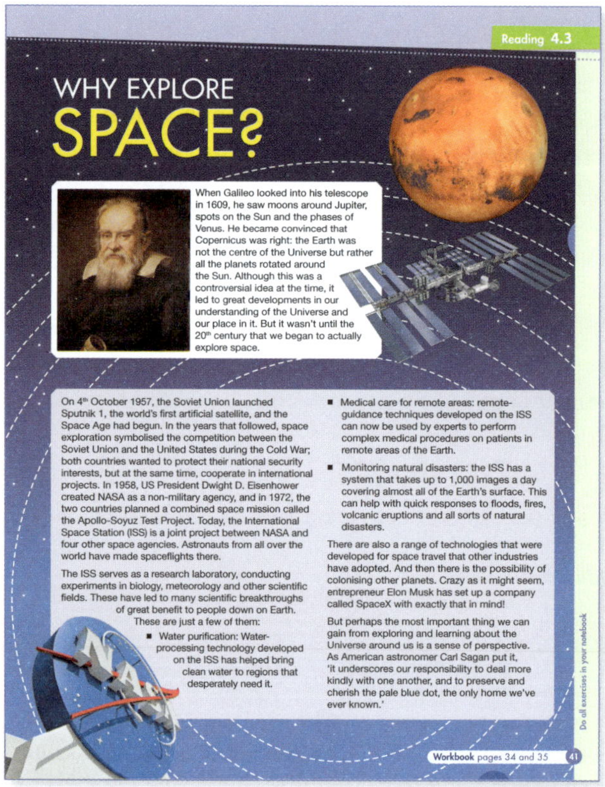
Reading 4.3

WHY EXPLORE SPACE?

When Galileo looked into his telescope in 1609, he saw moons around Jupiter, spots on the Sun and the phases of Venus. He became convinced that Copernicus was right: the Earth was not the centre of the Universe but rather all the planets rotated around the Sun. Although this was a controversial idea at the time, it led to great developments in our understanding of the Universe and our place in it. But it wasn't until the 20th century that we began to actually explore space.

On 4th October 1957, the Soviet Union launched Sputnik 1, the world's first artificial satellite, and the Space Age had begun. In the years that followed, space exploration symbolised the competition between the Soviet Union and the United States during the Cold War; both countries wanted to protect their national security interests, but at the same time, cooperate in international projects. In 1958, US President Dwight D. Eisenhower created NASA as a non-military agency, and in 1972, the two countries planned a combined space mission called the Apollo-Soyuz Test Project. Today, the International Space Station (ISS) is a joint project between NASA and four other space agencies. Astronauts from all over the world have made spaceflights there.

The ISS serves as a research laboratory, conducting experiments in biology, meteorology and other scientific fields. These have led to many scientific breakthroughs of great benefit to people down on Earth. These are just a few of them:
- Water purification: Water-processing technology developed on the ISS has helped bring clean water to regions that desperately need it.
- Medical care for remote areas: remote-guidance techniques developed on the ISS can now be used by experts to perform complex medical procedures on patients in remote areas of the Earth.
- Monitoring natural disasters: the ISS has a system that takes up to 1,000 images a day covering almost all of the Earth's surface. This can help with quick responses to floods, fires, volcanic eruptions and all sorts of natural disasters.

There are also a range of technologies that were developed for space travel that other industries have adopted. And then there is the possibility of colonising other planets. Crazy as it might seem, entrepreneur Elon Musk has set up a company called SpaceX with exactly that in mind!

But perhaps the most important thing we can gain from exploring and learning about the Universe around us is a sense of perspective. As American astronomer Carl Sagan put it, 'it underscores our responsibility to deal more kindly with one another, and to preserve and cherish the pale blue dot, the only home we've ever known.'

Do all exercises in your notebook

Workbook pages 34 and 35 41

ANSWER KEY

Pages 40-41

1 *Student's own answers*

2 To protect national security; To cooperate in international projects; To conduct experiments that have led to many scientific breakthroughs such as water-processing technology, remote-guidance techniques for medical procedures in remote areas and the monitoring of natural disasters; To investigate the possibility of colonising other planets; To gain a sense of perspective about our responsibilities to each other and to our planet.

3 **1** b **2** a **3** a **4** c **5** b

4 **1** the Cold War **2** a research laboratory **3** scientific breakthroughs **4** water purification **5** natural disasters

5 *Student's own answers*

6 **Arrogance:** arrogant; opposite; negative
Assertiveness: assertive; opposite; positive
Confidence: confident; opposite; positive
Modesty: modest; synonym; neutral
Shyness: shy; synonym; negative or neutral

7 **1** shyness **2** assertiveness **3** arrogance

8 *Student's own answers*

Remind students to do all the exercises in their notebook

LESSON FOCUS

Language in context Space exploration

Core values Humility

Resources

Teacher's i-solutions, Student's Book audio

→ See pages 36-37 **Literature**

Warmer

Write some space-related scenarios on the board. For example: *You're in the space station and you realise you're running out of food; You've been abandoned in a 'space habitat' on Mars as the crew in your mission don't think you're alive; You work for NASA and you realise a giant asteroid is heading for the Earth.* Put students in pairs, ask one of them to try to think of solutions using *I'd* clauses and the other to imagine further problems using But *What if* + past simple clauses.

1 Prompt students by asking what effects space exploration has already had. You could draw their attention to the title of the text and ask students to answer that question specifically.

2 1.39 (See page 174 for transcripts) Give students time to note the answer to the question and then compare in pairs.

READING TOOLS

Get students to read the **Reading tool** and tell them that in the next exercise they will have the chance to check their ability to recognise differently phrased information with the same meaning.

3 Remind students of the **Reading tool** and point out that the incorrect options will often look similar to parts of the text, but without having the same meaning.

4 Point out that students are looking for noun phrases with two words or more. See what phrases they remember before letting them read the text again to check.

5 Encourage students to give extended answers and ask them to report their partner's answers after the exercise to show that they were listening.

CORE VALUES Humility

6 Ask students what they think Carl Sagan meant by 'a sense of perspective' to lead into the subject of humility. If students aren't familiar with the words in the lozenges, give them examples not already in exercise 7 of behaviours that illustrate the words.

7 Ask students if they can think of any other examples of each type of behaviour without using the person's name, and see if they agree.

8 You could broaden the discussion to ask at what point confidence becomes arrogance and when humility could become problematic.

FAST FINISHERS Students can complete this exercise alone or in pairs.

FURTHER PRACTICE

Workbook pages 34-35

Remind students to do all the exercises in their notebook

CONTINUOUS ASSESSMENT Students can understand language related to space exploration.

4.4 Writing

A discursive essay

Focus on noun phrases

1 **Write noun phrases using the highlighted words in the correct form.**

1 The activity of **exploring space** is called *space exploration*.
2 When we **advance** current **technology** we are making … ….
3 **Technology** used in **medicine** is … ….
4 If you find a way to **solve** something **effectively**, you've found an … ….
5 If something has **benefitted** us **significantly**, it has brought … ….

2 **Read and check your answers from exercise 1. Then answer the questions.**

1 What question is the essay answering?
2 Is the writer's answer to the question *yes* or *no*?

Space exploration has many benefits for humanity. But do the benefits justify the enormous costs?

It is true that space research has brought many technological advances. We now have satellites to predict natural disasters. There is also medical technology that we wouldn't have if it weren't for agencies like NASA. In addition, supporters of space exploration suggest it helps protect us from asteroids.

However, apart from satellite technology, most of these benefits were not the focus of the research. If we spent the money directly on solving problems, we would have even more effective solutions. As for protection from extraplanetary objects, this can be done with existing technology.

In conclusion, space exploration has brought significant benefits, but in my opinion, our resources would be better directed at solving problems here on Earth.

Did you notice?

3 **What is the purpose of each paragraph? Write an outline of the essay.**

4 **Find linking expressions that are used to…**

1 introduce a new point.
2 contrast the points *for* with the points *against*.
3 acknowledge an exception.
4 conclude.
5 give the writer's main argument.

NOW YOU! → Workbook page 36

5 PLAN **You are going to write a discursive essay. Choose one of the questions below. Use your answer to exercise 3 to write a plan.**

- Do you think science should be a compulsory subject at school?
- Do we place too much importance on technology?
- The Space Race was a period of intense competition. Is competition the most effective way of making progress?

WRITING TOOLS

A good structure and use of linking language helps a reader to follow your arguments easily.

6 WRITE **Use your plan and the model to write your essay. Remember to use linking expressions.**

7 CHECK **Read your essay and check that it includes everything in your plan. Check that you have used linking language appropriately.**

PROJECT TASK 6 Comic strip

- Your group now has two comic strips: one that uses a myth to explain a natural phenomenon, and another one from a scientific perspective.
- Write a paragraph about the first comic, its setting, the plot, the characters, etc. Explain why you chose this myth to explain the natural phenomenon.
- Write another paragraph summarising the scientific explanation of your myth.
- Next, do the final task on page 44.

→ Workbook page 39

Do all exercises in your notebook

42 An essay / Noun phrases

ANSWER KEY

Page 42

1 **1** space exploration
2 technological advances
3 medical technology
4 effective solution
5 significant benefits

2 **1** Do the benefits of space exploration justify the costs?
2 No

3 **Paragraph 1:** introduce the topic and question
Paragraph 2: arguments for
Paragraph 3: arguments against
Paragraph 4: conclusion

4 **1** also, in addition
2 However
3 apart from
4 In conclusion
5 in my opinion

5 *Student's own answers*

6 *Student's own answers*

7 *Student's own answers*

FURTHER PRACTICE

Workbook page 36

LESSON FOCUS

Focus on Noun phrases
Writing A discursive essay
Project task 6 Write a paragraph about each of the comics

Resources
Teacher's i-solutions

Warmer

On the board, write a series of noun phrases that students have seen throughout the unit (e.g. *asteroid belt, memory device, space station, the Soviet Union* and any of the phrases from exercise 4, **Student's Book** page 40). Put students in pairs and get them to take turns to face the board and choose a phrase to define, and to face away from the board and try to guess the word that their partner has defined.

Focus on noun phrases

1 Point out that the main or head noun comes last and that the nouns or adjectives before it classify the main noun (for example, space exploration is a kind of exploration like deep sea exploration). Do not confirm or deny answers because they are in the text in exercise 2.

2 After students confirm their answers to exercise 1, let them read and then compare their answers to this exercise in pairs, discussing what they think of the arguments.

Did you notice?

3 Encourage students to notice how a general essay structure can be used for an essay on any topic.

4 Tell students that there are two expressions with the first function and one for each of the rest. Encourage them to keep a bank of useful linking expressions with examples and to order them by function.

5 PLAN You could put students in pairs or small groups to discuss the questions, so they have some ideas of which to choose and what arguments to use. Once students have finished their plan, encourage them to talk it through with a partner.

WRITING TOOLS

Get students to read the **Writing tool** and tell them to check these things when they have finished their essay.

6 WRITE Before students start writing, make a checklist on the board of any elements related to content, structure, language and style that they should bear in mind.

7 CHECK Once students have checked their own essays, they can swap with a partner and check theirs.

PROJECT TASK 6 Comic strip

Put students in their groups to collate their material and write the two paragraphs. Tell students that they need to keep their project notes together in their **Workbook** (page 39) or in their own notebook.

→ See pages 24-27 **Projects**

Remind students to do all the exercises in their notebook

 CONTINUOUS ASSESSMENT Students can use appropriate noun phrases to write a discursive essay.

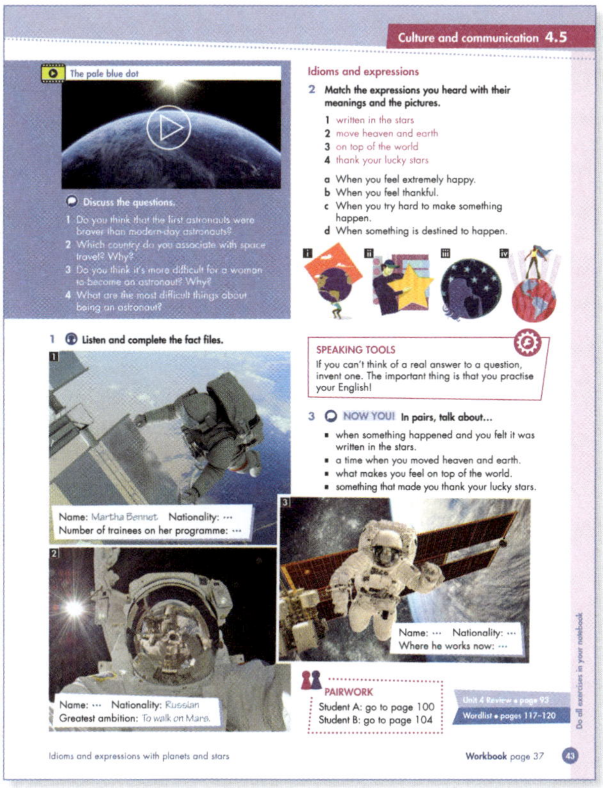
Culture and communication 4.5

The pale blue dot

Discuss the questions.
1 Do you think that the first astronauts were braver than modern-day astronauts?
2 Which country do you associate with space travel? Why?
3 Do you think it's more difficult for a woman to become an astronaut? Why?
4 What are the most difficult things about being an astronaut?

1 Listen and complete the fact files.

Name: Martha Bennet Nationality: ···
Number of trainees on her programme: ···

Name: ··· Nationality: Russian
Greatest ambition: To walk on Mars.

Name: ··· Nationality: ···
Where he works now: ···

Idioms and expressions
2 Match the expressions you heard with their meanings and the pictures.
1 written in the stars
2 move heaven and earth
3 on top of the world
4 thank your lucky stars
a When you feel extremely happy.
b When you feel thankful.
c When you try hard to make something happen.
d When something is destined to happen.

SPEAKING TOOLS
If you can't think of a real answer to a question, invent one. The important thing is that you practise your English!

3 NOW YOU! In pairs, talk about...
- when something happened and you felt it was written in the stars.
- a time when you moved heaven and earth.
- what makes you feel on top of the world.
- something that made you thank your lucky stars.

PAIRWORK
Student A: go to page 100
Student B: go to page 104

Unit 4 Review • page 93
Wordlist • pages 117–120

Do all exercises in your notebook.

Idioms and expressions with planets and stars
Workbook page 37
43

LESSON FOCUS

Idioms and expressions Planets and stars
Listening Completing fact files about astronauts
Speaking Asking and answering questions about personal experiences

Resources
Teacher's i-solutions, Student's Book audio, Culture video and worksheet

The pale blue dot

Video and worksheet available on the Richmond *Learning* Platform

- In pairs, ask students to complete the *What I know...* exercises on the **Culture video worksheet**.
- Show students the **Culture video** and ask them to complete the *What I learned...* exercises on the worksheet.
- In pairs, students compare answers.
- In small groups, tell students to complete the *What I wonder...* exercises on the worksheet.

ANSWER KEY

Page 43

1 **Name:** Martha Bennet
Nationality: British
Number of trainees on her programme: 19

Name: Vladimir Popov
Nationality: Russian
Greatest ambition: To walk on Mars

Name: David Feld
Nationality: Israeli
Where he works now: the (Kennedy) Space Center in Florida

2 **1** d; iii **2** c; i **3** a; iv **4** b; ii

3 *Student's own answers*

FURTHER PRACTICE AND UNIT ASSESSSMENT

Unit 4 Review **Student's Book** page 93
Workbook page 37
- **Reflect on your learning** page 37
- **Grammar reference and practice** pages 87 and 94
- **Wordlist and exercises** pages 99 and 103

Tests available to download and edit from the **Richmond *Learning* Platform**

→ See pages 40-41 **Assessment**

Warmer

Watch the **Culture video** and discuss the questions with the whole class. If you don't have video facilities, simply discuss the questions.

1 1.40 (See page 174 for transcripts) Tell students that they will hear three astronauts talk about themselves and their paths to becoming astronauts. Play the audio as many times as they need to complete the fact files. Fast finishers can look ahead at the idioms and expressions and write down the sentences that contain them.

Idioms and expressions

2 Ask if any students wrote the sentences with the expressions and write them on the board to help everybody guess their meanings.

SPEAKING TOOLS

Get students to read the **Speaking tool** and encourage them to put it into practice in the next exercise.

3 NOW YOU! To help reinforce the **Speaking tool**, ask students to come up with at least one invented answer giving them time to do so. Then they should tell each other their answers and guess each other's invented ones.

PAIRWORK **Student's Book** pages 100 and 104
See **Teacher's Book** page 100 for more information.
→ See pages 30-33 **Mediation**

Remind students to do all the exercises in their notebook.

CONTINUOUS ASSESSMENT Students can use idioms and expressions with planets and stars.

Unit 4 Review

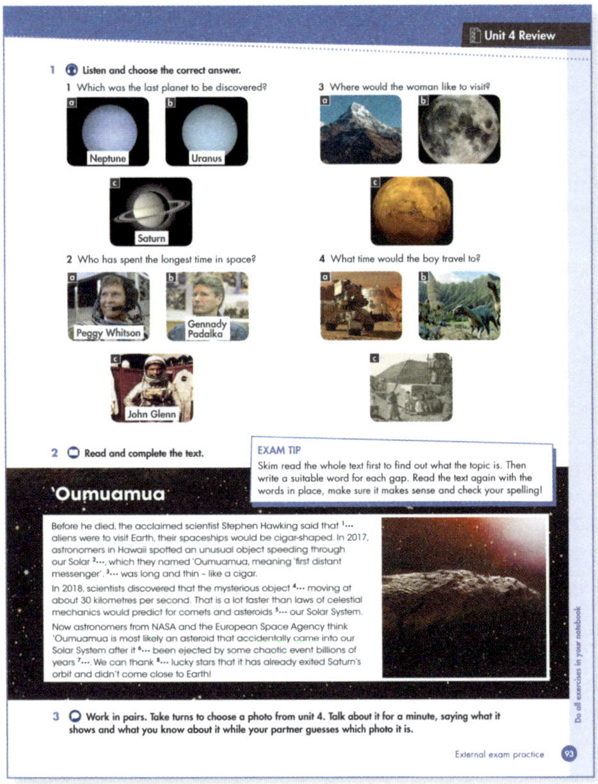
Unit 4 Review

1 Listen and choose the correct answer.

1 Which was the last planet to be discovered?

a Neptune b Uranus c Saturn

2 Who has spent the longest time in space?

a Peggy Whitson b Gennady Padalka c John Glenn

3 Where would the woman like to visit?

4 What time would the boy travel to?

2 Read and complete the text.

EXAM TIP
Skim read the whole text first to find out what the topic is. Then write a suitable word for each gap. Read the text again with the words in place, make sure it makes sense and check your spelling!

'Oumuamua

Before he died, the acclaimed scientist Stephen Hawking said that 1… aliens were to visit Earth, their spaceships would be cigar-shaped. In 2017, astronomers in Hawaii spotted an unusual object speeding through our Solar 2…, which they named 'Oumuamua, meaning 'first distant messenger'. 3… was long and thin – like a cigar.

In 2018, scientists discovered that the mysterious object 4… moving at about 30 kilometres per second. That is a lot faster than laws of celestial mechanics would predict for comets and asteroids 5… our Solar System.

Now astronomers from NASA and the European Space Agency think 'Oumuamua is most likely an asteroid that accidentally came into our Solar System after it 6… been ejected by some chaotic event billions of years 7…. We can thank 8… lucky stars that it has already exited Saturn's orbit and didn't come close to Earth!

3 Work in pairs. Take turns to choose a photo from unit 4. Talk about it for a minute, saying what it shows and what you know about it while your partner guesses which photo it is.

Do all exercises in your notebook

External exam practice 93

Student's Book page 93

ANSWER KEY

See page 182 for transcripts

1 2.35
1 a
2 b
3 b
4 a

2
1 if
2 System
3 It
4 was
5 in
6 had
7 ago
8 our

3 *Student's own answers*

Pairwork

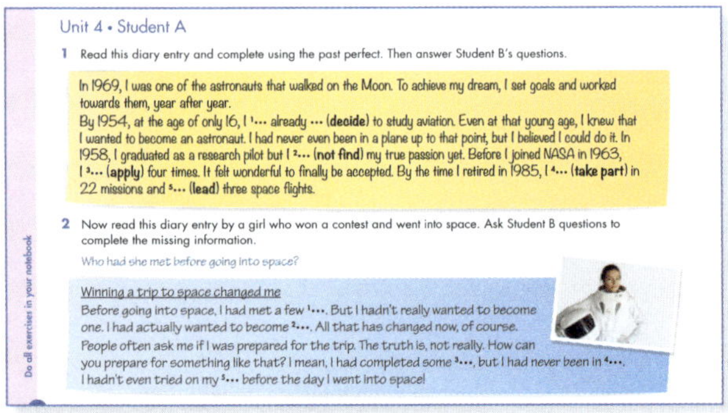
Unit 4 • Student A

1 Read this diary entry and complete using the past perfect. Then answer Student B's questions.

In 1969, I was one of the astronauts that walked on the Moon. To achieve my dream, I set goals and worked towards them, year after year.
By 1954, at the age of only 16, I 1… already … (**decide**) to study aviation. Even at that young age, I knew that I wanted to become an astronaut. I had never even been in a plane up to that point, but I believed I could do it. In 1958, I graduated as a research pilot but I 2… (**not find**) my true passion yet. Before I joined NASA in 1963, I 3… (**apply**) four times. It felt wonderful to finally be accepted. By the time I retired in 1985, I 4… (**take part**) in 22 missions and 5… (**lead**) three space flights.

2 Now read this diary entry by a girl who won a contest and went into space. Ask Student B questions to complete the missing information.

Who had she met before going into space?

Winning a trip to space changed me
Before going into space, I had met a few 1…. But I hadn't really wanted to become one. I had actually wanted to become 2…. All that has changed now, of course.
People often ask me if I was prepared for the trip. The truth is, not really. How can you prepare for something like that? I mean, I had completed some 3…, but I had never been in 4….
I hadn't even tried on my 5… before the day I went into space!

Do all exercises in your notebook

Student's Book page 100

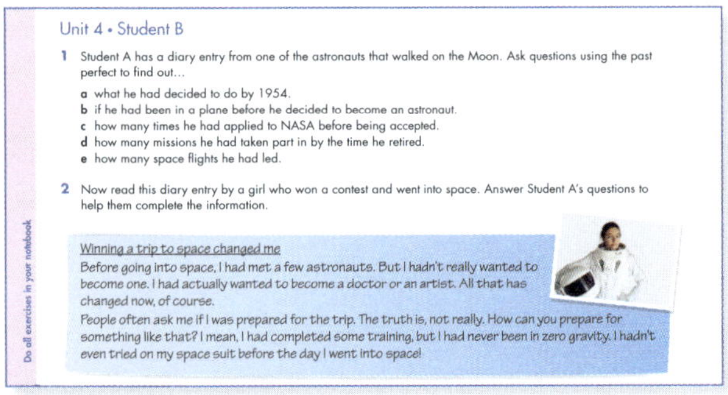
Unit 4 • Student B

1 Student A has a diary entry from one of the astronauts that walked on the Moon. Ask questions using the past perfect to find out…

a what he had decided to do by 1954.
b if he had been in a plane before he decided to become an astronaut.
c how many times he had applied to NASA before being accepted.
d how many missions he had taken part in by the time he retired.
e how many space flights he had led.

2 Now read this diary entry by a girl who won a contest and went into space. Answer Student A's questions to help them complete the information.

Winning a trip to space changed me
Before going into space, I had met a few astronauts. But I hadn't really wanted to become one. I had actually wanted to become a doctor or an artist. All that has changed now, of course.
People often ask me if I was prepared for the trip. The truth is, not really. How can you prepare for something like that? I mean, I had completed some training, but I had never been in zero gravity. I hadn't even tried on my space suit before the day I went into space!

Do all exercises in your notebook

Student's Book page 104

CEFR MEDIATION DESCRIPTOR

- **Relaying specific information in speech**
  Students can relay specific information given in straightforward informational texts.

- **Completing information**
  Tell students that one student has some complete information and questions about their partner's information, and the other student has incomplete information to help him/her formulate questions. Both texts are from astronauts' diaries. Give students time to read their task. Help Student A with any past perfect verb forms he/she doesn't know, and Student B with any question forms that he/she unsure of. Monitor them as they do the activity.

Remind students to do all the exercises in their notebook

Grammar reference

Unit 4 Grammar reference

Past perfect: negative and questions

Use the **past perfect** with the past simple to show that an action happened before another action in the past.	
Negative	Dinosaurs **hadn't been** around for millions of years by the time humans appeared on Earth.
Yes/No questions	**Had** a meteorite **killed** them?
Wh- questions	Why **had** they **been** extinct for so long?
Use time expressions like *by then, by the time, before that, already.*	

Past perfect questions are used in the same situations as the affirmative and negative forms: to talk about an action that occurred before another action in the past.

Why hadn't they learnt more English by the end of the summer? Because **they hadn't met** enough English speakers.

Zero, first and second conditionals

Use **zero conditional** for general truths and facts.	**If** you **travel** in space, you **float** because there's no gravity.
Use **first conditional** for real possibilities in the future.	**If** the Mars Rover **finds** water on Mars, scientists **will be** very excited.
Use **second conditional** for unlikely possibilities in the future.	**If** aliens **came** to our planet, they **would think** we were strange.

<u>**Zero conditional**</u>

The zero conditional is ***if/when*** + **present simple**, **present simple**. We use it to make universally true statements. We use it when we are certain of the consequence of an action.

If you drink poison, **you die**.

Ice melts when you heat it.

<u>**First conditional**</u>

The first conditional is ***if*** + **present simple**, ***will/won't*** + **infinitive**. We use it to describe situations that we think are possible in both the present and the future.

If she doesn't study, she won't pass her exams.

If we leave now, **we'll get** there on time.

In all types of conditionals, the meaning doesn't change if we reverse the order of the clauses. We use a comma to separate the clauses when the conditional clause comes first.

Conditional clause Main clause

If we train really hard, **we'll beat** them.

Main clause Conditional clause

We'll beat them **if we train** really hard.

Instead of using ***will*** alone in the main clause, we can use ***will probably***, ***probably won't*** or ***might***.

People **will probably live** a lot longer if our scientific knowledge improves.

We **probably won't be able to swim** in the sea if it becomes too polluted.

We **might end up** destroying our planet if we don't do something soon.

<u>**Second conditional**</u>

The second conditional is ***if*** + **past simple**, ***would/ could*** + **infinitive**. We use it to describe situations that are imaginary, unreal or unlikely.

If you lived on the moon, how **would you spend** your time? (imaginary situation)

If you came with us, **you'd have** a fantastic time. (unreal situation)

If she won the lottery, **she'd spend** all the money on clothes. (unlikely situation)

We often use the contracted form of the **subject** + **would**.

I would = I'd she would = she'd

it would = it'd they would = they'd

When we use the verb ***be*** in the ***if*** clause, we can always use ***were***, including for the first and third persons singular.

If I were a good swimmer, I'd try to swim the English Channel.

However, ***was*** is becoming more frequent in modern English.

If I was taller, I'd join the basketball team.

Second conditional for advice

We can use the second conditional form ***If I were you***, ***I would*** + **infinitive** as a way of giving advice.

I feel bad because I had a silly argument with my best friend.

If I were you, I'd call her and talk about it.

Do all exercises in your notebook

110 **Workbook** pages 93-96

Student's Book page 110

Wordlist

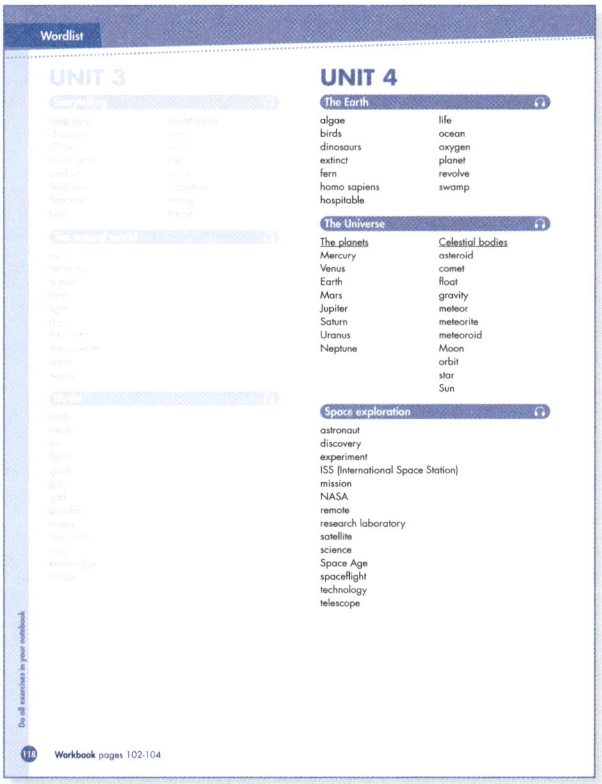

Wordlist

UNIT 3

UNIT 4

The Earth

algae
birds
dinosaurs
extinct
fern
homo sapiens
hospitable
life
ocean
oxygen
planet
revolve
swamp

The Universe

<u>The planets</u>
Mercury
Venus
Earth
Mars
Jupiter
Saturn
Uranus
Neptune

<u>Celestial bodies</u>
asteroid
comet
float
gravity
meteor
meteorite
meteoroid
Moon
orbit
star
Sun

Space exploration

astronaut
discovery
experiment
ISS (International Space Station)
mission
NASA
remote
research laboratory
satellite
science
Space Age
spaceflight
technology
telescope

Do all exercises in your notebook

118 **Workbook** pages 102-104

Student's Book page 118

2.48 2.49 2.50

Remind students to do all the exercises in their notebook

PROJECT: Comic strip

PROJECT: Comic strip

RECAP

- In this project, you made two comic strips: a myth about a natural phenomenon and a scientific explanation.
- In **units 3 and 4** you learnt the difference between a myth and a legend, and studied the structure of a story. You used language for telling stories, like verbs in past tenses, conditionals and reported speech. You also wrote a legend and learnt expressions related to myths, legends and astronomy.
- Now you are ready to present your comics!

TASK 1	**Decide on setting, characters and general plot.**
TASK 2	**Write versions of the story, with dialogue.**
TASK 3	**Edit the stories, taking the best parts from each one.**
TASK 4	**Create the comic.**
TASK 5	**Research the scientific explanation for the phenomenon.**
TASK 6	**Write a paragraph about each of your comics.**

FINAL TASK: Share your comics

- Present your comics. You will hold them up, but your classmates will not read them yet. Choose someone:
  - to explain why the group chose your myth and the techniques and materials used.
  - to present the characters, setting and plot of the mythical comic.
  - to present the scientific comic.
- After all of the presentations, display the comics around the classroom.
- In your group, walk around, read all the comics and discuss their strengths and weaknesses.
- As a class, vote to decide which is the best comic.

USEFUL EXPRESSIONS

Presenting
- We're excited to present our comic…
- To make our comic, we decided to…

Giving opinions
- From my point of view…
- One of the best aspects of our comic is…

21ST CENTURY SKILLS

Problem solving

Problem-solving is a skill that is needed in personal relationships, school life and work life. But it's not a skill that everybody has.

The steps are generally:
- define the problem
- find the cause
- identify a solution
- carry it out

These steps require other skills such as decision-making, risk management and creativity. That means that a person who is a good problem solver is a very valuable person in any team!

Do all exercises in your notebook

44 **Workbook** pages 38 and 39

Project • Units 3 and 4

EVALUATION

Answer the questions in your team.

1. If you made another comic together, what would you do differently?
2. What was the most difficult part of making the comics?
3. List some elements from other teams' comics that you liked.
4. Did you perform well as part of your team? What could you do better?

GO BEYOND

The FUNNIES

A comic is a strip of pictures, speech bubbles and caption boxes which tell a story. They became popular in magazines and newspapers in the late 19th century. Rudolph Dirks was one of the first comic artists to draw stars to show pain and thought balloons that look like clouds.

Comic strips can be entertaining, funny or political. The first comics were called 'The Funnies', and were used as a marketing strategy to attract readers to the Sunday newspapers. Although they began as small features in newspapers, comic books became an art form of their own.

Nowadays, the Japanese comic style called 'Manga' is growing in popularity and is widely enjoyed by children and adults of all ages. Many of Hollywood and TV's most popular characters also come from comics. The Fantastic Four and Superman, for example, are well-loved modern heroes who come from the Marvel Comics brand, which began in the 1930s.

Answer the questions in pairs.

1. Do you like reading comics? Which are your favourite ones?
2. What films can you name that are based on comics?
3. Why do you think people enjoy reading comics?
4. What elements does a good comic contain?

Do all exercises in your notebook

45

Workbook project task notes

PROJECT: Comic strip

Project • Units 3 and 4

Team members

________ ________ ________

TASK 1

Natural phenomenon: ________

Setting: ________

Characters: ________

Plot: ________

→ Student's book page 29

TASK 2

Introduction: ________

Conflict: ________

Climax: ________

Resolution: ________

→ Student's book page 31

TASK 3

Notes: ________

→ Student's book page 34

TASK 4

My task: ________

→ Student's book page 37

TASK 5

Scientific explanation: ________

My task: ________

→ Student's book page 39

TASK 6

Myth comic summary: ________

Scientific comic summary: ________

→ Student's book page 42

FINAL TASK

My role: ________

→ Student's book page 44

38 Project task notes

Project task notes 39

Remind students to do all the exercises in their notebook

PROJECT FOCUS

➔ See pages 24-27 **Projects**

Skills

- Collaborate to prepare and present two comic strips: a myth about a natural phenomenon and a scientific explanation
- Discuss and decide on a natural phenomenon to explain in the myth and the basics of the story
- Write a draft and dialogues for the story
- Read the drafts to combine the best elements into a collective story for the comic
- Delegate and carry out different drawing and writing tasks to then combine
- Research the scientific explanation for the natural phenomenon and use the same skills to produce another comic strip
- Write paragraphs summarising both comics
- Discuss evaluations of the project
- Read and discuss a text related to the project

CEFR mediation

Processing text in writing

Can summarise the main points made in straightforward informational texts on subjects of personal or current interest.

➔ See pages 30-33 **Mediation**

Preparation Remind students to bring their work from tasks 1-6 and their notes from the **Workbook** project task notes (pages 20-21) or their own notebook. Bring cue cards if needed for the presentation. Have students bring in their self-assessment diaries if you decided that you wanted them to keep one.

RECAP

Put students in their teams and read through the **Recap** as a class. Draw their attention to the project tasks and the unit objectives and ask which task helped achieve which objectives. Make sure they have all the materials and notes that they need (see **Preparation**) for the **Final task** and that they have completed any finishing touches to their comics.

FINAL TASK: Share your comics

Tell students they are now going to present their comics and display them in the classroom for everyone to read and discuss. Direct their attention to the **21st Century skill** (see next column). Read through the steps of the task and give them a short time to designate roles. Encourage them to use the **Useful language** and let them practise if you have time and think it will be of benefit.

It might be best to make the presentations short so students have more time to read them properly and discuss what they've read afterwards, but you could ask or encourage students to ask a quick question or two after each presentation to show and generate curiosity for what they will read in the comics. You could also encourage them to ask questions of the writers as they walk around and read their comics. Encourage students who finish reading quickly to make notes about the strengths and weakness of the comics, and when all students have finished have the class discuss comics that they thought stood out and why, and then vote on the best.

21ST CENTURY SKILLS

Read through the **21st Century skill** with the students and tell them that they will have time after sharing and discussing the comics as a class to assess their problem-solving skills and experiences in the **Evaluation** discussion.

➔ See pages 28-29 **21st Century skills**

EVALUATION

Before students discuss the questions in their teams, give them time to prepare notes about their experience in the project. Remind them to assess their own problem-solving skills and those of their team as part of the evaluation. Remind students to be supportive and give constructive criticism if necessary, with ideas on how to do things better next time. Monitor discussions, adding your own feedback where appropriate and noting common observations to then convey to the class as a whole. Have a class discussion about what students have learnt from the project, reminding them of the unit objectives, the **Core values** and the **Learning tools** sections of units 3 and 4, as well as the **21st Century skills** section of the **Project** pages.

If you have decided to use the evaluation exercise as a springboard for a student self-assessment diary (see **Evaluation** notes page 77), give them time to do this now and remind them to refer to the **Reflect on your learning** section of the **Workbook** if they have one.

➔ See pages 40-41 **Assessment**

GO BEYOND

Ask students to quickly read the text and tell you what 'the Funnies' refers to (in the second paragraph) and then get them to read the text in more detail and discuss answers to the questions below.

Remind students to do all the exercises in their notebook

5 UNSOLVED MYSTERIES

At the start of each unit and lesson, explain to the students what the objectives are.

Language objectives

Grammar

Modal verbs for speculation
- Students practise using *might, may, could* and *must* + *have* + past participle to speculate and to form hypotheses.

Third conditional
- Students practise conditional sentences to speculate about impossible situations in the past.

Vocabulary

Ancient monuments: *archaeologist, build, circular, construction, drawing, Egypt, England, geometric, huge, path, pharaoh, primitive, pyramid, stone, Stonehenge, structure, tomb, tonnes*
- Students use vocabulary for talking about and describing ancient monuments.

UFOs and aliens: *alien, being, clue, conspiracy theory, controversy, crash, debris, documentary, fake, footage, military, newspaper reports, spaceship, truth, UFO*
- Students use vocabulary related to UFOs and aliens.

Mysteries: *crop circles, evidence, fact, hoax, mysterious, pattern, phenomenon/phenomena, prove, theory*
- Students use vocabulary related to things that can't be explained.

Idioms and expressions

Secrets: *give the game away, spill the beans, keep someone in the dark, cover your tracks*
- Students look at idioms and expressions in the context of four opinions about dragons.

Recycled language

Modal verbs, Past participles, Past perfect

Skills objectives

Speaking

- Students discuss explanations of the mystery of Atlantis.
- Students share opinions about the Roswell UFO incident.
- Students discuss whether sentences are fact or opinion.
- Students share personal experiences using idioms and expressions.

Pronunciation: Students practise making contracted *'ve* sounds in modal perfects.

Pairwork: Students use various mediation techniques in order to tell tales and refute each other's mysterious stories.

Listening

- Students listen and complete texts about Stonehenge, the Egyptian pyramids and the Nazca lines.
- Students listen and take notes about the story of Atlantis.
- Students listen and complete a conversation about the Roswell UFO incident using expressions for opinions.
- Students listen and complete reports about UFO incidents.
- Students listen to take notes and complete sentences about dragons.

Reading

- Students skim a text to find explanations for the phenomenon of crop circles.
- Students read in detail to match people in a text to statements about them.
- Students decide if sentences in a text are fact or opinion, and identify the language the writer uses to present opinion.

Core values: Students reflect on their own **critical awareness** and discuss how to apply it in their reading.

Writing

- Students look at the language and structure of a review.
- Students plan, write and check a review of a museum.

Focus on Vocabulary for mystery: *claim, evidence, fake, prove, theory*

Remind students to do all the exercises in their notebook

Learning to learn tools

SPEAKING TOOLS Students practise using their listening skills to help their speaking performance.	**LISTENING TOOLS** Students practise listening for general meaning and for details.
READING TOOLS Students practise distinguishing between facts, unsupported opinions and supported opinions.	**WRITING TOOLS** Students practise considering their readers in order to make their writing more effective.

VOCABULARY TOOLS Students try using word cards to record vocabulary.

Project objectives: A mystery

Task 1 Students write about two mysteries and their possible explanations.

Task 2 Students write arguments against their team members' explanations.

Task 3 Students choose and research one of the mysteries.

Audiovisual objectives

Vlog: Students watch and listen to Robert talk about unsolved mysteries including the Loch Ness monster.

Culture: Students watch and listen to Robert talk about dragons.

Grammar animations: Students are presented with visual presentations of the unit grammar.

Key competences

LC **Linguistic**
pages 46-53

MST **Mathematical and Science and Technology**
pages 46-51, 53

DC **Digital**
pages 46-47, 49, 52-53

SCC **Social and Civic**
pages 48-53

CAE **Cultural awareness and expression**
pages 46-48, 52-53

LL **Learning to learn**
pages 47-48, 50, 52-53

IE **Sense of initiative and entrepreneurship**
pages 47, 49, 52

→ See pages 42-43 **Key competences**

CEFR Mediation

5.1 Facilitating collaborative interaction with peers
Can formulate and respond to suggestions and propose alternatives.

5.2 Encouraging conceptual talk
Can ask questions to invite people to clarify their reasoning.

5.3 Processing text in writing
Can summarise the main points in informational texts.

5.4 Linking to previous knowledge
Can explain something by drawing on people's experiences.

5.5 Note-taking
Can take notes in the form of a list of key points during a simple talk.

Project Facilitating delicate situations and disagreements
Can demonstrate understanding of the issues in a disagreement and ask for confirmation or clarification.

Unit review Facilitating collaborative interaction with peers
Can formulate and respond to suggestions, ask whether people agree and propose alternatives.

Pairwork Encouraging conceptual talk
Can ask questions to invite people to clarify their reasoning.

→ See pages 30-33 **Mediation**

Remind students to do all the exercises in their notebook

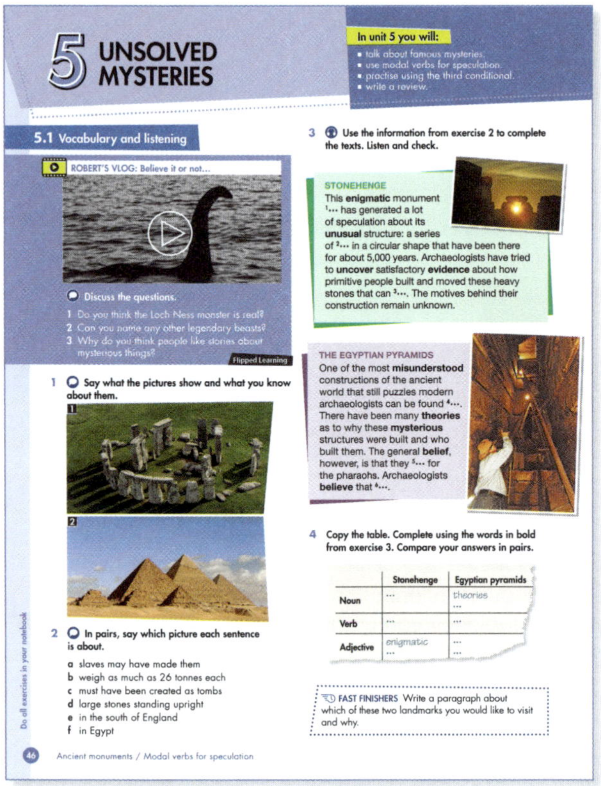

5 UNSOLVED MYSTERIES

In unit 5 you will:
- talk about famous mysteries.
- use modal verbs for speculation.
- practise using the third conditional.
- write a review.

5.1 Vocabulary and listening

ROBERT'S VLOG: Believe it or not…

Discuss the questions.
1 Do you think the Loch Ness monster is real?
2 Can you name any other legendary beasts?
3 Why do you think people like stories about mysterious things?

Flipped Learning

1 **Say what the pictures show and what you know about them.**

1

2

2 **In pairs, say which picture each sentence is about.**

a slaves may have made them
b weigh as much as 26 tonnes each
c must have been created as tombs
d large stones standing upright
e in the south of England
f in Egypt

3 **Use the information from exercise 2 to complete the texts. Listen and check.**

STONEHENGE
This **enigmatic** monument [1]… has generated a lot of speculation about its **unusual** structure: a series of [2]… in a circular shape that have been there for about 5,000 years. Archaeologists have tried to **uncover** satisfactory **evidence** about how primitive people built and moved these heavy stones that can [3]…. The motives behind their construction remain unknown.

THE EGYPTIAN PYRAMIDS
One of the most **misunderstood** constructions of the ancient world that still puzzles modern archaeologists can be found [4]…. There have been many **theories** as to why these **mysterious** structures were built and who built them. The general **belief**, however, is that they [5]… for the pharaohs. Archaeologists **believe** that [6]….

4 **Copy the table. Complete using the words in bold from exercise 3. Compare your answers in pairs.**

	Stonehenge	Egyptian pyramids
Noun	…	theories …
Verb	…	…
Adjective	enigmatic …	… …

FAST FINISHERS Write a paragraph about which of these two landmarks you would like to visit and why.

Do all exercises in your notebook

46 Ancient monuments / Modal verbs for speculation

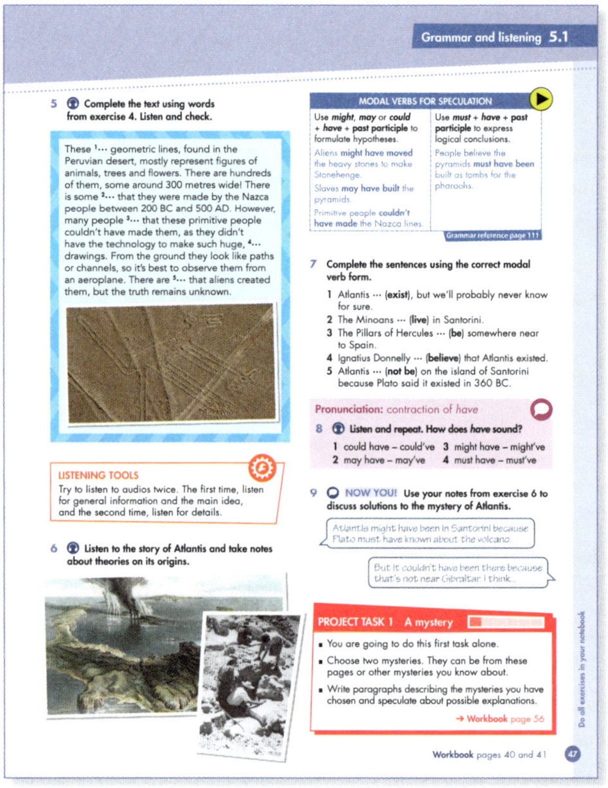

Grammar and listening 5.1

5 **Complete the text using words from exercise 4. Listen and check.**

These [1]… geometric lines, found in the Peruvian desert, mostly represent figures of animals, trees and flowers. There are hundreds of them, some around 300 metres wide! There is some [2]… that they were made by the Nazca people between 200 BC and 500 AD. However, many people [3]… that these primitive people couldn't have made them, as they didn't have the technology to make such huge, [4]… drawings. From the ground they look like paths or channels, so it's best to observe them from an aeroplane. There are [5]… that aliens created them, but the truth remains unknown.

LISTENING TOOLS
Try to listen to audios twice. The first time, listen for general information and the main idea, and the second time, listen for details.

6 **Listen to the story of Atlantis and take notes about theories on its origins.**

MODAL VERBS FOR SPECULATION

Use *might*, *may* or *could* + *have* + past participle to formulate hypotheses.	Use *must* + *have* + past participle to express logical conclusions.
Aliens **might have moved** the heavy stones to make Stonehenge. Slaves **may have built** the pyramids. Primitive people **couldn't have made** the Nazca lines.	People believe the pyramids **must have been** built as tombs for the pharaohs.

Grammar reference page 111

7 **Complete the sentences using the correct modal verb form.**

1 Atlantis … (**exist**), but we'll probably never know for sure.
2 The Minoans … (**live**) in Santorini.
3 The Pillars of Hercules … (**be**) somewhere near to Spain.
4 Ignatius Donnelly … (**believe**) that Atlantis existed.
5 Atlantis … (**not be**) on the island of Santorini because Plato said it existed in 360 BC.

Pronunciation: contraction of *have*

8 **Listen and repeat. How does *have* sound?**

1 could have – could've
2 may have – may've
3 might have – might've
4 must have – must've

9 NOW YOU! **Use your notes from exercise 6 to discuss solutions to the mystery of Atlantis.**

Atlantis might have been in Santorini because Plato must have known about the volcano.

But it couldn't have been there because that's not near Gibraltar I think…

PROJECT TASK 1 A mystery
- You are going to do this first task alone.
- Choose two mysteries. They can be from these pages or other mysteries you know about.
- Write paragraphs describing the mysteries you have chosen and speculate about possible explanations.

→ Workbook page 56

Do all exercises in your notebook

Workbook pages 40 and 41 47

ANSWER KEY

Pages 46-47

1 *Student's own answers*

2 **Picture 1:** b, d, e **Picture 2:** a, c, f

3
1 in the South of England
2 large stones standing upright
3 weigh as much as 26 tonnes each
4 in Egypt
5 must have been created as tombs
6 slaves may have made them

4

	Stonehenge	Egyptian pyramids
Noun	evidence	theories belief
Verb	uncover	believe
Adjective	enigmatic unusual	misunderstood mysterious

5
1 mysterious
2 evidence
3 believe
4 enigmatic
5 theories

6 *Student's own answers*

7
1 may/might/could have existed
2 must have lived
3 might/may/could have been
4 must have believed
5 couldn't have been

8 *Student's own answers*

9 *Student's own answers*

Remind students to do all the exercises in their notebook

LESSON FOCUS

Grammar Modal verbs for speculation
Vocabulary Ancient monuments
Listening Completing texts about Stonehenge, the Egyptian pyramids and the Nazca lines; Taking notes about the story of Atlantis.
Speaking Discussing the mystery of Atlantis
Project task 1 Write about two mysteries and their possible explanations

Resources

Teacher's i-solutions, Student's Book audio, Vlog and worksheets

Flipped Learning

ROBERTS'S VLOG: Believe it or not...

- Make sure to set up the **Flipped Learning** work with the students beforehand. **See pages 20-23 for complete Flipped Learning guidelines.**
- Ask students to put the **Flipped Learning worksheets** on their desks and walk around to check how many have completed the Flipped task.
- In pairs or small groups, ask students to compare and check the *Before you watch* ...and *While you watch...* exercises on the worksheet.
- Show students **Robert's Vlog** and ask volunteers to provide correct answers and clarify any doubts other students may have.
- Choose three or four students to read aloud their answers to the *After you watch...* exercises on the worksheet and encourage some class discussion.
- Move straight to exercise 1 on page 46.

Warmer

Watch Robert's Vlog and discuss the questions with the whole class. If you don't have video facilities, simply discuss the questions.

1 If possible, show students the pictures without the accompanying text and encourage them to speculate. Then tell them what the pictures are of and ask what they know about them.

2 Draw on students' answers from exercise 1 to get them started on this exercise and encourage them to speculate about the rest.

3 1.41 (See page 174 for transcripts) Point out that students are completing the texts with the exact phrases from exercise 2. Encourage them to guess the meanings of the words in bold from context and clarify where necessary.

4 Remind students that noting vocabulary in a way that reminds them of the context will help them to remember it.

FAST FINISHERS Students can complete this exercise alone or in pairs.

5 1.42 (See page 175 for transcripts) Ask students to scan the text to identify what the picture shows (geometric lines made in the Peruvian desert, either made by the Nazca people or possibly aliens). Let them complete the text before playing the audio.

LISTENING TOOLS

Get students to read the **Listening tool** and tell them they can apply it to the next exercise.

6 1.43 (See page 175 for transcripts) Ask students what they know about Atlantis. Tell them you will play the audio twice. After the first time, elicit what they have noted about the story. To help them note the details of the theories, you could write the following headings on the board: *Plato, Ignatius Donnelly, Santorini.*

Flipped Learning

MODAL VERBS FOR SPECULATION

Draw students' attention to the **Grammar table**. Remind students that they can use this as a quick reference while completing the exercises.

Show students the **Grammar animation** and/or refer students to the **Grammar reference** on page 111 for further information on form and use.

→ See page 23 for how to flip the **grammar lesson**

7 Refer students to the **Grammar table** as they do the exercise and ask them to give reasons for their choice of modal verbs, based on their notes from exercise 6.

Pronunciation

8 1.44 (See page 175 for transcripts) To give students some quick extra practice, write the modal verbs on the board and say short sentences in the past simple (and present perfect) for them to convert into modal sentences depending on the modal verb you point at on the board: *He went (might) - He might've gone; They knew (must) - They must've known,* etc.

9 **NOW YOU!** Draw attention to the sentences students completed in exercise 7 and encourage them to react to each other's ideas and give reasons, like in the examples in the speech bubbles.

PROJECT TASK 1 A mystery

Tell students that this project will be a team project but that the first task will be done alone. You can discuss other mysteries as a class to get them started. Remind students that they need to keep their project notes together in their **Workbook** (page 56) or in their own notebook.

→ See pages 24-27 **Projects**

FURTHER PRACTICE

Workbook pages 40-41
- **Grammar reference and practice** pages 88 and 94-95
- **Wordlist and exercises** pages 100 and 103

Remind students to do all the exercises in their notebook

CONTINUOUS ASSESSMENT Students can talk about ancient monuments and use modal verbs for speculation.

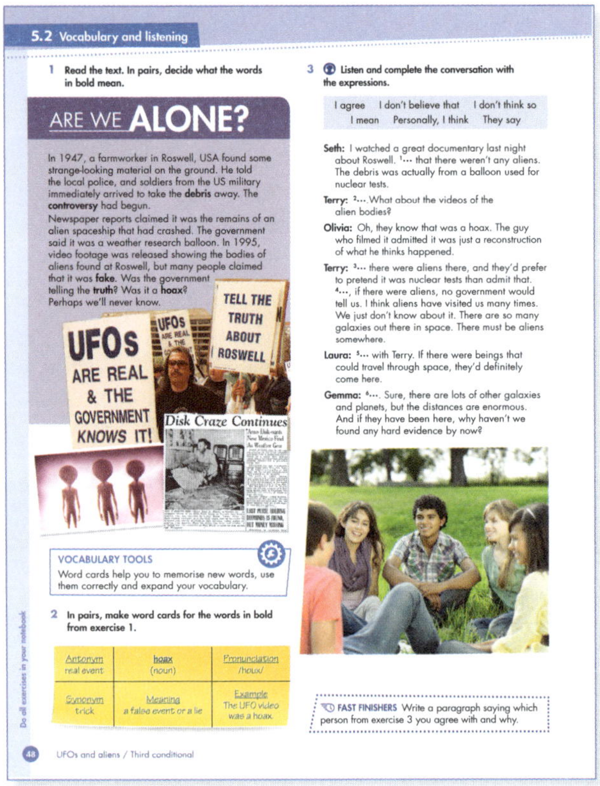

5.2 Vocabulary and listening

1 Read the text. In pairs, decide what the words in bold mean.

ARE WE ALONE?

In 1947, a farmworker in Roswell, USA found some strange-looking material on the ground. He told the local police, and soldiers from the US military immediately arrived to take the **debris** away. The **controversy** had begun.

Newspaper reports claimed it was the remains of an alien spaceship that had crashed. The government said it was a weather research balloon. In 1995, video footage was released showing the bodies of aliens found at Roswell, but many people claimed that it was **fake**. Was the government telling the **truth**? Was it a **hoax**? Perhaps we'll never know.

VOCABULARY TOOLS
Word cards help you to memorise new words, use them correctly and expand your vocabulary.

2 In pairs, make word cards for the words in bold from exercise 1.

Antonym real event	hoax (noun)	Pronunciation /həʊks/
Synonym trick	Meaning a false event or a lie	Example The UFO video was a hoax.

3 Listen and complete the conversation with the expressions.

I agree · I don't believe that · I don't think so · I mean · Personally, I think · They say

Seth: I watched a great documentary last night about Roswell. [1]… that there weren't any aliens. The debris was actually from a balloon used for nuclear tests.

Terry: [2]…. What about the videos of the alien bodies?

Olivia: Oh, they know that was a hoax. The guy who filmed it admitted it was just a reconstruction of what he thinks happened.

Terry: [3]… there were aliens there, and they'd prefer to pretend it was nuclear tests than admit that. [4]…, if there were aliens, no government would tell us. I think aliens have visited us many times. We just don't know about it. There are so many galaxies out there in space. There must be aliens somewhere.

Laura: [5]… with Terry. If there were beings that could travel through space, they'd definitely come here.

Gemma: [6]…. Sure, there are lots of other galaxies and planets, but the distances are enormous. And if they have been here, why haven't we found any hard evidence by now?

FAST FINISHERS Write a paragraph saying which person from exercise 3 you agree with and why.

Do all exercises in your notebook

48 UFOs and aliens / Third conditional

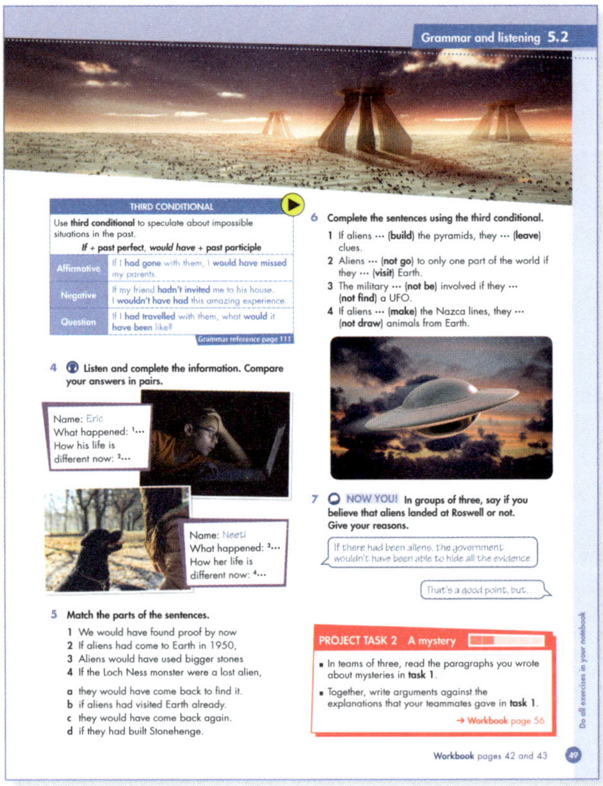

Grammar and listening 5.2

THIRD CONDITIONAL

Use **third conditional** to speculate about impossible situations in the past.

***If* + past perfect, *would have* + past participle**

Affirmative	If I **had gone** with them, I **would have missed** my parents.
Negative	If my friend **hadn't invited** me to his house, I **wouldn't have had** this amazing experience.
Question	If I **had travelled** with them, what **would** it **have been** like?

Grammar reference page 111

4 Listen and complete the information. Compare your answers in pairs.

Name: Eric
What happened: [1]…
How his life is different now: [2]…

Name: Neeti
What happened: [3]…
How her life is different now: [4]…

5 Match the parts of the sentences.

1 We would have found proof by now
2 If aliens had come to Earth in 1950,
3 Aliens would have used bigger stones
4 If the Loch Ness monster were a lost alien,

a they would have come back to find it.
b if aliens had visited Earth already.
c they would have come back again.
d if they had built Stonehenge.

6 Complete the sentences using the third conditional.

1 If aliens … (**build**) the pyramids, they … (**leave**) clues.
2 Aliens … (**not go**) to only one part of the world if they … (**visit**) Earth.
3 The military … (**not be**) involved if they … (**not find**) a UFO.
4 If aliens … (**make**) the Nazca lines, they … (**not draw**) animals from Earth.

7 NOW YOU! In groups of three, say if you believe that aliens landed at Roswell or not. Give your reasons.

If there had been aliens, the government wouldn't have been able to hide all the evidence.

That's a good point, but…

PROJECT TASK 2 A mystery

- In teams of three, read the paragraphs you wrote about mysteries in **task 1**.
- Together, write arguments against the explanations that your teammates gave in **task 1**.

→ Workbook page 56

Do all exercises in your notebook

Workbook pages 42 and 43 49

ANSWER KEY

Pages 48-49

1 *Suggested answers:*
debris: rubbish
controversy: disagreement
fake: false, imitation
truth: reality, fact
hoax: practical joke, trick

2 *Student's own answers*

3
1 They say
2 I don't believe that
3 Personally, I think
4 I mean
5 I agree
6 I don't think so

4
1 Eric went to a friend's house, but he wasn't there. He went to look for him and saw him with two tall creatures, walking towards a bright light. Eric followed them and they both woke up in their homes three days later.
2 He spends hours on the internet trying to find out what happened to them.
3 Neeti was walking her dog when she heard a humming sound. She felt herself being lifted into the air and heard a voice asking her if she wanted to travel in a spaceship. Then there was a loud bang and she woke up on the ground.
4 She walks her dog every day hoping to see them again and can't stop thinking what it would have been like if she'd gone with them.

5
1 b
2 c
3 d
4 a

6
1 had built; would have left
2 wouldn't have gone; had visited
3 wouldn't have been; hadn't found
4 had made; wouldn't have drawn

7 *Student's own answers*

Remind students to do all the exercises in their notebook

LESSON FOCUS

Grammar Third conditional
Vocabulary UFOs and aliens
Listening Completing a conversation about the Roswell UFO incident; Completing reports about UFO incidents
Speaking Sharing opinions about the Roswell UFO incident
Project task 2 Write arguments against team members' explanations

Resources
Teacher's i-solutions, Student's Book audio

Warmer

Put students in a circle and tell them to imagine themselves as part of an electric current that follows these rules: When a student uses the modal verb *might have been*, the student next to them must say something. They can either repeat *might have been* to keep the current going in the same direction, *must have done* to change direction or *couldn't have done* to jump one student forward in the same direction. Eliminate students who take too long or say something when it isn't their turn. Change the modal verbs for extra practice.

1 Ask students if they know anything about Roswell before getting them to read the text and discuss the vocabulary. Confirm or correct their definitions.

VOCABULARY TOOLS

Get students to read the **Vocabulary tool** and point out that you can also play revision games with word cards.

2 Tell students that they don't always need all of the information that's present on the example card, but that the more they write about a word, the better chance they have of remembering it and of using it correctly. Once they've made the cards, get them to take turns to pick up a card and read any information that doesn't include the actual word for their partner to guess.

3 1.45 (See page 175 for transcripts) Ask students for their general impressions of the Roswell incident but don't go into too much detail yet. To make the exercise smoother and more focused on listening, you could get them to write the expressions in the wordpool down first and number them as they hear them. Encourage them to record the expressions in their notebooks under headings like *Giving an opinion*, *Clarifying*, *Agreeing* and *Disagreeing*, and give them other useful expressions for each function if you wish.

FAST FINISHERS Students can complete this exercise alone or in pairs.

THIRD CONDITIONAL

Flipped Learning

Draw students' attention to the **Grammar table**. Remind students that they can use this as a quick reference while completing the exercises.

Show students the **Grammar animation** and/or refer students to the **Grammar reference** on page 111 for further information on form and use.

→ See page 23 for how to flip the **grammar lesson**

4 1.46 (See page 175 for transcripts) Tell students they are going to listen to two people talk about personal experiences related to alien contact. After they compare answers, ask them to match the sentences in the **Grammar table** with the people who said them (Eric said the second sentence and Neeti the other two)

5 Point out that, as with all conditionals, the *If* clause doesn't have to come first.

6 Refer students to the **Grammar table** to complete the exercise and get them to compare their answers in pairs for support. You could then ask them to say which of the sentences in exercises 5 and 6 they agree with and why.

7 NOW YOU! To ensure students use third conditional sentences correctly in this exercise, give them time to write a couple of third conditional sentences that support their opinion before they start the discussion. To extend the exercise, write the expressions of opinion from exercise 3 on the board and get them to swap partners and continue the discussion using the expressions.

PROJECT TASK 2 A mystery

Tell students to get their paragraphs from **task 1** and put them in groups of three to do this task. Remind students that they need to keep their project notes together in their **Workbook** (page 56) or in their own notebook.

→ See pages 24-27 **Projects**

FURTHER PRACTICE

Workbook pages 42-43
- **Grammar reference and practice** pages 88 and 94-95
- **Wordlist and exercises** pages 100 and 103

Vocabulary and Grammar worksheets available to download from the **Richmond***Learning***Platform**

→ See pages 38-39 **Mixed-ability classes**

Remind students to do all the exercises in their notebook

CONTINUOUS ASSESSMENT Students can talk about UFOs and aliens, and use the third conditional.

5.3 Reading

1 In groups of three, say what the photos show. Read the introduction and check.

2 In your group, write a list of possible explanations for crop circles.

READING TOOLS
When you read, try to distinguish between facts, subjective opinions and opinions that show a logical interpretation of facts. Then you can form better informed opinions yourself.

3 Read the text and make a list of the explanations the writer gives. Compare them to your answers in exercise 2.

4 Complete the sentences with names from the article.
1 ··· made a few crop circles themselves.
2 ··· found evidence that some crop circles were not made by humans.
3 ··· noted that the formation of some crop circles had changed the crops.
4 ··· found strange changes in the soil in a crop circle.
5 ··· suggested that the circles are messages from other beings.

5 In pairs, look at the six numbered sentences and decide if they are presented as fact or opinion.

6 Identify the language the writer uses to highlight that a statement is an opinion.

7 Answer the question in the title.

CROP CIRCLES:

[1] A crop circle is a pattern of flattened crops, like wheat or barley, that suddenly appears in a field. They first started appearing in the 1970s, although some people say there is evidence of them as early as the 17th century. Most of them have been found in England, but they have appeared in countries around the world. We don't know what, or who, creates them, but there are many mysterious theories.

As the years have gone by, the crop circles have become more and more complex. Symbolic shapes have also appeared in the patterns. [2] For these reasons, some people argue that they couldn't be

Do all exercises in your notebook

50 Language in context / Mysteries

Reading 5.3

hoax or unsolved mystery?

a hoax made by humans. They believe that they are created by some sort of higher intelligence! Molecular biologist Horace Drew has theorised that they might be messages of hope for humanity from either aliens or time travellers.

[3] In 1991, two Englishmen named Doug Bower and Dave Chorley caused a sensation by announcing that the whole thing was an elaborate hoax: they had created the first crop circles using wood and rope in 1978. They even made one in front of journalists. They didn't claim that they had made all of the circles, just the first few, and then others must have copied them. They said that they had wanted people to believe a UFO had landed and made the circles.

[4] Most crop circle researchers now admit that the vast majority of circles must be man-made. There is even a UK arts collective called Circlemakers who dedicate their time to making them for art and business. [5] But some still claim that there are a few that cannot have been made by humans.

Biophysicist William Levengood said that he discovered differences in the crops inside and outside the circles that could not be attributed to human activity. He also said he'd found tiny spheres of iron in the crops, something that would suggest intense heat.

Furthermore, mineralogist Sampath Iyengar studied the soil from a crop circle in Canada and found evidence of temperatures so high that humans could not have produced them and they should have killed the crops.

So, are crop circles an unsolved mystery or a hoax? Just because we know that humans have made many, doesn't mean that they are all man-made. It is true that the only proven cause is humans, that we love a mystery and that many people make money out of books and documentaries about mysterious phenomena. [6] But it's also true that if there were evidence of contact from aliens, our governments might not want us to know about it. Something to think about!

CORE VALUES Critical awareness

8 Answer the questions in pairs.
1 Do you believe everything you read? How do you decide what not to believe?
2 How important are these factors in deciding whether to believe something?
- the source (who said/wrote it and where)
- how credible the evidence is
- how logical the arguments are
- how it makes you feel
- how balanced it seems
3 How much would you believe of these statements? Give reasons.
- (In a car advert) With the latest in Auto Emergency Braking, this is the safest luxury car on the road.
- (A politician on a national news programme) Unemployment is now at 6%. We have created more jobs than any government in recent history.
- (On a social media posting complete with photo) Great white shark attacks coast guard helicopter!

FAST FINISHERS Write a short fake news story.

Workbook pages 44 and 45

Do all exercises in your notebook

51

ANSWER KEY

Pages 50-51

1 The photos on the right show crop circles. These are patterns of flattened crops in fields, usually of cereals like wheat. The photo at the bottom of the page shows wheat.

2 *Student's own answers*

3 They are created by some sort of higher intelligence.
They might be messages from either aliens or time travellers.
They are an elaborate hoax, started by two Englishmen and then copied by others.
They are man-made, some for art and business.

4 **1** Doug Bower and Dave Chorley
2 William Levengood
3 William Levengood
4 Sampath Iyengar
5 Horace Drew

5 **1** fact
2 opinion
3 fact
4 fact
5 opinion
6 opinion

6 some people say; some people argue; they believe that; they might be; some still claim

7 *Student's own answers*

8 *Student's own answers*

Remind students to do all the exercises in their notebook

LESSON FOCUS

Language in context Mysteries

Core values Critical awareness

Resources

Teacher's i-solutions, Student's Book audio

→ See pages 36-37 **Literature**

Warmer

Choose one of the mysteries from the unit and talk about it for students to guess which mystery it is. Students can then continue in pairs or small groups.

1 If possible, show students the photos (or any photos of crop circles) and ask what they think they are before they open their books. Use the photos to explain any vocabulary from the introduction they don't understand.

2 Write some of the students' explanations on the board to compare with the text in the next exercise.

READING TOOLS

Get students to read the **Reading tool** and tell them they will apply it in exercise 5.

3 1.47 (See page 175 for transcripts) Refer to the list you wrote on the board in exercise 2. Answer any vocabulary questions that students have.

4 Tell students this is a scanning exercise and see how quickly they can complete it.

5 Give time for students to discuss the reasons for their decisions and see if they notice the language referred to in the next exercise as a lead into it.

6 Point out that the word *claim* casts more doubt on the statement. Ask students if they think the text is fair and balanced.

7 If students seem interested, extend the exercise by focusing their attention on the last paragraph of the text as a starting point for a discussion of their answer.

CORE VALUES Critical awareness

8 Encourage students to give specific examples from personal experience to answer the questions. You could end by getting them to summarise the discussion by writing a couple of sentences of advice on how to be critically aware.

FAST FINISHERS Students can complete this exercise alone or in pairs.

FURTHER PRACTICE
Workbook pages 44-45

Remind students to do all the exercises in their notebook

CONTINUOUS ASSESSMENT Students can understand vocabulary about mysteries in a text about crop circles.

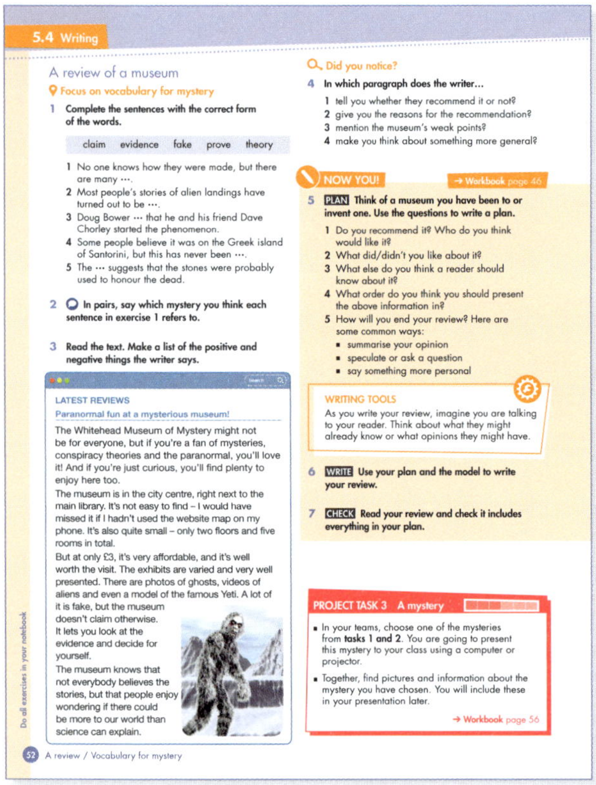

5.4 Writing

A review of a museum

Focus on vocabulary for mystery

1 **Complete the sentences with the correct form of the words.**

claim evidence fake prove theory

1 No one knows how they were made, but there are many ···.
2 Most people's stories of alien landings have turned out to be ···.
3 Doug Bower ··· that he and his friend Dave Chorley started the phenomenon.
4 Some people believe it was on the Greek island of Santorini, but this has never been ···.
5 The ··· suggests that the stones were probably used to honour the dead.

2 **In pairs, say which mystery you think each sentence in exercise 1 refers to.**

3 **Read the text. Make a list of the positive and negative things the writer says.**

LATEST REVIEWS

Paranormal fun at a mysterious museum!

The Whitehead Museum of Mystery might not be for everyone, but if you're a fan of mysteries, conspiracy theories and the paranormal, you'll love it! And if you're just curious, you'll find plenty to enjoy here too.

The museum is in the city centre, right next to the main library. It's not easy to find – I would have missed it if I hadn't used the website map on my phone. It's also quite small – only two floors and five rooms in total.

But at only £3, it's very affordable, and it's well worth the visit. The exhibits are varied and very well presented. There are photos of ghosts, videos of aliens and even a model of the famous Yeti. A lot of it is fake, but the museum doesn't claim otherwise. It lets you look at the evidence and decide for yourself.

The museum knows that not everybody believes the stories, but that people enjoy wondering if there could be more to our world than science can explain.

Did you notice?

4 **In which paragraph does the writer…**

1 tell you whether they recommend it or not?
2 give you the reasons for the recommendation?
3 mention the museum's weak points?
4 make you think about something more general?

NOW YOU! → Workbook page 46

5 **PLAN Think of a museum you have been to or invent one. Use the questions to write a plan.**

1 Do you recommend it? Who do you think would like it?
2 What did/didn't you like about it?
3 What else do you think a reader should know about it?
4 What order do you think you should present the above information in?
5 How will you end your review? Here are some common ways:
- summarise your opinion
- speculate or ask a question
- say something more personal

WRITING TOOLS

As you write your review, imagine you are talking to your reader. Think about what they might already know or what opinions they might have.

6 **WRITE Use your plan and the model to write your review.**

7 **CHECK Read your review and check it includes everything in your plan.**

PROJECT TASK 3 A mystery

- In your teams, choose one of the mysteries from **tasks 1 and 2**. You are going to present this mystery to your class using a computer or projector.
- Together, find pictures and information about the mystery you have chosen. You will include these in your presentation later.

→ Workbook page 56

Do all exercises in your notebook

52 A review / Vocabulary for mystery

ANSWER KEY

Page 52

1
1 theories
2 fake
3 claims/claimed
4 proved
5 evidence

2 *Suggested answers:*
1 the Pyramids, the Nazca lines
2 Roswell
3 Crop circles
4 Atlantis
5 Stonehenge

3 **Positive:** Fans of mysteries, conspiracy theories and the paranormal will love it; People who are just curious will also enjoy it; It's affordable; The exhibits are varied and well presented; It lets you look at the evidence and decide for yourself.
Negative: It might not be for everyone; It's not easy to find; It's quite small.

4
1 first paragraph
2 third paragraph
3 second paragraph
4 fourth paragraph

5 *Student's own answers*

6 *Student's own answers*

7 *Student's own answers*

FURTHER PRACTICE

Workbook page 46

LESSON FOCUS

Focus on Vocabulary for mystery

Writing A review of a museum

Project task 3 Choose and research one of the mysteries

Preparation Word cards

Resources

Teacher's i-solutions

Warmer

Get students to prepare more word cards like those on page 48 of the **Student's Book** for the other words in the Wordlist. Put students in groups of three to test each other on their word cards. You could make it a competition to see which group can guess most words in a time limit, with each member picking up one card at a time to describe.

Focus on vocabulary for mystery

1 Get students to do this and the next exercise before you correct their answers. Remind them they may have to change the word forms.

2 Give a couple of possible answers to the first question using modal verbs for speculation in the present to encourage students to get some extra practice.

3 Ask students what museum the writer is reviewing (The Whitehead Museum of Mystery) and let them compare answers in pairs if you have time.

Did you notice?

4 Point out that this isn't the only structure for a review, but that each paragraph has, as it should, a clear purpose and that the recommendation is clear.

5 **PLAN** Once students have finished their plan, encourage them to talk it through with a partner.

WRITING TOOLS

Get students to read the **Writing tool**. You could get them to give a spoken review to a classmate after they've written their plan to see if their classmate's response highlights any changes they need to make.

6 **WRITE** Before students start writing, make a checklist on the board of any elements related to content, structure, language and style that they should bear in mind.

7 **CHECK** Once students have checked their own reviews, they can swap with a partner and check theirs.

PROJECT TASK 3 A mystery

Put students in their groups again to discuss how to proceed. Tell students that they need to keep their project notes together in their **Workbook** (page 56) or in their own notebook.

→ See pages 24-27 **Projects**

Remind students to do all the exercises in their notebook

 CONTINUOUS ASSESSMENT Students can write a review of a museum.

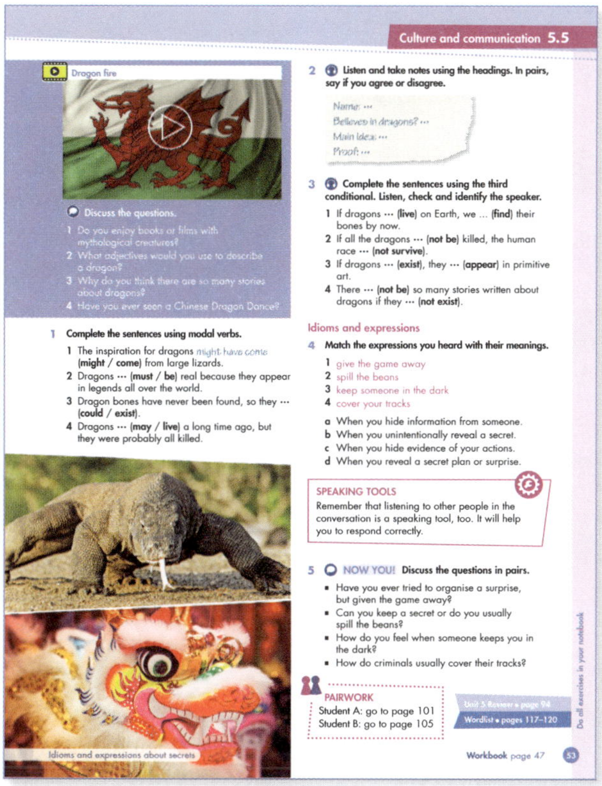
Culture and communication 5.5

Dragon fire

Discuss the questions.

1 Do you enjoy books or films with mythological creatures?
2 What adjectives would you use to describe a dragon?
3 Why do you think there are so many stories about dragons?
4 Have you ever seen a Chinese Dragon Dance?

1 Complete the sentences using modal verbs.

1 The inspiration for dragons might have come (might / come) from large lizards.
2 Dragons ··· (must / be) real because they appear in legends all over the world.
3 Dragon bones have never been found, so they ··· (could / exist).
4 Dragons ··· (may / live) a long time ago, but they were probably all killed.

Idioms and expressions about secrets

2 Listen and take notes using the headings. In pairs, say if you agree or disagree.

Name: ···
Believes in dragons? ···
Main idea: ···
Proof: ···

3 Complete the sentences using the third conditional. Listen, check and identify the speaker.

1 If dragons ··· (live) on Earth, we ... (find) their bones by now.
2 If all the dragons ··· (not be) killed, the human race ··· (not survive).
3 If dragons ··· (exist), they ··· (appear) in primitive art.
4 There ··· (not be) so many stories written about dragons if they ··· (not exist).

Idioms and expressions

4 Match the expressions you heard with their meanings.

1 give the game away
2 spill the beans
3 keep someone in the dark
4 cover your tracks

a When you hide information from someone.
b When you unintentionally reveal a secret.
c When you hide evidence of your actions.
d When you reveal a secret plan or surprise.

SPEAKING TOOLS
Remember that listening to other people in the conversation is a speaking tool, too. It will help you to respond correctly.

5 NOW YOU! Discuss the questions in pairs.

- Have you ever tried to organise a surprise, but given the game away?
- Can you keep a secret or do you usually spill the beans?
- How do you feel when someone keeps you in the dark?
- How do criminals usually cover their tracks?

PAIRWORK
Student A: go to page 101
Student B: go to page 105

Unit 5 Review • page 94
Wordlist • pages 117–120

Do all exercises in your notebook

Workbook page 47

53

ANSWER KEY

Page 53

1 **1** might have come **2** must have been **3** couldn't have existed **4** may have lived

2 Refer to page 195 of the **Teacher's Book**.

3 **1** had lived on Earth; would have found bones by now; Anna
2 hadn't been; wouldn't have survived; Tom
3 had existed; would have appeared; Jamie
4 wouldn't have been; hadn't existed; Mark

4 **1** d **2** b **3** a **4** c

5 *Student's own answers*

FURTHER PRACTICE AND UNIT ASSESSMENT

Unit 5 Review **Student's Book** page 94
Workbook page 47
- Reflect on your learning page 47
- Grammar reference and practice pages 88 and 94-95
- Wordlist and exercises pages 100 and 103

Tests available to download and edit from the **Richmond***Learning***Platform**

→ See pages 40-41 **Assessment**

LESSON FOCUS

Idioms and expressions Secrets
Listening Taking notes and completing sentences
Speaking Sharing personal experiences using idioms and expressions

Resources
Teacher's i-solutions, Student's Book audio, Culture video and worksheet

Dragon fire

Video and worksheet available on the Richmond*Learning***Platform**

- In pairs, ask students to complete the *What I know...* exercises on the **Culture video worksheet**.
- Show students the **Culture video** and ask them to complete the *What I learned...* exercises on the worksheet.
- In pairs, students compare answers.
- In small groups, tell students to complete the *What I wonder...* exercises on the worksheet.

Warmer

Watch the **Culture video** and discuss the questions with the whole class. If you don't have video facilities, simply discuss the questions.

1 Ask students what types of dragon are featured in the photos (a Komodo dragon and a Chinese New Year dragon). Tell them that, in the next exercise, they will hear people talk about whether dragons really existed. Get them to complete the sentences.

2 1.48 (See page 176 for transcripts) Tell students they will hear four people giving their opinion. Let them compare their notes and discuss in pairs after they listen to the audio.

3 1.49 (See page 176 for transcripts) Get students to do the exercise from memory and from their knowledge of the grammar. Let them refer to the **Grammar table** on page 49 of the **Student's Book** if they want to. Play the audio and stop after each sentence for them to check.

Idioms and expressions

4 Remind students of the context of the expressions to help them decide meanings.

SPEAKING TOOLS

Get students to read the **Speaking tool** and tell them that you will check that they are applying it.

5 NOW YOU! After students complete the discussion, ask individuals to report what their partners said.

PAIRWORK **Student's Book** pages 101 and 105
See **Teacher's Book** page 114 for more information.
→ See pages 30-33 **Mediation**

Remind students to do all the exercises in their notebook

Unit 5 Review

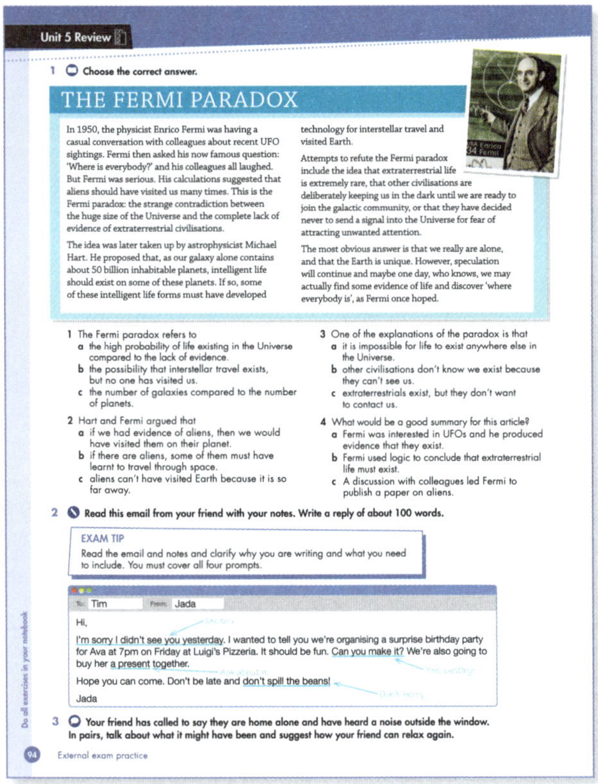
Unit 5 Review

1 Choose the correct answer.

THE FERMI PARADOX

In 1950, the physicist Enrico Fermi was having a casual conversation with colleagues about recent UFO sightings. Fermi then asked his now famous question: 'Where is everybody?' and his colleagues all laughed. But Fermi was serious. His calculations suggested that aliens should have visited us many times. This is the Fermi paradox: the strange contradiction between the huge size of the Universe and the complete lack of evidence of extraterrestrial civilisations.

The idea was later taken up by astrophysicist Michael Hart. He proposed that, as our galaxy alone contains about 50 billion inhabitable planets, intelligent life should exist on some of these planets. If so, some of these intelligent life forms must have developed technology for interstellar travel and visited Earth.

Attempts to refute the Fermi paradox include the idea that extraterrestrial life is extremely rare, that other civilisations are deliberately keeping us in the dark until we are ready to join the galactic community, or that they have decided never to send a signal into the Universe for fear of attracting unwanted attention.

The most obvious answer is that we really are alone, and that the Earth is unique. However, speculation will continue and maybe one day, who knows, we may actually find some evidence of life and discover 'where everybody is', as Fermi once hoped.

1 The Fermi paradox refers to
  a the high probability of life existing in the Universe compared to the lack of evidence.
  b the possibility that interstellar travel exists, but no one has visited us.
  c the number of galaxies compared to the number of planets.

2 Hart and Fermi argued that
  a if we had evidence of aliens, then we would have visited them on their planet.
  b if there are aliens, some of them must have learnt to travel through space.
  c aliens can't have visited Earth because it is so far away.

3 One of the explanations of the paradox is that
  a it is impossible for life to exist anywhere else in the Universe.
  b other civilisations don't know we exist because they can't see us.
  c extraterrestrials exist, but they don't want to contact us.

4 What would be a good summary for this article?
  a Fermi was interested in UFOs and he produced evidence that they exist.
  b Fermi used logic to conclude that extraterrestrial life must exist.
  c A discussion with colleagues led Fermi to publish a paper on aliens.

2 Read this email from your friend with your notes. Write a reply of about 100 words.

EXAM TIP
Read the email and notes and clarify why you are writing and what you need to include. You must cover all four prompts.

To: Tim From: Jada

Hi,

I'm sorry I didn't see you yesterday. I wanted to tell you we're organising a surprise birthday party for Ava at 7pm on Friday at Luigi's Pizzeria. It should be fun. Can you make it? We're also going to buy her a present together.

Hope you can come. Don't be late and don't spill the beans!

Jada

3 Your friend has called to say they are home alone and have heard a noise outside the window. In pairs, talk about what it might have been and suggest how your friend can relax again.

Do all exercises in your notebook

94 External exam practice

Student's Book page 94

ANSWER KEY

1 **1** a
2 b
3 c
4 b

2 *Student's own answers*

3 *Student's own answers*

Pairwork

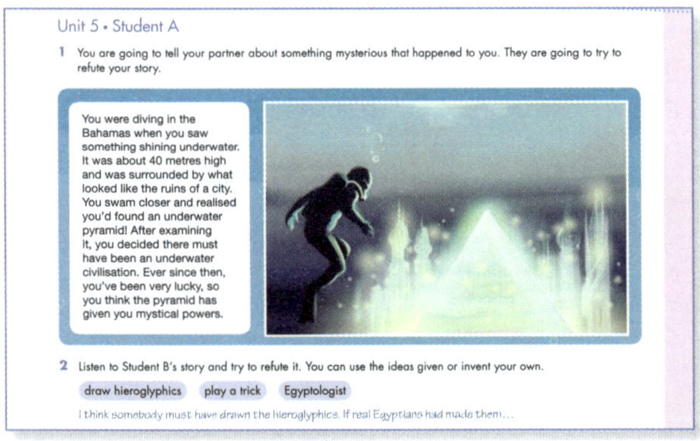
Unit 5 • Student A

1 You are going to tell your partner about something mysterious that happened to you. They are going to try to refute your story.

You were diving in the Bahamas when you saw something shining underwater. It was about 40 metres high and was surrounded by what looked like the ruins of a city. You swam closer and realised you'd found an underwater pyramid! After examining it, you decided there must have been an underwater civilisation. Ever since then, you've been very lucky, so you think the pyramid has given you mystical powers.

2 Listen to Student B's story and try to refute it. You can use the ideas given or invent your own.

draw hieroglyphics | play a trick | Egyptologist

I think somebody must have drawn the hieroglyphics. If real Egyptians had made them…

Student's Book page 101

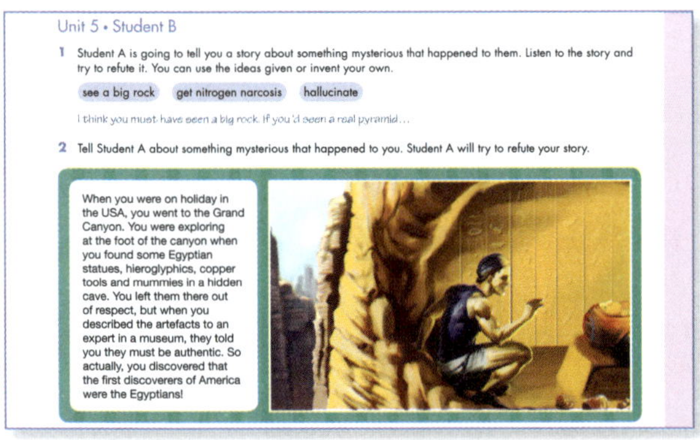
Unit 5 • Student B

1 Student A is going to tell you a story about something mysterious that happened to them. Listen to the story and try to refute it. You can use the ideas given or invent your own.

see a big rock | get nitrogen narcosis | hallucinate

I think you must have seen a big rock. If you'd seen a real pyramid…

2 Tell Student A about something mysterious that happened to you. Student A will try to refute your story.

When you were on holiday in the USA, you went to the Grand Canyon. You were exploring at the foot of the canyon when you found some Egyptian statues, hieroglyphics, copper tools and mummies in a hidden cave. You left them there out of respect, but when you described the artefacts to an expert in a museum, they told you they must be authentic. So actually, you discovered that the first discoverers of America were the Egyptians!

Student's Book page 105

CEFR MEDIATION DESCRIPTOR

- **Collaborating to construct meaning**
  Students can consider two different sides of an issue, giving arguments for and against, and propose a solution or compromise.

- **Refuting a story**
  Tell students that they each have a mysterious story to tell their partner as if it really happened. Their partners will try to refute the story and they have to insist that it was real, giving the best reasons they can. Encourage them to use modal perfects and the third conditional like in the example sentences given.

Remind students to do all the exercises in their notebook

Modal verbs for speculation

Use ***might***, ***may*** or ***could*** + ***have*** + **past participle** to formulate hypotheses.	Use ***must*** + ***have*** + **past participle** to express logical conclusions.
Aliens **might have moved** the heavy stones to make Stonehenge. Slaves **may have built** the pyramids. Primitive people **couldn't have made** the Nazca lines.	People believe the pyramids **must have been** built as tombs for the pharaohs.

We use modal verbs with the present perfect to speculate about whether something was true in the past or not.

We use ***may/might/could*** + ***have*** + **past participle** to say that we think that it's possible that something happened or was true in the past.

I don't feel great. I **might have caught** a cold.

James didn't come to class on time. He **might have slept** through his alarm.

We use ***may/might*** + ***not*** + ***have*** + **past participle** when we think it's possible something didn't happen.

The storm isn't that bad. The football match **might not have been** cancelled.

We use ***must*** + ***have*** + **past participle** to say that we think that it's almost certain that something happened or was true in the past.

I **must have left** my coat at your house. I remember taking it off there.

We use ***can/could*** + ***not*** + ***have*** + **past participle** to dismiss possibilities in the past.

You **couldn't have left** your coat at my house because you were wearing it this afternoon.

We use ***should*** + ***have*** + **past participle** when someone didn't do something in the past, and we think it was a mistake or bad decision. We use it when it is too late to change the situation.

You **should have looked** in a few different shops before you bought your laptop.

We use ***should*** + ***not*** + ***have*** + **past participle** to say that someone did something in the past and we think it was a mistake or bad decision.

You **shouldn't have joined** the rowing team. You're afraid of the water!

Third conditional

Use **third conditional** to speculate about impossible situations in the past.

If + **past perfect**, ***would have*** + **past participle**

Affirmative	If I **had gone** with them, I **would have missed** my parents.
Negative	If my friend **hadn't invited** me to his house, I **wouldn't have had** this amazing experience.
Question	If I **had travelled** with them, what **would** it **have been** like?

We use the third conditional to talk about hypothetical situations in the past.

We **wouldn't have taken** a taxi if you **had told** us that there was a bus.

We can put either part of the sentence first without changing the meaning. When we begin with the conditional clause, we must use a comma to separate the parts. When we begin with the main clause, we don't use a comma.

Conditional clause — Main clause

If **I'd had** time, I **would have gone** shopping on Saturday.

Main clause — Conditional clause

I **would have gone** shopping on Saturday if **I'd had** time.

Do all exercises in your notebook

Workbook pages 93-96 111

Student's Book page 111

UNIT 5

Ancient monuments

archaeologist
build
circular
construction
drawing
Egypt
England
geometric
huge
path
pharaoh
primitive
pyramid
stone
Stonehenge
structure
tomb
tonnes

UFOs and aliens

alien
being
clue
conspiracy theory
controversy
crash
debris
documentary
fake
footage
military
newspaper reports
spaceship
truth
UFO

Mysteries

crop circles
evidence
fact
hoax
mysterious
pattern
phenomenon / phenomena
prove
theory

Do all exercises in your notebook

Workbook pages 102-104 119

19Student's Book page 118

2.51 2.52 2.53

Remind students to do all the exercises in their notebook

6 SUPER SLEUTHS

At the start of each unit and lesson, explain to the students what the objectives are.

Language objectives

Grammar

Verb patterns
- Students practise using verbs with specific grammatical patterns.

Tag questions: various tenses
- Students practise using positive and negative question tags in a variety of tenses.

Vocabulary

Phrasal verbs: *figure out, find out, give up, look for, look into*
- Students practise phrasal verbs in context.

Detective work: *alibi, clue, criminal, deduction, evidence, hunch, illegal, lawyer, private detective, red herring, sleuth, steal, suspect, unsolved, witness*
- Students use a range of vocabulary related to detective work.

Investigation: *analyse, check, conclusion, cover-up, disappearance, discuss, interview, missing, notice, police officer, solve, stick to*
- Students encounter vocabulary related to crime investigation.

Idioms and expressions

Coming to conclusions: *put two and two together, the penny drops, hit the nail on the head, jump to conclusions*
- Students look at idioms and expressions related to coming to conclusions in the context of a talk about Agatha Christie.

Recycled language

All tenses, Infinitives, *-ing* forms

Skills objectives

Speaking

- Students interpret a pie chart.
- Students discuss a case of vandalism.
- Students write and perform the end of a crime story.
- Students discuss a short courtroom drama.
- Students complete and perform a short interaction using idioms and expressions.

Pronunciation: Students practise rising and falling tag question intonation.

Pairwork: Students use various mediation techniques to role play an interview between a detective and a suspect.

Listening

- Students answer multiple-choice questions about a short detective story.
- Students listen complete a short report about three suspects in a case of vandalism.
- Students listen to the end of a crime story to compare against their own versions.
- Students listen and complete a short court-room drama.
- Students listen and complete fact files about two famous fictional detectives.

Reading

- Students read and analyse a detective story.
- Students guess the meanings of words in context and use them to complete sentences.
- Students order letters to make words to match their definitions.

Core values: Students reflect on the value of **withholding judgement** and different ways to ensure that they don't jump to conclusions.

Writing

- Students look at features of a detective story, including clues and direct speech.
- Students plan, write and check a short detective story.

Focus on verb forms

Remind students to do all the exercises in their notebook

Learning to learn tools

SPEAKING TOOLS Students practise reading from a text and holding it at chin-height to help project their voices.	LISTENING TOOLS Students practise preparing themselves for listening tasks by reading the multiple-choice options first.
READING TOOLS Students practise guessing the meanings of words from context.	WRITING TOOLS Students reflect on the value of well-placed clues in a detective story.

Project objectives: A mystery

Task 4 Students invent some false facts about their mystery.

Task 5 Students survey their classmates and create a pie chart.

Task 6 Students choose the best explanation for their mystery.

Audiovisual objectives

Vlog: Students watch and listen to Holly talk about riddles.

Culture: Students watch and listen to Holly talk about real-life superheroes.

Grammar animations: Students are presented with visual presentations of the unit grammar.

Key competences

LC **Linguistic**
pages 54-61

MST **Mathematical and Science and Technology**
pages 54-55, 57, 60

DC **Digital**
pages 54-55, 57, 61

SCC **Social and Civic**
pages 54-58, 61

CAE **Cultural awareness and expression**
pages 54, 56-57, 61

LL **Learning to learn**
pages 54, 56, 58, 60

IE **Sense of initiative and entrepreneurship**
pages 55, 57, 60

→ See pages 42-43 **Key competences**

CEFR Mediation

6.1 Explaining data in speech
Can interpret and describe information in diagrams.

6.2 Expressing a personal response to creative texts
Can briefly explain opinions provoked by a text and describe the personality of a character.

6.3 Analysis and criticism of creative texts
Can point to and explain the significance of events and the connection between them.

6.4 Processing text in speech
Can summarise the main points in written texts.

6.5 Relaying specific information in writing
Can write specific information from spoken texts.

Project Facilitating delicate situations and disagreement
Can demonstrate understanding of the issues in a disagreement and ask for confirmation or clarification.

Unit review Facilitating collaborative interaction with peers
Can formulate and respond to suggestions, ask whether people agree and propose alternatives.

Pairwork Processing text in speech
Can summarise the main content of simple texts.

→ See pages 30-33 **Mediation**

Remind students to do all the exercises in their notebook

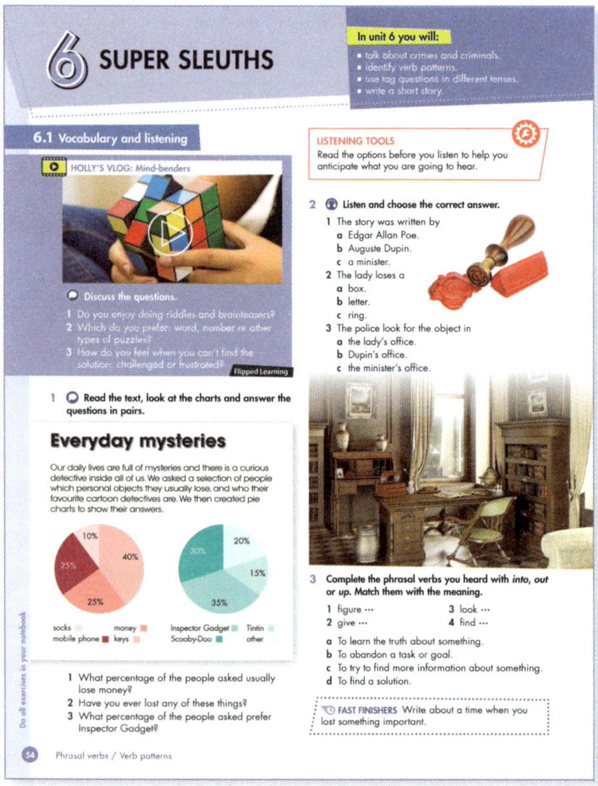
6 SUPER SLEUTHS

In unit 6 you will:
- talk about crimes and criminals.
- identify verb patterns.
- use tag questions in different tenses.
- write a short story.

6.1 Vocabulary and listening

HOLLY'S VLOG: Mind-benders

Discuss the questions.
1 Do you enjoy doing riddles and brainteasers?
2 Which do you prefer: word, number or other types of puzzles?
3 How do you feel when you can't find the solution: challenged or frustrated?

Flipped Learning

1 Read the text, look at the charts and answer the questions in pairs.

Everyday mysteries

Our daily lives are full of mysteries and there is a curious detective inside all of us. We asked a selection of people which personal objects they usually lose, and who their favourite cartoon detectives are. We then created pie charts to show their answers.

1 What percentage of the people asked usually lose money?
2 Have you ever lost any of these things?
3 What percentage of the people asked prefer Inspector Gadget?

LISTENING TOOLS
Read the options before you listen to help you anticipate what you are going to hear.

2 Listen and choose the correct answer.
1 The story was written by
a Edgar Allan Poe.
b Auguste Dupin.
c a minister.
2 The lady loses a
a box.
b letter.
c ring.
3 The police look for the object in
a the lady's office.
b Dupin's office.
c the minister's office.

3 Complete the phrasal verbs you heard with *into*, *out* or *up*. Match them with the meaning.
1 figure ··· 3 look ···
2 give ··· 4 find ···
a To learn the truth about something.
b To abandon a task or goal.
c To try to find more information about something.
d To find a solution.

FAST FINISHERS Write about a time when you lost something important.

Do all exercises in your notebook

54 Phrasal verbs / Verb patterns

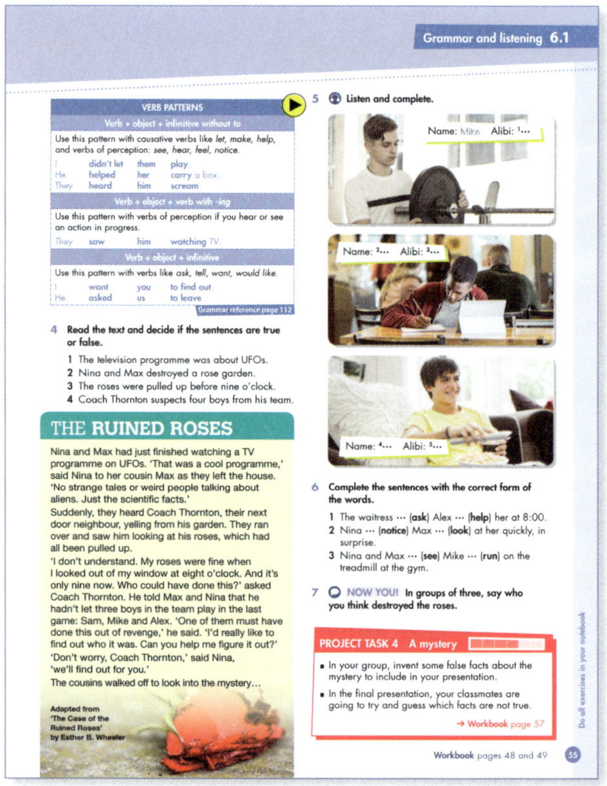
Grammar and listening 6.1

VERB PATTERNS

Verb + object + infinitive without *to*
Use this pattern with causative verbs like *let, make, help*, and verbs of perception: *see, hear, feel, notice*.
I didn't let them play
He helped her carry a box
They heard him scream

Verb + object + verb with *-ing*
Use this pattern with verbs of perception if you hear or see an action in progress.
They saw him watching TV

Verb + object + infinitive
Use this pattern with verbs like *ask, tell, want, would like*.
I want you to find out
He asked us to leave

Grammar reference page 112

4 Read the text and decide if the sentences are true or false.
1 The television programme was about UFOs.
2 Nina and Max destroyed a rose garden.
3 The roses were pulled up before nine o'clock.
4 Coach Thornton suspects four boys from his team.

THE RUINED ROSES

Nina and Max had just finished watching a TV programme on UFOs. 'That was a cool programme,' said Nina to her cousin Max as they left the house. 'No strange tales or weird people talking about aliens. Just the scientific facts.'
Suddenly, they heard Coach Thornton, their next door neighbour, yelling from his garden. They ran over and saw him looking at his roses, which had all been pulled up.
'I don't understand. My roses were fine when I looked out of my window at eight o'clock. And it's only nine now. Who could have done this?' asked Coach Thornton. He told Max and Nina that he hadn't let three boys in the team play in the last game: Sam, Mike and Alex. 'One of them must have done this out of revenge,' he said. 'I'd really like to find out who it was. Can you help me figure it out?'
'Don't worry, Coach Thornton,' said Nina, 'we'll find out for you.'
The cousins walked off to look into the mystery...

Adapted from 'The Case of the Ruined Roses' by Esther B. Wheeler

5 Listen and complete.

Name: Mike Alibi: [1]···
Name: [2]··· Alibi: [3]···
Name: [4]··· Alibi: [5]···

6 Complete the sentences with the correct form of the words.
1 The waitress ··· (ask) Alex ··· (help) her at 8:00.
2 Nina ··· (notice) Max ··· (look) at her quickly, in surprise.
3 Nina and Max ··· (see) Mike ··· (run) on the treadmill at the gym.

7 NOW YOU! In groups of three, say who you think destroyed the roses.

PROJECT TASK 4 A mystery
- In your group, invent some false facts about the mystery to include in your presentation.
- In the final presentation, your classmates are going to try and guess which facts are not true.

→ Workbook page 57

Do all exercises in your notebook

Workbook pages 48 and 49 55

ANSWER KEY

Pages 54-55

1 **1** 25%
2 *Student's own answers*
3 35%

2 **1** a **2** b **3** c

3 **1** out; d
2 up; b
3 into; c
4 out; a

4 **1** True
2 False
3 True
4 False

5 **1** The receptionist at the gym says he was there all the time.
2 Alex
3 The waitress at the café confirmed he was there.
4 Sam
5 He says he was at home, watching the TV programme about UFOs.

6 **1** asked; to help
2 noticed; look
3 saw; running

7 Sam stole the roses. When Nina asked him about the aliens, she was inventing something she knew wasn't in the video to check whether he had watched it. He fell for it, so he was lying.

Remind students to do all the exercises in their notebook

LESSON FOCUS

Grammar Verb patterns
Vocabulary Phrasal verbs
Listening Answering multiple-choice questions; Completing a short report
Speaking Interpreting a pie chart; Discussing a case of vandalism
Project task 4 Invent some false facts about the mystery

Resources

Teacher's i-solutions, Student's Book audio, Vlog and worksheet

Flipped Learning

HOLLY'S VLOG: Mind-benders

- Make sure to set up the **Flipped Learning** work with the students beforehand. **See pages 20-23 for complete Flipped Learning guidelines**.
- Ask students to put the **Flipped Learning worksheets** on their desks and walk around to check how many have completed the Flipped task.
- In pairs or small groups, ask students to compare and check the *Before you watch...* and *While you watch...* exercises on the worksheet.
- Show students **Holly's Vlog** and ask volunteers to provide correct answers and clarify any doubts other students may have.
- Choose three or four students to read aloud their answers to the *After you watch...* exercises on the worksheet and encourage some class discussion.
- Move straight to exercise 1 on page 54.

Warmer

Watch Holly's Vlog and discuss the questions with the whole class. If you don't have video facilities, simply discuss the questions.

1 Tell students they are going to read, interpret and discuss the results of two surveys about everyday mysteries. Elicit students' answers for question 2.

LISTENING TOOLS

Get students to read the **Listening tool** and tell them to apply it to the next exercise.

2 2.1 (See page 176 for transcripts) Tell students they are going to hear a short detective story. Let them read the questions and then play the audio twice if students need it.

3 Play the sentences containing the phrasal verbs to help the students guess their meanings.

FAST FINISHERS Students can complete this exercise alone or in pairs.

Flipped Learning

VERB PATTERNS

Draw students' attention to the **Grammar table**. Remind students that they can use this as a quick reference while completing the exercises.

Show students the **Grammar animation** and/or refer students to the **Grammar reference** on page 112 for further information on form and use.

➔ See page 23 for how to flip the **grammar lesson**

4 Tell students that they are going to read the first part of a short mystery. Let them compare their answers in pairs.

5 2.2 (See page 176 for transcripts) Tell students they are going to hear Nina and Max interview three suspects. Check that they know what an *alibi* is and play the audio for them to complete the information.

6 Tell students that the sentences are about the story they just heard and refer to them to the **Grammar table** to help them complete the sentences.

7 **NOW YOU!** Point out that Nina is the one who said she knew who it was. You may like to play the audio again to prompt them.

PROJECT TASK 4 A mystery

Put students in their groups to discuss what false facts to include in their mystery. Remind students that they need to keep their project notes together in their **Workbook** (page 57) or in their own notebook.

➔ See pages 24-27 **Projects**

FURTHER PRACTICE

Workbook pages 48-49
- **Grammar reference and practice** pages 89 and 95
- **Wordlist and exercises** pages 100 and 103

Remind students to do all the exercises in their notebook

6.2 Vocabulary and listening

6.2 Vocabulary and listening

1 Read the text and match the underlined words with their meanings.

Solving mysteries

Detective fiction is a popular literary genre. The traditional detective story includes an unsolved crime and clues that may turn out to be a red herring. Usually the sleuth solves the mystery using deduction, curiosity and often, a hunch. Detectives interview witnesses and ask each suspect to provide an alibi. The writer often includes misleading information so that the reader is surprised by the final solution.

1 A synonym for *detective*.
2 Information that helps to solve a mystery.
3 A guess or a feeling.
4 False evidence that diverts attention from the truth.
5 Someone who sees an event happen.
6 Evidence which shows that a person wasn't present at the time an illegal act was committed.

SPEAKING TOOLS

When you are reading something aloud to an audience, hold the text up at chin height. This will remind you to keep your head up so the audience can hear you.

2 Use the underlined words from exercise 1 to complete the text.

THE STOLEN WALLET

Samantha loved solving mysteries and considered herself to be a good, amateur 1…. One day, somebody broke her neighbour's window and stole his wallet. She found the wallet in the park the next day. She needed to find a suspect. Near the wallet, she found an earring that belonged to a girl from school, Heather. The earring turned out to be a 2…. Heather had an excellent 3… because she was visiting her aunt in another town when the wallet was stolen.

Next, she tried to find a 4…. A waiter from a nearby café said a boy in a green blazer had come in with a lot of money and bought food for all his friends the same day as the wallet was stolen. 'Those are great 5… !' said Samantha. Now she had a 6… that the criminal was a boy at her school.

3 NOW YOU! In groups of three, write and perform the end of *The Stolen Wallet*.

Before you write, plan the plot, setting, characters, props, etc.

4 Listen to the end of the story and answer the questions in your group.

1 Is this ending similar to the one you invented?
2 Why did the criminal steal the money?
3 How much money did he steal?
4 Were you surprised by the ending?

FAST FINISHERS Write the conversation that Samantha and Heather might have had.

Do all exercises in your notebook

56 Detective work / Tag Questions: various tenses

Grammar and vocabulary 6.2

TAG QUESTIONS: VARIOUS TENSES

Use **tag questions** to confirm agreement or ask for information.

Positive statement → negative tag	Negative statement → positive tag
He **went** to the police station, **didn't he?**	You **didn't take** all the money, **did you?**
They **had stolen** his wallet, **hadn't they?**	You **haven't seen** my camera, **have you?**
They **could** be the criminals, **couldn't they?**	She **couldn't have been** at the scene of the crime, **could she?**
She **was eating** in a restaurant when the money was stolen, **wasn't she?**	He **wasn't** really on holiday last week, **was he?**

Grammar reference page 112

5 Complete the conversation using tag questions. Listen and check.

Lawyer: Veronica Moore, you were the secretary of the Bluewater Tennis Club, 1…?
Suspect: Yes, I was.
Lawyer: A witness says that on the night of 20th February, he saw you carrying boxes and a big black bag out of the tennis club office. You haven't returned to the club since that day, 2…?
Suspect: No, I haven't. I quit because I hated the job. I was taking the things from my desk and my tennis rackets to my car.
Lawyer: But that wasn't all you took, 3…? You were hiding money in the tennis bag, 4…?
Suspect: I wasn't hiding anything. The manager of the tennis club often let me borrow money. I always gave it back.
Lawyer: Yes, but this time you had taken a very large amount, 5…? And you threatened my witness, 6…?
Suspect: Err, you can't prove anything though, 7…?
Lawyer: I'm afraid we can. What you didn't notice is that our witness swapped your bag with his. So actually, we're looking at all the evidence we need, 8…?

6 Answer the questions in pairs.

1 What is the name of the criminal?
2 What was the evidence?
3 How did the lawyer get the bag?
4 Why do you think the woman stole the money?

Pronunciation: tag question intonation

7 Listen and repeat. Does the tag question go up or down?

Asking a question:
1 You're coming to the party, **aren't you?**
2 He didn't steal the money, **did he?**

Confirming:
3 You've been to England, **haven't you?**
4 That film isn't very good, **is it?**

8 Choose the correct option and say the sentences.

1 I heard a noise downstairs! The wind made the door slam, **haven't** / **didn't** it?
2 It could be a thief, **couldn't** / **could** it?
3 That was the sound of a car leaving, **didn't** / **wasn't** it?
4 You haven't seen my mobile phone, **have** / **did** you?
5 They were together all day, **were** / **weren't** they?

PROJECT TASK 5 A mystery

- You are going to ask for your classmates' opinions about your mystery.
- Create a list of questions related to your mystery to ask your classmates. The questions need to have a limited list of answers (*yes*, *no* or *not sure*, for example).
- Create pie charts to show your classmates' answers.

→ Workbook page 57

Do all exercises in your notebook

Workbook pages 50 and 51 57

ANSWER KEY

Pages 56-57

1 1 sleuth 2 clues 3 hunch 4 red herring 5 witness 6 alibi

2 1 sleuth 2 red herring 3 alibi 4 witness 5 clues 6 hunch

3 *Student's own answers*

4
1 *Student's own answers*
2 He stole the money to buy snacks for a group of his classmates because he wanted them to like him.
3 30 euros
4 *Student's own answers*

5 1 weren't you 2 have you 3 was it 4 weren't you 5 hadn't you 6 didn't you 7 can you 8 aren't we

6
1 Veronica Moore
2 The bag of money that the criminal was going to steal
3 The witness had swapped the suspect's bag.
4 *Suggested answer:* She stole the money because she hated the job and she often borrowed money from the manager of the tennis club, so she thought it wouldn't matter.

7 1 up 2 up 3 down 4 down

8 1 didn't 2 couldn't 3 wasn't 4 have 5 weren't

Remind students to do all the exercises in their notebook

LESSON FOCUS

Grammar Tag questions: various tenses
Vocabulary Detective work
Listening Comparing different versions of a story; Completing a short courtroom drama
Speaking Writing and performing the ending of a story; Discussing a short courtroom drama
Project task 5 Survey classmates and create a pie chart
Resources
Teacher's i-solutions, Student's Book audio

Warmer

Put students in pairs and ask one of them to turn away from the board. Tell them that you are going to write a sentence with a verb pattern on the board. The student facing the board must start a conversation with their partner in which they use the sentence. Suggested sentences: *They didn't let me play; We helped her do it; I wanted you to know.*

1 Ask students if they read crime fiction and what kind of plots or plot devices crime fiction novels usually have.

2 Tell students they are going to read the beginning of a short detective story that they will later write and perform the ending of. Let them complete the exercise.

SPEAKING TOOLS

Get students to read the **Speaking tool** and tell them to apply it in their performance in exercise 3.

3 NOW YOU! Give students a time limit and encourage them to make sure their endings are consistent with the story so far.

4 2.3 (See page 177 for transcripts) Ask students which version of the story they liked best and why.

FAST FINISHERS Students can complete this exercise alone or in pairs.

TAG QUESTIONS: VARIOUS TENSES

Flipped Learning

Draw students' attention to the **Grammar table**. Remind students that they can use this as a quick reference while completing the exercises.

Show students the **Grammar animation** and/or refer students to the **Grammar reference** on page 112 for further information on form and use.

→ See page 23 for how to flip the **grammar lesson**

5 2.4 (See page 177 for transcripts) Refer students to the **Grammar table** as they do the exercise. Then play the audio for them to check their answers.

6 After students have done the exercise, elicit a range of possible motives.

Pronunciation

7 2.5 (See page 177 for transcripts) You could play the audio through once, to see if students can hear the difference and the effect it has, before playing it again for them to listen and repeat.

8 To extend this exercise, get students to write a short dialogue with one of the sentences from the exercise. Tell them to decide if the intonation goes up or down and get them to perform their dialogues.

PROJECT TASK 5 A mystery

Put students in their groups to write and perform the survey, and to report the results. Remind students that they need to keep their project notes together in their **Workbook** (page 57) or in their own notebook.

→ See pages 24-27 **Projects**

FURTHER PRACTICE

Workbook pages 50-51
- **Grammar reference and practice** pages 89 and 95
- **Wordlist and exercises** pages 100 and 103

Vocabulary and Grammar worksheets available to download from the **Richmond***Learning***Platform**

→ See pages 38-39 **Mixed-ability classes**

Remind students to do all the exercises in their notebook

CONTINUOUS ASSESSMENT Students can talk about detective work and use tag questions in various tenses.

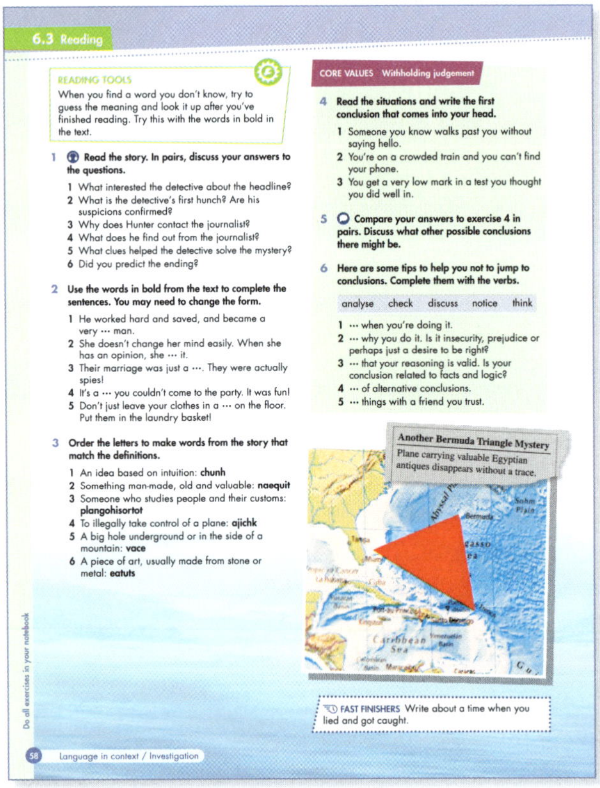

6.3 Reading

READING TOOLS
When you find a word you don't know, try to guess the meaning and look it up after you've finished reading. Try this with the words in bold in the text.

1 Read the story. In pairs, discuss your answers to the questions.
1 What interested the detective about the headline?
2 What is the detective's first hunch? Are his suspicions confirmed?
3 Why does Hunter contact the journalist?
4 What does he find out from the journalist?
5 What clues helped the detective solve the mystery?
6 Did you predict the ending?

2 Use the words in bold from the text to complete the sentences. You may need to change the form.
1 He worked hard and saved, and became a very ··· man.
2 She doesn't change her mind easily. When she has an opinion, she ··· it.
3 Their marriage was just a ···. They were actually spies!
4 It's a ··· you couldn't come to the party. It was fun!
5 Don't just leave your clothes in a ··· on the floor. Put them in the laundry basket!

3 Order the letters to make words from the story that match the definitions.
1 An idea based on intuition: **chunh**
2 Something man-made, old and valuable: **naequit**
3 Someone who studies people and their customs: **plangohisortot**
4 To illegally take control of a plane: **ajichk**
5 A big hole underground or in the side of a mountain: **vace**
6 A piece of art, usually made from stone or metal: **eatuts**

CORE VALUES Withholding judgement

4 Read the situations and write the first conclusion that comes into your head.
1 Someone you know walks past you without saying hello.
2 You're on a crowded train and you can't find your phone.
3 You get a very low mark in a test you thought you did well in.

5 Compare your answers to exercise 4 in pairs. Discuss what other possible conclusions there might be.

6 Here are some tips to help you not to jump to conclusions. Complete them with the verbs.

analyse check discuss notice think

1 ··· when you're doing it.
2 ··· why you do it. Is it insecurity, prejudice or perhaps just a desire to be right?
3 ··· that your reasoning is valid. Is your conclusion related to facts and logic?
4 ··· of alternative conclusions.
5 ··· things with a friend you trust.

Another Bermuda Triangle Mystery
Plane carrying valuable Egyptian antiques disappears without a trace.

FAST FINISHERS Write about a time when you lied and got caught.

Do all exercises in your notebook

58 Language in context / Investigation

Reading 6.3

A SUSPICIOUS MYSTERY

The headline caught Detective David Hunter's attention – *Airplane carrying priceless antiques goes missing in the Bermuda Triangle.*

He had always been interested in disappearances in the Bermuda Triangle and suspected that some of them were **cover-ups** for crimes. He had a hunch that there was something strange about this story. Among the passengers on the plane was a **wealthy** businesswoman who had just acquired the precious cargo, and an amateur anthropologist.

'Hmm – a suspect! The anthropologist would probably know how much those treasures are worth,' Hunter thought, and he decided to contact the journalist who had written the story.

The journalist opened the door, and the detective introduced himself: 'David Hunter, private detective.' 'Dab Pike,' the journalist replied, 'what can I do for you?'

'In your Bermuda Triangle story, you mentioned that there was an anthropologist on board.' 'Yes, Ignatius Wittington. Interesting man. It's a **shame** he's disappeared, really.'
'Ah, so you've met him?' asked Hunter.

'Well, the acquisition of the antiques was a story in itself,' said Pike. 'I was there before the flight to interview Philomena Stock, the woman who had just acquired the collection. Wittington was there and I spoke to him briefly too.'

'Did he seem to know anything about the collection?' Hunter asked. 'Yes, Ignatius knew all about it.' The journalist paused. A light seemed to go on in his head. 'You think Ignatius Wittington might have... what... hijacked the plane to steal the antiques?!'
'I'm a detective, Mr Pike. We have to look into all the possibilities,' said Hunter. Pike gave Hunter a look that suggested the detective was wasting his time. 'I think you'll find it's just another mysterious Bermuda Triangle disappearance. Now, if you'll excuse me, I have a flight to catch'.

Upon returning to his office, Hunter looked up the coordinates for the plane's last known location and saw that there was a small island nearby. Following his hunch, he decided to go there immediately. As he approached the island by boat, he heard cries for help coming from inside a cave. He ran in and found a huge **pile** of Egyptian antiques, Ignatius Wittington and Philomena Stock tied up, and guarding over them, Dab Pike.

'Mr Pike. I thought I might find you here. Which is why I brought a few friends with me,' said Hunter, pointing at the three police officers behind him. Pike looked shocked, so Hunter explained. 'I began to suspect you when you said you knew about the antiques before the flight. Later, you tried to convince me to **stick to** the Bermuda Triangle theory. Finally, I noticed a golden statue of a pharaoh in your office... much like that one there!' The detective pointed to an identical golden statue on top of the pile of antiques.

And so, the mystery was solved. Dab Pike was sent to prison and Hunter returned to his office in New York, happy in the knowledge of a job well done.

Do all exercises in your notebook

Workbook pages 52 and 53 59

ANSWER KEY

Pages 58-59

1
1 He had always been interested in disappearances in the Bermuda Triangle.
2 His first hunch is that there is something strange about the story and that the anthropologist on the plane is a possible suspect. His suspicion that there is something strange about the story is confirmed. His suspicion that the anthropologist is the criminal is not confirmed.
3 To find out more about his suspect: the anthropologist.
4 He finds out that the anthropologist was called Ignatius Wittington and that the woman who had acquired the treasures was called Philomena Stock. He also finds out that the journalist had spoken to both of them before the flight and that Wittington knew all about the collection.
5 The journalist told the detective he knew about the antiques before the flight, then tried to convince him to stick to the Bermuda Triangle theory. The detective also noticed a golden statue on the journalist's bookshelf.
6 *Student's own answers*

2
1 wealthy
2 sticks to
3 cover-up
4 shame
5 pile

3
1 hunch
2 antique
3 anthropologist
4 hijack
5 cave
6 statue

4 *Student's own answers*

5 *Student's own answers*

6
1 Notice
2 Analyse
3 Check
4 Think
5 Discuss

Remind students to do all the exercises in their notebook

LESSON FOCUS

Language in context Investigation

Core values Withholding judgement

Resources

Teacher's i-solutions, Student's Book audio

→ See pages 36-37 **Literature**

Warmer

Put students in pairs and ask each student to write four tag questions to ask their partner. Two should be about things that they are fairly sure of and two should be about things they suspect are true, but are not sure. Ask which way the intonation should go (down for the first two and up for the last two) and tell them to ask each other their questions.

READING TOOLS

Tell students to read the **Reading tool**. Ask them if they already do this and how much it helps. Tell them to apply it in exercises 2 and 3.

1 2.6 (See page 177 for transcripts) To add to the suspense of the story, you could get students to close their books and listen to the audio, stopping at key points in the story to ask the questions before they continue.

2 For any words that students can't guess, prompt with questions about the context to help them.

3 You could give students the first letter of each word to help them.

CORE VALUES Withholding judgement

4 To make sure students write the first thing that comes into their head, get them to close their books and read out the situations one by one, giving them a short time limit to complete each one.

5 Elicit some of the students' first impressions and then ask them to think of at least two other options for each. Ask if they think their first impressions were more cynical than the ideas they came up with afterwards.

6 You could point out that we are programmed to jump to conclusions and that sometimes these can be right, but that we should try to recognise patterns of incorrect judgements and be prepared to rethink our conclusions.

FAST FINISHERS Students can complete this exercise alone or in pairs.

FURTHER PRACTICE

Workbook pages 52-53

Remind students to do all the exercises in their notebook

CONTINUOUS ASSESSMENT Students can understand vocabulary for investigation in a detective story.

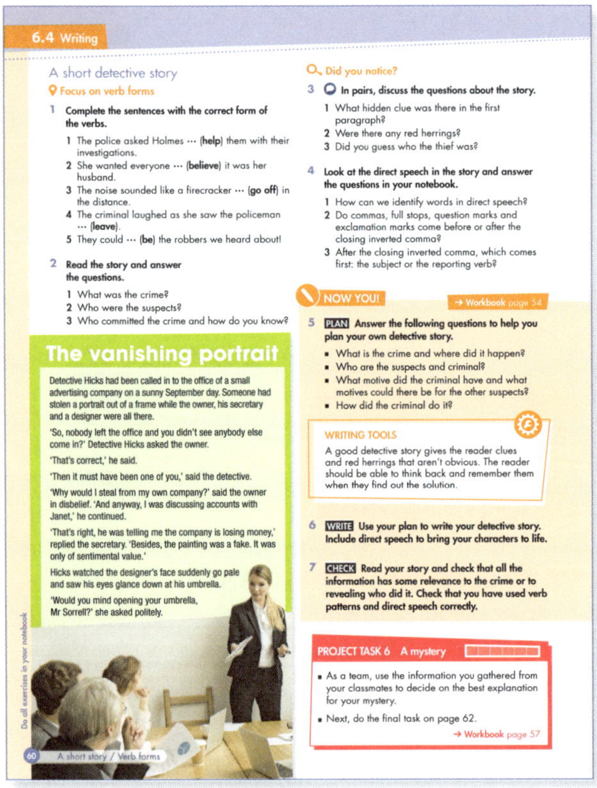

6.4 Writing

A short detective story

Focus on verb forms

1 **Complete the sentences with the correct form of the verbs.**

1 The police asked Holmes ··· (**help**) them with their investigations.
2 She wanted everyone ··· (**believe**) it was her husband.
3 The noise sounded like a firecracker ··· (**go off**) in the distance.
4 The criminal laughed as she saw the policeman ··· (**leave**).
5 They could ··· (**be**) the robbers we heard about!

2 **Read the story and answer the questions.**

1 What was the crime?
2 Who were the suspects?
3 Who committed the crime and how do you know?

The vanishing portrait

Detective Hicks had been called in to the office of a small advertising company on a sunny September day. Someone had stolen a portrait out of a frame while the owner, his secretary and a designer were all there.

'So, nobody left the office and you didn't see anybody else come in?' Detective Hicks asked the owner.

'That's correct,' he said.

'Then it must have been one of you,' said the detective.

'Why would I steal from my own company?' said the owner in disbelief. 'And anyway, I was discussing accounts with Janet,' he continued.

'That's right, he was telling me the company is losing money,' replied the secretary. 'Besides, the painting was a fake. It was only of sentimental value.'

Hicks watched the designer's face suddenly go pale and saw his eyes glance down at his umbrella.

'Would you mind opening your umbrella, Mr Sorrell?' she asked politely.

Did you notice?

3 **In pairs, discuss the questions about the story.**

1 What hidden clue was there in the first paragraph?
2 Were there any red herrings?
3 Did you guess who the thief was?

4 **Look at the direct speech in the story and answer the questions in your notebook.**

1 How can we identify words in direct speech?
2 Do commas, full stops, question marks and exclamation marks come before or after the closing inverted comma?
3 After the closing inverted comma, which comes first: the subject or the reporting verb?

NOW YOU! → Workbook page 54

5 PLAN **Answer the following questions to help you plan your own detective story.**

- What is the crime and where did it happen?
- Who are the suspects and criminal?
- What motive did the criminal have and what motives could there be for the other suspects?
- How did the criminal do it?

WRITING TOOLS

A good detective story gives the reader clues and red herrings that aren't obvious. The reader should be able to think back and remember them when they find out the solution.

6 WRITE **Use your plan to write your detective story. Include direct speech to bring your characters to life.**

7 CHECK **Read your story and check that all the information has some relevance to the crime or to revealing who did it. Check that you have used verb patterns and direct speech correctly.**

PROJECT TASK 6 A mystery

- As a team, use the information you gathered from your classmates to decide on the best explanation for your mystery.
- Next, do the final task on page 62.

→ Workbook page 57

Do all exercises in your notebook

60 A short story / Verb forms

ANSWER KEY

Pages 60

1 **1** to help **2** to believe **3** going off **4** leaving **5** be

2 **1** A portrait has been stolen.
2 The owner of an advertising company, his secretary and a designer.
3 The designer committed the crime. His face goes pale when he hears that the painting was a fake and he looks at his umbrella, where he has hidden the painting.

3 **1** The writer says it is a sunny day, which means the designer doesn't need an umbrella.
2 The company is losing money.
3 *Student's own answers*

4 **1** They're inside inverted commas.
2 Before
3 The subject comes before the verb if it's a pronoun and afterwards if not.

5 *Student's own answers*

6 *Student's own answers*

7 *Student's own answers*

FURTHER PRACTICE

Workbook page 54

LESSON FOCUS

Focus on Verb forms

Writing A short detective story

Project task 6 Choose the best explanation for the mystery

Resources

Teacher's i-solutions

Warmer

Give a spoken summary of one of the stories in the unit and see if students can remember the story. Students continue the activity in pairs or small groups.

Focus on verb forms

1 Point out that they are all patterns students have come across in the last two units.

2 Ask students to compare their answers in pairs and then continue the next exercise before you correct their answers.

Did you notice?

3 Remind students of the meaning of *red herring* from exercise 1 on page 56 of the **Student's Book**, and ask them what they liked and what they didn't like about the story.

4 Give students time to find examples of each and compare answers in pairs.

5 PLAN Tell students that they can research an already existing story if they want to, but that they must write it in their own words. Once they have finished their plan, encourage them to talk it through with a partner.

WRITING TOOLS

Get students to read the **Writing tool** and point out that this is difficult to do but makes for a better story.

6 WRITE Before students start writing, make a checklist on the board of any elements related to content, structure, language and style that they should bear in mind.

7 CHECK Once students have checked their own stories, they can swap with a partner and check theirs.

PROJECT TASK 6 A mystery

Put students back into their groups for this task. Tell students that they need to keep their project notes together in their **Workbook** (page 57) or in their own notebook.

→ See pages 24-27 **Projects**

Remind students to do all the exercises in their notebook

 CONTINUOUS ASSESSMENT Students can use appropriate verb forms to write a short detective story.

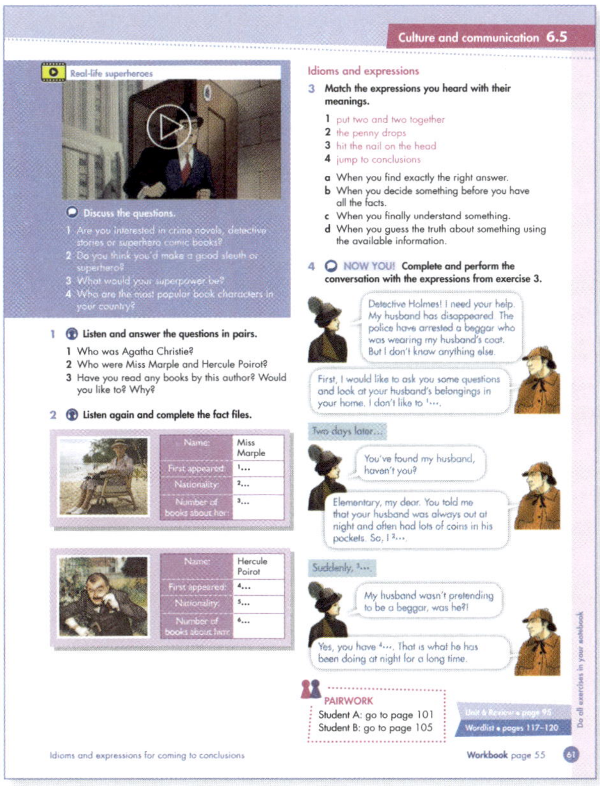

Culture and communication 6.5

Real-life superheroes

Discuss the questions.

1 Are you interested in crime novels, detective stories or superhero comic books?
2 Do you think you'd make a good sleuth or superhero?
3 What would your superpower be?
4 Who are the most popular book characters in your country?

1 Listen and answer the questions in pairs.

1 Who was Agatha Christie?
2 Who were Miss Marple and Hercule Poirot?
3 Have you read any books by this author? Would you like to? Why?

2 Listen again and complete the fact files.

Name:	Miss Marple
First appeared:	1...
Nationality:	2...
Number of books about her:	3...

Name:	Hercule Poirot
First appeared:	4...
Nationality:	5...
Number of books about him:	6...

Idioms and expressions

3 Match the expressions you heard with their meanings.

1 put two and two together
2 the penny drops
3 hit the nail on the head
4 jump to conclusions

a When you find exactly the right answer.
b When you decide something before you have all the facts.
c When you finally understand something.
d When you guess the truth about something using the available information.

4 NOW YOU! Complete and perform the conversation with the expressions from exercise 3.

Detective Holmes! I need your help. My husband has disappeared. The police have arrested a beggar who was wearing my husband's coat. But I don't know anything else.

First, I would like to ask you some questions and look at your husband's belongings in your home. I don't like to 1....

Two days later...

You've found my husband, haven't you?

Elementary, my dear. You told me that your husband was always out at night and often had lots of coins in his pockets. So, I 2....

Suddenly, 3....

My husband wasn't pretending to be a beggar, was he?!

Yes, you have 4.... That is what he has been doing at night for a long time.

PAIRWORK
Student A: go to page 101
Student B: go to page 105

Unit 6 Review • page 95
Wordlist • pages 117–120

Do all exercises in your notebook

Idioms and expressions for coming to conclusions

Workbook page 55 61

ANSWER KEY

Page 61

1 **1** She was one of the most important authors in the history of detective fiction.
2 They were two detectives that featured in her novels.
3 *Student's own answers*

2 **1** 1927
2 English
3 12 novels (and 20 short stories)
4 1920
5 Belgian
6 30 novels (and nearly 60 short stories)

3 **1** d **2** c **3** a **4** b

4 **1** jump to conclusions
2 put two and two together
3 the penny dropped
4 hit the nail on the head

FURTHER PRACTICE AND UNIT ASSESSMENT

Unit 6 Review Student's Book page 95
Workbook page 55
- **Reflect on your learning** page 55
- **Grammar reference and practice** pages 88 and 95
- **Wordlist and exercises** pages 100 and 103

Tests available to download and edit from the **Richmond***Learning***Platform**

➔ See pages 40-41 **Assessment**

LESSON FOCUS

Idioms and expressions Coming to conclusions
Listening Completing fact files about detectives
Speaking Completing and performing a short interaction

Resources

Teacher's i-solutions, Student's Book audio, Culture video and worksheet

Real-life superheroes

Video and worksheet available on the Richmond*Learning*Platform

- In pairs, ask students to complete the *What I know...* exercises on the **Culture video worksheet**.
- Show students the **Culture video** and ask them to complete the *What I learned...* exercises on the worksheet.
- In pairs, students compare answers.
- In small groups, tell students to complete the *What I wonder...* exercises on the worksheet.

Warmer

Watch the **Culture video** and discuss the questions with the whole class. If you don't have video facilities, simply discuss the questions.

1 2.7 (See page 178 for transcripts) Ask if students can answer any of the questions before listening and then ask them to take notes to compare in pairs. You could get them to do this and the next exercise at the same time, and go through the answers together afterwards.

2 2.8 (See page 178 for transcripts) Remind students they are listening for quite specific information for the fact files and play the audio again if necessary.

Idioms and expressions

3 Say or write the sentences with the expressions in them from exercise 2 for students to guess their meanings.

4 NOW YOU! Ask if students recognise the detective in the illustration and then let them complete the conversation. Encourage them to read as little as possible as they perform the conversation. You could get students to perform the conversation without their books and with two prompters reminding them of their lines.

PAIRWORK Student's Book pages 101 and 105
See **Teacher's Book** page 126 for more information.
➔ See pages 30-33 **Mediation**

Remind students to do all the exercises in their notebook

CONTINUOUS ASSESSMENT Students can use idioms and expressions for coming to conclusions.

Unit 6 Review

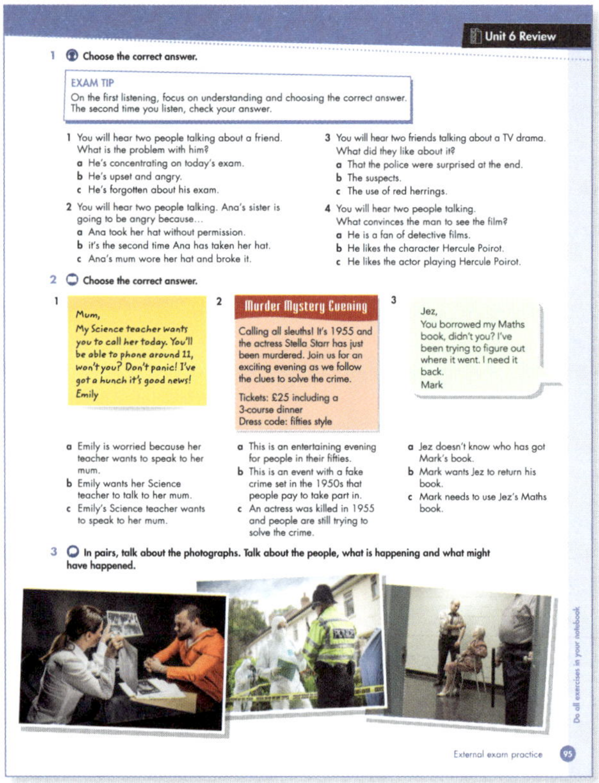

Unit 6 Review

1 Choose the correct answer.

EXAM TIP
On the first listening, focus on understanding and choosing the correct answer. The second time you listen, check your answer.

1 You will hear two people talking about a friend. What is the problem with him?
a He's concentrating on today's exam.
b He's upset and angry.
c He's forgotten about his exam.

2 You will hear two people talking. Ana's sister is going to be angry because…
a Ana took her hat without permission.
b it's the second time Ana has taken her hat.
c Ana's mum wore her hat and broke it.

3 You will hear two friends talking about a TV drama. What did they like about it?
a That the police were surprised at the end.
b The suspects.
c The use of red herrings.

4 You will hear two people talking. What convinces the man to see the film?
a He is a fan of detective films.
b He likes the character Hercule Poirot.
c He likes the actor playing Hercule Poirot.

2 Choose the correct answer.

1
Mum,
My Science teacher wants you to call her today. You'll be able to phone around 11, won't you? Don't panic! I've got a hunch it's good news!
Emily

a Emily is worried because her teacher wants to speak to her mum.
b Emily wants her Science teacher to talk to her mum.
c Emily's Science teacher wants to speak to her mum.

2
Murder Mystery Evening
Calling all sleuths! It's 1955 and the actress Stella Starr has just been murdered. Join us for an exciting evening as we follow the clues to solve the crime.
Tickets: £25 including a 3-course dinner
Dress code: fifties style

a This is an entertaining evening for people in their fifties.
b This is an event with a fake crime set in the 1950s that people pay to take part in.
c An actress was killed in 1955 and people are still trying to solve the crime.

3
Jez,
You borrowed my Maths book, didn't you? I've been trying to figure out where it went. I need it back.
Mark

a Jez doesn't know who has got Mark's book.
b Mark wants Jez to return his book.
c Mark needs to use Jez's Maths book.

3 In pairs, talk about the photographs. Talk about the people, what is happening and what might have happened.

Do all exercises in your notebook

External exam practice 95

Student's Book page 95

ANSWER KEY

See page 183 for transcripts

1 2.36
1 a
2 a
3 c
4 c

2 **1** c
2 b
3 b

3 *Student's own answers*

Pairwork

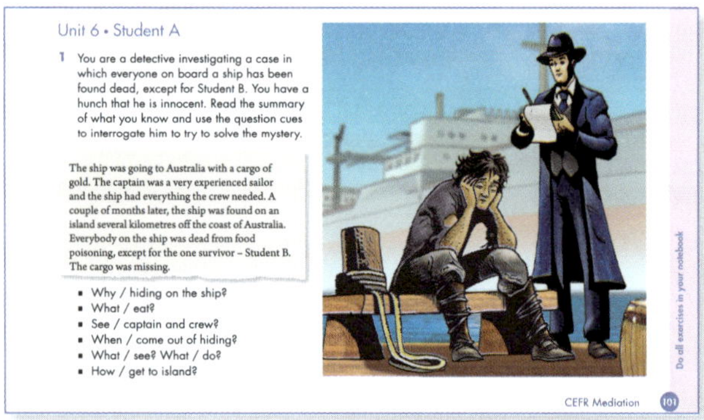

Unit 6 • Student A

1 You are a detective investigating a case in which everyone on board a ship has been found dead, except for Student B. You have a hunch that he is innocent. Read the summary of what you know and use the question cues to interrogate him to try to solve the mystery.

The ship was going to Australia with a cargo of gold. The captain was a very experienced sailor and the ship had everything the crew needed. A couple of months later, the ship was found on an island several kilometres off the coast of Australia. Everybody on the ship was dead from food poisoning, except for the one survivor – Student B. The cargo was missing.

- Why / hiding on the ship?
- What / eat?
- See / captain and crew?
- When / come out of hiding?
- What / see? What / do?
- How / get to island?

Do all exercises in your notebook

CEFR Mediation 101

Student's Book page 101

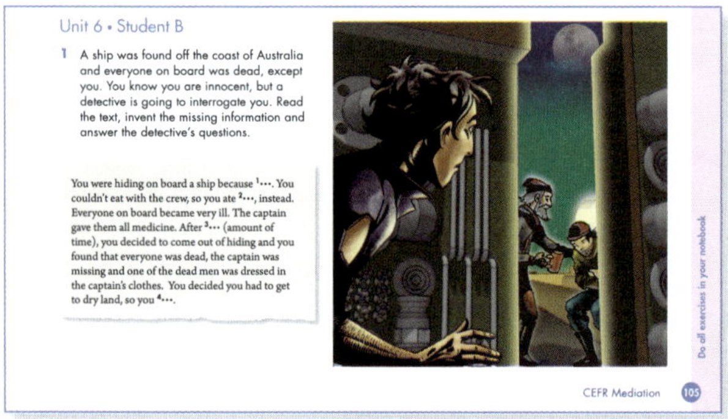

Unit 6 • Student B

1 A ship was found off the coast of Australia and everyone on board was dead, except you. You know you are innocent, but a detective is going to interrogate you. Read the text, invent the missing information and answer the detective's questions.

You were hiding on board a ship because [1]…. You couldn't eat with the crew, so you ate [2]…, instead. Everyone on board became very ill. The captain gave them all medicine. After [3]… (amount of time), you decided to come out of hiding and you found that everyone was dead, the captain was missing and one of the dead men was dressed in the captain's clothes. You decided you had to get to dry land, so you [4]….

Do all exercises in your notebook

CEFR Mediation 105

Student's Book page 105

CEFR MEDIATION DESCRIPTOR

- **Encouraging conceptual talk**
  Students can ask questions to invite people to clarify their reasoning.

- **Interpreting clues**
  Tell students that they have information for two different roles in the same case: Student A is the detective and B the suspect. Give them time to prepare their roles before they start.

Remind students to do all the exercises in their notebook

Unit 6 Grammar reference

Verb patterns

Verb + object + infinitive without *to*			
Use this pattern with causative verbs like *let, make, help,* and verbs of perception: *see, hear, feel, notice.*			
I	didn't let	them	play.
He	helped	her	carry a box.
They	heard	him	scream.
Verb + object + verb with -*ing*			
Use this pattern with verbs of perception if you hear or see an action in progress.			
They	saw	him	watching TV.
Verb + object + infinitive			
Use this pattern with verbs like *ask, tell, want, would like.*			
I	want	you	to find out.
He	asked	us	to leave.

The verb ***let*** is never followed by the infinitive with ***to***.
My mother **let me go** to a concert alone last weekend.
NOT ~~My mother let me to go to a concert alone last weekend.~~

Help is a causative verb which can be followed by the infinitive without ***to***, or the infinitive with ***to***. There is no difference in meaning, but it sounds more formal with ***to***.
I **helped** my grandfather **to water** his plants.
I **helped** my grandfather **water** his plants.

Apart from object pronouns (**me**, **you**, **him**, **her**, **it**, **us**, **you** and **them**), these verb patterns are often used in combination with common indefinite pronouns like ***anybody/anyone***, ***somebody/someone***, ***everybody/everyone***, ***nobody/no one***, ***either/neither*** and ***others***.
She **wanted everybody** to sing along.
I **saw somebody** waiting for the bus.
I never **let others** tell me what to do.

Tag questions: various tenses

Use **tag questions** to confirm agreement or ask for information.

Positive statement → negative tag	Negative statement → positive tag
He **went** to the police station, **didn't he**?	You **didn't take** all the money, **did you**?
They **had stolen** his wallet, **hadn't they**?	You **haven't seen** my camera, **have you**?
They **could** be the criminals, **couldn't they**?	She **couldn't have been** at the scene of the crime, **could she**?
She **was eating** in a restaurant when the money was stolen, **wasn't she**?	He **wasn't** really on holiday last week, **was he**?

We use tag questions to check answers when we think the statement might be true.
You live in London, **don't you**?
Your parents bought a new car, **didn't they**?

The tag questions reflect the grammar of the statement that precede it. Here are some rules for forming question tags and some examples.
Positive statements have negative tags.
Geena was there, **wasn't she**?
Negative statements have positive tags.
She doesn't know we're here, **does she**?

We use an auxiliary verb or ***be*** in the same tense as the statement.
You won the game, **didn't you**?
We always use a pronoun in the **tag**, not a name or noun.
Jenny'll help us, won't **she**?

Do all exercises in your notebook

112 **Workbook** pages 93-96

Student's Book page 112

Wordlist

UNIT 6

Phrasal verbs

figure out
find out
give up
look for
look into

Detective work

alibi
clue
criminal
deduction
evidence
hunch
illegal
lawyer
private detective
red herring
sleuth
steal
suspect
unsolved
witness

Investigation

analyse
check
conclusion
cover-up
disappearance
discuss
interview
missing
notice
police officer
solve
stick to

Do all exercises in your notebook

Workbook pages 102-104 119

Student's Book page 119
2.51 2.52 2.53

Remind students to do all the exercises in their notebook

PROJECT: A mystery

PROJECT: A mystery

RECAP

- In this project, you have researched information and opinions about a famous mystery. You have surveyed your classmates and decided on a likely explanation.
- In **units 5 and 6** you talked about famous mysteries such as the Loch Ness Monster. You learnt how to use modal verbs for speculation and you also practised using tag questions and phrasal verbs such as 'to figure out'. You practised expressions like 'Personally, I think that...', you read an article about crop circles, and you learnt idioms about secrets.
- Now you are ready to present a mystery to the class!

TASK 1 Write about two mysteries and their possible explanations.

TASK 2 Write arguments against your team members' explanations.

TASK 3 Choose and research one of the mysteries.

TASK 4 Invent some false facts about the mystery.

TASK 5 Survey your classmates and create pie charts.

TASK 6 Choose the best explanation for your mystery.

FINAL TASK: Present your mystery

- Decide which software you are going to use to present your mystery to the class.
- Think about the other elements would you like to include, e.g. music, handouts, props, etc.
- Decide who will present each slide of the presentation.
- Write questions to ask your audience at the end of the presentation.

USEFUL EXPRESSIONS

- Our presentation is about…
- Now we're going to talk about…
- In this slide we can see…
- According to…
- Are there any questions?

21ST CENTURY SKILLS

Critical thinking

Thanks to modern communication technology, we have access to unlimited amounts of information, ideas and opinions. Because of this, it is very important that we analyse the information we receive. Thinking critically about who created the information and what their motive might be is a good place to start. Also, make sure to question controversial 'facts' and find other sources that support what you have read.

Do all exercises in your notebook

62 Workbook pages 56 and 57

Project • Units 5 and 6

EVALUATION

Answer the questions in your team.

1 What difficulties did you have? How did you solve them?
2 Was it easy for a group of people to work on one document?
3 List some elements from other teams' presentations that you would like to use in the future.
4 Do you prefer giving presentations with or without digital support?

GO BEYOND

PRESENTATION SKILLS

In the past, presentations in schools and businesses were delivered using blackboards or paper flip charts. As technology developed, people started to use overhead projectors and interactive whiteboards. This way of presenting material is a great way to engage the audience and clearly express your ideas. Also, the presenter can send the digital presentation to the audience afterwards.

Here are some tips for creating excellent presentations:

- Research the topic first; work on the presentation later. Don't waste your time making poor content look great.
- Don't include a lot of text on the screen; only use key words or short sentences.
- Choose a large, clear font and contrasting colours for the background and text.
- Look at your audience, make eye contact and make sure they can hear you. Don't look at the screen too much.
- Save your presentation on several devices and email it to yourself to avoid last-minute problems.

Answer the questions in pairs.

1 Do you think teachers should use lots of digital presentations?
2 What are the advantages and disadvantages of presenting information in this way?
3 How do you think presentations will be given in the future?
4 Think of a few more tips for creating excellent presentations.

Do all exercises in your notebook

63

Workbook project task notes

PROJECT: A mystery

Project • Units 5 and 6

TASK 1

Mystery 1: ____________________

Mystery 2: ____________________

→ Student's book page 47

TASK 2

Team members:

______ ______ ______

Counterarguments: ____________________

→ Student's book page 49

TASK 3

Our chosen mystery: ____________________

→ Student's book page 52

56 Project task notes

TASK 4

False facts: ____________________

→ Student's book page 55

TASK 5

Ideas for questions: ____________________

→ Student's book page 57

TASK 6

The best explanation: ____________________

→ Student's book page 60

FINAL TASK

Software we will use: ____________________

Other elements to include: ____________________

My task: ____________________

→ Student's book page 62

Project task notes 57

Remind students to do all the exercises in their notebook

PROJECT FOCUS

➔ See pages 24-27 **Projects**

Skills

- Collaborate to prepare and give a presentation about a mystery
- Write paragraphs describing mysteries and speculating about explanations
- Collaborate to write arguments against the explanations
- Research and write about a mystery
- Write some false facts about the mystery
- Carry out a survey and create pie charts to show the findings
- Reach consensus on an explanation using the survey data
- Discuss evaluations of the project
- Read and discuss a text related to the project

CEFR mediation

Facilitating delicate situations and disagreements

Can demonstrate understanding of the key issues in a disagreement on a familiar topic and make simple requests for confirmation and/or clarification.

➔ See pages 30-33 **Mediation**

Preparation Remind students to bring their work from tasks 1-6 and their notes from the **Workbook** project task notes (pages 20-21) or their own notebook. Bring cue cards if needed for the presentation. Have students bring in their self-assessment diaries if you decided that you wanted them to keep one.

RECAP

Put students in their teams and read through the **Recap** as a class. Draw their attention to the project tasks and the unit objectives and ask which task helped achieve which objectives. Make sure they have all the materials and notes that they need (see **Preparation**) for the **Final task**.

FINAL TASK: Present your mystery

Tell students they are now going to finalise and give their presentations. Direct their attention to the **21st Century skill** (see next column). Read through the steps for the final preparation and give them a time limit for each presentation and for the preparation. Encourage them to use the **Useful expressions** and remind them to include the list of facts to ask the class to determine which are false. Monitor as they finalise to make sure everyone is collaborating as best they can.

Introduce and end each presentation with applause to help confidence and generate enthusiasm and interest, and prepare and ask a question after each to prompt the students to ask questions too. Make sure the section where the audience guesses the false facts is brief. Ask each team how they felt about their presentation immediately afterwards and give some short, supportive and constructive feedback, especially about the delivery since that might help the next teams present more effectively. You could also end each by asking if the class agrees with the teams' conclusions about the mystery they presented, and perhaps end the whole session by asking which mystery they found most intriguing and which presentation they thought was best.

21ST CENTURY SKILLS

Read through the **21st Century skill** with them. Ask if they found any controversial or questionable information in their research and what made them question it. Ask if they did further research to check the facts and if that helped them refute the information (or confirm that it was in fact true).

➔ See pages 28-29 **21st Century skills**

EVALUATION

Before students answer the questions, draw their attention to the tips in **Go beyond** and ask them to take them into consideration as they do the evaluation. Give them time to prepare notes in answer to the questions and remind them to be supportive and give constructive feedback to each other in the discussions. Monitor discussions, adding your own feedback where appropriate and noting common observations to then convey to the class as a whole.

Have a class discussion about what students have learnt from the project, reminding them of the unit objectives, the **Core values** and the **Learning tools** sections of units 5 and 6, as well as the **21st Century skills** section of the **Project** pages.

If you have decided to use the evaluation exercise as a springboard for a student self-assessment diary (see **Evaluation** notes page 77), give them time to do this now and remind them to refer to the **Reflect on your learning** section of the **Workbook** if they have one.

➔ See pages 40-41 **Assessment**

GO BEYOND

Ask students if there were any tips that they think they will remember to apply in future presentations, and then get them to read the text in more detail and discuss answers to the questions below. Elicit any other tips students come up with and make sure you have some of your own (for example, have an introductory slide for the audience to know the overall content, use a logical flow of information and make clear transitions between slides, prepare concept-checking questions for the audience if appropriate). Write them on the board.

Remind students to do all the exercises in their notebook

7 DIGITAL COMMUNICATION

At the start of each unit and lesson, explain to the students what the objectives are.

Language objectives

Grammar

The passive voice
- Students practise the passive voice in a variety of tenses.

Modal verbs with the passive voice
- Students practise the passive voice with modal verbs.

Vocabulary

Communication I: *app, attachment, computer literate, contact, email account, GPS, junk mail, message, real-time, social media, vlog, mobile phone, email*
- Students use vocabulary for digital communication.

The internet: *chatroom, download, install, online, platform, software, spam, user-friendly, virus, webcam, website*
- Students use vocabulary related to the internet.

Academic honesty: *assessment, assignment, cheating, e-learning, expel, get away with something, pass a test, plagiarism, punishment*
- Students encounter vocabulary related to academic honesty.

Idioms and expressions

Communication: *keep someone in the loop, get off on the wrong foot; be on the same wavelength, get straight to the point*
- Students look at idioms and expressions related to communication in the context of an IM conversation.

Recycled language

Various tenses, Modal verbs

Skills objectives

Speaking

- Students discuss and assess their email and messaging habits.
- Students discuss technology in the classroom.
- Students reach a consensus on rules for a class chatroom.
- Students discuss cheating at school.
- Students discuss their own experiences with communication.

Pronunciation: Students practise the diphthong /eɪ/ and practise distinguishing when they hear it.

Pairwork: Students use various mediation techniques to help each other complete a text about mobile phones or laptops.

Listening

- Students listen and complete a text about mobile phones.
- Students listen and complete a text about emails.
- Students listen and write sentences about emails.
- Students listen and take notes about technology in the classroom.
- Students listen and choose options in an IM conversation.

Reading

- Students read and match headings to paragraphs.
- Students read in detail to answer multiple-choice questions.
- Students come up with their own definitions for words in a text.

Core values: Students assess different dishonest acts and discuss the value of **honesty**.

Writing

- Students look at how processes are described and explained.
- Students write, plan and check a description of how something works.

Focus on the passive

Remind students to do all the exercises in their notebook

Learning to learn tools	
SPEAKING TOOLS Students practise using expressions to introduce opinions.	LISTENING TOOLS Students practise a strategy for paying attention to specific words in order to complete a text.
READING TOOLS Students practise finding evidence in a text to support an answer and to eliminate wrong answers.	WRITING TOOLS Students practise paraphrasing information they find in research.

Project objectives: Campaign

Task 1 Students write reports on technology that is beneficial in modern society.

Task 2 Students list the advantages and disadvantages of using technology in the classroom.

Task 3 Students write a campaign proposal.

Audiovisual objectives

Vlog: Students watch and listen to Emma talk about social media.

Culture: Students watch and listen to Emma talk about online communities.

Grammar animations: Students are presented with visual presentations of the unit grammar.

Key competences

Linguistic
pages 64-71

Mathematical and Science and Technology
pages 64-71

Digital
pages 64-71

Social and Civic
pages 65-71

Cultural awareness and expression
pages 64, 67, 71

Learning to learn
pages 64, 66, 68, 70

Sense of initiative and entrepreneurship
pages 65, 67, 70

→ See pages 42-43 Key competences

CEFR Mediation

7.1 Encouraging conceptual talk
Can ask questions to invite people to clarify their reasoning.

7.2 Facilitating collaborative interaction with peers
Can make and respond to suggestions and propose alternatives.

7.3 Adapting language
Can paraphrase more simply the main points in short written texts.

7.4 Processing text in writing
Can summarise information in texts of general interest and paraphrase short passages simply.

7.5 Relaying specific information in writing
Can write specific information from spoken texts.

Project Overall mediation
Can collaborate with interest and empathy to achieve a common goal and can convey the main points of text in simple language.

Unit review Facilitating collaborative interaction with peers
Can collaborate in shared tasks and work towards a common goal.

Pairwork Facilitating collaborative interaction with peers
Can make and respond to suggestions and propose alternatives.

→ See pages 30-33 Mediation

Remind students to do all the exercises in their notebook

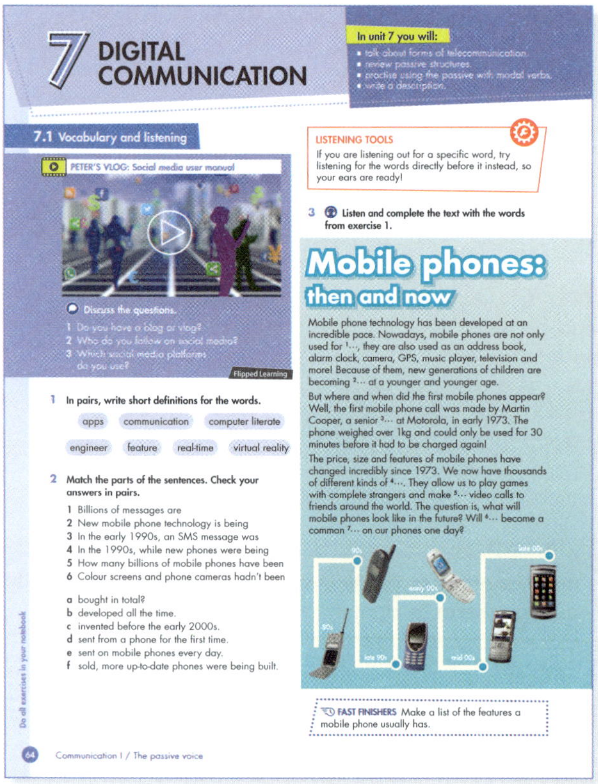
7 DIGITAL COMMUNICATION

In unit 7 you will:
- talk about forms of telecommunication.
- review passive structures.
- practise using the passive with modal verbs.
- write a description.

7.1 Vocabulary and listening

PETER'S VLOG: Social media user manual

Discuss the questions.
1 Do you have a blog or vlog?
2 Who do you follow on social media?
3 Which social media platforms do you use?

Flipped Learning

1 In pairs, write short definitions for the words.

apps communication computer literate engineer feature real-time virtual reality

2 Match the parts of the sentences. Check your answers in pairs.

1 Billions of messages are
2 New mobile phone technology is being
3 In the early 1990s, an SMS message was
4 In the 1990s, while new phones were being
5 How many billions of mobile phones have been
6 Colour screens and phone cameras hadn't been

a bought in total?
b developed all the time.
c invented before the early 2000s.
d sent from a phone for the first time.
e sent on mobile phones every day.
f sold, more up-to-date phones were being built.

LISTENING TOOLS
If you are listening out for a specific word, try listening for the words directly before it instead, so your ears are ready!

3 Listen and complete the text with the words from exercise 1.

Mobile phones: then and now

Mobile phone technology has been developed at an incredible pace. Nowadays, mobile phones are not only used for [1]..., they are also used as an address book, alarm clock, camera, GPS, music player, television and more! Because of them, new generations of children are becoming [2]... at a younger and younger age.

But where and when did the first mobile phones appear? Well, the first mobile phone call was made by Martin Cooper, a senior [3]... at Motorola, in early 1973. The phone weighed over 1kg and could only be used for 30 minutes before it had to be charged again!

The price, size and features of mobile phones have changed incredibly since 1973. We now have thousands of different kinds of [4].... They allow us to play games with complete strangers and make [5]... video calls to friends around the world. The question is, what will mobile phones look like in the future? Will [6]... become a common [7]... on our phones one day?

FAST FINISHERS Make a list of the features a mobile phone usually has.

Do all exercises in your notebook

64 Communication 1 / The passive voice

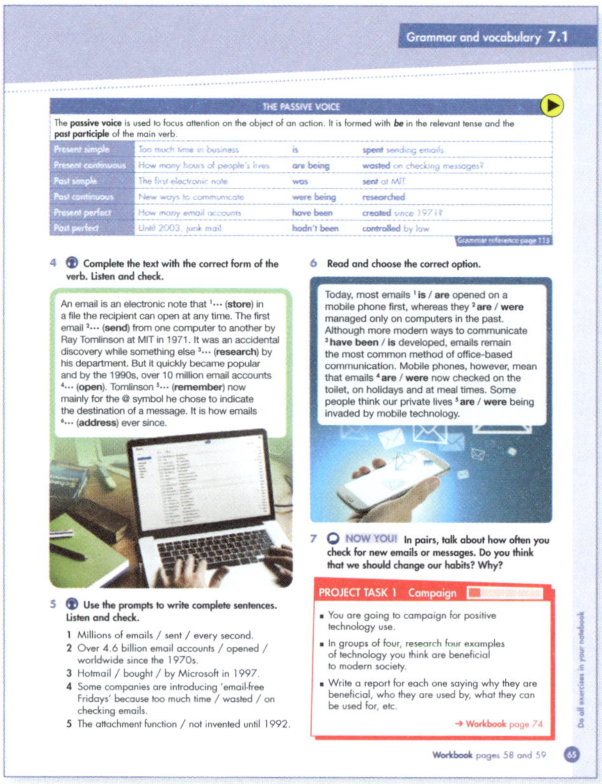
Grammar and vocabulary 7.1

THE PASSIVE VOICE

The **passive voice** is used to focus attention on the object of an action. It is formed with **be** in the relevant tense and the **past participle** of the main verb.

Present simple	Too much time in business	is	spent sending emails.
Present continuous	How many hours of people's lives	are being	wasted on checking messages?
Past simple	The first electronic note	was	sent at MIT.
Past continuous	New ways to communicate	were being	researched.
Present perfect	How many email accounts	have been	created since 1971?
Past perfect	Until 2003, junk mail	hadn't been	controlled by law.

Grammar reference page 113

4 Complete the text with the correct form of the verb. Listen and check.

An email is an electronic note that [1]... (**store**) in a file the recipient can open at any time. The first email [2]... (**send**) from one computer to another by Ray Tomlinson at MIT in 1971. It was an accidental discovery while something else [3]... (**research**) by his department. But it quickly became popular and by the 1990s, over 10 million email accounts [4]... (**open**). Tomlinson [5]... (**remember**) now mainly for the @ symbol he chose to indicate the destination of a message. It is how emails [6]... (**address**) ever since.

5 Use the prompts to write complete sentences. Listen and check.

1 Millions of emails / sent / every second.
2 Over 4.6 billion email accounts / opened / worldwide since the 1970s.
3 Hotmail / bought / by Microsoft in 1997.
4 Some companies are introducing 'email-free Fridays' because too much time / wasted / on checking emails.
5 The attachment function / not invented until 1992.

6 Read and choose the correct option.

Today, most emails [1]**is / are** opened on a mobile phone first, whereas they [2]**are / were** managed only on computers in the past. Although more modern ways to communicate [3]**have been / is** developed, emails remain the most common method of office-based communication. Mobile phones, however, mean that emails [4]**are / were** now checked on the toilet, on holidays and at meal times. Some people think our private lives [5]**are / were** being invaded by mobile technology.

7 NOW YOU! In pairs, talk about how often you check for new emails or messages. Do you think that we should change our habits? Why?

PROJECT TASK 1 Campaign
- You are going to campaign for positive technology use.
- In groups of four, research four examples of technology you think are beneficial to modern society.
- Write a report for each one saying why they are beneficial, who they are used by, what they can be used for, etc.

→ Workbook page 74

Do all exercises in your notebook

Workbook pages 58 and 59 65

ANSWER KEY

Pages 64-65

1 *Suggested answers:*

apps: computer programmes we use on a mobile phone
communication: exchanging information
computer literate: the ability to use computers with skill and knowledge
engineer: someone who designs or develops computer systems
feature: characteristic
real-time: instantaneous
virtual reality: a simulated environment produced by a computer

2 **1** e **2** b **3** d **4** f **5** a **6** c

3
1 communication
2 computer literate
3 engineer
4 apps
5 real-time
6 virtual reality
7 feature

4
1 is stored
2 was sent
3 was being researched
4 had been opened
5 is remembered
6 have been addressed

5
1 Millions of emails are sent every second.
2 Over 4.6 billion email accounts have been opened worldwide since the 1970s.
3 Hotmail was bought by Microsoft in 1997.
4 Some companies are introducing 'email-free Fridays' because too much time is being wasted on checking emails.
5 The attachment function was not invented until 1992.

6
1 are
2 were
3 have been
4 are
5 are

7 *Student's own answers*

Remind students to do all the exercises in their notebook

LESSON FOCUS

Grammar The passive voice

Vocabulary Communication I

Listening Completing a text about mobile phones; Completing a text about emails

Speaking Discussing and assessing emailing and messaging

Project task 1 Write a report on technology that is beneficial to society

Resources

Teacher's i-solutions, Student's Book audio, Vlog and worksheet

Flipped Learning

EMMA'S VLOG: Social media user manual

- Make sure to set up the **Flipped Learning** work with the students beforehand. **See pages 20-23 for complete Flipped Learning guidelines**.
- Ask students to put the **Flipped Learning worksheets** on their desks and walk around to check how many have completed the Flipped task.
- In pairs or small groups, ask students to compare and check the *Before you watch...* and *While you watch...* exercises on the worksheet.
- Show students **Emma's Vlog** and ask volunteers to provide correct answers and clarify any doubts other students may have.
- Choose three or four students to read aloud their answers to the *After you watch...* exercises on the worksheet and encourage some class discussion.
- Move straight to exercise 1 on page 64.

Warmer

Watch Emma's Vlog and discuss the questions with the whole class. If you don't have video facilities, simply discuss the questions.

1 Get students to write definitions for the words they know and then compare with a partner. Give them the definitions for any words they don't know.

2 Ask students which technological device the sentences are about (mobile phones) and let them do the exercise. You could point out that all the sentences are in the passive, which they will look at on the next page.

LISTENING TOOLS

Get students to read the **Listening tool** and tell them to apply it to exercise 3.

3 2.9 (See page 178 for transcripts) Let students skim the text before playing the audio.

FAST FINISHERS Students can complete this exercise alone or in pairs.

Flipped Learning

THE PASSIVE VOICE

Draw students' attention to the **Grammar table**. Remind students that they can use this as a quick reference while completing the exercises.

Show students the **Grammar animation** and/or refer students to the **Grammar reference** on page 113 for further information on form and use.

→ See page 23 for how to flip the **grammar lesson**

4 2.10 (See page 178 for transcripts) Get students to refer to the **Grammar table** as they do the exercise.

5 2.11 (See page 178 for transcripts) Tell students to check the time expressions in each sentence so they know which tense to use.

6 Ask students what big change in email use is mentioned here (accessing email via a smartphone) and get them to do the exercise.

7 NOW YOU! You could offer students the statistic that, the average North American checks their phone around 100 times a day. Ask them to compare their use and continue the discussion.

PROJECT TASK 1 Campaign

Organise students into teams of 4 and go through the steps of the task together. Remind students that they need to keep their project notes together in their **Workbook** (page 74) or in their own notebook.

→ See pages 24-27 **Projects**

FURTHER PRACTICE

Workbook pages 58-59
- **Grammar reference and practice** pages 90 and 95-96
- **Wordlist and exercises** pages 101 and 104

Remind students to do all the exercises in their notebook

CONTINUOUS ASSESSMENT Students can talk about communication and use the passive voice.

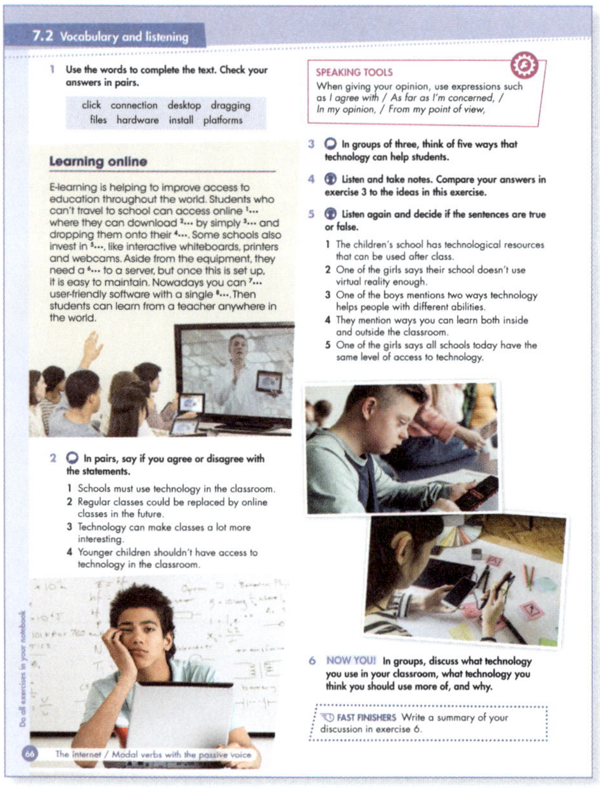

7.2 Vocabulary and listening

1 **Use the words to complete the text. Check your answers in pairs.**

click connection desktop dragging files hardware install platforms

Learning online

E-learning is helping to improve access to education throughout the world. Students who can't travel to school can access online [1]··· where they can download [2]··· by simply [3]··· and dropping them onto their [4]···. Some schools also invest in [5]···, like interactive whiteboards, printers and webcams. Aside from the equipment, they need a [6]··· to a server, but once this is set up, it is easy to maintain. Nowadays you can [7]··· user-friendly software with a single [8]···. Then students can learn from a teacher anywhere in the world.

2 **In pairs, say if you agree or disagree with the statements.**

1 Schools must use technology in the classroom.
2 Regular classes could be replaced by online classes in the future.
3 Technology can make classes a lot more interesting.
4 Younger children shouldn't have access to technology in the classroom.

SPEAKING TOOLS
When giving your opinion, use expressions such as *I agree with / As far as I'm concerned, / In my opinion, / From my point of view,*

3 **In groups of three, think of five ways that technology can help students.**

4 **Listen and take notes. Compare your answers in exercise 3 to the ideas in this exercise.**

5 **Listen again and decide if the sentences are true or false.**

1 The children's school has technological resources that can be used after class.
2 One of the girls says their school doesn't use virtual reality enough.
3 One of the boys mentions two ways technology helps people with different abilities.
4 They mention ways you can learn both inside and outside the classroom.
5 One of the girls says all schools today have the same level of access to technology.

6 NOW YOU! **In groups, discuss what technology you use in your classroom, what technology you think you should use more of, and why.**

FAST FINISHERS Write a summary of your discussion in exercise 6.

Do all exercises in your notebook

66 The internet / Modal verbs with the passive voice

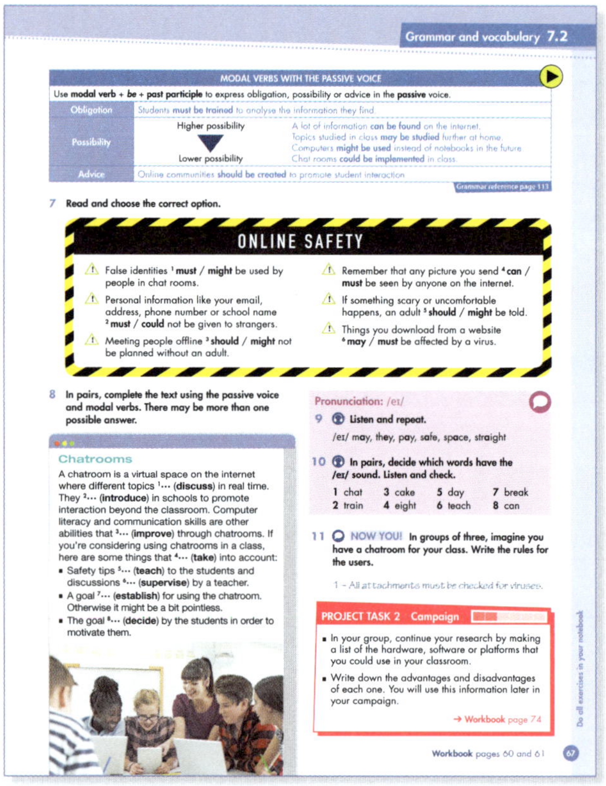

Grammar and vocabulary 7.2

MODAL VERBS WITH THE PASSIVE VOICE		
Use **modal verb** + *be* + **past participle** to express obligation, possibility or advice in the **passive** voice.		
Obligation		Students **must be trained** to analyse the information they find.
Possibility	Higher possibility ▼ Lower possibility	A lot of information **can be found** on the internet. Topics studied in class **may be studied** further at home. Computers **might be used** instead of notebooks in the future. Chat rooms **could be implemented** in class.
Advice		Online communities **should be created** to promote student interaction.

Grammar reference page 113

7 **Read and choose the correct option.**

ONLINE SAFETY

- False identities [1] **must** / **might** be used by people in chat rooms.
- Personal information like your email, address, phone number or school name [2] **must** / **could** not be given to strangers.
- Meeting people offline [3] **should** / **might** not be planned without an adult.
- Remember that any picture you send [4] **can** / **must** be seen by anyone on the internet.
- If something scary or uncomfortable happens, an adult [5] **should** / **might** be told.
- Things you download from a website [6] **may** / **must** be affected by a virus.

8 **In pairs, complete the text using the passive voice and modal verbs. There may be more than one possible answer.**

Chatrooms

A chatroom is a virtual space on the internet where different topics [1]··· (**discuss**) in real time. They [2]··· (**introduce**) in schools to promote interaction beyond the classroom. Computer literacy and communication skills are other abilities that [3]··· (**improve**) through chatrooms. If you're considering using chatrooms in a class, here are some things that [4]··· (**take**) into account:

- Safety tips [5]··· (**teach**) to the students and discussions [6]··· (**supervise**) by a teacher.
- A goal [7]··· (**establish**) for using the chatroom. Otherwise it might be a bit pointless.
- The goal [8]··· (**decide**) by the students in order to motivate them.

Pronunciation: /eɪ/

9 **Listen and repeat.**

/eɪ/ may, they, pay, safe, space, straight

10 **In pairs, decide which words have the /eɪ/ sound. Listen and check.**

1 chat 3 cake 5 day 7 break
2 train 4 eight 6 teach 8 can

11 NOW YOU! **In groups of three, imagine you have a chatroom for your class. Write the rules for the users.**

1 – All attachments must be checked for viruses.

PROJECT TASK 2 Campaign

- In your group, continue your research by making a list of the hardware, software or platforms that you could use in your classroom.
- Write down the advantages and disadvantages of each one. You will use this information later in your campaign.

→ Workbook page 74

Workbook pages 60 and 61 67

Do all exercises in your notebook

ANSWER KEY

Pages 66-67

1
1 platforms
2 files
3 dragging
4 desktop
5 hardware
6 connection
7 install
8 click

2 *Student's own answers*

3 *Student's own answers*

4 *Student's own answers*

5
1 True
2 False
3 True
4 True
5 False

6 *Student's own answers*

7
1 might
2 must
3 should
4 can
5 should
6 may

8
1 can / may be discussed
2 could / can be introduced
3 could / might / can be improved
4 should be taken
5 must / should be taught
6 must / should be supervised
7 should be established
8 could / can be decided

9 *Student's own answers*

10 train, cake, eight, day, break

11 *Student's own answers*

Remind students to do all the exercises in their notebook

LESSON FOCUS

Grammar Modal verbs with the passive voice

Vocabulary The internet

Listening Taking notes on a presentation about technology

Speaking Discussing technology in the classroom; Reaching a consensus about a class chatroom

Project task 2 List the advantages and disadvantages of using technology in the classroom

Resources

Teacher's i-solutions, Student's Book audio

Warmer

Put students into pairs or small groups to discuss which technological devices they have and what they use them for. Elicit the most common devices/uses from the class.

1 Ask how popular e-learning was as an option in the Warmer and what types of e-learning students use. Check that students understand the words in the wordpool and let them complete the exercise.

2 Encourage students to give reasons based on their own experience. Listen out for students' use of expressions of opinion to highlight for the **Speaking tool**.

SPEAKING TOOLS

Write on the board any expressions of opinion you heard students use in exercise 2 and then get them to read the **Speaking tool**.

3 To highlight the **Speaking tool**, you could get students to choose an expression of opinion to use in this exercise. Write some of their answers on the board for the next exercise.

4 2.12 (See page 178 for transcripts) Tell the class they will hear a group of students give a presentation about how technology helps learning. They will hear it twice and the first time they should take notes to compare with their own ideas.

5 2.13 (See page 178 for transcripts) Let students read the sentences before playing the audio again and discuss answers in pairs afterwards.

6 NOW YOU! Encourage students to refer to what they read and heard about technology in the classroom and to present some of their views to the class using the opinion expressions from the **Speaking tool.**

FAST FINISHERS Students can complete this exercise alone or in pairs.

MODAL VERBS WITH THE PASSIVE VOICE

Flipped Learning

Draw students' attention to the **Grammar table**. Remind students that they can use this as a quick reference while completing the exercises.

Show students the **Grammar animation** and/or refer students to the **Grammar reference** on page 113 for further information on form and use.

→ See page 23 for how to flip the **grammar lesson**

7 Get students to refer to the **Grammar table** as they do the exercise and ask them if they know any other useful advice for safety online.

8 Tell students that this time they must use the whole passive structure. Ask what comes after the modal verb (*be* + past participle). When they've finished, ask what experience they have of chatrooms.

Pronunciation

9 2.14 (See page 178 for transcripts) Exaggerate the two sounds of the diphthong to make sure students can hear and pronounce it.

10 2.15 (See page 178 for transcripts) Let students say the words to themselves before they listen, check and repeat.

11 NOW YOU! Get students to choose someone to write the rules, or you choose someone in each group who doesn't always participate as much, and tell them that they have to reach a consensus on the rules before writing them.

PROJECT TASK 2 Campaign

Put students back in their groups to continue their research of the pros and cons of technology. Remind students that they need to keep their project notes together in their **Workbook** (page 74) or in their own notebook.

→ See pages 24-27 **Projects**

FURTHER PRACTICE

Workbook pages 60-61
- **Grammar reference and practice** pages 90 and 95-96
- **Wordlist and exercises** pages 101 and 104

Vocabulary and Grammar worksheets available to download and edit from the **Richmond** *Learning* **Platform**

→ See pages 38-39 **Mixed-ability classes**

Remind students to do all the exercises in their notebook

CONTINUOUS ASSESSMENT Students can talk about the internet and use modal verbs with the passive voice.

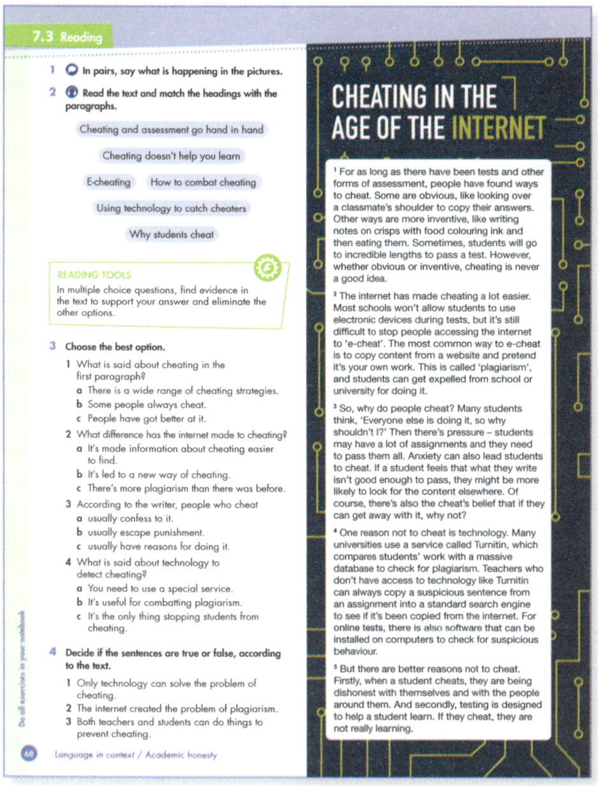

7.3 Reading

1 In pairs, say what is happening in the pictures.

2 Read the text and match the headings with the paragraphs.

Cheating and assessment go hand in hand

Cheating doesn't help you learn

E-cheating

How to combat cheating

Using technology to catch cheaters

Why students cheat

READING TOOLS
In multiple choice questions, find evidence in the text to support your answer and eliminate the other options.

3 Choose the best option.

1 What is said about cheating in the first paragraph?
 a There is a wide range of cheating strategies.
 b Some people always cheat.
 c People have got better at it.
2 What difference has the internet made to cheating?
 a It's made information about cheating easier to find.
 b It's led to a new way of cheating.
 c There's more plagiarism than there was before.
3 According to the writer, people who cheat
 a usually confess to it.
 b usually escape punishment.
 c usually have reasons for doing it.
4 What is said about technology to detect cheating?
 a You need to use a special service.
 b It's useful for combatting plagiarism.
 c It's the only thing stopping students from cheating.

4 Decide if the sentences are true or false, according to the text.

1 Only technology can solve the problem of cheating.
2 The internet created the problem of plagiarism.
3 Both teachers and students can do things to prevent cheating.

Do all exercises in your notebook

68 Language in context / Academic honesty

CHEATING IN THE AGE OF THE INTERNET

1 For as long as there have been tests and other forms of assessment, people have found ways to cheat. Some are obvious, like looking over a classmate's shoulder to copy their answers. Other ways are more inventive, like writing notes on crisps with food colouring ink and then eating them. Sometimes, students will go to incredible lengths to pass a test. However, whether obvious or inventive, cheating is never a good idea.

2 The internet has made cheating a lot easier. Most schools won't allow students to use electronic devices during tests, but it's still difficult to stop people accessing the internet to 'e-cheat'. The most common way to e-cheat is to copy content from a website and pretend it's your own work. This is called 'plagiarism', and students can get expelled from school or university for doing it.

3 So, why do people cheat? Many students think, 'Everyone else is doing it, so why shouldn't I?' Then there's pressure – students may have a lot of assignments and they need to pass them all. Anxiety can also lead students to cheat. If a student feels that what they write isn't good enough to pass, they might be more likely to look for the content elsewhere. Of course, there's also the cheat's belief that if they can get away with it, why not?

4 One reason not to cheat is technology. Many universities use a service called Turnitin, which compares students' work with a massive database to check for plagiarism. Teachers who don't have access to technology like Turnitin can always copy a suspicious sentence from an assignment into a standard search engine to see if it's been copied from the internet. For online tests, there is also software that can be installed on computers to check for suspicious behaviour.

5 But there are better reasons not to cheat. Firstly, when a student cheats, they are being dishonest with themselves and with the people around them. And secondly, testing is designed to help a student learn. If they cheat, they are not really learning.

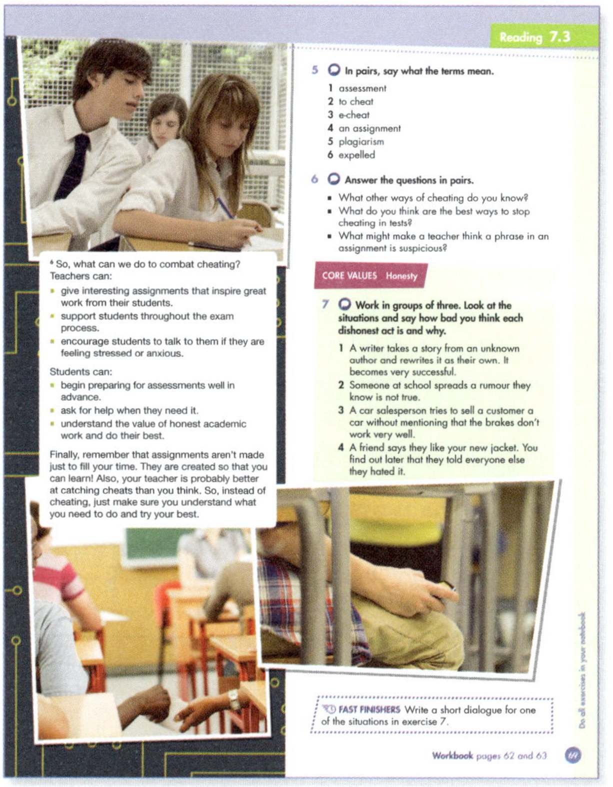

6 So, what can we do to combat cheating? Teachers can:

- give interesting assignments that inspire great work from their students.
- support students throughout the exam process.
- encourage students to talk to them if they are feeling stressed or anxious.

Students can:

- begin preparing for assessments well in advance.
- ask for help when they need it.
- understand the value of honest academic work and do their best.

Finally, remember that assignments aren't made just to fill your time. They are created so that you can learn! Also, your teacher is probably better at catching cheats than you think. So, instead of cheating, just make sure you understand what you need to do and try your best.

Reading 7.3

5 In pairs, say what the terms mean.

1 assessment
2 to cheat
3 e-cheat
4 an assignment
5 plagiarism
6 expelled

6 Answer the questions in pairs.

- What other ways of cheating do you know?
- What do you think are the best ways to stop cheating in tests?
- What might make a teacher think a phrase in an assignment is suspicious?

CORE VALUES Honesty

7 Work in groups of three. Look at the situations and say how bad you think each dishonest act is and why.

1 A writer takes a story from an unknown author and rewrites it as their own. It becomes very successful.
2 Someone at school spreads a rumour they know is not true.
3 A car salesperson tries to sell a customer a car without mentioning that the brakes don't work very well.
4 A friend says they like your new jacket. You find out later that they told everyone else they hated it.

FAST FINISHERS Write a short dialogue for one of the situations in exercise 7.

Workbook pages 62 and 63 69

Do all exercises in your notebook

ANSWER KEY

Pages 68-69

1 *Student's own answers*

2 **1** Cheating and assessment go hand in hand
2 E-cheating
3 Why students cheat
4 Using technology to catch cheaters
5 Cheating doesn't help you learn
6 How to combat cheating

3 **1** a **2** b **3** c **4** b

4 **1** False
2 False
3 True

5 *Suggested answers:*
1 assessment: evaluation
2 to cheat: to behave dishonestly for some gain
3 to e-cheat: to use technology to cheat
4 an assignment: a task
5 plagiarism: to use someone else's work or words and pretend it's/they are your own
6 expelled: ordered to leave (the room, the school)

6 *Student's own answers*

7 *Student's own answers*

Remind students to do all the exercises in their notebook

LESSON FOCUS

Language in context Academic honesty

Core values Honesty

Resources

Teacher's i-solutions, Student's Book audio

→ See pages 36-37 **Literature**

Warmer

Put students in pairs and get them to think of a form of technology, then ask them to write some rules for how to use it correctly. They should then read them out for another pair to guess which form of technology it is.

1 Elicit that the students in the picture are cheating and discuss how, but don't go into other ways of cheating yet, as this will come up in exercise 6. Ask students how they think technology has influenced cheating.

2 2.16 (See page 179 for transcripts) Tell students this is an exercise in skimming a text and that they will read in more detail in the next exercise.

READING TOOLS

Get students to read the **Reading tool** and tell them to help each other apply it to the next exercise.

3 Give students the time they need to complete the exercise and then check their answers in pairs. Remind them of the **Reading tool**.

4 Students can continue this exercise in pairs. Make sure they justify their answers using the text.

5 You could direct students' attention to the 'Academic honesty' section of the **Wordlist** and get them to find and guess those words too. Check their definitions.

6 Refer students to the ways of cheating mentioned in the text to get them started. Elicit answers to the second and third questions after they've finished.

CORE VALUES Honesty

7 This could lead into a discussion of whether intentions or consequences are more important and when it might be preferable not to be completely honest.

FAST FINISHERS Students can complete this exercise alone or in pairs.

FURTHER PRACTICE

Workbook pages 62-63

Remind students to do all the exercises in their notebook

CONTINUOUS ASSESSMENT Students can understand a text about academic honesty.

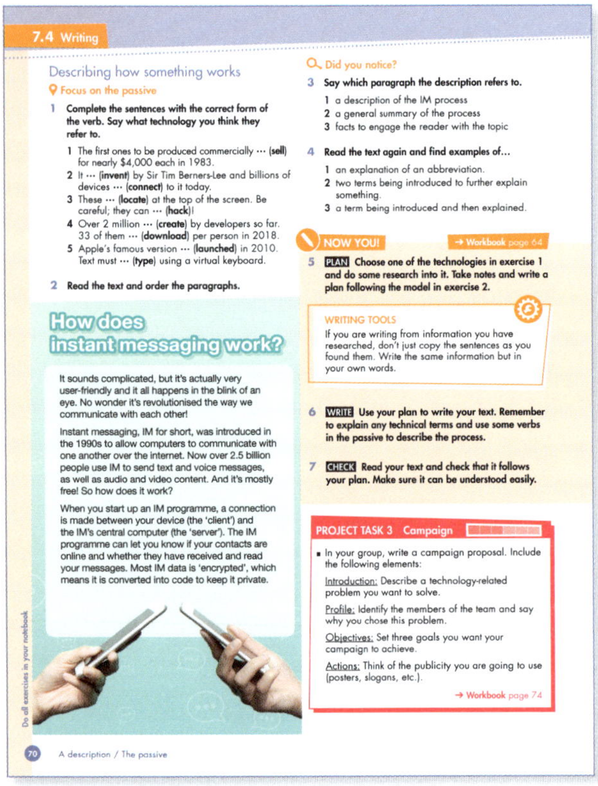
7.4 Writing

Describing how something works

Focus on the passive

1 **Complete the sentences with the correct form of the verb. Say what technology you think they refer to.**
 1 The first ones to be produced commercially ··· (**sell**) for nearly $4,000 each in 1983.
 2 It ··· (**invent**) by Sir Tim Berners-Lee and billions of devices ··· (**connect**) to it today.
 3 These ··· (**locate**) at the top of the screen. Be careful; they can ··· (**hack**)!
 4 Over 2 million ··· (**create**) by developers so far. 33 of them ··· (**download**) per person in 2018.
 5 Apple's famous version ··· (**launched**) in 2010. Text must ··· (**type**) using a virtual keyboard.

2 **Read the text and order the paragraphs.**

How does instant messaging work?

It sounds complicated, but it's actually very user-friendly and it all happens in the blink of an eye. No wonder it's revolutionised the way we communicate with each other!

Instant messaging, IM for short, was introduced in the 1990s to allow computers to communicate with one another over the internet. Now over 2.5 billion people use IM to send text and voice messages, as well as audio and video content. And it's mostly free! So how does it work?

When you start up an IM programme, a connection is made between your device (the 'client') and the IM's central computer (the 'server'). The IM programme can let you know if your contacts are online and whether they have received and read your messages. Most IM data is 'encrypted', which means it is converted into code to keep it private.

Did you notice?

3 **Say which paragraph the description refers to.**
 1 a description of the IM process
 2 a general summary of the process
 3 facts to engage the reader with the topic

4 **Read the text again and find examples of…**
 1 an explanation of an abbreviation.
 2 two terms being introduced to further explain something.
 3 a term being introduced and then explained.

NOW YOU! → Workbook page 64

5 PLAN **Choose one of the technologies in exercise 1 and do some research into it. Take notes and write a plan following the model in exercise 2.**

WRITING TOOLS
If you are writing from information you have researched, don't just copy the sentences as you found them. Write the same information but in your own words.

6 WRITE **Use your plan to write your text. Remember to explain any technical terms and use some verbs in the passive to describe the process.**

7 CHECK **Read your text and check that it follows your plan. Make sure it can be understood easily.**

PROJECT TASK 3 Campaign
- In your group, write a campaign proposal. Include the following elements:
 Introduction: Describe a technology-related problem you want to solve.
 Profile: Identify the members of the team and say why you chose this problem.
 Objectives: Set three goals you want your campaign to achieve.
 Actions: Think of the publicity you are going to use (posters, slogans, etc.).
 → Workbook page 74

Do all exercises in your notebook

70 A description / The passive

ANSWER KEY

Page 70

1 1 were sold; mobile phones
2 was invented; are connected; the internet
3 are located; be hacked; webcams
4 have been created; were downloaded; phone apps
5 was launched; be typed; tablet

2 2, 3, 1

3 1 second paragraph
2 third paragraph
3 first paragraph

4 1 Instant messaging, IM for short
2 your device (the 'client') and IM's central computer (the 'server')
3 'encrypted', which means it is converted into code to keep it private

5 *Student's own answers*

6 *Student's own answers*

7 *Student's own answers*

FURTHER PRACTICE

Workbook page 64

LESSON FOCUS

Focus on The passive
Writing Describing how something works
Project task 3 Write a campaign proposal

Resources
Teacher's i-solutions

Preparation Images of logos, icons of apps and tech companies

Warmer

Show students the images of icons and logos and see how many they recognise and what they know about the apps and companies behind them.

Focus on the passive

1 Let students do the exercise alone and then compare their answers in pairs. Ask them to justify their guesses as to which technology each sentence refers to.

2 You could do this first exercise quickly as a class and give students more time to do exercises 3 and 4 in pairs.

Did you notice?

3 Let students compare their answers in pairs and ask them what facts are mentioned to engage the reader.

4 Remind students that in explaining a process they should use strategies like these to explain technical terms.

5 **PLAN** Once students have finished their plan, encourage them to talk it through with a partner. Encourage partners to make suggestions about what terms need to be explained.

WRITING TOOLS

Get students to read the **Writing tool** and advise them to be aware of this advice in the writing task.

6 **WRITE** Before students start writing, make a checklist on the board of any elements related to content, structure, language and style that they should bear in mind.

7 **CHECK** Once students have checked their own descriptions, they can swap with a partner and check theirs.

PROJECT TASK 3 Campaign

Put students in their groups to write the proposal. Make sure each member has a part to play. Tell students that they need to keep their project notes together in their **Workbook** (page 74) or in their own notebook.

→ See pages 24-27 **Projects**

Remind students to do all the exercises in their notebook

CONTINUOUS ASSESSMENT Students can use the passive to describe how something works.

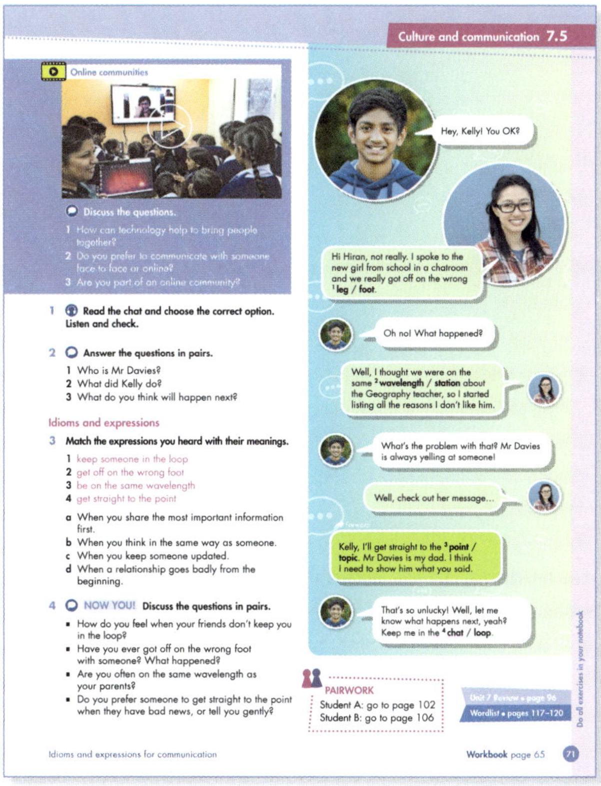

Culture and communication 7.5

Online communities

Discuss the questions.

1 How can technology help to bring people together?
2 Do you prefer to communicate with someone face to face or online?
3 Are you part of an online community?

1 Read the chat and choose the correct option. Listen and check.

Hey, Kelly! You OK?

Hi Hiran, not really. I spoke to the new girl from school in a chatroom and we really got off on the wrong [1] **leg / foot**.

Oh no! What happened?

Well, I thought we were on the same [2] **wavelength / station** about the Geography teacher, so I started listing all the reasons I don't like him.

What's the problem with that? Mr Davies is always yelling at someone!

Well, check out her message…

Kelly, I'll get straight to the [3] **point / topic**. Mr Davies is my dad. I think I need to show him what you said.

That's so unlucky! Well, let me know what happens next, yeah? Keep me in the [4] **chat / loop**.

2 Answer the questions in pairs.

1 Who is Mr Davies?
2 What did Kelly do?
3 What do you think will happen next?

Idioms and expressions

3 Match the expressions you heard with their meanings.

1 keep someone in the loop
2 get off on the wrong foot
3 be on the same wavelength
4 get straight to the point

a When you share the most important information first.
b When you think in the same way as someone.
c When you keep someone updated.
d When a relationship goes badly from the beginning.

4 NOW YOU! Discuss the questions in pairs.

- How do you feel when your friends don't keep you in the loop?
- Have you ever got off on the wrong foot with someone? What happened?
- Are you often on the same wavelength as your parents?
- Do you prefer someone to get straight to the point when they have bad news, or tell you gently?

PAIRWORK
Student A: go to page 102
Student B: go to page 106

Unit 7 Review • page 96
Wordlist • pages 117–120

Do all exercises in your notebook

Idioms and expressions for communication

Workbook page 65 71

ANSWER KEY

Page 71

1 **1** foot
2 wavelength
3 point
4 loop

2 **1** The Geography teacher
2 She told the new girl from school that she didn't like Mr Davies and then she found out he was the new girl's dad.
3 *Student's own answers*

3 **1** c **2** d **3** b **4** a

4 *Student's own answers*

FURTHER PRACTICE AND UNIT ASSESSMENT

Unit 7 Review **Student's Book** page 96
Workbook page 65
- Reflect on your learning page 65
- Grammar reference and practice pages 90 and 95-96
- Wordlist and exercises pages 101 and 104

Tests available to download and edit from the **Richmond***Learning***Platform**

→ See pages 40-41 **Assessment**

LESSON FOCUS

Idioms and expressions Communication
Listening Taking notes and choosing options in a conversation
Speaking Discussing experiences of communication

Resources

Teacher's i-solutions, Student's Book audio, Culture video and worksheet

Online communities

- In pairs, ask students to complete the *What I know…* exercises on the **Culture video worksheet.**
- Show students the **Culture video** and ask them to complete the *What I learned…* exercises on the worksheet.
- In pairs, students compare answers.
- In small groups, tell students to complete the *What I wonder…* exercises on the worksheet.

Warmer

Watch the **Culture video** and discuss the questions with the whole class. If you don't have video facilities, simply discuss the questions.

1 2.17 (See page 179 for transcripts) Let students read the chat and check their answers after playing the audio. Ask which expressions they knew or guessed correctly.

2 Let students answer the questions, playing the audio again if you think it helps. Elicit answers to the last question.

Idioms and expressions

3 Encourage students to use the text to help them. You could also encourage them to draw the expressions in a way that helps them remember them.

4 NOW YOU! Ask a few students to tell the class about their partner's answers.

PAIRWORK **Student's Book** pages 102 and 106
See **Teacher's Book** page 140 for more information.

→ See pages 30-33 **Mediation**

Remind students to do all the exercises in their notebook

Unit 7 Review

Unit 7 Review

1 Read the text and complete with the correct form of the words.

active advertise agent automatic be converse feel frighten real

IS BIG BROTHER LISTENING TO YOU?

Have you ever been talking to a friend about something and then found that when you next go online, it's being [1]advertised to you? It's certainly happened to me, and it's not a pleasant [2]…. So let's get straight to the point: are our devices listening to us?

Most social media apps say they don't [3]… have access to your data, but they may use your smartphone to record you if you say something that's considered a 'trigger', like 'Hey, Siri'. The problem is that no one [4]… knows what these triggers are. A normal [5]… about wanting some new jeans could [6]… a recording. I tried an experiment in which I said some phrases that could be triggers and mentioned needing cheap clothes. Almost immediately, I was [7]… sold all sorts of deals from budget clothing shops.

Experts say we shouldn't be too [8]… about this because the information is only going to advertising [9]… but it does make you wonder: if they can get the information so easily, surely anyone can.

2 Write an essay using all the notes and giving reasons for your point of view. Write between 140–190 words.

EXAM TIP
Make sure you use the notes provided and that you give explanations for your point of view.

Some parents who work in the big technology companies in California are sending their children to tech-free primary schools.
From what age should technology be used in the classroom?

Notes
Write about:
1 learning how to use technology
2 playing, making friends and traditional schooling
3 (your own ideas)

3 In pairs, compare the photos and say what you think the people are enjoying about the games. Then say which type of game you prefer and why.

Do all exercises in your notebook

96 External exam practice

Student's Book page 96

ANSWER KEY

1 **1** advertised **2** feeling **3** automatically **4** really **5** conversation **6** activate **7** being **8** frightened **9** agencies

2 *Student's own answers*

3 *Student's own answers*

Pairwork

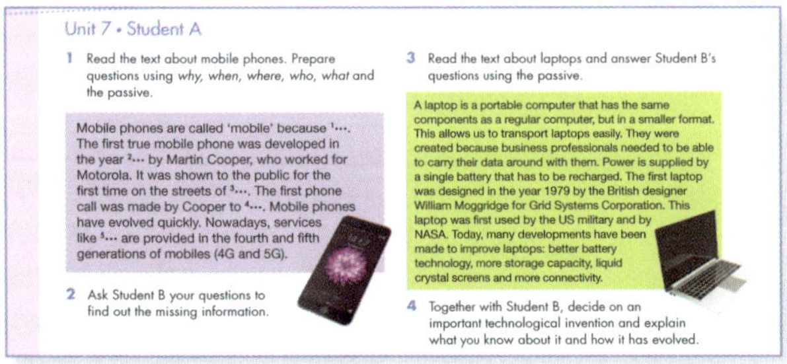

Unit 7 • Student A

1 Read the text about mobile phones. Prepare questions using *why, when, where, who, what* and the passive.

Mobile phones are called 'mobile' because [1]…. The first true mobile phone was developed in the year [2]… by Martin Cooper, who worked for Motorola. It was shown to the public for the first time on the streets of [3]…. The first phone call was made by Cooper to [4]…. Mobile phones have evolved quickly. Nowadays, services like [5]… are provided in the fourth and fifth generations of mobiles (4G and 5G).

2 Ask Student B your questions to find out the missing information.

3 Read the text about laptops and answer Student B's questions using the passive.

A laptop is a portable computer that has the same components as a regular computer, but in a smaller format. This allows us to transport laptops easily. They were created because business professionals needed to be able to carry their data around with them. Power is supplied by a single battery that has to be recharged. The first laptop was designed in the year 1979 by the British designer William Moggridge for Grid Systems Corporation. This laptop was first used by the US military and by NASA. Today, many developments have been made to improve laptops: better battery technology, more storage capacity, liquid crystal screens and more connectivity.

4 Together with Student B, decide on an important technological invention and explain what you know about it and how it has evolved.

Student's Book page 102

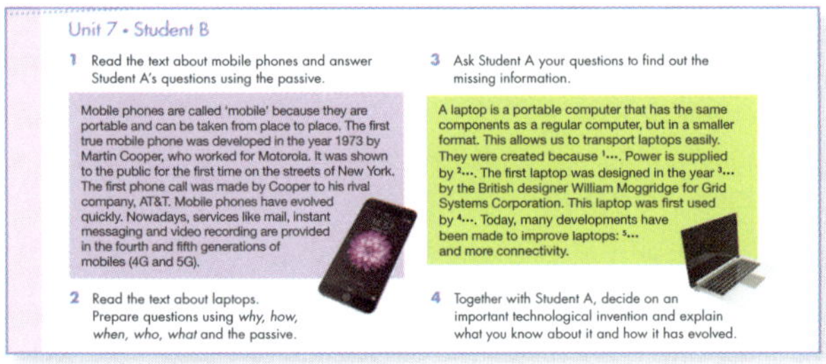

Unit 7 • Student B

1 Read the text about mobile phones and answer Student A's questions using the passive.

Mobile phones are called 'mobile' because they are portable and can be taken from place to place. The first true mobile phone was developed in the year 1973 by Martin Cooper, who worked for Motorola. It was shown to the public for the first time on the streets of New York. The first phone call was made by Cooper to his rival company, AT&T. Mobile phones have evolved quickly. Nowadays, services like mail, instant messaging and video recording are provided in the fourth and fifth generations of mobiles (4G and 5G).

2 Read the text about laptops. Prepare questions using *why, how, when, who, what* and the passive.

3 Ask Student A your questions to find out the missing information.

A laptop is a portable computer that has the same components as a regular computer, but in a smaller format. This allows us to transport laptops easily. They were created because [1]…. Power is supplied by [2]…. The first laptop was designed in the year [3]… by the British designer William Moggridge for Grid Systems Corporation. This laptop was first used by [4]…. Today, many developments have been made to improve laptops: [5]… and more connectivity.

4 Together with Student A, decide on an important technological invention and explain what you know about it and how it has evolved.

Student's Book page 106

CEFR MEDIATION DESCRIPTOR

- **Facilitating collaborative interaction with peers**
  Students can make and respond to suggestions and propose alternatives.

- **Requesting information**
  Tell students they each have one complete and one incomplete text about technology. They have to ask each other questions in the passive in order to complete both texts. Give them time to prepare their questions before they start.

Remind students to do all the exercises in their notebook

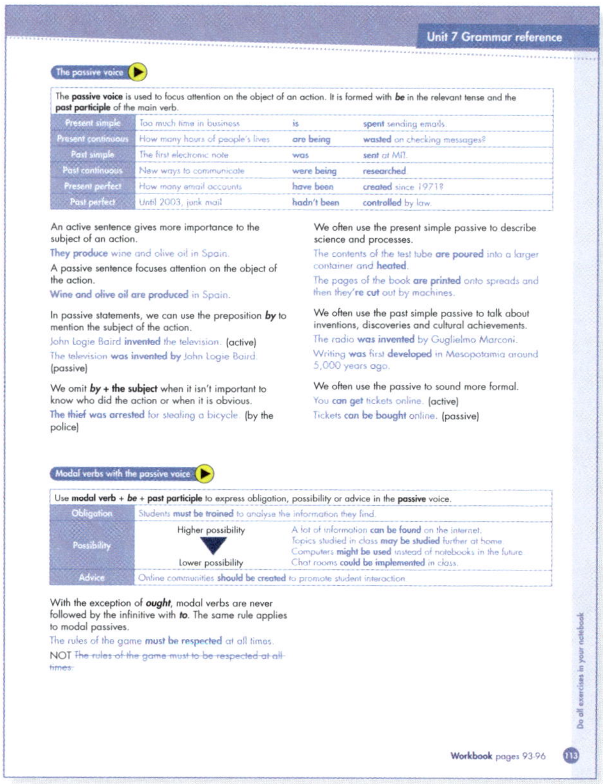

Unit 7 Grammar reference

The passive voice

The **passive voice** is used to focus attention on the object of an action. It is formed with ***be*** in the relevant tense and the **past participle** of the main verb.

Present simple	Too much time in business	**is**	**spent** sending emails.
Present continuous	How many hours of people's lives	**are being**	**wasted** on checking messages?
Past simple	The first electronic note	**was**	**sent** at MIT.
Past continuous	New ways to communicate	**were being**	**researched**.
Present perfect	How many email accounts	**have been**	**created** since 1971?
Past perfect	Until 2003, junk mail	**hadn't been**	**controlled** by law.

An active sentence gives more importance to the subject of an action.

They produce wine and olive oil in Spain.

A passive sentence focuses attention on the object of the action.

Wine and olive oil are produced in Spain.

In passive statements, we can use the preposition ***by*** to mention the subject of the action.

John Logie Baird **invented** the television. (active)

The television **was invented by** John Logie Baird. (passive)

We omit ***by* + the subject** when it isn't important to know who did the action or when it is obvious.

The thief was arrested for stealing a bicycle. (by the police)

We often use the present simple passive to describe science and processes.

The contents of the test tube **are poured** into a larger container and **heated**.

The pages of the book **are printed** onto spreads and then they**'re cut** out by machines.

We often use the past simple passive to talk about inventions, discoveries and cultural achievements.

The radio **was invented** by Guglielmo Marconi.

Writing **was** first **developed** in Mesopotamia around 5,000 years ago.

We often use the passive to sound more formal.

You **can get** tickets online. (active)

Tickets **can be bought** online. (passive)

Modal verbs with the passive voice

Use **modal verb** + ***be*** + **past participle** to express obligation, possibility or advice in the **passive** voice.

Obligation	Students **must be trained** to analyse the information they find.	
Possibility	Higher possibility ▼ Lower possibility	A lot of information **can be found** on the internet. Topics studied in class **may be studied** further at home. Computers **might be used** instead of notebooks in the future. Chat rooms **could be implemented** in class.
Advice	Online communities **should be created** to promote student interaction.	

With the exception of ***ought***, modal verbs are never followed by the infinitive with ***to***. The same rule applies to modal passives.

The rules of the game **must be respected** at all times.

NOT ~~The rules of the game must to be respected at all times.~~

Do all exercises in your notebook

Workbook pages 93-96 113

Student's Book page 113

Wordlist

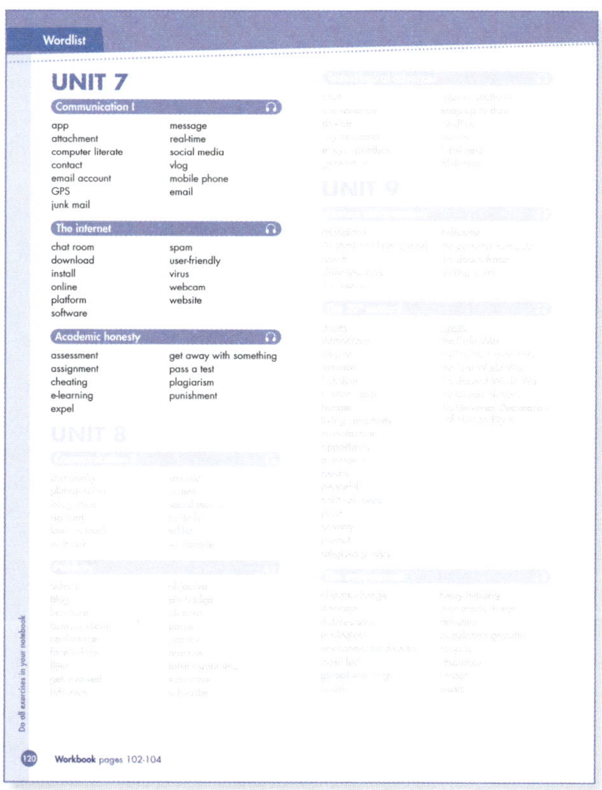

Wordlist

UNIT 7

Communication I

app
attachment
computer literate
contact
email account
GPS
junk mail
message
real-time
social media
vlog
mobile phone
email

The internet

chat room
download
install
online
platform
software
spam
user-friendly
virus
webcam
website

Academic honesty

assessment
assignment
cheating
e-learning
expel
get away with something
pass a test
plagiarism
punishment

Do all exercises in your notebook

120 Workbook pages 102-104

Student's Book page 120

2.57 2.58 2.59

Remind students to do all the exercises in their notebook

8 TECHNOLOGY VS. SOCIETY

At the start of each unit and lesson, explain to the students what the objectives are.

Language objectives

Grammar

Relative clauses: defining

- Students practise using defining relative clauses to give essential information about nouns.

Relative clauses: non-defining

- Students practise using non-defining relative clauses to give extra, non-essential information about nouns.

Vocabulary

Communication II: *community, globalisation, integration, isolated, keep in touch, multitask, satellite, screen, social media, solitude, tablet, worldwide*

- Students expand their use of vocabulary for communication.

Publicity: *advert, blog, brochure, bumper sticker, conference, face-to-face, flyer, get involved, influence, objective, pin badge, placard, poster, privacy, promote, raise awareness, subjective, subscribe*

- Students use vocabulary to describe different types of publicity.

Technological advances: *chat, conversation, device, digital addict, encyclopaedias, generation, internet platform, keep up to date, landline, library, loneliness, Millennial*

- Students encounter vocabulary to describe technological advances.

Idioms and expressions

Technology: *bells and whistles, a cog in the machine, hit the panic button, like a well-oiled machine*

- Students look at idioms and expressions related to technology in the context of a classroom conversation.

Recycled language

Expressions for opinions, agreement and disagreement, Passive voice, Modal verbs, Linking language, First conditional

Skills objectives

Speaking

- Students respond to opinions they hear about the problems of technology in society.
- Students discuss technological issues that may be a problem for teenagers.
- Students rank different types of publicity campaigns in terms of effectiveness.
- Students discuss which inventions in the history of communication technology were important.
- Students decide whether they agree with a text related to information and communications technology.
- Students talk about a robotics project.

Pronunciation: Students practise the /ɔ:/ and /ɔɪ/ sounds.

Pairwork: Students use a variety of mediation techniques to find six differences in two similar pictures of people using technology.

Listening

- Students listen and complete three texts about technology in society.
- Students listen and complete a text about publicity.
- Students listen to a class conversation about a technological project and answer multiple-choice questions.

Reading

- Students read and list points made in an article.
- Students read in detail to correct false information.
- Students read and decide whether or not they agree with the points a writer makes.

Core values: Students discuss different ways of **socialising** and the effects of certain behaviour on others during face-to-face conversations.

Writing

- Students write a short paragraph about a problem related to technology.
- Students write conversations using idioms and expressions.
- Students plan, write and check a list of 'how-to' tips.

Focus on language of cause and effect

Remind students to do all the exercises in their notebook

Learning to learn tools

SPEAKING TOOLS Students practise using expressions of agreement and disagreement.	LISTENING TOOLS Students practise noticing and copying word stress and tone of voice from audios, to help learn how to use new expressions correctly.
READING TOOLS Students practise taking notes with a specific purpose.	WRITING TOOLS Students practise using reference words to make their writing clearer and more fluent.

VOCABULARY TOOLS Students practise writing dictionary definitions of words in their notebooks.

Project objectives: Campaign

Task 4 Students think about digital support for their campaigns.

Task 5 Students create a logo, a slogan and publicity for their campaigns.

Task 6 Students write outlines for their campaign speeches.

Audiovisual objectives

Vlog: Students watch and listen to Robert talk about having a day without using electricity.

Culture: Students watch and listen to Robert talk about the benefits technology has brought us.

Grammar animations: Students are presented with visual presentations of the unit grammar.

Key competences

LC **Linguistic**
pages 72-79

MST **Mathematical and Science and Technology**
pages 72-74, 76-77, 79

DC **Digital**
pages 72-75, 79

SCC **Social and Civic**
pages 72-79

CAE **Cultural awareness and expression**
pages 72, 75-77, 79

LL **Learning to learn**
pages 72, 75-77, 79

IE **Sense of initiative and entrepreneurship**
pages 73, 75, 78

→ See pages 42-43 **Key competences**

CEFR Mediation

8.1 Encouraging conceptual talk
Can ask questions to invite people to clarify their reasoning.

8.2 Facilitating collaborative interaction with peers
Can collaborate on a shared task by making and responding to suggestions.

8.3 Facilitating collaborative interaction with peers
Can ask others to contribute their expertise and experience in a discussion.

8.4 Facilitating collaborative interaction with peers
Can work towards a common goal by asking and answering simple questions.

8.5 Relaying specific information in writing
Can write specific information from spoken texts.

Project Overall mediation
Can collaborate with interest and empathy to achieve a common goal and can convey the main points of a text in simple language.

Unit review Facilitating collaborative interaction with peers
Can collaborate on a shared task by making and responding to suggestions.

Pairwork Facilitating collaborative interaction with peers
Can work towards a common goal by asking and answering simple questions.

→ See pages 30-33 **Mediation**

Remind students to do all the exercises in their notebook

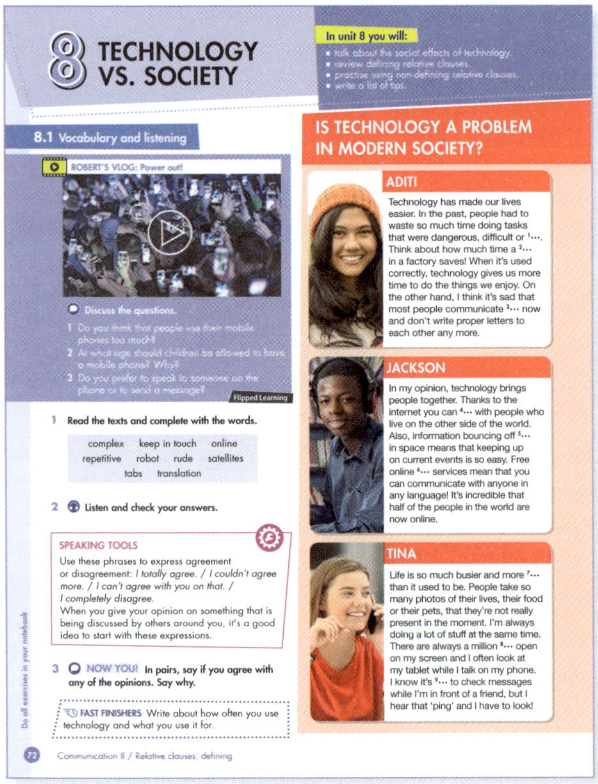

8 TECHNOLOGY VS. SOCIETY

In unit 8 you will:
- talk about the social effects of technology.
- review defining relative clauses.
- practise using non-defining relative clauses.
- write a list of tips.

8.1 Vocabulary and listening

ROBERT'S VLOG: Power out!

Discuss the questions.
1 Do you think that people use their mobile phones too much?
2 At what age should children be allowed to have a mobile phone? Why?
3 Do you prefer to speak to someone on the phone or to send a message?

Flipped Learning

1 Read the texts and complete with the words.

complex keep in touch online repetitive robot rude satellites tabs translation

2 Listen and check your answers.

SPEAKING TOOLS
Use these phrases to express agreement or disagreement: *I totally agree. / I couldn't agree more. / I can't agree with you on that. / I completely disagree.*
When you give your opinion on something that is being discussed by others around you, it's a good idea to start with these expressions.

3 NOW YOU! In pairs, say if you agree with any of the opinions. Say why.

FAST FINISHERS Write about how often you use technology and what you use it for.

IS TECHNOLOGY A PROBLEM IN MODERN SOCIETY?

ADITI
Technology has made our lives easier. In the past, people had to waste so much time doing tasks that were dangerous, difficult or [1]…. Think about how much time a [2]… in a factory saves! When it's used correctly, technology gives us more time to do the things we enjoy. On the other hand, I think it's sad that most people communicate [3]… now and don't write proper letters to each other any more.

JACKSON
In my opinion, technology brings people together. Thanks to the internet you can [4]… with people who live on the other side of the world. Also, information bouncing off [5]… in space means that keeping up on current events is so easy. Free online [6]… services mean that you can communicate with anyone in any language! It's incredible that half of the people in the world are now online.

TINA
Life is so much busier and more [7]… than it used to be. People take so many photos of their lives, their food or their pets, that they're not really present in the moment. I'm always doing a lot of stuff at the same time. There are always a million [8]… open on my screen and I often look at my tablet while I talk on my phone. I know it's [9]… to check messages while I'm in front of a friend, but I hear that 'ping' and I have to look!

Do all exercises in your notebook

72 Communication II / Relative clauses: defining

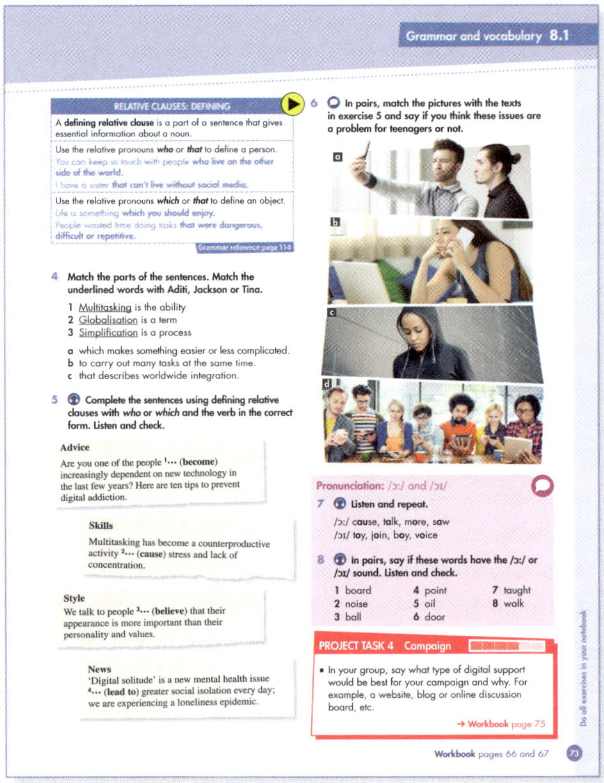

Grammar and vocabulary 8.1

RELATIVE CLAUSES: DEFINING
A **defining relative clause** is a part of a sentence that gives essential information about a noun.
Use the relative pronouns ***who*** or ***that*** to define a person.
You can keep in touch with people **who live on the other side of the world.**
I have a sister **that can't live without social media.**
Use the relative pronouns ***which*** or ***that*** to define an object.
Life is something **which you should enjoy.**
People wasted time doing tasks **that were dangerous, difficult or repetitive.**
Grammar reference page 114

4 Match the parts of the sentences. Match the underlined words with Aditi, Jackson or Tina.
1 Multitasking is the ability
2 Globalisation is a term
3 Simplification is a process
a which makes something easier or less complicated.
b to carry out many tasks at the same time.
c that describes worldwide integration.

5 Complete the sentences using defining relative clauses with *who* or *which* and the verb in the correct form. Listen and check.

Advice
Are you one of the people [1]… **(become)** increasingly dependent on new technology in the last few years? Here are ten tips to prevent digital addiction.

Skills
Multitasking has become a counterproductive activity [2]… **(cause)** stress and lack of concentration.

Style
We talk to people [3]… **(believe)** that their appearance is more important than their personality and values.

News
'Digital solitude' is a new mental health issue [4]… **(lead to)** greater social isolation every day; we are experiencing a loneliness epidemic.

6 In pairs, match the pictures with the texts in exercise 5 and say if you think these issues are a problem for teenagers or not.

a b c d

Pronunciation: /ɔː/ and /ɔɪ/
7 Listen and repeat.
/ɔː/ cause, talk, more, saw
/ɔɪ/ toy, join, boy, voice
8 In pairs, say if these words have the /ɔː/ or /ɔɪ/ sound. Listen and check.
1 board 2 noise 3 ball 4 point 5 oil 6 door 7 taught 8 walk

PROJECT TASK 4 Campaign
- In your group, say what type of digital support would be best for your campaign and why. For example, a website, blog or online discussion board, etc.
→ Workbook page 75

Workbook pages 66 and 67 73

Do all exercises in your notebook

ANSWER KEY

Pages 72-73

1
1 repetitive
2 robot
3 online
4 keep in touch
5 satellites
6 translation
7 complex
8 tabs
9 rude

2 *Student's own answers*

3 *Student's own answers*

4
1 b; Tina
2 c; Jackson
3 a; Aditi

5
1 who is becoming
2 which causes
3 who believe
4 which is leading to

6
a Style
b Skills
c News
d Advice

7 *Student's own answers*

8 *Student's own answers*

Remind students to do all the exercises in their notebook

LESSON FOCUS

Grammar Relative clauses: defining
Vocabulary Communication II
Listening Opinions about technology in society
Speaking Responding to opinions; A discussion of technological issues
Project task 4 Digital support for the campaign

Resources

Teacher's i-solutions, Student's Book audio, Vlog and worksheets

Flipped Learning

ROBERT'S VLOG: Power out!

- Make sure to set up the **Flipped Learning** work with the students beforehand. **See pages 20-23 for complete Flipped Learning guidelines**.
- Ask students to put the **Flipped Learning worksheets** on their desks and walk around to check how many have completed the Flipped task.
- In pairs or small groups, ask students to compare and check the *Before you watch...* and *While you watch...* exercises on the worksheet.
- Show students **Robert's Vlog** and ask volunteers to provide correct answers and clarify any doubts other students may have.
- Choose three or four students to read aloud their answers to the *After you watch...* exercises on the worksheet and encourage some class discussion.
- Move straight to exercise 1 on page 72.

Warmer

Watch Robert's Vlog and discuss the questions with the whole class. If you don't have video facilities, simply discuss the questions.

1 Tell students they will read and hear three students' opinions about technology in society. Check that they understand the words and expression in the wordpool and let them complete the texts.

2 2.18 (See page 179 for transcripts) After students have finished the exercise, check that they understand the opinions that were given.

SPEAKING TOOLS

Get students to read the **Speaking tool** and encourage them to keep a list of expressions. Remind them they looked at similar expressions on pages 66 and 48 of the **Student's Book**.

3 NOW YOU! Encourage students to use the expressions they wrote for the **Speaking tool**. You could give them a chance to answer as naturally as possible with one partner, and then swap partners to practise the expressions.

FAST FINISHERS Students can complete this exercise alone or in pairs.

Flipped Learning

RELATIVE CLAUSES: DEFINING

Draw students' attention to the **Grammar table**. Remind students that they can use this as a quick reference while completing the exercises.

Show students the **Grammar animation** and/or refer students to the **Grammar reference** on page 114 for further information on form and use.

→ See page 23 for how to flip the **grammar lesson**

4 You may like to do this as a class exercise to round up the discussion from exercise 3.

5 2.19 (See page 179 for transcripts) Refer students to the **Grammar table** as they do the exercise.

6 Encourage students to use words from the text when giving their opinion. Elicit which ones they think are big problems and which ones they think are not.

Pronunciation

7 2.20 (See page 179 for transcripts) Make sure students make the first sound as a long vowel sound and the second as a diphthong.

8 2.21 (See page 179 for transcripts) Let students say the words to each other to see what they think they sound like before playing the audio to check.

PROJECT TASK 4 Campaign

Put students in their groups to discuss the questions and reach a consensus. Remind students that they need to keep their project notes together in their **Workbook** (page 75) or in their own notebook.

→ See pages 24-27 **Projects**

FURTHER PRACTICE

Workbook pages 66-67
- **Grammar reference and practice** pages 91 and 96
- **Wordlist and exercises** pages 101 and 104

Remind students to do all the exercises in their notebook

CONTINUOUS ASSESSMENT Students can talk about communication and use defining relative clauses.

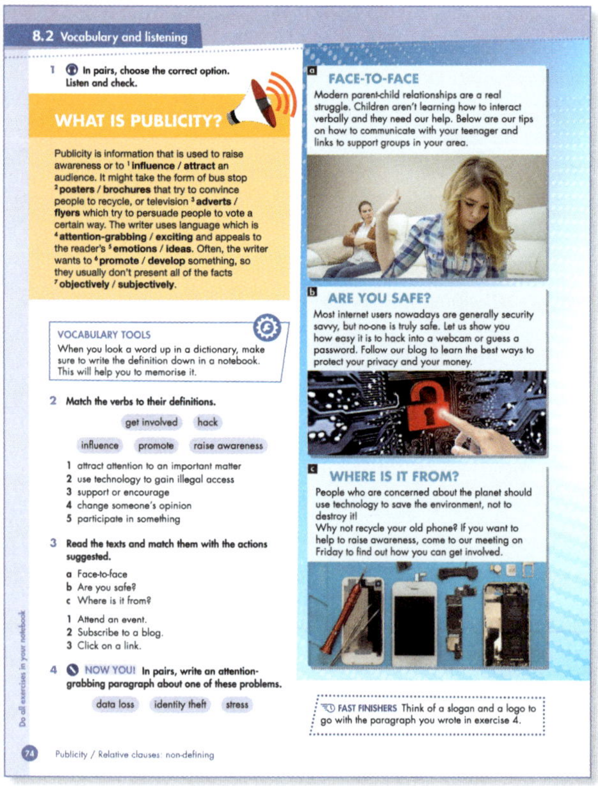

8.2 Vocabulary and listening

1 In pairs, choose the correct option. Listen and check.

WHAT IS PUBLICITY?

Publicity is information that is used to raise awareness or to [1] **influence / attract** an audience. It might take the form of bus stop [2] **posters / brochures** that try to convince people to recycle, or television [3] **adverts / flyers** which try to persuade people to vote a certain way. The writer uses language which is [4] **attention-grabbing / exciting** and appeals to the reader's [5] **emotions / ideas**. Often, the writer wants to [6] **promote / develop** something, so they usually don't present all of the facts [7] **objectively / subjectively**.

VOCABULARY TOOLS
When you look a word up in a dictionary, make sure to write the definition down in a notebook. This will help you to memorise it.

2 Match the verbs to their definitions.

get involved hack influence promote raise awareness

1 attract attention to an important matter
2 use technology to gain illegal access
3 support or encourage
4 change someone's opinion
5 participate in something

3 Read the texts and match them with the actions suggested.

a Face-to-face
b Are you safe?
c Where is it from?

1 Attend an event.
2 Subscribe to a blog.
3 Click on a link.

4 NOW YOU! In pairs, write an attention-grabbing paragraph about one of these problems.

data loss identity theft stress

a **FACE-TO-FACE**
Modern parent-child relationships are a real struggle. Children aren't learning how to interact verbally and they need our help. Below are our tips on how to communicate with your teenager and links to support groups in your area.

b **ARE YOU SAFE?**
Most internet users nowadays are generally security savvy, but no-one is truly safe. Let us show you how easy it is to hack into a webcam or guess a password. Follow our blog to learn the best ways to protect your privacy and your money.

c **WHERE IS IT FROM?**
People who are concerned about the planet should use technology to save the environment, not to destroy it!
Why not recycle your old phone? If you want to help to raise awareness, come to our meeting on Friday to find out how you can get involved.

FAST FINISHERS Think of a slogan and a logo to go with the paragraph you wrote in exercise 4.

Do all exercises in your notebook

74 Publicity / Relative clauses: non-defining

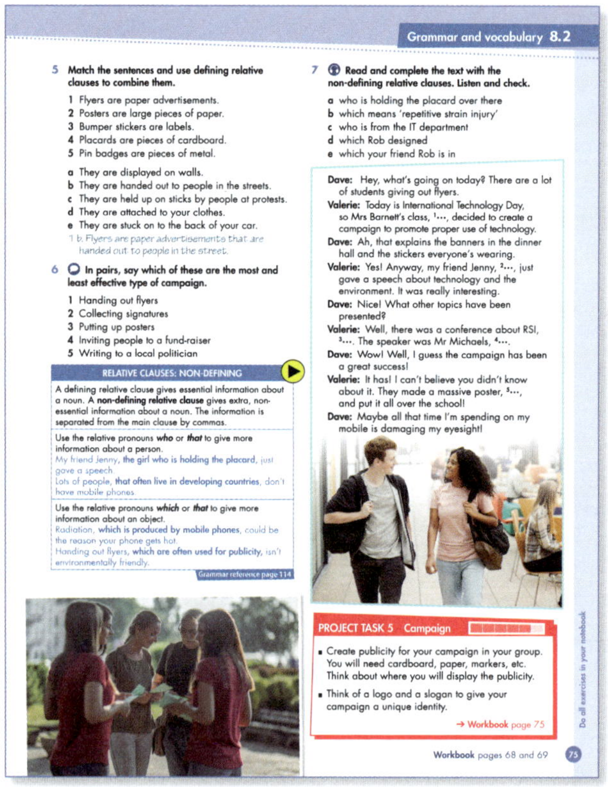

Grammar and vocabulary 8.2

5 Match the sentences and use defining relative clauses to combine them.

1 Flyers are paper advertisements.
2 Posters are large pieces of paper.
3 Bumper stickers are labels.
4 Placards are pieces of cardboard.
5 Pin badges are pieces of metal.

a They are displayed on walls.
b They are handed out to people in the streets.
c They are held up on sticks by people at protests.
d They are attached to your clothes.
e They are stuck on to the back of your car.

1 b. Flyers are paper advertisements that are handed out to people in the street.

6 In pairs, say which of these are the most and least effective type of campaign.

1 Handing out flyers
2 Collecting signatures
3 Putting up posters
4 Inviting people to a fund-raiser
5 Writing to a local politician

RELATIVE CLAUSES: NON-DEFINING

A defining relative clause gives essential information about a noun. A **non-defining relative clause** gives extra, non-essential information about a noun. The information is separated from the main clause by commas.

Use the relative pronouns *who* or *that* to give more information about a person.
My friend Jenny, **the girl who is holding the placard**, just gave a speech.
Lots of people, **that often live in developing countries**, don't have mobile phones.

Use the relative pronouns *which* or *that* to give more information about an object.
Radiation, **which is produced by mobile phones**, could be the reason your phone gets hot.
Handing out flyers, **which are often used for publicity**, isn't environmentally friendly.

Grammar reference page 114

7 Read and complete the text with the non-defining relative clauses. Listen and check.

a who is holding the placard over there
b which means 'repetitive strain injury'
c who is from the IT department
d which Rob designed
e which your friend Rob is in

Dave: Hey, what's going on today? There are a lot of students giving out flyers.
Valerie: Today is International Technology Day, so Mrs Barnett's class, [1]…, decided to create a campaign to promote proper use of technology.
Dave: Ah, that explains the banners in the dinner hall and the stickers everyone's wearing.
Valerie: Yes! Anyway, my friend Jenny, [2]…, just gave a speech about technology and the environment. It was really interesting.
Dave: Nice! What other topics have been presented?
Valerie: Well, there was a conference about RSI, [3]…. The speaker was Mr Michaels, [4]….
Dave: Wow! Well, I guess the campaign has been a great success!
Valerie: It has! I can't believe you didn't know about it. They made a massive poster, [5]…, and put it all over the school!
Dave: Maybe all that time I'm spending on my mobile is damaging my eyesight!

PROJECT TASK 5 Campaign
- Create publicity for your campaign in your group. You will need cardboard, paper, markers, etc. Think about where you will display the publicity.
- Think of a logo and a slogan to give your campaign a unique identity.

→ Workbook page 75

Workbook pages 68 and 69 75

Do all exercises in your notebook

ANSWER KEY

Pages 74-75

1 **1** influence
2 posters
3 adverts
4 attention-grabbing
5 emotions
6 promote
7 objectively

2 **1** raise awareness
2 hack
3 promote
4 influence
5 get involved

3 **a** 1
b 2
c 3

4 *Student's own answers*

5 **1** b; Flyers are paper advertisements that are handed out to people in the street.
2 a; Posters are large pieces of paper that/which are displayed on walls.
3 e; Bumper stickers are labels that/which are stuck on to the back of your car.
4 c; Placards are pieces of cardboard that/which are held up on sticks by people at protests.
5 d; Pin badges are pieces of metal that/which are attached to your clothes.

6 *Student's own answers*

7 **1** e
2 a
3 b
4 c
5 d

Remind students to do all the exercises in their notebook

LESSON FOCUS

Grammar Relative clauses: non-defining
Vocabulary Publicity
Listening Completing a text about publicity
Speaking Ranking types of publicity campaign in terms of effectiveness
Project task 5 Create a logo, a slogan and publicity for the campaigns

Resources
Teacher's i-solutions, Student's Book audio

Warmer

Choose a word or a person from pages 72 and 73 of the **Student's Book**. Define the word or describe the person using a defining relative clause, and have the students guess who or what it is. Students can continue in pairs or small groups. You could also broaden the task out to include other vocabulary or famous people from the book.

1 2.22 (See page 180 for transcripts) Before students open their books, ask how they would define 'publicity'. Then ask them to open their books, compare their definitions with the first sentence of the text and complete the exercise.

VOCABULARY TOOLS

Get students to read the **Vocabulary tool**. Ask them to look up the word 'hack' from exercise 2 in a monolingual dictionary and ask them what type of information it gives, in addition to the definition: For example, pronunciation, part of speech, example sentences, etc. Point out that 'hack' can be a verb as well as a noun and encourage them to write both meanings in their notebooks.

2 Elicit that 'hack' is defined in item 2 as a verb and let students continue the exercise. Encourage them to look up any less familiar words in a dictionary to find extra information about their use that might be helpful.

3 Tell students that the texts are examples of publicity and that they have to skim them to match them with the actions they suggest. Explain any unfamiliar vocabulary.

4 NOW YOU! Encourage students to use the texts in exercise 3 as a model.

FAST FINISHERS Students can complete this exercise alone or in pairs.

5 Point out to the students that the sentences they will form are definitions of different types of publicity. You could check understanding by letting them translate them. Ask students if they have ever owned or made any of the items.

6 Remind students of their preparations for the campaign project and ask which type of publicity they are thinking of using. You could show them different examples of campaigns to focus this discussion: campaigning for more investment in technology for schools, for example.

RELATIVE CLAUSES: NON-DEFINING

Flipped Learning

Draw students' attention to the **Grammar table**. Remind students that they can use this as a quick reference while completing the exercises.

Show students the **Grammar animation** and/or refer students to the **Grammar reference** on page 114 for further information on form and use.

→ See page 23 for how to flip the **grammar lesson**

7 2.23 (See page 180 for transcripts) Remind students to refer to the **Grammar table** if they are unsure. Let them look over the text and clarify any doubts before playing the audio and completing the exercise.

PROJECT TASK 5 Campaign

Put students back in their groups to continue with the project. Make sure they have all the materials they need to create the publicity for their campaign. Remind students that they need to keep their project notes together in their **Workbook** (page 75) or in their own notebook

→ See pages 24-27 **Projects**

FURTHER PRACTICE

Workbook pages 68-69
- **Grammar reference and practice** pages 91 and 96
- **Wordlist and exercises** pages 101 and 104

Vocabulary and Grammar worksheets available to download and edit from the **Richmond** *Learning* **Platform**

→ See pages 38-39 **Mixed-ability classes**

CONTINUOUS ASSESSMENT Students can talk about publicity and use non-defining relative clauses.

Remind students to do all the exercises in their notebook

8.3 Reading

1 Look at the pictures. In pairs, name the inventions and guess when they were invented. Say why you think they were an important invention.

1440s 1870s 1980s 1990s

READING TOOLS
When taking notes, make sure you include only information that is relevant to the question.

2 Read the article and write a list of the ways technology has changed society.

3 Decide if the sentences are true or false. Correct the false ones.

1 Generation Z refers to people who were born after the internet became popular.
2 People born before Generation Z use different technologies to communicate than Generation Zers.
3 Generation Zers are better at multitasking than other generations.
4 Surveys say that 40% of adults today think Generation Z are digital addicts.
5 The writer thinks face-to-face conversations are important.

4 In pairs, find what the writer says about these things. Say if you agree with the writer.

- the future of work
- the downside of internet platforms
- tolerance
- digital addiction
- face-to-face conversations

CORE VALUES Socialising

5 Discuss the questions in groups.

1 What differences are there between an online chat and a face-to-face conversation?
2 How many reasons can you think of for having a conversation?
3 What effect does it have on you when someone does these things in conversation with you?
- looks you in the eye
- uses your name
- interrupts you
- laughs
- looks at their phone

FAST FINISHERS Choose an item of technology from exercise 1 and write about how it has changed people's lives.

76 Language in context / Technological advances

Reading 8.3

THE INFORMATION AND COMMUNICATION REVOLUTION

If you were born after 1995, you belong to a generation that's called Generation Z, which means you don't remember a time without the internet. This means you are a 'digital native'. You may even have had your own phone since you were about 13. You probably chat with your friends more by messaging them than by talking to them in person. Perhaps your parents sometimes ask you to put your phone down.

Your parents are either Generation X (born between the early 1960s and the early 1980s) or Millennials (born between the early 1980s and the mid-1990s) and they do remember a time without the internet. They are 'digital immigrants'. They remember going to the library to look things up in encyclopaedias. They probably stayed in touch with friends by calling them on a landline phone. They would have had to dial the number every time and, because of this, your parents might still remember some of their friends' telephone numbers. (Go on – ask them!)

There have been more developments in information and communication technology in the last few decades than ever before. These developments have fundamentally changed the way we behave. Information is more instantly available, and we have become better at finding the information we want. Generation Zers, in particular, have become skilled multitaskers. Having the internet in our pockets means we can access cultural content from all over the world. As a result, young people are becoming more global and more tolerant. In one survey of adults over the age of 35, the majority of said they felt that teenagers today have more in common with teenagers from other countries than with adults from their own country.

Not all changes are so positive. Surveys have found that 40% of Generation Zers describe themselves as digital addicts. Using digital devices a lot is not a problem in itself. It becomes an issue when we use them so much that we no longer interact with the people and places around us. Some experts say Generation Z are at a greater risk of loneliness than previous generations.

So, what does the future hold and how should we approach it? New generations of workers will have to keep up to date with technological advances and be able to change careers, when necessary. We must be aware that internet platforms can be used to manipulate, and we should learn to analyse and question the information we receive via online media.

Most importantly, we should enjoy the many benefits that the information and communication revolution has brought to our lives, while continuing to form strong social relationships in the world around us. Meeting people face-to-face, having conversations and developing relationships can be challenging, but they are also some of the most rewarding human experiences.

Workbook pages 70 and 71 77

ANSWER KEY

Pages 76-77

1 **1** The printing press; 1440s; *Student's own answers*
2 The world wide web; 1980s; *Student's own answers*
3 The telephone; 1870s; *Student's own answers*
4 The smartphone; 1990s; *Student's own answers*

2 *Suggested answers:*
People now chat to their friends more by messaging than talking in person or using a landline phone.
People can look things up on the internet instead of going to the library.
Information is instantly available and we have become more efficient at finding things out.
Young people have become skilled multitaskers.
We can access cultural content from all over the world.
Young people are becoming more global and tolerant.
Many young people have become digital addicts.
Generation Z are at greater risk of loneliness than previous generations.

3 **1** True
2 False. They used different technologies in the past.
3 True
4 False. Surveys say that 40% of Generation Z describe themselves as digital addicts.
5 True

4 *Student's own answers*

5 *Student's own answers*

Remind students to do all the exercises in their notebook

LESSON FOCUS

Language in context Technological advances

Core values Socialising

Resources

Teacher's i-solutions, Student's Book audio

→ See pages 36-37 **Literature**

Warmer

Think of an invention that's not in exercise 1 (e.g. the car) and describe it using increasingly more specific, passive sentences: *It was invented over a hundred years ago; It's still used by many people around the world every day; It's being made more and more by machines and robots; It's used for private transport.* Write some inventions on the board and let students continue in pairs or small groups.

1 Help students identify the inventions if necessary, so that they can move on to the discussion of their importance.

READING TOOLS

Get students to read the **Reading tool** and tell them to apply it to the next exercise.

2 2.24 (See page 180 for transcripts) Tell students that this is an opportunity to practise the **Reading tool**. Help them by saying there are eight main ways that technology has changed society.

3 Give students time to read in detail before answering the question and comparing in pairs. Check that they refer to the text when justifying their answers.

4 After students respond to the writer's points, encourage them to expand on their own opinions using the list of expressions for opinion, agreeing and disagreeing, from page 72 of the **Student's Book**.

CORE VALUES Socialising

5 Differences between face-to-face conversations and online chats are that, in a face-to-face conversation, you can:

- see the other person's facial expressions and body langauge.
- understand why they pause before responding.
- listen to their tone of voice.
- have physical contact if appropriate or necessary.

Reasons for having a conversation can include:

- sharing information.
- getting someone to do something (or to stop them doing something).
- developing relationships.
- developing your knowledge of the world and other people.

For the last question, elicit the positive and negative effects of each option.

FAST FINISHERS Students can complete this exercise alone or in pairs.

FURTHER PRACTICE

Workbook pages 70-71

Remind students to do all the exercises in their notebook

CONTINUOUS ASSESSMENT Students can understand a text about advances in information technology.

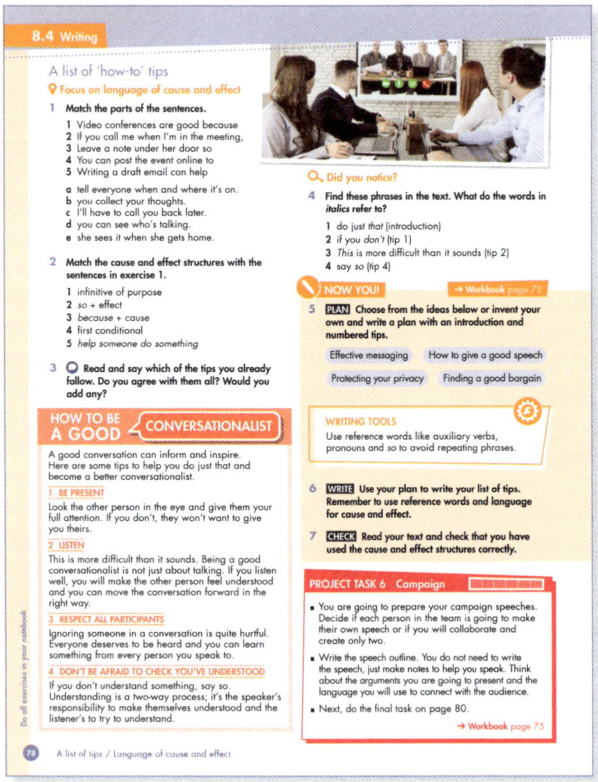

8.4 Writing

A list of 'how-to' tips

Focus on language of cause and effect

1 **Match the parts of the sentences.**

1 Video conferences are good because
2 If you call me when I'm in the meeting,
3 Leave a note under her door so
4 You can post the event online to
5 Writing a draft email can help

a tell everyone when and where it's on.
b you collect your thoughts.
c I'll have to call you back later.
d you can see who's talking.
e she sees it when she gets home.

2 **Match the cause and effect structures with the sentences in exercise 1.**

1 infinitive of purpose
2 *so* + effect
3 *because* + cause
4 first conditional
5 *help someone do something*

3 **Read and say which of the tips you already follow. Do you agree with them all? Would you add any?**

HOW TO BE A GOOD CONVERSATIONALIST

A good conversation can inform and inspire. Here are some tips to help you do just that and become a better conversationalist.

1 BE PRESENT
Look the other person in the eye and give them your full attention. If you don't, they won't want to give you theirs.

2 LISTEN
This is more difficult than it sounds. Being a good conversationalist is not just about talking. If you listen well, you will make the other person feel understood and you can move the conversation forward in the right way.

3 RESPECT ALL PARTICIPANTS
Ignoring someone in a conversation is quite hurtful. Everyone deserves to be heard and you can learn something from every person you speak to.

4 DON'T BE AFRAID TO CHECK YOU'VE UNDERSTOOD
If you don't understand something, say so. Understanding is a two-way process; it's the speaker's responsibility to make themselves understood and the listener's to try to understand.

Did you notice?

4 **Find these phrases in the text. What do the words in *italics* refer to?**

1 do just *that* (introduction)
2 if you *don't* (tip 1)
3 *This* is more difficult than it sounds (tip 2)
4 say *so* (tip 4)

NOW YOU! → Workbook page 72

5 **PLAN Choose from the ideas below or invent your own and write a plan with an introduction and numbered tips.**

Effective messaging | How to give a good speech | Protecting your privacy | Finding a good bargain

WRITING TOOLS
Use reference words like auxiliary verbs, pronouns and *so* to avoid repeating phrases.

6 **WRITE Use your plan to write your list of tips. Remember to use reference words and language for cause and effect.**

7 **CHECK Read your text and check that you have used the cause and effect structures correctly.**

PROJECT TASK 6 Campaign

- You are going to prepare your campaign speeches. Decide if each person in the team is going to make their own speech or if you will collaborate and create only two.
- Write the speech outline. You do not need to write the speech, just make notes to help you speak. Think about the arguments you are going to present and the language you will use to connect with the audience.
- Next, do the final task on page 80.

→ Workbook page 75

Do all exercises in your notebook

78 A list of tips / Language of cause and effect

LESSON FOCUS

Focus on Language of cause and effect

Writing A list of 'how-to' tips

Project task 6 Write outlines for the campaign speeches

Resources

Teacher's i-solutions

Warmer

On the left-hand side of the board, write things that are connected with the unit, for example: *Taking selfies; Handing out flyers*. Then write a list to the right of not obviously connected consequences, like: *Happiness; Wealth*. Put students in pairs to come up with ways in which one of things on the left could lead to one of the things on the right.

Focus on language of cause and effect

1 You could get students to do this and the next exercise in pairs. You could also ask them to imagine what contexts the sentences might appear in.

2 To extend the exercise, get students to write example sentences of their own using structures they are less familiar with. They could write sentences leaving gaps for the key words in order to test their classmates.

3 Put students in pairs or small groups for this exercise. Draw their attention back to their discussion on socialising in the **Core values** section of this unit.

Did you notice?

4 Give students time to find the answers to the best of their ability before checking. Point out the type of structure or information each reference word can refer to: the first two refer to verb phrases and the last two refer to full statements.

5 **PLAN** Once students have finished their plan, encourage them to talk it through with a partner.

WRITING TOOLS

Get students to read the **Writing tool** and ask them to find examples of each type of reference word in exercise 4.

6 **WRITE** Before students start writing, make a checklist on the board of any elements related to content, structure, language and style that they should bear in mind.

7 **CHECK** Once students have checked their own lists, they can swap with a partner and check theirs.

PROJECT TASK 6 Campaign

Put students in their groups again. Encourage them to challenge themselves, so that students who may be a little reticent should give speeches if possible and whoever isn't speaking should be active in the writing. Check that they are only writing notes, and not full sentences. Tell students that they need to keep their project notes together in their **Workbook** (page 75) or in their own notebook.

→ See pages 24-27 **Projects**

ANSWER KEY

Page 78

1 1 d 2 c 3 e 4 a 5 b

2 1 4a 2 3e 3 1d 4 2c 5 5b

3 *Student's own answers*

4
1 inform and inspire
2 look the other person in the eye and give them your full attention
3 listen
4 if you don't understand something

5 *Student's own answers*

6 *Student's own answers*

7 *Student's own answers*

FURTHER PRACTICE

Workbook page 72

Remind students to do all the exercises in their notebook

 CONTINUOUS ASSESSMENT Students can use language of cause and effect to write a list of 'how-to' tips.

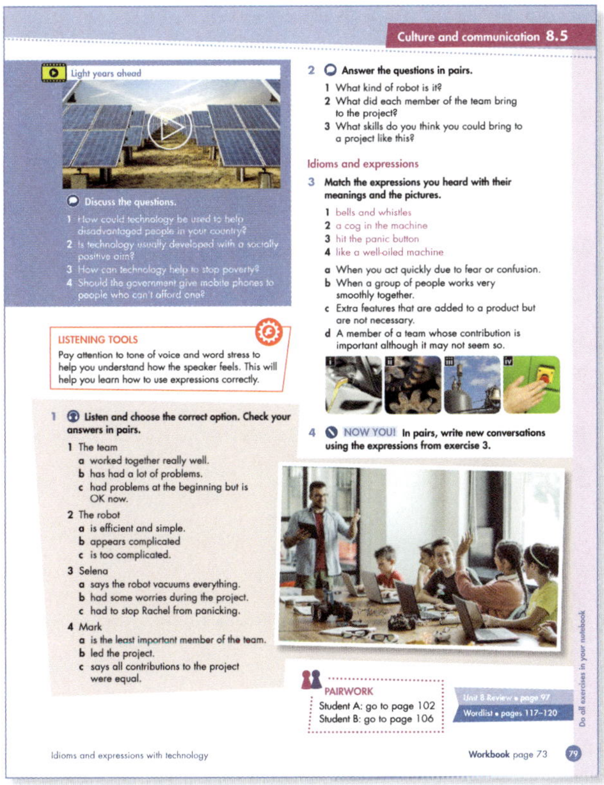

Culture and communication 8.5

Light years ahead

Discuss the questions.

1 How could technology be used to help disadvantaged people in your country?
2 Is technology usually developed with a socially positive aim?
3 How can technology help to stop poverty?
4 Should the government give mobile phones to people who can't afford one?

LISTENING TOOLS
Pay attention to tone of voice and word stress to help you understand how the speaker feels. This will help you learn how to use expressions correctly.

1 **Listen and choose the correct option. Check your answers in pairs.**

1 The team
  a worked together really well.
  b has had a lot of problems.
  c had problems at the beginning but is OK now.
2 The robot
  a is efficient and simple.
  b appears complicated
  c is too complicated.
3 Selena
  a says the robot vacuums everything.
  b had some worries during the project.
  c had to stop Rachel from panicking.
4 Mark
  a is the least important member of the team.
  b led the project.
  c says all contributions to the project were equal.

2 **Answer the questions in pairs.**

1 What kind of robot is it?
2 What did each member of the team bring to the project?
3 What skills do you think you could bring to a project like this?

Idioms and expressions

3 **Match the expressions you heard with their meanings and the pictures.**

1 bells and whistles
2 a cog in the machine
3 hit the panic button
4 like a well-oiled machine

a When you act quickly due to fear or confusion.
b When a group of people works very smoothly together.
c Extra features that are added to a product but are not necessary.
d A member of a team whose contribution is important although it may not seem so.

i ii iii iv

4 NOW YOU! **In pairs, write new conversations using the expressions from exercise 3.**

PAIRWORK
Student A: go to page 102
Student B: go to page 106

Unit 8 Review • page 97
Wordlist • pages 117–120

Do all exercises in your notebook

Idioms and expressions with technology

Workbook page 73 79

ANSWER KEY

Page 79

1 **1** a
2 b
3 b
4 c

2 **1** a vacuum cleaner
2 Selena - brainstorming, Mark – knowledge about robotics, Rachel – organisational skills
3 *Student's own answers*

3 **1** c; iii
2 d; ii
3 a; iv
4 b; i

4 *Student's own answers*

FURTHER PRACTICE AND UNIT ASSESSMENT

Unit 8 Review **Student's Book** page 97
Workbook page 73
- Reflect on your learning **Workbook** page 73
- Grammar reference and practice pages 91 and 96
- Wordlist and exercises pages 101 and 104

Tests available to download and edit from the **Richmond***Learning***Platform**

→ See pages 40-41 **Assessment**

LESSON FOCUS

Idioms and expressions Technology
Listening Multiple-choice questions about a technological project
Speaking A discussion about a robotics project

Resources

Teacher's i-solutions, Student's Book audio; Culture video worksheet

Light years ahead

- In pairs, ask students to compare/complete the *What I know...* exercises on the **Culture video worksheet**.
- Show students the **Culture video** and ask them to check/complete the *What I learned...* exercises on the worksheet. If students are completing the exercises for the first time, they will need to watch the video twice.
- In pairs, students compare answers.
- In small groups, tell students to complete/discuss the *What I wonder...* exercises on the worksheet.

Warmer

Watch the **Culture video** and discuss the questions with the whole class. If you don't have video facilities, simply discuss the questions.

LISTENING TOOLS

Get students to read the **Listening tool** and tell them you will give them a second listening of the audio so they can practise.

1 2.25 (See page 180 for transcripts) Tell students they are going to listen to a class talk about a robotics project and tell them to focus on answering the questions. Give them time to read the questions before playing the audio.

2 After students discuss their answers, elicit answers for question 3 and compare this to their discussions in the **Warmer**.

Idioms and expressions

3 To practise the **Listening tool**, play the audio again, stopping after each expression to guess meaning and note word stress.

4 NOW YOU! Get students to perform their conversations for other pairs. Then choose some pairs to perform their conversations for the class.

PAIRWORK **Student's Book** pages 102 and 106
See **Teacher's Book** page 152 for more information.
→ See pages 30-33 **Mediation**

Remind students to do all the exercises in their notebook

CONTINUOUS ASSESSMENT Students can use idioms and expressions with technology.

Unit 8 Review

Unit 8 Review

1 Listen and complete the sentences.

1 Gina uses the term ··· as another way to describe Generation Z.
2 She has ··· all her social media accounts.
3 She believes that posting and following people on social media is ···.
4 She would rather spend time with ··· than follow people on the internet.
5 She uses the word ··· to describe how she began feeling when looking at other people's posts.
6 She says researchers are examining the effect of social media on our ···.

2 Complete the second sentence so that it has a similar meaning to the first, using the word given. Use between two and five words.

EXAM TIP
You must use the word given without changing it, and up to four more words. Remember that contractions count as two words. If in doubt, guess.

1 My brother is studying computer game design at university.
HAVE
I have a brother who is studying computer game design at university.
2 You should change your password regularly to avoid being hacked.
DON'T
Your computer can easily be hacked ··· change your password regularly.
3 It's important during face-to-face conversations to look people in the eye.
YOU
··· people in the eye when you speak to them face to face.
4 Tech companies are adding new features to the new generation of smartphones.
ADDED
New features ··· new generation of smartphones.
5 Nowadays, you don't have to remember any phone numbers.
PEOPLE
In the past, ··· remember lots of phone numbers.

3 Imagine your school is going to start some lunchtime activities to encourage students' social skills. In pairs, discuss which might be the most interesting to attend and match the names to the pictures.

debating class · drama club · English conversation · team building

Do all exercises in your notebook

External exam practice 97

Student's Book page 97

ANSWER KEY

See page 183 for transcript

1 2.37
1 digital generation
2 deleted
3 an addiction
4 her friends
5 down
6 mental health

2 **1** have a brother who
2 if you don't
3 You should look
4 are being added to the
5 people had to

3 *Student's own answers*

Pairwork

Unit 8 • Student A

1 You and Student B have pictures of the same block of flats. Take turns asking questions in order to find six differences.
In flat 101, is there a woman talking on a mobile phone?

Student's Book page 102

Unit 8 • Student B

1 You and Student A have pictures of the same block of flats. Take turns asking questions in order to find six differences.
In flat 102, is there a boy listening to music on his radio?

Student's Book page 106

CEFR MEDIATION DESCRIPTOR

- **Encouraging conceptual talk**
  Students can ask questions to invite people to clarify their reasoning.

- **Interpreting similarities and differences**
  Tell students that they have information about a two different blocks of flats. Explain that they have to take turns at asking each other questions in order to identify six differences.

Remind students to do all the exercises in their notebook

Unit 8 Grammar reference

Relative clauses: defining

A **defining relative clause** is a part of a sentence that gives essential information about a noun.

Use the relative pronouns ***who*** or ***that*** to define a person.
You can keep in touch with people **who live on the other side of the world.**
I have a sister **that can't live without social media.**

Use the relative pronouns ***which*** or ***that*** to define an object.
Life is something **which you should enjoy.**
People wasted time doing tasks **that were dangerous, difficult or repetitive.**

We use relative clauses to give extra information in a sentence. In defining relative clauses, we give essential, extra information by linking parts of the sentence with ***which/that, who/that, where*** or ***whose***.

The woman **that gave the talk was very interesting**.
This is the exercise **which the teacher gave us**.
The set is the place **where a film is made**.

When ***who, which*** or ***that*** is the object in the relative clause, we can leave it out.

Can you bring me the book **(that) I bought yesterday**?
The student **(who) you saw** studies at Oxford University.
I've lost the skirt **(which) I bought in London**.

When the relative clause refers to a situation, not a specific thing, we always use ***which***.

I overslept, **which** meant that I arrived really late.

We never use ***which*** to refer to a person, we always use ***who***.

The girl **who** is reading the newspaper is in my class.
NOT ~~The girl which is reading the newspaper is in my class.~~

We don't use a pronoun (e.g. ***him, them***) in addition to ***who, which*** or ***that***.

She is the woman **who** you met at the party.
NOT ~~She is the woman who you met her at the party.~~

Relative clauses: non-defining

A defining relative clause gives essential information about a noun. A **non-defining relative clause** gives extra, non-essential information about a noun. The information is separated from the main clause by commas.

Use the relative pronouns ***who*** or ***that*** to give more information about a person.
My friend Jenny, **the girl who is holding the placard,** just gave a speech.
Lots of people, **that often live in developing countries**, don't have mobile phones.

Use the relative pronouns ***which*** or ***that*** to give more information about an object.
Radiation, **which is produced by mobile phones**, could be the reason your phone gets hot.
Handing out flyers, **which are often used for publicity,** isn't environmentally friendly.

In non-defining relative clauses, the clause gives optional extra information.

My friend Mario, **who went to the same school as me,** lives in Madrid.
The car, **which can reach speeds of over 300 km an hour**, is very expensive.
The new head teacher, **who moved here from a school in London**, seems like a pretty nice guy.

We can use **quantifiers + *of which/of whom*** in non-defining relative clauses.

She's got loads of clothes, **most of which** she never wears.
I've got four brothers, **all of whom** live in London.
Their camp has several activities to choose from, **some of which** sound really exciting!

Do all exercises in your notebook

114 **Workbook** pages 93-96

Student's Book page 114

Wordlist

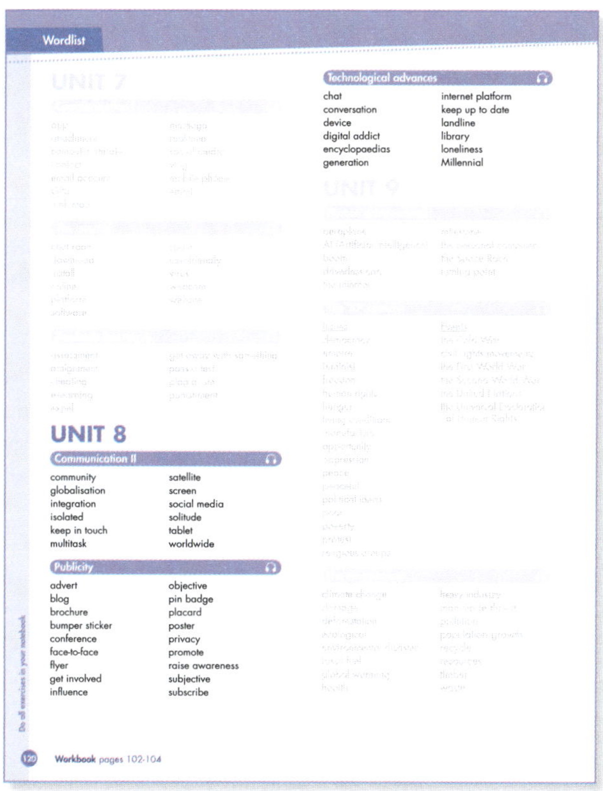

Wordlist

UNIT 8

Communication II

community, globalisation, integration, isolated, keep in touch, multitask, satellite, screen, social media, solitude, tablet, worldwide

Publicity

advert, blog, brochure, bumper sticker, conference, face-to-face, flyer, get involved, influence, objective, pin badge, placard, poster, privacy, promote, raise awareness, subjective, subscribe

Technological advances

chat, conversation, device, digital addict, encyclopaedias, generation, internet platform, keep up to date, landline, library, loneliness, Millennial

Do all exercises in your notebook

120 **Workbook** pages 102-104

Student's Book page 120

2.60 2.61 2.62

Remind students to do all the exercises in their notebook

PROJECT: Campaign

PROJECT: Campaign

RECAP

- In this project, you have written a campaign proposal and created publicity and speeches to promote the campaign.
- In **units 7 and 8**, you also learnt vocabulary related to technology, reviewed the passive voice and relative clauses, read texts about technology and communication, and wrote a speech and 'how-to tips'.
- Now you are ready to launch your campaign!

TASK 1 Write reports on technology that is beneficial in modern society.
TASK 2 List the advantages and disadvantages of using technology in the classroom.
TASK 3 Write a campaign proposal.
TASK 4 Think about digital support for your campaign.
TASK 5 Create a logo, slogan and publicity for your campaign.
TASK 6 Write outlines for your campaign speeches.

FINAL TASK: Launch your campaign

- You are going to launch your campaign for positive technology use and present your material to the class.
- Choose someone to:
  - manage the launch and explain your proposal.
  - deliver the speeches (two students).
  - present the publicity that your team has made.
- When all the teams have presented their campaigns, the class will vote for the best campaign.
- The winning team could develop the campaign and launch it for the whole school.

USEFUL EXPRESSIONS

- Today, we're here to listen to...
- After you have listened, please vote…
- We would like to present our proposal…
- We think this would be beneficial because…
- We believe this is feasible because…

21ST CENTURY SKILLS

Online security

Any frequent user of technology knows that there are risks involved, from hacking to viruses and false identities. If your phone regularly overheats, your battery life suddenly slows, or your friends receive emails from you that you didn't send, your device may have been attacked.

Keeping antivirus software on your device up-to-date, covering your camera and carefully choosing which links you click on are all ways of protecting yourself.

Do all exercises in your notebook

GO BEYOND
POLITICAL CAMPAIGNS

In democratic countries, political campaigns are an important part of the election process. During the months before an election, politicians often travel around the country, meeting people and giving speeches. The campaign speeches focus on big issues, such as the economy, health care, the environment, national security and education.

Politicians traditionally appeared on television, on the radio and in printed media. Nowadays, social media has become an important campaign tool. However, certain platforms have been accused of interfering with the voting process, as they have the power to influence voters' decisions by manipulating their newsfeeds and the links they see.

As political campaigns become more like a form of entertainment, many people feel that the serious job of choosing a leader for a country has become a secondary purpose. Some politicians exploit voters' emotions and fears rather than presenting the information that people really need.

It is our responsibility to question and analyse the information we are given and make up our own minds.

Answer the questions in pairs.

1 What do you think makes a political campaign succeed or fail?
2 Do politicians run campaigns in your country? What are they like?
3 Have you or someone in your family ever participated in a political campaign before? How were you/they involved?
4 Do you think that political campaigns ensure that voters have all the information they need to make an educated decision? How can this be improved?

EVALUATION

Answer the questions in your team.

1 Do you think that you achieved the objectives of your campaign?
2 What were the strongest and weakest elements of your campaign?
3 Do you think that each member of the team had the correct role? Why?
4 Why do you think that the winning campaign was chosen?

Do all exercises in your notebook

Workbook project task notes

PROJECT: Campaign

Team members

________ ________ ________ ________

TASK 1

Technology 1: ____________________
Technology 2: ____________________
Technology 3: ____________________
Technology 4: ____________________

→ Student's book page 65

TASK 2

Technology we could use in our classroom: ____________________

→ Student's book page 67

TASK 3

Campaign proposal notes: ____________________

→ Student's book page 70

TASK 4

Digital support ideas: ____________________

→ Student's book page 73

TASK 5

Where we will display the publicity: ____________________

Slogan: ____________________

→ Student's book page 75

TASK 6

Speech outline: ____________________

→ Student's book page 78

FINAL TASK

The part I will present: ____________________

→ Student's book page 80

Remind students to do all the exercises in their notebook

PROJECT FOCUS

→ See pages 24-27 **Projects**

Skills

- Collaborate to prepare and launch a campaign
- Research and write about the benefits of four types of technology
- Research and compile a list of technologies for the classroom, with the advantages and disadvantages of each
- Write a campaign proposal
- Reach consensus about digital support for the campaign
- Create publicity for the campaign, including a logo and slogan
- Prepare and deliver speeches
- Discuss evaluations of the project
- Read and discuss a text related to the project

CEFR mediation

Overall mediation

Can collaborate with interest and empathy, asking and answering simple questions, formulating and responding to suggestions, checking agreement and proposing alternatives to achieve a common goal, and can convey the main points of text in simple language.

→ See pages 30-33 **Mediation**

Preparation Remind students to bring their work from tasks 1-6 and their notes from the **Workbook** project task notes (pages 20-21) or their own notebook. Bring cue cards if needed for the presentation. Have students bring in their self-assessment diaries if you decided that you wanted them to keep one.

RECAP

Put students in their teams and read through the **Recap** as a class. Draw their attention to the project tasks and the unit objectives and ask which task helped achieve which objectives. Make sure they have all the materials and notes that they need (see **Preparation**) for the **Final task**.

FINAL TASK: Launch your campaign

Tell students they are now going to launch their campaigns. Read through the steps of the task and agree on time limits for each launch and for the final preparation. If you can, include time for a short practice run and encourage them to use the **Useful expressions**. Make sure everyone is collaborating. If they are presenting information using technology, remind them of the presentation tips they read on page 63.

Before the first campaign launch, remind them they will be voting on the best at the end and if you are going to make the vote the basis for a real school campaign remind them of that too. In any case, suggest they vote based on how convincing the campaign proposals are, and encourage them to take notes as they watch to help them decide. Before the final vote, you could have a brief discussion to create a shortlist of nominations to make the vote seem more meaningful. Afterwards, direct their attention to the **21st Century skill**.

21ST CENTURY SKILLS

Read through the text and ask students which of the advice given they follow. Ask them if they remember any other tips on online security in the two units (see page 67) or if they have any other useful advice to share.

→ See pages 28-29 **21st Century skills**

EVALUATION

Before students discuss the questions in their teams, give them time to prepare notes about their experience in the project. Remind students to be supportive and give constructive feedback. Monitor discussions, noting comments you think are worth asking them to report to the class.

Have a class discussion about what students have learnt from the project, reminding them of the unit objectives, the **Core values** and the **Learning tools** sections of units 7 and 8, as well as the **21st Century skills** section of the **Project** pages.

If you have decided to use the evaluation exercise as a springboard for a student self-assessment diary (see **Evaluation** notes page 77), give them time to do this now and remind them to refer to the **Reflect on your learning** section of the **Workbook** if they have one.

→ See pages 40-41 **Assessment**

GO BEYOND

Ask students if they've ever watched a political campaign and what they think of them. Since politics can be a sensitive topic, before students read the texts and discuss answers perhaps remind them to respect each other's views and suggest that they keep the conversation general or more about foreign politics if they prefer. You could also focus a class discussion on question 4 and elicit effective ways of informing and persuading members of the general public, perhaps using petitions as an example.

CONTINUOUS ASSESSMENT Students can collaborate to prepare and launch a campaign.

9 CHANGING TIMES

At the start of each unit and lesson, explain to the students what the objectives are.

Language objectives

Grammar

So* and *such

- Students practise using *so* and *such* for emphasis.

***So* with quantifiers**

- Students practise using *so* with quantifiers and nouns for emphasis.

So* and *neither

- Students practise using *so* and *neither* to express agreement or similarities.

Vocabulary

Human achievements: *aeroplane, AI (Artificial Intelligence), boom, driverless cars, the internet, milestone, the personal computer, the Space Race, turning point*

- Students practise vocabulary related to human achievements.

The 20th century: Issues: *democracy, empire, feminist, freedom, human rights, hunger, living conditions, manufacture, opportunity, oppression, peace, peaceful, political ideas, poor, poverty, protest, religious groups,* Events: *the Cold War, civil rights movements, the First World War, the Second World War, the United Nations, the Universal Declaration of Human Rights*

- Students practise vocabulary for issues and events in the 20th century.

The environment: *climate change, damage, deforestation, ecological, environmental disaster, fossil fuel, global warming, health, heavy industry, man-made threat, pollution, population growth, recycle, resources, timber, waste*

- Students encounter vocabulary related to the environment.

Idioms and expressions

Change: *shake things up, start from scratch, change for the better, make matters worse*

- Students look at idioms and expressions related to change in a talk about the 20th century

Recycled language

Narrative tenses, 2nd and 3rd conditionals, Adjectives, Quantifiers and countable and uncountable nouns, Linking expressions

Skills objectives

Speaking

- Students share opinions about the future.
- Students compare predictions for the near future.
- Students discuss environmental threats and solutions to environmental problems.
- Students discuss how the world is changing, using idioms and expressions.

Pronunciation: Students practise the /ɜː/ sound and look at typical spelling patterns that produce it.

Pairwork: Students take notes on two different texts about the pros and cons of vlogging and compare their points and opinions.

Listening

- Students listen and complete a historical timeline.
- Students listen and complete a conversation about important events in the 20th century.
- Students listen and complete a text about the causes and consequences of historical events.
- Students listen and complete a conversation about two important historical figures.
- Students listen to answer multiple-choice questions in a talk about the 20th century.

Reading

- Students skim a text to match a summary of the main argument.
- Students read a text to find statements that support the main argument.
- Students read a text to find words, phrases and sentences that help structure the argument.

Core values: Students discuss quotes about **thinking globally** and reflect on the value of it.

Writing

- Students look at the structure and linking language of an essay.
- Students plan, write and check a discursive essay about humanity and progress.

Focus on essay structure

Remind students to do all the exercises in their notebook

Learning to learn tools

SPEAKING TOOLS Students practise giving extended answers to get more practice at speaking.	LISTENING TOOLS Students practise listening first for key words and then for details.
READING TOOLS Students develop a knowledge of essay structure to help facilitate comprehension.	WRITING TOOLS Students practise using a range of structural devices to make their essay writing clearer and more convincing.

Review task objectives: Quiz

Review Task 1 Students plan a quiz about the language content of the **Student's Book**. They decide which two students will focus on vocabulary questions and which two will focus on grammar questions, as well as what type of questions to ask.

Review Task 2 Students write the questions and the answers.

Review Task 3 Students exchange quizzes with other teams.

Audiovisual objectives

Vlog: Students watch and listen to Holly talk about our ancestors and historical turning points.

Culture: Students watch and listen to Holly talk about six different generations alive today.

Grammar animations: Students are presented with visual presentations of the unit grammar.

Key competences

LC **Linguistic**
pages 82-89

MST **Mathematical and Science and Technology**
pages 82-83, 86-87

DC **Digital**
pages 82-85, 89

SCC **Social and Civic**
pages 82-85

CAE **Cultural awareness and expression**
pages 82-85, 89

LL **Learning to learn**
pages 82, 85, 86, 88

IE **Sense of initiative and entrepreneurship**
pages 83, 85, 88

→ See pages 42-43 **Key competences**

CEFR Mediation

9.1 Relaying specific information in writing
Can write specific information from spoken texts.

9.2 Facilitating collaborative interaction with peers
Can make and respond to suggestions.

9.3 Processing text in writing
Can summarise the main points in informational texts.

9.4 Processing text in writing
Can pick out and reproduce key words and phrases or short sentences from a short text.

9.5 Facilitating pluricultural space
Can exchange information about values and attitudes to culture in a simple way.

Review Facilitating collaborative interaction with peers
Can define the task in basic terms in a discussion and ask others to contribute their expertise and experience.

Unit review Relaying specific information in writing
Can relay specific information from spoken texts.

Pairwork Overall mediation
Can collaborate to achieve a common goal and can convey the main points of a text in simple language.

→ See pages 30-33 **Mediation**

Remind students to do all the exercises in their notebook

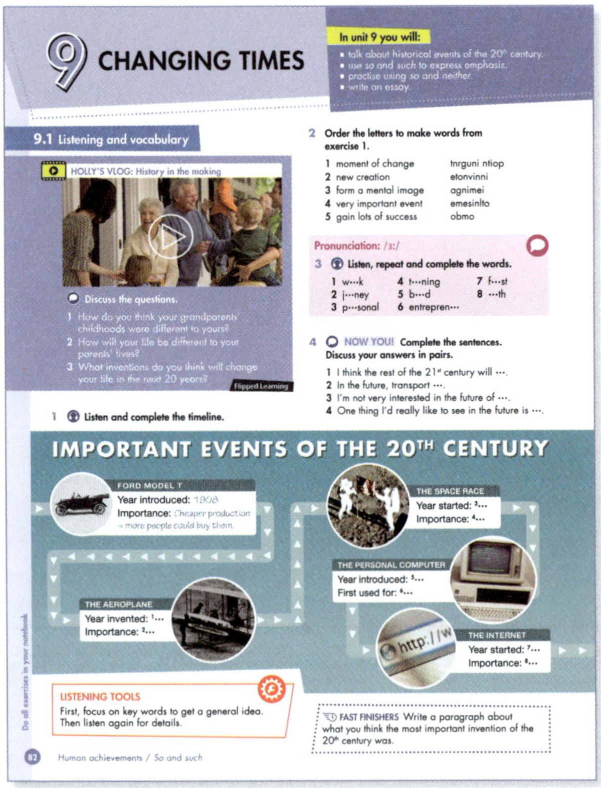
9 CHANGING TIMES

In unit 9 you will:
- talk about historical events of the 20th century.
- use so and such to express emphasis.
- practise using so and neither.
- write an essay.

9.1 Listening and vocabulary

HOLLY'S VLOG: History in the making

Discuss the questions.
1 How do you think your grandparents' childhoods were different to yours?
2 How will your life be different to your parents' lives?
3 What inventions do you think will change your life in the next 20 years?

1 Listen and complete the timeline.

2 Order the letters to make words from exercise 1.
1 moment of change — tnrguni ntiop
2 new creation — etonvinni
3 form a mental image — agnimei
4 very important event — emesinlto
5 gain lots of success — obmo

Pronunciation: /ɜː/
3 Listen, repeat and complete the words.
1 w…k 2 j…ney 3 p…sonal 4 t…ning 5 b…d 6 entrepren… 7 f…st 8 …th

4 NOW YOU! Complete the sentences. Discuss your answers in pairs.
1 I think the rest of the 21st century will …
2 In the future, transport …
3 I'm not very interested in the future of …
4 One thing I'd really like to see in the future is …

IMPORTANT EVENTS OF THE 20TH CENTURY
FORD MODEL T — Year introduced: 1908 — Importance: Cheaper production = more people could buy them.
THE AEROPLANE — Year invented: 1… — Importance: 2…
THE SPACE RACE — Year started: 3… — Importance: 4…
THE PERSONAL COMPUTER — Year introduced: 5… — First used for: 6…
THE INTERNET — Year started: 7… — Importance: 8…

LISTENING TOOLS
First, focus on key words to get a general idea. Then listen again for details.

FAST FINISHERS Write a paragraph about what you think the most important invention of the 20th century was.

82 Human achievements / So and such

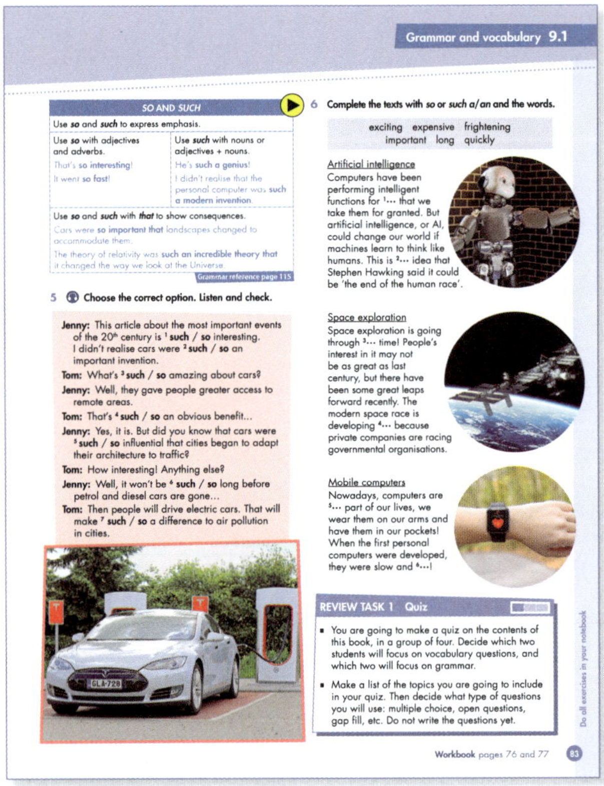
Grammar and vocabulary 9.1

SO AND SUCH
Use so and such to express emphasis.
Use so with adjectives and adverbs. That's so interesting! It went so fast!
Use such with nouns or adjectives + nouns. He's such a genius! I didn't realise that the personal computer was such a modern invention.
Use so and such with that to show consequences.
Cars were so important that landscapes changed to accommodate them.
The theory of relativity was such an incredible theory that it changed the way we look at the Universe.
Grammar reference page 115

5 Choose the correct option. Listen and check.
Jenny: This article about the most important events of the 20th century is 1 such / so interesting. I didn't realise cars were 2 such / so an important invention.
Tom: What's 3 such / so amazing about cars?
Jenny: Well, they gave people greater access to remote areas.
Tom: That's 4 such / so an obvious benefit…
Jenny: Yes, it is. But did you know that cars were 5 such / so influential that cities began to adapt their architecture to traffic?
Tom: How interesting! Anything else?
Jenny: Well, it won't be 6 such / so long before petrol and diesel cars are gone…
Tom: Then people will drive electric cars. That will make 7 such / so a difference to air pollution in cities.

6 Complete the texts with so or such a/an and the words.
exciting expensive frightening important long quickly

Artificial intelligence
Computers have been performing intelligent functions for 1… that we take them for granted. But artificial intelligence, or AI, could change our world if machines learn to think like humans. This is 2… idea that Stephen Hawking said it could be 'the end of the human race'.

Space exploration
Space exploration is going through 3… time! People's interest in it may not be as great as last century, but there have been some great leaps forward recently. The modern space race is developing 4… because private companies are racing governmental organisations.

Mobile computers
Nowadays, computers are 5… part of our lives, we wear them on our arms and have them in our pockets! When the first personal computers were developed, they were slow and 6…!

REVIEW TASK 1 Quiz
- You are going to make a quiz on the contents of this book, in a group of four. Decide which two students will focus on vocabulary questions, and which two will focus on grammar.
- Make a list of the topics you are going to include in your quiz. Then decide what type of questions you will use: multiple choice, open questions, gap fill, etc. Do not write the questions yet.

Workbook pages 76 and 77 83

ANSWER KEY

Pages 82-83

1
1 1903
2 meant the conquest of the air
3 1955
4 brought universal benefits, including GPS, accurate weather predictions and satellite internet access
5 the 1970s
6 word processing, databases, spreadsheets and games
7 the 1960s
8 gave us easy and widespread access to information and contact with other users

2
1 turning point
2 invention
3 imagine
4 milestone
5 boom

3
1 work
2 journey
3 personal
4 turning
5 bird
6 entrepreneur
7 first
8 earth

4 *Student's own answers*

5
1 so
2 such
3 so
4 such
5 so
6 so
7 such

6
1 so long
2 such a frightening
3 such an exciting
4 so quickly
5 such an important
6 so expensive

Remind students to do all the exercises in their notebook

LESSON FOCUS

Grammar *So* and *such*

Vocabulary Human achievements

Listening Completing a historical timeline; Completing a conversation about the 20th century

Speaking Sharing opinions about the future

Review task 1 Students plan a quiz about the language content of the Student's Book

Resources

Teacher's i-solutions, Student's Book audio, Vlog and worksheets

Flipped Learning

HOLLY'S'S VLOG: History in the making

- Make sure to set up the **Flipped Learning** work with the students beforehand. **See pages 20-23 for complete Flipped Learning guidelines**.
- Ask students to put the **Flipped Learning worksheets** on their desks and walk around to check how many have completed the Flipped task.
- In pairs or small groups, ask students to compare and check the *Before you watch...* and *While you watch...* exercises on the worksheet.
- Show students **Holly's Vlog** and ask volunteers to provide correct answers and clarify any doubts that other students may have.
- Choose three or four students to read aloud their answers to the *After you watch...* exercises on the worksheet and encourage some class discussion.
- Move straight to exercise 1 on page 82.

Warmer

Watch Holly's Vlog and discuss the questions with the whole class. If you don't have video facilities, simply discuss the questions.

1 2.26 (See page 180 for transcripts) Tell students to keep their books closed. Tell them that they are going to hear people describing important events in the 20th century. Ask them to take notes about the events. Ask them to open their books, and then play the audio for them to complete the exercise.

LISTENING TOOLS

Get students to read the **Listening tool** and point out that they have just done this and ask them to reflect on how it helped them with the exercise.

2 Play the audio again or show students the transcript to help them do the exercise.

Pronunciation

3 2.27 (See page 181 for transcripts) Get students to make the sound first and then try to guess the words before you play the audio.

4 NOW YOU! Model your own answers to prompt them. After they have finished, find out who had answers in common.

FAST FINISHERS Students can complete this exercise alone or in pairs.

Flipped Learning

SO AND *SUCH*

Draw students' attention to the **Grammar table**. Remind students that they can use this as a quick reference while completing the exercises.

Show students the **Grammar animation** and/or refer students to the **Grammar reference** on page 115 for further information on form and use.

→ See page 23 for how to flip the **grammar lesson**

5 2.28 (See page 181 for transcripts) Ask students which invention the two people are talking about (the car). Refer them to the **Grammar table** to do the exercise and then ask them what they think about electric cars.

6 Encourage students to notice that if they find a noun straight after the word gap they need to use *such a/an*. Ask which of the areas of technology they think will have the biggest impact on our future.

REVIEW TASK 1 Quiz

Organise students into teams of 4 and tell them they are going to prepare quizzes to exchange with each other to help them revise the language content of the book. Go through the task together.

FURTHER PRACTICE

Workbook pages 76-77
- **Grammar reference and practice** pages 92 and 96
- **Wordlist and exercises** pages 101 and 104

Remind students to do all the exercises in their notebook

CONTINUOUS ASSESSMENT Students can talk about human achievements and use *so* and *such*.

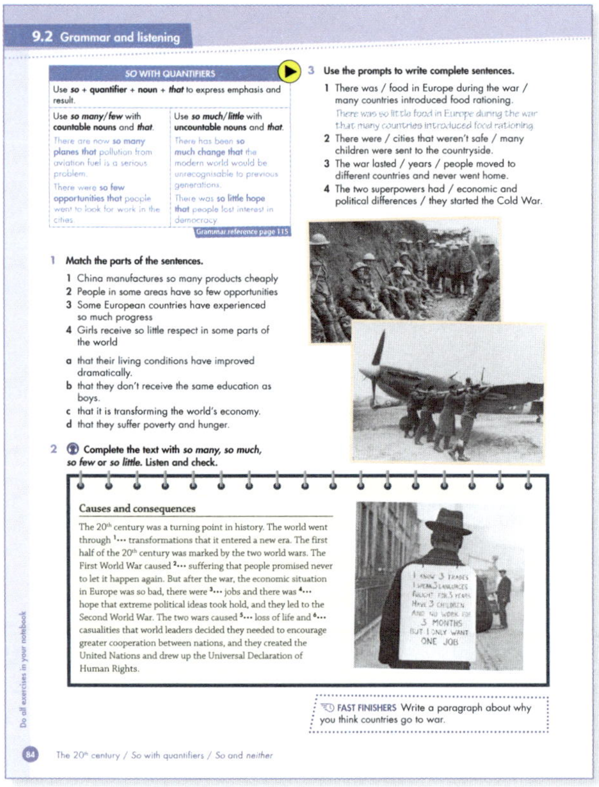
9.2 Grammar and listening

SO WITH QUANTIFIERS

Use *so* + quantifier + noun + *that* to express emphasis and result.

Use *so many/few* with countable nouns and *that*.	Use *so much/little* with uncountable nouns and *that*.
There are now so many planes that pollution from aviation fuel is a serious problem. There were so few opportunities that people went to look for work in the cities.	There has been so much change that the modern world would be unrecognisable to previous generations. There was so little hope that people lost interest in democracy.

Grammar reference page 115

1 Match the parts of the sentences.

1 China manufactures so many products cheaply
2 People in some areas have so few opportunities
3 Some European countries have experienced so much progress
4 Girls receive so little respect in some parts of the world

a that their living conditions have improved dramatically.
b that they don't receive the same education as boys.
c that it is transforming the world's economy.
d that they suffer poverty and hunger.

2 Complete the text with *so many, so much, so few* or *so little*. Listen and check.

Causes and consequences

The 20th century was a turning point in history. The world went through ¹… transformations that it entered a new era. The first half of the 20th century was marked by the two world wars. The First World War caused ²… suffering that people promised never to let it happen again. But after the war, the economic situation in Europe was so bad, there were ³… jobs and there was ⁴… hope that extreme political ideas took hold, and they led to the Second World War. The two wars caused ⁵… loss of life and ⁶… casualties that world leaders decided they needed to encourage greater cooperation between nations, and they created the United Nations and drew up the Universal Declaration of Human Rights.

3 Use the prompts to write complete sentences.

1 There was / food in Europe during the war / many countries introduced food rationing.
There was so little food in Europe during the war that many countries introduced food rationing.
2 There were / cities that weren't safe / many children were sent to the countryside.
3 The war lasted / years / people moved to different countries and never went home.
4 The two superpowers had / economic and political differences / they started the Cold War.

FAST FINISHERS Write a paragraph about why you think countries go to war.

Do all exercises in your notebook

84 The 20th century / So with quantifiers / So and neither

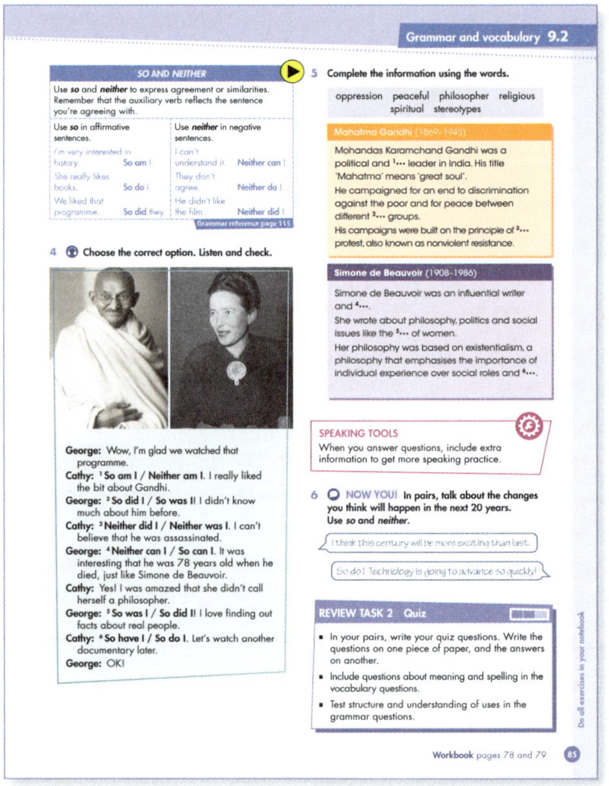
Grammar and vocabulary 9.2

SO AND NEITHER

Use *so* and *neither* to express agreement or similarities. Remember that the auxiliary verb reflects the sentence you're agreeing with.

Use *so* in affirmative sentences.	Use *neither* in negative sentences.
I'm very interested in history. So am I.	I can't understand it. Neither can I.
She really likes books. So do I.	They don't agree. Neither do I.
We liked that programme. So did they.	He didn't like the film. Neither did I.

Grammar reference page 115

4 Choose the correct option. Listen and check.

George: Wow, I'm glad we watched that programme.
Cathy: ¹**So am I / Neither am I.** I really liked the bit about Gandhi.
George: ²**So did I / So was I!** I didn't know much about him before.
Cathy: ³**Neither did I / Neither was I.** I can't believe that he was assassinated.
George: ⁴**Neither can I / So can I.** It was interesting that he was 78 years old when he died, just like Simone de Beauvoir.
Cathy: Yes! I was amazed that she didn't call herself a philosopher.
George: ⁵**So was I / So did I!** I love finding out facts about real people.
Cathy: ⁶**So have I / So do I.** Let's watch another documentary later.
George: OK!

5 Complete the information using the words.

oppression peaceful philosopher religious spiritual stereotypes

Mahatma Gandhi (1869–1948)

Mohandas Karamchand Gandhi was a political and ¹… leader in India. His title 'Mahatma' means 'great soul'.
He campaigned for an end to discrimination against the poor and for peace between different ²… groups.
His campaigns were built on the principle of ³… protest, also known as nonviolent resistance.

Simone de Beauvoir (1908–1986)

Simone de Beauvoir was an influential writer and ⁴….
She wrote about philosophy, politics and social issues like the ⁵… of women.
Her philosophy was based on existentialism, a philosophy that emphasises the importance of individual experience over social roles and ⁶….

SPEAKING TOOLS
When you answer questions, include extra information to get more speaking practice.

6 NOW YOU! In pairs, talk about the changes you think will happen in the next 20 years. Use *so* and *neither*.

I think this century will be more exciting than last.
So do I. Technology is going to advance so quickly!

REVIEW TASK 2 Quiz

- In your pairs, write your quiz questions. Write the questions on one piece of paper, and the answers on another.
- Include questions about meaning and spelling in the vocabulary questions.
- Test structure and understanding of uses in the grammar questions.

Do all exercises in your notebook

Workbook pages 78 and 79 85

ANSWER KEY

Pages 84-85

1
1 c
2 d
3 a
4 b

2
1 so many
2 so much
3 so few
4 so little
5 so much
6 so many

3
1 There was so little food in Europe during the war that many countries introduced food rationing.
2 There were so many cities that weren't safe that many children were sent to the countryside.
3 The war lasted so many years that people moved to different countries and never went home.
4 The two superpowers had so many economic and political differences that they started the Cold War.

4
1 So am I
2 So did I
3 Neither did I
4 Neither can I
5 So was I
6 So do I

5
1 spiritual
2 religious
3 peaceful
4 philosopher
5 oppression
6 stereotypes

6 *Student's own answers*

Remind students to do all the exercises in their notebook

LESSON FOCUS

Grammar *So* with quantifiers; *So* and *neither*

Vocabulary The 20th century

Listening Completing a text about historical events; Completing a conversation about historical figures

Speaking Comparing predictions for the future

Review task 2 Write the questions and the answers to the quiz

Resources

Teacher's i-solutions, Student's Book audio

Warmer

Give students a series of sentence beginnings with *so* + adjective + *that* and get them to complete the sentences. You could give points for sentences that are the most common in class or for sentences that no one else has, but that you think make sense. Sentence beginnings could include: *Sam was so clever that…; The robot is so small that…; The spacecraft can travel so fast that…; etc.*

SO WITH QUANTIFIERS

Draw students' attention to the **Grammar table**. Remind students that they can use this as a quick reference while completing the exercises.

Show students the **Grammar animation** and/or refer students to the **Grammar reference** on page 115 for further information on form and use.

→ See page 23 for how to flip the **grammar lesson**

1 Ask students to think of the likely result of each sentence beginning before they do the exercise.

2 2.29 (See page 181 for transcripts) Ask students if they know what period of history the photo represents (The Great Depression). Ask them to scan the text to find the other three historical events it mentions (The two world wars and the creation of the UN). Get students to complete the exercise and tell you how each event in turn led to the next in their own words.

3 Refer students to the **Grammar table** as they do the exercise.

FAST FINISHERS Students can complete this exercise alone or in pairs.

4 2.30 (See page 181 for transcripts) Ask students to identify the two historical figures (Gandhi and Simone de Beauvoir) and point out that they only have to find out whether the people are agreeing in the affirmative or in the negative. Ask them what the auxiliary verbs in each answer refer to in the conversation.

5 Give definitions for any words the students aren't familiar with before they complete the texts. Then ask what influences they think Gandhi and Simone de Beauvoir have had on society.

SPEAKING TOOLS

Get students to read the **Speaking tool** and ask them to put it into practice in the next exercise.

6 **NOW YOU!** Make sure students give reasons for their answers. Ask a few pairs of students what predictions they agreed on after they complete the exercise.

REVIEW TASK 2 Quiz

Put students back in their groups, make sure they know which pair is doing which questions and get them to continue preparing the quiz.

FURTHER PRACTICE

Workbook pages 78-79
- **Grammar reference and practice** pages 92 and 96
- **Wordlist and exercises** pages 101 and 104

Vocabulary and Grammar worksheets available to download from the **Richmond***Learning***Platform**

→ See pages 38-39 **Mixed-ability classes**

CONTINUOUS ASSESSMENT Students can talk about the 20th century, and use *So* with quantifiers and *So* and *neither* to express agreement and similarities.

Remind students to do all the exercises in their notebook

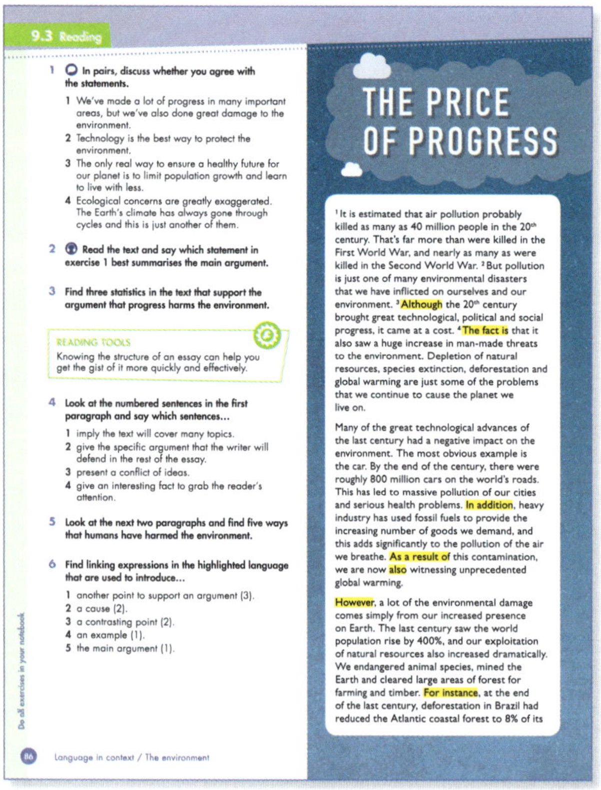

1 In pairs, discuss whether you agree with the statements.

1 We've made a lot of progress in many important areas, but we've also done great damage to the environment.
2 Technology is the best way to protect the environment.
3 The only real way to ensure a healthy future for our planet is to limit population growth and learn to live with less.
4 Ecological concerns are greatly exaggerated. The Earth's climate has always gone through cycles and this is just another of them.

2 Read the text and say which statement in exercise 1 best summarises the main argument.

3 Find three statistics in the text that support the argument that progress harms the environment.

READING TOOLS
Knowing the structure of an essay can help you get the gist of it more quickly and effectively.

4 Look at the numbered sentences in the first paragraph and say which sentences…

1 imply the text will cover many topics.
2 give the specific argument that the writer will defend in the rest of the essay.
3 present a conflict of ideas.
4 give an interesting fact to grab the reader's attention.

5 Look at the next two paragraphs and find five ways that humans have harmed the environment.

6 Find linking expressions in the highlighted language that are used to introduce…

1 another point to support an argument (3).
2 a cause (2).
3 a contrasting point (2).
4 an example (1).
5 the main argument (1).

Do all exercises in your notebook

THE PRICE OF PROGRESS

[1] It is estimated that air pollution probably killed as many as 40 million people in the 20th century. That's far more than were killed in the First World War, and nearly as many as were killed in the Second World War. [2] But pollution is just one of many environmental disasters that we have inflicted on ourselves and our environment. [3] Although the 20th century brought great technological, political and social progress, it came at a cost. [4] The fact is that it also saw a huge increase in man-made threats to the environment. Depletion of natural resources, species extinction, deforestation and global warming are just some of the problems that we continue to cause the planet we live on.

Many of the great technological advances of the last century had a negative impact on the environment. The most obvious example is the car. By the end of the century, there were roughly 800 million cars on the world's roads. This has led to massive pollution of our cities and serious health problems. In addition, heavy industry has used fossil fuels to provide the increasing number of goods we demand, and this adds significantly to the pollution of the air we breathe. As a result of this contamination, we are now also witnessing unprecedented global warming.

However, a lot of the environmental damage comes simply from our increased presence on Earth. The last century saw the world population rise by 400%, and our exploitation of natural resources also increased dramatically. We endangered animal species, mined the Earth and cleared large areas of forest for farming and timber. For instance, at the end of the last century, deforestation in Brazil had reduced the Atlantic coastal forest to 8% of its

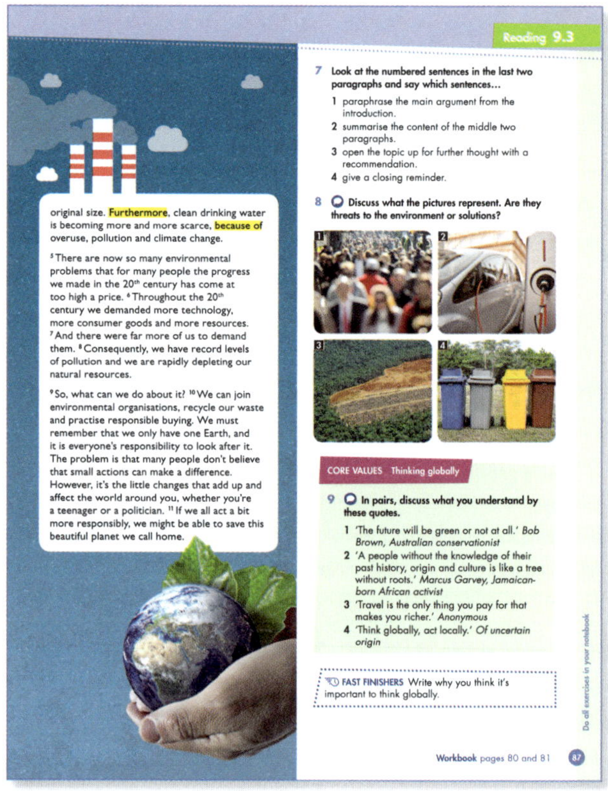

original size. Furthermore, clean drinking water is becoming more and more scarce, because of overuse, pollution and climate change.

[5] There are now so many environmental problems that for many people the progress we made in the 20th century has come at too high a price. [6] Throughout the 20th century we demanded more technology, more consumer goods and more resources. [7] And there were far more of us to demand them. [8] Consequently, we have record levels of pollution and we are rapidly depleting our natural resources.

[9] So, what can we do about it? [10] We can join environmental organisations, recycle our waste and practise responsible buying. We must remember that we only have one Earth, and it is everyone's responsibility to look after it. The problem is that many people don't believe that small actions can make a difference. However, it's the little changes that add up and affect the world around you, whether you're a teenager or a politician. [11] If we all act a bit more responsibly, we might be able to save this beautiful planet we call home.

7 Look at the numbered sentences in the last two paragraphs and say which sentences…

1 paraphrase the main argument from the introduction.
2 summarise the content of the middle two paragraphs.
3 open the topic up for further thought with a recommendation.
4 give a closing reminder.

8 Discuss what the pictures represent. Are they threats to the environment or solutions?

1 2 3 4

CORE VALUES Thinking globally

9 In pairs, discuss what you understand by these quotes.

1 'The future will be green or not at all.' *Bob Brown, Australian conservationist*
2 'A people without the knowledge of their past history, origin and culture is like a tree without roots.' *Marcus Garvey, Jamaican-born African activist*
3 'Travel is the only thing you pay for that makes you richer.' *Anonymous*
4 'Think globally, act locally.' *Of uncertain origin*

FAST FINISHERS Write why you think it's important to think globally.

Do all exercises in your notebook

ANSWER KEY

Pages 86-87

1 *Student's own answers*

2 Statement 1

3 *Suggested answers: (any three of…)*
1 In the 20th century, it is estimated that 40 million people died because of air pollution.
2 At the end of the last century, there were roughly 800 million cars in the world.
3 In the last century, the population rose by 400%.
4 By the end of the last century, the Atlantic coastal forest of Brazil had been reduced to 8% of its original size.

4 **1** 2 **2** 4 **3** 3 **4** 1

5 *Suggested answers: (any five of…)*
1 The number of cars on the road has led to massive air pollution.
2 Heavy industry has added significantly to pollution and global warming.
3 The rise in the world's population means our exploitation of natural resources has increased.
4 Animal species have become endangered.
5 The Earth has been over-mined.
6 Clearing large areas for farming and timber has led to deforestation in Brazil.
7 Clean drinking water is becoming scarce because of overuse, pollution and climate change.

6 **1** In addition, also, furthermore
2 As a result of, because of
3 Although, however
4 For instance
5 The fact is

7 **1** 5 **3** 9, 10
2 6, 7, 8 **4** 11

8 *Suggested answers:*
1 overpopulation; threat (we use more resources and pollute the environment).
2 electric cars; solution (solves the fossil fuel problem, although the electricity has to come from renewable sources).
3 deforestation; threat (it leads to the extinction of species and more polluted air).
4 recycling; solution (reuses waste, although we should also try to produce less non-organic rubbish)

9 *Suggested answers:*
1 We will either learn to take care of the environment or we'll have no future.
2 We need to know our history, origin and culture in order to survive and evolve.
3 Travel makes us smarter, wiser and happier.
4 We should consider the impact our actions have all over the world and start by taking small steps to improve the world in our local communities.

Remind students to do all the exercises in their notebook

LESSON FOCUS

Language in context The environment

Core values Thinking globally

Resources

Teacher's i-solutions, Student's Book audio

Preparation Prepare a list of sentences about history for students to practise *So* and *Neither* for agreement

→ See pages 36-37 **Literature**

Warmer

Say one of the sentences you prepared. Sentences could include: *I didn't know cars were such an important invention; I thought computers were more recent; I've seen a film about Gandhi; I think history helps us to learn from mistakes.* Elicit answers to the first one: *Neither did I/I did* and then continue eliciting agreement or disagreement, checking students' use of auxiliaries and *So* and *Neither*.

1 Ask students what topic the statements all have in common (the environment) and get them to discuss them. Ask which statement aligns most closely with their own view.

2 2.31 (See page 181 for transcripts) Give students a time limit to answer this question and get them to say where they got their answer from (most likely from sentences 3 and 4). Compare this briefly with their ideas in exercise 1.

3 Get students to find these answers in pairs and explain how they support the argument.

READING TOOLS

Get students to read the **Reading tool** and point out that the introduction often contains a summary of the main argument of an essay.

4 Remind them of the **Reading tool** and point out that this is a typical structure for an introduction.

5 Discuss which of these they think has the greatest impact.

6 Point out the grammar and punctuation of the linking expressions and encourage students to find other examples online and write them in their notebooks.

7 Point out that this is also a typical structure for a conclusion and that, as well as opening up with a recommendation, writers often open up with rhetorical questions, general observations and personal comments.

8 Point out that there are no definite answers and elicit possible answers from students.

CORE VALUES Thinking globally

9 End the discussion by asking which quote they like most and why.

FAST FINISHERS Students can complete this exercise alone or in pairs.

FURTHER PRACTICE

Workbook pages 80-81

Remind students to do all the exercises in their notebook

CONTINUOUS ASSESSMENT Students can understand a text about environmental damage.

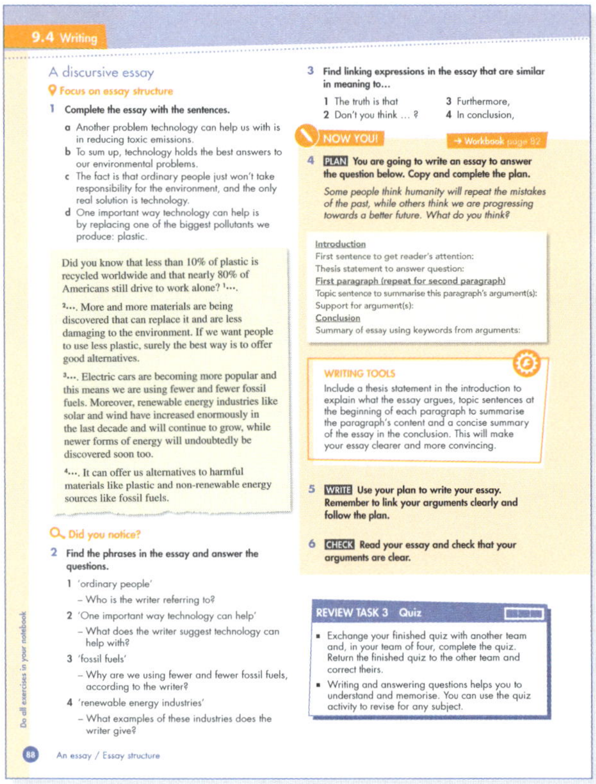

9.4 Writing

A discursive essay

Focus on essay structure

1 Complete the essay with the sentences.

a Another problem technology can help us with is in reducing toxic emissions.
b To sum up, technology holds the best answers to our environmental problems.
c The fact is that ordinary people just won't take responsibility for the environment, and the only real solution is technology.
d One important way technology can help is by replacing one of the biggest pollutants we produce: plastic.

Did you know that less than 10% of plastic is recycled worldwide and that nearly 80% of Americans still drive to work alone? [1]….

[2]…. More and more materials are being discovered that can replace it and are less damaging to the environment. If we want people to use less plastic, surely the best way is to offer good alternatives.

[3]…. Electric cars are becoming more popular and this means we are using fewer and fewer fossil fuels. Moreover, renewable energy industries like solar and wind have increased enormously in the last decade and will continue to grow, while newer forms of energy will undoubtedly be discovered soon too.

[4]…. It can offer us alternatives to harmful materials like plastic and non-renewable energy sources like fossil fuels.

Did you notice?

2 Find the phrases in the essay and answer the questions.

1 'ordinary people'
– Who is the writer referring to?
2 'One important way technology can help'
– What does the writer suggest technology can help with?
3 'fossil fuels'
– Why are we using fewer and fewer fossil fuels, according to the writer?
4 'renewable energy industries'
– What examples of these industries does the writer give?

3 Find linking expressions in the essay that are similar in meaning to…

1 The truth is that
2 Don't you think … ?
3 Furthermore,
4 In conclusion,

NOW YOU! → Workbook page 82

4 PLAN You are going to write an essay to answer the question below. Copy and complete the plan.

Some people think humanity will repeat the mistakes of the past, while others think we are progressing towards a better future. What do you think?

Introduction
First sentence to get reader's attention:
Thesis statement to answer question:
First paragraph (repeat for second paragraph)
Topic sentence to summarise this paragraph's argument(s):
Support for argument(s):
Conclusion
Summary of essay using keywords from arguments:

WRITING TOOLS

Include a thesis statement in the introduction to explain what the essay argues, topic sentences at the beginning of each paragraph to summarise the paragraph's content and a concise summary of the essay in the conclusion. This will make your essay clearer and more convincing.

5 WRITE Use your plan to write your essay. Remember to link your arguments clearly and follow the plan.

6 CHECK Read your essay and check that your arguments are clear.

REVIEW TASK 3 Quiz

- Exchange your finished quiz with another team and, in your team of four, complete the quiz. Return the finished quiz to the other team and correct theirs.
- Writing and answering questions helps you to understand and memorise. You can use the quiz activity to revise for any subject.

Do all exercises in your notebook

88 An essay / Essay structure

ANSWER KEY

Page 88

1 1 c
2 d
3 a
4 b

2 1 People who don't recycle and the 80% of Americans who drive to work alone.
2 It can help by replacing plastic with other materials that are less damaging to the environment.
3 Electric cars are becoming more popular.
4 Solar and wind.

3 1 The fact is that
2 Surely
3 Moreover
4 To sum up

4 *Student's own answers*

5 *Student's own answers*

6 *Student's own answers*

7 *Student's own answers*

FURTHER PRACTICE

Workbook page 82

LESSON FOCUS

Focus on Essay structure
Writing A discursive essay
Review task 3 Exchange quizzes with other teams

Resources
Teacher's i-solutions

Warmer

Put students in pairs and tell them you're going to test their knowledge of linking language. Ask them to write as many expressions as they can for the following linking functions: giving the main argument, introducing an example, giving another point, introducing a cause, introducing an effect, contrasting, and concluding. Give one function at a time and give them a time limit to see who can come up with the most expressions.

Focus on essay structure

1 Remind students of where they found the main argument articulated most clearly in the reading and find the first sentence (c) before you let them continue on their own.

Did you notice?

2 Ask students to discuss their answers in pairs. Make sure they get their answers from specific parts of the text so they can see how the text is linked.

3 Get students to add these linking expressions to their previous list of linking language in their notebooks.

4 **PLAN** Check that students use the plan outline. Once students have finished their plan, encourage them to talk it through with a partner.

WRITING TOOLS

Get students to read the **Writing tool** and point these features out in the model.

5 **WRITE** Before students start writing, make a checklist on the board of any elements related to content, structure, language and style that they should bear in mind.

6 **CHECK** Once students have checked their own essays, they can swap with a partner and check theirs.

REVIEW TASK 3 Quiz

Put students in their groups and pair each group up with another to exchange quizzes. If you get them to write their answers on a separate piece of paper, they can rotate and continue doing other group's quizzes and then have a class vote on which group got the most correct answers and who had the best quiz.

Remind students to do all the exercises in their notebook

 CONTINUOUS ASSESSMENT Students can write a structured, discursive essay.

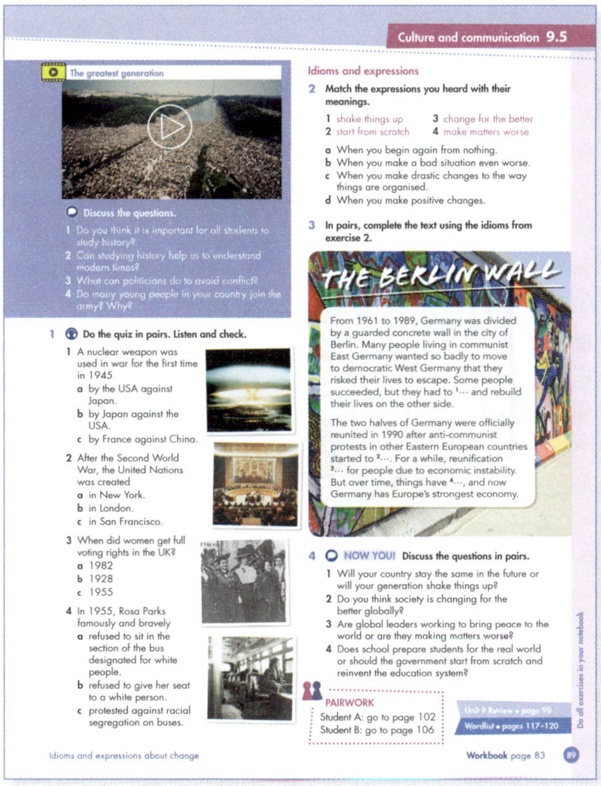

Culture and communication 9.5

The greatest generation

Discuss the questions.

1 Do you think it is important for all students to study history?
2 Can studying history help us to understand modern times?
3 What can politicians do to avoid conflict?
4 Do many young people in your country join the army? Why?

1 Do the quiz in pairs. Listen and check.

1 A nuclear weapon was used in war for the first time in 1945
 a by the USA against Japan.
 b by Japan against the USA.
 c by France against China.
2 After the Second World War, the United Nations was created
 a in New York.
 b in London.
 c in San Francisco.
3 When did women get full voting rights in the UK?
 a 1982
 b 1928
 c 1955
4 In 1955, Rosa Parks famously and bravely
 a refused to sit in the section of the bus designated for white people.
 b refused to give her seat to a white person.
 c protested against racial segregation on buses.

Idioms and expressions

2 Match the expressions you heard with their meanings.

1 shake things up
2 start from scratch
3 change for the better
4 make matters worse

a When you begin again from nothing.
b When you make a bad situation even worse.
c When you make drastic changes to the way things are organised.
d When you make positive changes.

3 In pairs, complete the text using the idioms from exercise 2.

THE BERLIN WALL

From 1961 to 1989, Germany was divided by a guarded concrete wall in the city of Berlin. Many people living in communist East Germany wanted so badly to move to democratic West Germany that they risked their lives to escape. Some people succeeded, but they had to [1]… and rebuild their lives on the other side.

The two halves of Germany were officially reunited in 1990 after anti-communist protests in other Eastern European countries started to [2]…. For a while, reunification [3]… for people due to economic instability. But over time, things have [4]…, and now Germany has Europe's strongest economy.

4 NOW YOU! Discuss the questions in pairs.

1 Will your country stay the same in the future or will your generation shake things up?
2 Do you think society is changing for the better globally?
3 Are global leaders working to bring peace to the world or are they making matters worse?
4 Does school prepare students for the real world or should the government start from scratch and reinvent the education system?

PAIRWORK
Student A: go to page 102
Student B: go to page 106

Unit 9 Review • page 98
Wordlist • pages 117–120

Do all exercises in your notebook

Idioms and expressions about change

Workbook page 83

89

LESSON FOCUS

Idioms and expressions Change

Listening Answering multiple-choice questions about the 20th century

Speaking A discussion of how the world is changing

Resources

Teacher's i-solutions, Student's Book audio, Culture video and worksheets

The greatest generation

Video and worksheet available on the Richmond*Learning*Platform

- In pairs, ask students to complete the *What I know...* exercises on the **Culture video worksheet**.
- Show students the **Culture video** and ask them to complete the *What I learned...* exercises on the worksheet.
- In pairs, students compare answers.
- In small groups, tell students to complete the *What I wonder...* exercises on the worksheet.

ANSWER KEY

Page 89

1 1 a
2 c
3 b
4 b

2 1 c
2 a
3 d
4 b

3 1 start from scratch
2 shake things up
3 made matters worse
4 changed for the better

4 *Student's own answers*

Warmer

Watch the **Culture video** and discuss the questions with the whole class. If you don't have video facilities, simply discuss the questions.

1 2.32 (See page 182 for transcripts) Get the students to do the quiz before playing the audio. After they check their answers, you could get them to write questions for each other based on other information in the audio and play it a second time.

Idioms and expressions

2 Ask questions to check students' understanding of the expressions in context: *What made matters worse?* (German war reparation payments); *What was started from scratch?* (The UN); *What was a change for the better?* (Women gaining independence); *How did Rosa Parks shake things up?* (She forced people to reconsider racial segregation).

3 Ask students if they know what the Berlin Wall was and get them to check their ideas against the text as they do the exercise.

4 NOW YOU! When students have finished discussing their ideas in pairs, ask volunteers to give an extended answer to one of the questions and ask their classmates to ask them questions about their opinions.

FURTHER PRACTICE AND UNIT ASSESSSMENT

Unit 9 Review Student's Book page 98
Workbook page 83
- **Reflect on your learning** page 83
- **Grammar reference and practice** pages 92 and 96
- **Wordlist and exercises** pages 101 and 104

Tests available to download and edit from the **Richmond*Learning*Platform**

➔ See pages 40-41 **Assessment**

PAIRWORK Student's Book pages 102 and 106
See **Teacher's Book** page 166 for more information.

➔ See pages 30-33 **Mediation**

Remind students to do all the exercises in their notebook

CONTINUOUS ASSESSMENT Students can use idioms and expressions about change.

Unit 9 Review

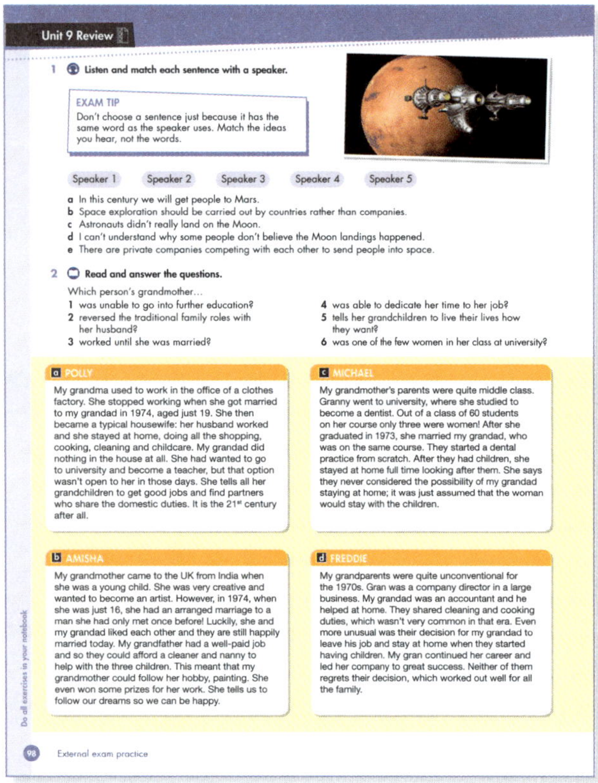
Unit 9 Review

1 Listen and match each sentence with a speaker.

EXAM TIP
Don't choose a sentence just because it has the same word as the speaker uses. Match the ideas you hear, not the words.

Speaker 1 Speaker 2 Speaker 3 Speaker 4 Speaker 5

a In this century we will get people to Mars.
b Space exploration should be carried out by countries rather than companies.
c Astronauts didn't really land on the Moon.
d I can't understand why some people don't believe the Moon landings happened.
e There are private companies competing with each other to send people into space.

2 Read and answer the questions.

Which person's grandmother…
1 was unable to go into further education?
2 reversed the traditional family roles with her husband?
3 worked until she was married?
4 was able to dedicate her time to her job?
5 tells her grandchildren to live their lives how they want?
6 was one of the few women in her class at university?

a POLLY
My grandma used to work in the office of a clothes factory. She stopped working when she got married to my grandad in 1974, aged just 19. She then became a typical housewife: her husband worked and she stayed at home, doing all the shopping, cooking, cleaning and childcare. My grandad did nothing in the house at all. She had wanted to go to university and become a teacher, but that option wasn't open to her in those days. She tells all her grandchildren to get good jobs and find partners who share the domestic duties. It is the 21st century after all.

b AMISHA
My grandmother came to the UK from India when she was a young child. She was very creative and wanted to become an artist. However, in 1974, when she was just 16, she had an arranged marriage to a man she had only met once before! Luckily, she and my grandad liked each other and they are still happily married today. My grandfather had a well-paid job and so they could afford a cleaner and nanny to help with the three children. This meant that my grandmother could follow her hobby, painting. She even won some prizes for her work. She tells us to follow our dreams so we can be happy.

c MICHAEL
My grandmother's parents were quite middle class. Granny went to university, where she studied to become a dentist. Out of a class of 60 students on her course only three were women! After she graduated in 1973, she married my grandad, who was on the same course. They started a dental practice from scratch. After they had children, she stayed at home full time looking after them. She says they never considered the possibility of my grandad staying at home; it was just assumed that the woman would stay with the children.

d FREDDIE
My grandparents were quite unconventional for the 1970s. Gran was a company director in a large business. My grandad was an accountant and he helped at home. They shared cleaning and cooking duties, which wasn't very common in that era. Even more unusual was their decision for my grandad to leave his job and stay at home when they started having children. My gran continued her career and led her company to great success. Neither of them regrets their decision, which worked out well for all the family.

Do all exercises in your notebook

98 External exam practice

Student's Book page 98

ANSWER KEY

See page 184 for transcripts

1 2.38
a Speaker 4
b Speaker 5
c Speaker 1
d Speaker 3
e Speaker 2

2 **1** a
2 d
3 a
4 d
5 b
6 c

Pairwork

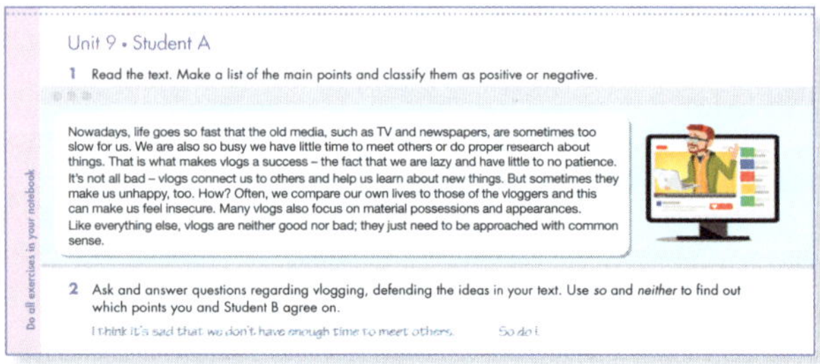
Unit 9 • Student A

1 Read the text. Make a list of the main points and classify them as positive or negative.

Nowadays, life goes so fast that the old media, such as TV and newspapers, are sometimes too slow for us. We are also so busy we have little time to meet others or do proper research about things. That is what makes vlogs a success – the fact that we are lazy and have little to no patience.
It's not all bad – vlogs connect us to others and help us learn about new things. But sometimes they make us unhappy, too. How? Often, we compare our own lives to those of the vloggers and this can make us feel insecure. Many vlogs also focus on material possessions and appearances.
Like everything else, vlogs are neither good nor bad; they just need to be approached with common sense.

2 Ask and answer questions regarding vlogging, defending the ideas in your text. Use *so* and *neither* to find out which points you and Student B agree on.

I think it's sad that we don't have enough time to meet others. So do I.

Do all exercises in your notebook

Student's Book page 102

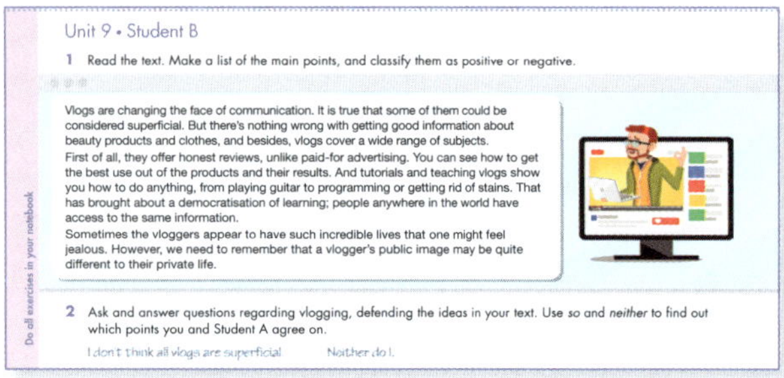
Unit 9 • Student B

1 Read the text. Make a list of the main points, and classify them as positive or negative.

Vlogs are changing the face of communication. It is true that some of them could be considered superficial. But there's nothing wrong with getting good information about beauty products and clothes, and besides, vlogs cover a wide range of subjects.
First of all, they offer honest reviews, unlike paid-for advertising. You can see how to get the best use out of the products and their results. And tutorials and teaching vlogs show you how to do anything, from playing guitar to programming or getting rid of stains. That has brought about a democratisation of learning; people anywhere in the world have access to the same information.
Sometimes the vloggers appear to have such incredible lives that one might feel jealous. However, we need to remember that a vlogger's public image may be quite different to their private life.

2 Ask and answer questions regarding vlogging, defending the ideas in your text. Use *so* and *neither* to find out which points you and Student A agree on.

I don't think all vlogs are superficial. Neither do I.

Do all exercises in your notebook

Student's Book page 106

CEFR MEDIATION DESCRIPTOR

- **Adapting language**
  Students can paraphrase more simply the main points made in short, straightforward spoken or written texts on familiar subjects.

- **Defending ideas**
  Tell students that they each have a different text about the same topic – vlogging – and that they have to make notes on their text to compare the information given and their own opinions. You could ask volunteers to summarise the main points of their discussions.

Grammar reference

So and such

Use **so** and **such** to express emphasis.	
Use **so** with adjectives and adverbs. That's **so interesting**! It went **so fast**!	Use **such** with nouns or adjectives + nouns. He's **such a genius**! I didn't realise that the personal computer was **such a modern invention**.
Use **so** and **such** with **that** to show consequences. Cars were **so important that** landscapes changed to accommodate them. The theory of relativity was **such an incredible theory that** it changed the way we look at the Universe.	

Sometimes, we can construct the same meaning using either ***so*** or ***such***, but we must structure the sentence in different ways.

so* + adjective/adverb + *that	***such* + noun phrase + *that***
We were **so tired that** we had to stop walking.	It was **such a tiring day that** we had to stop walking.
The coat was **so expensive that** I decided not to buy it.	It was **such an expensive coat that** I decided not to buy it.
It was **so wet that** we had to stay in and read.	It was **such a wet afternoon that** we had to stay in and read.

So with quantifiers

Use ***so* + quantifier + noun + *that*** to express emphasis and result.	
Use ***so many/few*** with **countable nouns** and ***that***. There are now **so many planes that** pollution from aviation fuel is a serious problem. There were **so few opportunities that** people went to look for work in the cities.	Use ***so much/little*** with **uncountable nouns** and ***that***. There has been **so much change** that the modern world would be unrecognisable to previous generations. There was **so little hope that** people lost interest in democracy.

In modern English, the quantifiers ***a lot of/lots of*** have become more common than ***much/many*** in affirmative sentences. However, when we use a quantifier in combination with ***so***, we always use ***much/many***.

There are **so many** languages I would like to learn.

There are **lots of** languages I would like to learn.

I'm planning on eating **so much** pizza when I go Italy next month.

NOT ~~I'm planning on eating so lots of pizza when I go to Italy next month.~~

So and neither

Use ***so*** and ***neither*** to express agreement or similarities. Remember that the auxiliary verb reflects the sentence you're agreeing with.			
Use ***so*** in affirmative sentences.		Use ***neither*** in negative sentences.	
I'm very interested in history.	**So am** I.	I can't understand it.	**Neither can** I.
She really likes books.	**So do** I.	They don't agree.	**Neither do** I.
We liked that programme.	**So did** they.	He didn't like the film.	**Neither did** I.

The ***so/neither* + auxiliary + pronoun** means the same as the **pronoun + *too/neither*** structure. ***Me too***, for example, can mean the same things as ***so do I***, ***so did I***, ***so was I***, depending on the verb tense the statement is in.

I had a great weekend!

Me too! OR **So did I!**

I've never met anyone from Germany.

Me neither. OR **Neither have I.**

My parents both work long hours.

Mine too. OR **So do mine!**

Do all exercises in your notebook

Student's Book page 115

Wordlist

UNIT 9

Human achievements

aeroplane
AI (Artificial Intelligence)
boom
driverless cars
the internet
milestone
the personal computer
the Space Race
turning point

The 20th century

Issues
democracy
empire
feminist
freedom
human rights
hunger
living conditions
manufacture
opportunity
oppression
peace
peaceful
political ideas
poor
poverty
protest
religious groups

Events
the Cold War
civil rights movements
the First World War
the Second World War
the United Nations
the Universal Declaration of Human Rights

The environment

climate change
damage
deforestation
ecological
environmental disaster
fossil fuel
global warming
health
heavy industry
man-made threat
pollution
population growth
recycle
resources
timber
waste

Do all exercises in your notebook

Student's Book page 120

2.63 2.64 2.65

Remind students to do all the exercises in their notebook

Track 1.1 Get started! page 7, exercise 1

I didn't do much during the Easter holidays and my Dad wasn't happy about it. In May, he suggested I set some summer holiday goals for myself.

So, in June, I volunteered at the nursing home where my Mum works. I learned so much and I met people who are very different to me, people who have overcome struggles in their lives. It also challenged the stereotypes I had about elderly people.

I'm proud that I have achieved so much this summer. It makes me feel more confident about the year ahead, too.

Track 1.2 Get started! page 8, exercise 1

I've been asked to manage a fundraising campaign for girls' education. It's such an important issue! Did you know that around 130 million girls do not have access to education? If only we were doing more to raise awareness. I wish I had got involved a long time ago.

At first, I was worried that I wouldn't have time for the campaign. I decided to ask my parents for help with time management. They helped me to prioritise my tasks and now I feel much more confident. It's going to be a great year!

Track 1.3 Get started! page 9, exercise 1

In the future, I hope to go to university and get a degree, but it's really difficult to decide what to study. I'm feeling a bit stressed out.

Last week, I decided to talk to a teacher about my options. She was great. She suggested that I make a list of the projects I've enjoyed, the hobbies that are important to me and the things I'm good at. It has really helped. Now I'm excited about going to university and getting a job I love, one day!

Track 1.4 Unit 1, page 10, exercise 3

Woman 1: So, as you know, the purpose of this meeting is to discuss the employee of the year. The idea is to reward someone for particularly good work and to show that the company recognises the efforts of all its employees. So, who are the nominees this year, and what are each of their merits?

Man 1: Well, I'd like to nominate Jana Fisher, the human resources officer. I think she's proven to be a very thoughtful and sociable team member over the past year. She always seems to be available to listen to any problems our staff have.

Woman 1: And what has she done to convince you of that?

Man 1: Well, she's solved a difficult conflict between two of our graphic designers, a Conflict that went on for months before she came. Now they're working together again happily. And she's also set up a social programme to help improve staff relations.

Almost half of our employees have signed up already and it only started two months ago.

Woman 1: Impressive. Are there any other nominees?

Woman 2: Yes. I think our accountant Sam Vitelli deserves a nomination. Before he started last year our accounts were, quite frankly, a disaster. He's made sure that all our financial records are accurate and up to date. And he's helped us save over ten thousand pounds in unnecessary expenses. He's systematic and meticulous, and he's doing a fantastic job.

Man 1: I agree.

Man 2: And I'd like to nominate Christina Brent, our web designer. She's extremely enthusiastic and creative, and she's won two awards for the design of our web page. She's also increased the number of hits on our homepage by 50%. I think she's basically helped us all to believe in the company again.

Woman 1: She certainly has been an inspiration. Right, well, we have our three nominations. Let's vote, shall we?

Track 1.5 Unit 1, page 11, exercise 6

1

If you chose the sentences marked 'a', you probably have good self-awareness. You know yourself very well and make good decisions. Have you thought about becoming a project manager or running your own business?

2

If you chose the sentences marked 'b', you have good linguistic and communication skills. You can use words very well to express yourself. You must be quite a chatterbox or maybe even a poet! You could be a journalist or write slogans for companies.

3

If you chose the sentences marked 'c', you have good numeracy and logical thinking skills. You're good at maths and solving problems. Have you thought about becoming a scientist, a computer programmer or a banker?

4

If you chose the sentences marked 'd', you have good visual-spatial abilities. You understand the world in images and can manipulate them easily in your mind. For you, as the saying goes, 'a picture is worth a thousand words'. You could work in advertising or become a designer or perhaps an engineer.

Track 1.6 Unit 1, page 12, exercise 1

Woman 1: Hi everyone! The entrepreneurs we're discussing today are Bill Gates, Coco Chanel and Dan Wieden.

Man 1: Yeah, so Bill Gates is one of the richest people in the world and the co founder of Microsoft. He launched the company in 1975 and since then the company has developed, manufactured and sold services to businesses worldwide.

Woman 1: What does Bill Gates do now?

Man 1: Well, now he runs a charity focused on healthcare, education and ending poverty.

Woman 1: How long has he had the charity?

Man 1: He started it in the year 2000 with his wife, Melinda.

Woman 1: How about the second entrepreneur?

Man 1: It's Coco Chanel, the fashion designer. She created the Chanel brand and the famous double-C logo.

Woman 1: When was that?

Man 1: She created the brand in 1910 and the logo in 1925. Her designs really Revolutionized the fashion industry.

Woman 1: How did Chanel's designs change fashion?

Man 1: Well, she made it fashionable for women to wear more practical, comfortable clothes.

Woman 1: All right! And last, but not least, who is Dan Wieden?

Man 1: He owns an advertising agency and he created Nike's slogan 'Just do it' in 1988.
Woman: What does the Nike slogan represent?
Man 1: It represents the 'can do' attitude of the company. He didn't create the famous 'swoosh' logo, though.
Woman 1: Didn't he? Who did?
Man 1: It was a graphic design student called Carolyn Davidson.
Woman 1: Has Wieden created any other famous slogans?
Man 1: Oh yes, he's created lots more since then. Anyway, it's now time for an advertisement break...

Track 1.7 Unit 1, page 12, exercise 2
See previous track

Track 1.8 Unit 1, page 13, exercise 4
Adam: This afternoon we have successful local entrepreneur Ryan Harris with us in the studio. What's your advice for creating a successful business?
Ryan: For one thing, you have to make sure you choose the right product. That means you should identify a specific need your product or service meets. Put simply, you must make sure you're answering some need in the market. That is the key. Once you've chosen your product or service, you need to create a logo and a slogan. The logo must be simple and original. The style depends on the market it is aimed at. Generally, you should use contrasting colours. Finally, the slogan... it must be short and concise... catchy. Remember, you have only a couple of seconds to catch your audience's attention. You could begin by writing a paragraph or making a list of qualities you want to express, then reduce the information until you have a short phrase... also known as a slogan. And that's it!
Adam: Thanks Ryan! And that's all for today. Thank you for listening!

Track 1.9 Unit 1, page 13, exercise 5
Boy 1: Hi, I'm Alex Gomez. I'm 16 years old and I'm currently attending high school. In my family we have always worried about people in need, so my brother and I have come up with the idea of a charity for students who don't have enough money to buy books or food. We haven't done much yet... well, we've thought of a slogan. It's going to be 'Together we're better'. We've created teams for collecting donated items and we've made a proposal to the head teacher to open a service office where students can donate old books, money, food, etc. I've started a campaign at school and in the neighbourhood asking people to join in.
Girl 1: I'm Rose Jones and I'm 16 years old. I love computers. I was really tired of how Slow our computers at school were and I thought there must be loads of people like me. Since I like to fix and upgrade computers, I started my own computer repair business. I've created a logo, which is a smiling computer. It's blue and red, my favourite colours. I've made a list of the most common problems computers have and I've used my savings to pay friends who know about computers to work for me, too.
Boy 2: Hello, I'm Liam Scott. I'm 15 years old. How did I come up with this project? Well, in my town people like partying a lot, so I thought it was a great idea to start a company to sell party stuff like balloons, flowers, hats and things online. So far, I've made some party E-cards that my clients loved; the cards have the slogan 'There's no party better'. I've helped my friends to plan their parties because I know what teenagers like when it comes to partying. I've hired friends and family members to be the hosts at people's parties too. What's next? Well, I'm going to run an advertising campaign with special offers!

Track 1.10 Unit 1, page 13, exercise 7
Listen and repeat.
/əʊ/ both, logo, no, only, show, slogan

Track 1.11 Unit 1, page 13, exercise 8

1 south	**3** open	**5** most	**7** should
2 note	**4** wood	**6** hello	**8** also

Track 1.12 Unit 1, page 14, exercise 2
Brain Power
Our brains are truly amazing. Although the average human brain only weighs about 1.5kg, it contains about 86 billion nerve cells called 'neurons', and each of these create trillions of connections, forming a mass that will process all of our life experiences.
From when we're born until we're in our 20s, these connections continue developing.
Not only that, but each person develops unique combinations of connections. Some connections become stronger, and we abandon others. This process is essential to our ability to learn.
Our brains are very adaptable and continue adapting throughout our lives. This is called 'brain plasticity'. Plasticity makes some brain regions bigger than others, specifically the regions that control what we do most. For example, the region that controls the right leg for a right-footed football player will be larger than the region that controls his or her left leg. This plasticity can also help our brains deal with injury. If one region of the brain is damaged, another region can assume its function.
This means that all of our brains work differently, and that there are various kinds of intelligence. Psychologist Howard Gardner has identified eight intelligences the brain can develop.
Bodily-kinaesthetic: control your body or hands well and can use movement to help memory.
Interpersonal: communicate well and empathise with other people's feelings and experiences.
Intrapersonal: understand yourself and can predict your reactions and emotions.
Verbal-linguistic: Are good at reading, writing, telling stories and learning languages.
Logical-mathematical: can understand numbers and systems, and use logical reasoning.
Musical: are sensitive to patterns, rhythms or sounds and can create or and compose music.
Naturalistic: understand and relate to the natural world and your surroundings
Visual-spatial: have good spatial judgement and can visualise things in your mind You can probably identify which intelligences you are strong in, and which you are weaker in. Knowing your strengths and weakness can help you develop personalised learning strategies, as well as identify jobs you could be good at. Recognising your own unique range of skills can help to build your self-esteem,

too. Also, because of brain plasticity, you can develop the intelligences you are weaker in. That is what many successful people have done. Play to your strengths and work on your weaknesses!

Track 1.13 Unit 1, page 17, exercise 1

1
Hey, my name's Sarah and I've got a hard decision to make. I can't decide what to study next year. I went to a nature summer camp last summer. Now I know I'd love to do forestry work, but my mum wants me to be a lawyer like her. I know that I have naturalistic intelligence and I want to work outdoors. So, I'm totally on the fence. Why is it so hard to decide?

2
Hey, Paul here. I'm stuck. We're working on a project in class and I think I'm in the wrong group. My group is working on a business proposal, but the other group has decided to create a charity to help people. That sounds much better to me, but I know that if I change groups my team will probably be annoyed. I've had this kind of problem before. Why did we choose money over helping people? I'm going to sleep o it and decide tomorrow.

3
Hello, it's Bruce. I'm a writer for the school blog. One of our writers has written an article and we can't decide whether or not to publish it. A girl in our class is in trouble for spraying graffiti, but it wasn't her - it was a boy in a different class. We have always written the truth, but this time it doesn't feel good. We're having a vote this afternoon, but until we know the result, the jury's out.

4
Hi, I'm Liz. At the moment, I'm working on a team project... can you guess my problem? Yes, I'm the only one doing any work! I can't decide whether or not to tell my teacher that the other students aren't doing their share. I'm in two minds about what to do. On the one hand, if I tell my teacher, she can make the other students do some work. But on the other hand, my teammates might get really angry. Do I tell the teacher?

Track 1.14 Unit 1, page 17, exercise 2
See previous track

Track 1.15 Unit 2, page 18, exercise 2

Dreams can come true
Walt Disney had business ideas from a very young age. By the time he died in 1966, he had created a multimillion-dollar business empire, made countless films, and built the world's most successful theme park.
Disney's success didn't come easily. He experienced lots of failure. He was fired from his job at a Kansas newspaper in 1919; they said that he wasn't imaginative enough! In 1922, he started Laugh-O-Gram Studio; it went bankrupt in one year.
His failures are not well known, but we all know about Walt Disney's achievements. He created Mickey Mouse in 1928. Before he produced Snow White and the Seven Dwarfs in 1937, there had never been a full-length, hand-drawn animated feature film.
A friend remembered him standing outside an amusement park in Kansas as a child and saying, 'I'm going to have a park like this one day'. Disneyland opened in 1955 and after two months, it had already received over one million visitors! In 1971, some years after Walt died, his brother Roy opened the Magic Kingdom.

Track 1.16 Unit 2, page 20, exercise 1
Jennifer Lopez was a professional dancer for many years and had appeared on television shows as a dancer before she decided to start acting. In 2001, she became the first person to have a number one film and album in the same week. She now owns a production company, companies that sell clothes and perfumes and a charitable foundation. Jennifer Lopez was named the most powerful celebrity in the world in 2012.
J.R.R. Tolkien is the well-loved author of The Hobbit and The Lord of the Rings. Tolkien was a university professor who wrote novels, short stories and poems. He fought in the First World War and created a secret code so that his wife could track his location through his letters to her. He started writing The Hobbit in 1930 and finished two years later, in 1932. His other masterpiece, The Lord of the Rings, took 12 years to complete!
Michael Jordan tried out for his high school basketball team, but at 180 centimetres tall, he was considered too short to play. A few years later, he had grown to 198 centimetres and he joined the Chicago Bulls. He retired in 1993 and joined the Chicago White Sox baseball team, but he returned to basketball in 1995. In 1999, ESPN named Michael Jordan number one in a list of the top 50 North American athletes of the 20th century.
Mexican artist Frida Kahlo was seriously hurt in a bus accident when she was 18 and was forced to stay in bed for long periods. During this time, she taught herself to paint and developed her unusual style. Her most famous paintings are her self-portraits The Two Fridas and The Broken Column. Kahlo lived in the USA from 1930 to 1933, but then returned home to Mexico where she lived in a house called 'The Blue House'. It is now an art museum dedicated to her life and work.

Track 1.17 Unit 2, page 20, exercise 2
See previous track

Track 1.18 Unit 2, page 20, exercise 3

Listen and repeat.
/ɒ/ from, hobbit, restaurant, stop, want, watch.

Track 1.19 Unit 2, page 20, exercise 4

1 found	**5** on
2 out	**6** book
3 what	**7** focus
4 job	**8** problem

Track 1.20 Unit 2, page 21, exercise 6
Marc Chavannes and Al Fielding created bubble wrap in 1957. They had designed it as a new style of textured wallpaper, but it was a complete commercial disaster. Following that, they tried to sell the bubble wrap as insultation for homes. But that was as unpopular as the wallpaper idea had been. In 1960, IBM decided to use it to package their new computers for transport. Finally, after three years and several business failures, bubble wrap had become a hit!

Track 1.21 Unit 2, page 22, exercise 2

Secrets to success

Every year, hundreds of books are published on the subject of success and self-help. Most of these books focus on money, but some also discuss how to be good at school, sports, relationships, happiness and life in general. And regardless of what you want to succeed in, the characteristics and tools you will need are often the same. So, what are the secrets to success?

Success means something different to everyone. It's not enough to want to be richer or happier; you need to set specific goals. A study at Harvard Business School asked graduates of the class of 1979 how many had written out goals for their future and outlined a plan to achieve them. They found that only 13% had written down their goals and only 3% had a specific plan. Ten years later, the 13% were earning twice as much as those who had no written goals, and the 3% were earning ten times as much!

Once you know your goals and have a plan to achieve them, you have to carry out the plan. This is the hard part. Many people start out with the best intentions, but get distracted or lose heart. Setting realistic goals and choosing something you are passionate about helps. But even then, there will be times when you will fail or where it all starts to seem too much. Psychologist Angela Duckworth has identified a common factor in successful people. She calls it 'grit'. She defines grit as 'perseverance and passion for long-term goals'. Her findings suggest that this is more important for success than intelligence. Some people, it seems, are born with it, but what should the rest of us do?

The key seems to be to develop good habits. Remind yourself of your goals regularly and stay focused. When you fail or encounter an obstacle, think about what you can learn from the situation. Don't let problems or comparing yourself with others demotivate you. And remember to appreciate how much progress you've already made. It can be hard to stay motivated, but it's very important. As Confucius once said, 'It does not matter how slowly you go, as long as you do not stop.'

Track 1.22 Unit 2, page 22, exercise 5

achieve, achievement, achievable
distract, distraction, distracted
fail, failure, failed, failing
focus, focus, focused
intelligence, intelligent
motivate, motivation, motivated
passion, passionate
persevere, perseverance, persevering
succeed, success, successful

Track 1.23 Unit 2, page 25, exercise 1

1

I play the saxophone and I want to be a famous jazz musician when I'm older. Anyway, last year I went for an audition, but I fell at the first hurdle! I had rehearsed for 3 hours every day up to the audition and I was feeling confident, but I walked up onto the stage and… I froze. My hands were sweating and I felt sick. I played really badly! But I'm not going to give up – I'm going to try again this year.

2

I've always been really bad at computers. We had an exam last week in my technology class and I was really stressed. I had failed the practice exam and I was determined not to fail the real one! My friend Jessica helped me study and I worked really hard. I watched tutorials and read articles online to help me understand. I was so happy when I got the results I had passed with flying colours!

3

I've just won a photography award! Last year, mum paid for me to do a wildlife photography course. I had always loved taking photos. And a few years ago, I became interested in animal conservation. We learnt about how to find the right light, and how to create context and tone. I've discovered my calling! As soon as I took this photo for the competition, I knew the award was in the bag; and sure enough, I won!

4

Last year our team didn't play well and we were all disappointed. Our team had gone to the dogs and we got knocked out of the championship early. But this year has been incredible. Last weekend we played in the semi-final and we won! I hadn't been playing very well but the coach put me on anyway and I scored three goals – three! The new coach is great. She really helped me to believe in myself. I'm so glad I didn't give up last year.

Track 1.24 Unit 2, page 25, exercise 2

See previous track

Track 1.25 Unit 3, page 28, exercise 4

William Tell is a folk hero. His story is from a small town in Switzerland. The legend says that Gessler, the tyrannical ruler of the town, demanded that all the people in the town bow down in front of him to show their respect. One day, William Tell and his son were passing by Gessler and they refused to bow. Gessler was offended that he had been disrespected. Gessler told William Tell that he was going to kill him and his son. The only way William Tell could save himself and his son was to shoot an apple off the top of the son's head with his bow and arrow, from a long distance away. He aimed and fired, and cleanly shot the apple off his son's head, then used his second arrow to kill Gessler and set all the people in the town free. These three characters, William Tell, his son and Gessler live on in the memories of the Swiss to the present day.

Track 1.26 Unit 3, page 29, exercise 5

Angela: Hey, Pete. You look tired. Did you go to bed late?

Pete: Yes. I was reading about the Trojan War for History class. We've got the test tomorrow, remember?

Angela: Oh no! I forgot. Is it complicated?

Pete: A bit. I can give you a summary and then tonight you can study.

Angela: Thanks, Pete! It all happened in ancient Greece, right?

Pete: Well, the Trojan War was between the Greeks and the city of Troy. The soldiers were fighting for a woman named Helen, who was married to the King of Sparta. The gods made Helen fall in love with Paris, the Prince of Troy, and he took her away to live with him in Troy. The war began when the king of Sparta went to Troy with his army to rescue her.

Angela: And who won the war in the end?
Pete: Well it lasted for ten years. Paris killed the Greek warrior Achilles by shooting him in the heel, his only weak spot. Then finally the Greeks defeated the Trojans, partly thanks to a clever trick.
Angela: Oh yeah, the Trojan horse! We were talking about that in class when the bell rang.
Pete: The Greeks pretended the wooden horse was a peace offering for the people of Troy, to end the war. As the Greeks were sailing away, the Trojans pulled the horse inside the city walls…
Angela: …and some of the Greeks were hiding inside!
Pete: Exactly! And they defeated the Trojan army.
Angela: What a great story!

Track 1.27 **Unit 3, page 30, exercise 2**

Listen and repeat.
/k/ carve, check, clay, folk, kind, queen
/ks/ box, climax, exercise, ox, six, text

Track 1.28 **Unit 3, page 30, exercise 3**
Narrator: At the beginning of time, the gods decided to create humans.
Female deity: Let's create people so that they can enjoy the beautiful planet that we have made.
Male deity 1: Yes! Let's use wet clay! We can easily mould it into shapes.
Female deity: Oh no! They're dissolving in the water!
Narrator: After a while, they decided to try wood.
Female deity: Earlier today, I was walking on the Earth and I saw the trees. They're so strong and tall. Let's carve people from wood.
Narrator: Unfortunately, the wooden people had no souls.
Male deity 2: Oh dear! They're completely mindless! People made of wood can't appreciate the beauty of the Earth.
Narrator: Finally…
Male deity 2: So, what material should we use?
Female deity: How about corn? It's nutritious and it grows naturally, in harmony with the Earth. People made of corn will be good-hearted.
Narrator: The people made of corn were kind and healthy, and the gods were satisfied.

Track 1.29 **Unit 3, page 31, exercise 5**
One day, the god Di Jun told his wife, Xi He, that they needed to have children to bring light to the universe. They had ten sons. One day, one of the sons was talking to Mother Earth. She asked him what he and his brothers did all day. He explained that every day one of the brothers travelled through the sky in a chariot to bring light to the humans. However, one day the brothers grew bored of doing the same thing every day. One of them suggested that they all went to the Earth and played together for a change. All but one brother agreed.
The next morning, the brothers visited Earth together. Mother Earth started to cry out that she was dying because it was too hot, and she asked them to leave the Earth. However, the brothers weren't listening.
Their father, Di Jun, became angry and he tried to stop them too. Finally, he sent for the godly archer, Hou Yi. Di Jun told Hou Yi that his children were burning the Earth and they weren't listening to him. He asked Hou Yi to stop them. The archer used his bow and arrow to stop the children. The next day, only the boy who hadn't wanted all the brothers to visit the Earth together remained. He cried that he was lonely, and he missed his brothers. His tears filled the lakes and rivers of the world.

Track 1.30 **Unit 3, page 32, exercise 2**

Thor and the stolen hammer
According to Norse mythology, the gods were created when the land of fire and the land of ice collided. Odin, the god of knowledge, battle and death, was married to Frigg, a goddess who could see into the future. They had a son called Thor who had become the god of thunder and strength, and a protector of humanity. He had a powerful hammer that he used against his enemies.
One day, Thor discovered that his hammer was missing. He asked his friend, Loki, a half-god who could change form, to look for the hammer. Loki turned into a falcon, flew to the land of giants and discovered that Thor's hammer had been taken by Thrym, the king of the giants. Thrym said he would only return it if Freyja, the beautiful goddess of love, married him.
Loki flew back home and told Thor and together, they made a plan. They decided to put a wedding veil on Thor, dress him up as Freyja and pretend to marry Thrym.
Before the ceremony, Thrym became suspicious of Freyja's behaviour. Loki told him that she was just nervous about the wedding. He suggested that he bring the hammer and begin the wedding ceremony immediately.
As soon as Thrym put the hammer down on the table, Thor took of his disguise, grabbed it and took his revenge.

Pandora's box
According to Greek mythology, Zeus, the god of the sky, lightening, thunder and justice, told two Titans, the brothers Prometheus and Epimetheus, to go down to Earth and create humans and animals. Prometheus created man in the image of the gods, and Epimetheus created the animals.
Epimetheus gave each animal he created a gift. But by the time Prometheus finished creating humans, there weren't any gifts left. So, he decided to steal fire from the gods and give it to the humans. When Zeus found out, he was angry and decided to punish both Prometheus and Epimetheus.
He chained Prometheus to a mountain and tormented him. But Epimetheus' punishment was worse. First, he created the first human woman, Pandora, and made her curious and beautiful. Epimetheus fell in love with her and they got married. As a wedding present, Zeus gave the couple a box but told them not to open it.
One day, curiosity got the better of Pandora and she opened the box, releasing evil, pain and disease into the world.
To make matters worse, the only thing that did not escape from the box was hope. It remained trapped inside and could not provide any remedy for mankind's pain.

Track 1.31 **Unit 3, page 35, exercise 1**
Male interviewer: Hello and welcome to our show, Magical Myths. Today we're talking To Melanie Abbot, a Professor of Legendary and Mythical Literature. Welcome, Professor.
Woman: Good morning.
Male interviewer: Today you're going to talk to us about King Arthur, right? Who was he?

Woman: That's right. Well, King Arthur is a character from a beloved British legend. Some historians disagree about whether or not he ever really existed. However, most experts agree that he was probably a real king whose story has grown and been added to over the centuries.
Male interviewer: Excalibur is part of the legend of King Arthur, right? Who was he?
Woman: Well, actually Excalibur was King Arthur's magical sword. He famously pulled it out of a stone when he was a boy. Other people had tried, but the legend was that only the 'true King of England' could pull it out.
Male interviewer: Wow! Well, I know that Merlin and Guinevere were people – who were they?
Woman: Well, Guinevere was King Arthur's wife and Merlin was a wizard who helped King Arthur throughout his life. The other important people in this story were Sir Lancelot and the other 'Knights of the Round Table'.
Male interviewer: Who were they?
Woman: They were the men who served King Arthur in battles. The 'Round Table refers to their meeting room. In the past, kings and queens always stood at the end of a table, to show their power. King Arthur had a round table, to show that there was equality between all the members of his group.
Male interviewer: Ohh... now I understand the expression 'To have a round-table discussion'. A discussion where everyone's opinions are equal.
Woman: Exactly! This common, everyday expression actually comes from the legend of King Arthur!

Track 1.32 Unit 3, page 35, exercise 2
Male interviewer: I suppose that a 'round-table discussion' isn't the only expression we Use which comes from myths and legends, is it?
Woman: You're right! For example, many people use the expression 'to open Pandora's box' but don't remember the story it came from.
Male interviewer: Can you remind us?
Woman: Of course! In Greek mythology, Pandora was the first woman on Earth. There are many different stories about her, but generally they say that Zeus gave her a box on Mount Olympus and told her not to open it. She did, and all the evil in the world flew out. The only thing left inside the box when she closed the lid was hope.
Male interviewer: What a sad story! So, the expression refers to when your curiosity about something creates a lot of unexpected problems.
Woman: Exactly! And my favourite expression is 'the Midas touch'. This story is from a Place that is now modern-day Turkey. King Midas helped the god Dionysus and was rewarded with one wish. Midas wished that everything he touched would turn to gold. Sadly, one day he forgot and touched his beloved daughter, Zoe, and she turned to gold too!
Male interviewer: But we use the expression to talk about people who are good at making money, or who are particularly successful, right?
Woman: Yes! But most people don't know the real, sad story the expression comes from. Another expression I like is 'Achilles heel'. This is another story from Greece. When Achilles was a baby, his mother dipped his body into a magical river to protect him. He became exceptionally strong, but one heel didn't touch the water, so it remained his only weak point. The god Apollo knew about this weakness and used it to defeat him in battle.
Male interviewer: So, your 'Achilles heel' is your greatest weakness.
Woman: Exactly! Fascinating, right?
Male interviewer: Absolutely. Will you come back on the show next week and tell us about some more interesting things about myths and legends?
Woman: Of course!

Track 1.33 Unit 4, page 36, exercise 1
For thousands of years, humanity has tried to make sense of what we see in the night sky. The study of this is called astronomy, and it has taught us a lot about the Universe. We live in a galaxy that is called the Milky Way. There are billions of stars here and one of the brightest is our Sun. We call everything that revolves around the Sun the Solar System. It includes our Earth and our Moon, along with seven other planets and their moons. It also includes a collection of rocks between Mars and Jupiter called the asteroid belt, as well as objects made of ice and dust with bright burning tails that we call comets.

Track 1.34 Unit 4, page 38, exercise 1
Do you know the difference between an asteroid, a meteoroid, a meteor and a meteorite? They might have similar sounding names, but they are different. Let's start with asteroid and meteoroid. These are both rocky bodies that orbit the sun and there are millions of them in space. The simple difference between asteroids and meteoroids is their size. Meteoroids are pieces of rock that have broken off an asteroid, so asteroids are much bigger than meteoroids. Most meteoroids are small enough to fit in your hand, in fact. Next, we have meteors. These are meteoroids that enter the Earth's atmosphere and burn brightly as they vaporise. Meteors are also called 'shooting stars' because they look like stars travelling very fast across the sky. But don't confuse a meteor with a comet. Comets are not in our atmosphere; their tail is burning because of the heat from the sun. Finally, we have meteorites. These are fragments of meteors that survive their passage through the atmosphere and land on Earth. Perhaps you've seen a meteorite in a museum. They look a lot like normal rocks. In fact 90% of meteorites are simply made of rock, but some are made of metal. Others are made of both and you can see pieces of coloured metal in the rock.

Track 1.35 Unit 4, page 38, exercise 2
See previous track

Track 1.36 Unit 4, page 38, exercise 3
Listen and repeat.
/uː/ blue, Jupiter, Moon, Neptune
/ʊ/ could, look, pull, Uranus

Track 1.37 Unit 4, page 38, exercise 4
1 few
2 put
3 book
4 good
5 group
6 who
7 through
8 fruit

Track 1.38 Unit 4, page 38, exercise 5

Teacher: Good morning students, and welcome to our class about the Solar System. To begin with, let me ask you a basic question. How many planets are there in our Solar System? Robert?

Boy 1: Well, there are eight planets. Mercury, Venus, Earth, Mars, Jupiter, Saturn, Uranus and Neptune. Pluto is now considered a different kind of planet called a 'dwarf planet'.

Teacher: That's right. I see you've done some research. Now, who can give me some information about one particular planet? Ashley?

Girl 1: My favourite planet is Venus, the brightest planet in the sky. Venus was the goddess of love and beauty in Roman mythology. It was named after her because it's so bright and beautiful. Venus has almost the same gravity as the Earth, so if you went to Venus you would have a similar weight as you have on Earth.

Teacher: That's interesting. Anyone else?

Girl 2: I know about Mercury. Mercury was named after the messenger of the gods because it's the fastest planet in the Solar System. Mercury is also the smallest planet. And it's so hot on Mercury, we wouldn't be able to survive there.

Teacher: Thanks, Camille. Did you know that NASA's spacecraft Messenger orbited Mercury for four years and sent back thousands of images of the planet's surface? Messenger eventually crashed into the surface of Mercury, but if NASA send another spacecraft, we will be able to get even more information. All right, is there anyone interested in Mars? Carl?

Boy 2: Well, it is red because the surface is covered in red dust. Mars was named after The Roman god of war, because of its colour. Mars has had a lot of meteor impacts so there are thousands of craters. Mrs Flynn, do you think it will be possible to live on Mars some day?

Teacher: Well, if Mars didn't have poisonous gases in its atmosphere, maybe we could live there. Some people think that we will be able to live on Mars one day, but I wouldn't like to!

Track 1.39 Unit 4, page 40, exercise 2

Why explore space?

When Galileo looked into his telescope in 1609, he saw moons around Jupiter, spots on the Sun and the phases of Venus. He became convinced that Coperniucs was right: the Earth was not the centre of the Universe but rather all the planets rotated around the Sun. Although this was a controversial idea at the time, it led to great developments in our understanding of the Universe and our place in it. But it wasn't until the 20th century that we began to actually explore space.

On 4th October 1957, the Soviet Union launched Sputnik 1, the world's first artificial satellite, and the Space Age had begun. In the years that followed, space exploration symbolised the competition between the Soviet Union and the United States during the Cold War; both countries wanted to protect their national security interests, but at the same time, cooperate in international projects. In 1958, US President Dwight D. Eisenhower created NASA as a non-military agency, and in 1972, the two countries planned a combined space mission called the Apollo-Soyuz Test Project. Today, the International Space Station (ISS) is a joint project between NASA and four other space agencies. Astronauts from all over the world have made spaceflights there.

The ISS serves as a research laboratory, conducting experiments in biology, meteorology and other scientific fields. These have led to many scientific breakthroughs of great benefit to people down on Earth. These are just a few of them:

Water purification: Water-processing technology developed on the ISS has helped bring clean water to regions that desperately need it.

Medical care for remote areas: remote-guidance techniques developed on the ISS can now be used by experts to perform complex medical procedures on patients in remote areas of the Earth.

Monitoring natural disasters: the ISS has a system that takes up to 1,000 images a day covering almost all of the Earth's surface. This can help with quick responses to floods, fires, volcanic eruptions and all sorts of natural disasters.

There are also a range of technologies that were adopted for space travel that other industries have developed. And then there is the possibility of colonising other planets. Crazy as it might seem, entrepreneur Elon Musk has set up a company called SpaceX with exactly that in mind!

But perhaps the most important thing we can gain from exploring and learning about the Universe around us is a sense of perspective. As American astronomer Carl Sagan put it, 'it underscores our responsibility to deal more kindly with one another, and to preserve and cherish the pale blue dot, the only home we've ever known.'

Track 1.40 Unit 4, page 43, exercise 1

Hi. I'm Martha Bennet. I'm British. I studied physics and mathematics at university. I had been one of the most important football players in my city, but I chose science over a football career. I applied to the NASA Training Program on an impulse. I thought that I would never get in, but I guess I should thank my lucky stars because I became one of the 19 trainees that year. I can still remember the day I flew for the first time in a spaceship and walked in space. Now, I work at NASA Headquarters and I still love my job.

Hello. I'm Vladimir Popov and I was born in Russia. When I was 30, I joined an aero club and learnt to fly a light aeroplane. I was so good at flying that my teacher said it was written in the stars that I was going to be a famous aviator. I'd always been interested in space and the planets. A few years later, I was selected to participate in the Russian space programme. When I got the good news, I was on top of the world. I was so excited! Now, my greatest ambition is to walk on Mars one day. If I could do that, I would be the luckiest man alive.

My name is David Feld and I'm from Israel, but I've lived in the USA for a long time. I wanted to work at the technology centre for the military, but it was very difficult to get in. Finally, I decided to try and join NASA. I hadn't imagined being an astronaut but suddenly it was my only dream. I had to move heaven and earth to get in. Being an astronaut was the best experience of my life and I'm currently working at the Space Center in Florida.

Track 1.41 Unit 5, page 46, exercise 3

Stonehenge

This enigmatic monument in the south of England has generated a lot of speculation about its unusual structure: a series of large stones standing upright in a circular shape that have been there for about 5,000 years. Archaeologists have tried to uncover satisfactory evidence about how primitive people built and moved these heavy stones that can weigh as much as 26 tonnes each. The motives behind their construction remain unknown.

The Egyptian pyramids
One of the most misunderstood constructions of the ancient world that still puzzles modern archaeologists can be found in Egypt. There have been many theories as to why these mysterious structures were built and who built them. The general belief, however, is that they must have been created as tombs for the pharaohs. Archaeologists believe that slaves may have made them.

Track 1.42 **Unit 5, page 47, exercise 5**
These mysterious geometric lines, found in the Peruvian desert, mostly represent figures of animals, trees and flowers. There are hundreds of them, some around 300 metres wide! There is some evidence that they were made by the Nazca people between 200 BC and 500 AD. However, many people believe that these primitive people couldn't have made them, as they didn't have the technology to make such huge, enigmatic drawings. From the ground, they look like paths or channels, so it's best to observe them from an aeroplane. There are theories that aliens created them, but the truth remains unknown.

Track 1.43 **Unit 5, page 47, exercise 6**
The story of Atlantis comes from the writings of the ancient Greek philosopher Plato. He described a Utopian civilisation that lived on an island which was like an earthly paradise. The people on the island, however, became arrogant and greedy and the gods punished them by making the entire island disappear in a single day and night.

Even in Plato's time, a lot of people thought it was a myth that he told to warn people about the dangers of becoming morally corrupt.

But many people throughout history have also believed the story and many have tried to find the location of Atlantis, mainly around the Mediterranean Sea or just off the Atlantic coast of Europe or Africa. Plato said that Atlantis was just past the Pillars of Hercules, which historians think is the Strait of Gibraltar, the narrow area of sea that connects the Mediterranean with the Atlantic. Plato also said it existed about 9,000 years before his time, in 360 BC. In 1882 the American writer Ignatius Donnelly suggested that Atlantis was in fact the Garden of Eden and that it had been destroyed by the Great Flood described in the Bible. Other people believe that the Greek island Santorini was once Atlantis. This island was the location of a volcanic eruption that caused a tsunami in the 16th century BC. In 1964 a team of archaeologists were doing research on Santorini when they found houses, and the remains of people and objects from the ancient Minoan civilisation preserved inside volcanic rock and ash.

Historians and scientists may never agree on the truth behind the lost civilisation of Atlantis, but the story will almost certainly continue to inspire us for many years to come.

Track 1.44 **Unit 5, page 47, exercise 8**
1 could have, could've
2 may have, may've
3 might have, might've
4 must have, must've

Track 1.45 **Unit 5, page 48, exercise 3**
Seth: I watched a great documentary last night about Roswell. They say that there weren't any aliens. The debris was actually from a balloon used for nuclear tests.

Terry: I don't believe that. What about the videos of the alien bodies?

Olivia: Oh, they know that was a hoax. The guy who filmed it admitted it was just a reconstruction of what he thinks happened.

Terry: Personally, I think there were aliens there, and they'd prefer to pretend it was nuclear tests than admit that. I mean, if there were aliens, no government would tell us. I think aliens have visited us many times. We just don't know about it. There are so many galaxies out there in space. There must be aliens somewhere.

Laura: I agree with Terry. If there were beings that could travel through space, they'd definitely come here.

Gemma: I don't think so. Sure, there are lots of other galaxies and planets, but the distances are enormous. And if they have been here, why haven't we found any hard evidence by now?

Track 1.46 **Unit 5, page 49, exercise 4**
One day, my friend called me and told me to meet him at his house, but when I arrived, he wasn't there. I walked into the fields by his house to look for him and I suddenly saw him with two very tall creatures. They were walking towards a really bright light. I followed him and… we woke up in our own homes three days later. The police and our parents had been looking for us everywhere, but we don't remember anything more than a warm, bright light. Now I'm crazy about UFOs and aliens, I spend hours on the internet every day trying to find out what happened to us. If my friend hadn't invited me to his house, I wouldn't have had this amazing experience.

One day I was walking with my dog when he started barking and behaving really strangely. Suddenly I heard an indescribable sound, like a low frequency humming and I felt myself being lifted into the air. I felt a warm, loving presence and heard a voice in my head asking if I wanted to travel in a spaceship. Then suddenly, there was a loud bang and I woke up on the ground. I'm glad I didn't leave Earth. If I had gone with them, I would have missed my parents. But I walk my dog every day hoping to see them again. I can't stop thinking, if I had gone with them, what would it have been like?

Track 1.47 **Unit 5, page 50, exercise 3**

Crop Circles: hoax or unsolved mystery?
A crop circle is a pattern of flattened crops, like wheat or barley, that suddenly appears in a field. They first started appearing in the 1970s, although some people say there is evidence of them as early as the 17th century. Most of them have been found in England, but they have appeared in countries around the world. We don't know what, or who, creates them, but there are many mysterious theories.

As the years have gone by, the crop circles have become more and more complex. Symbolic shapes have also appeared in the patterns. For these reasons, some people argue that they couldn't be a hoax made by humans. They believe that they are created by some sort of higher intelligence! Molecular biologist Horace Drew has theorised that they might be messages of hope for humanity from either aliens or time travellers.

In 1991, two Englishmen named Doug Bower and Dave Chorley caused a sensation by announcing that the whole thing was an elaborate hoax: they had created the first crop circles using wood and rope in 1978. They even made one in front of journalists. They didn't claim that they had made all of the circles, just the first few, and then others must have copied them. They said that they had wanted people to believe a UFO had landed and made the circles.

Most crop circle researchers now admit that the vast majority of circles must be man-made. There is even a UK arts collective called Circlemakers who dedicate their time to making them for art and business. But some still claim that there are a few that cannot have been made by humans.

Biophysicist William Levengood said that he discovered differences in the crops inside and outside the circles that could not be attributed to human activity. He also said he'd found tiny spheres of iron in the crops, something that would suggest intense heat.

Furthermore, mineralogist Sampath Iyengar studied the soil from a crop circle in Canada and found evidence of temperatures so high that humans could not have produced them and they should have killed the crops.

So, are crop circles an unsolved mystery or a hoax? Just because we know that humans have made many, doesn't mean that they are all man-made. It is true that the only proven cause is humans, that we love a mystery and that many people make money out of books and documentaries about mysterious phenomena. But it's also true that if there were evidence of contact from aliens, our governments might not want us to know about it. Something to think about!

Track 1.48 **Unit 5, page 53, exercise 2**

Hey, Jamie here. I don't believe in dragons. I think people in ancient times wanted to invent a scary creature to make their stories more interesting. The inspiration for dragons might have come from large lizards. If dragons had existed, they would have appeared in primitive art, too. Furthermore, if there had been dragons, scientists would have found bones. Unless they have found them and they're keeping us in the dark, but I don't think it's likely.

Hi, it's Tom. I believe that dragons may have lived a long time ago, but they were probably all killed. It's sad but maybe if all the dragons hadn't been killed, the human race wouldn't have survived. There are many stories about them, and they always try to eat everyone in the village! I know we haven't found any skeletons, but people could have taken the bones for luck and accidentally covered their tracks.

My name's Anna. I don't believe in dragons because if dragons had lived on Earth we would have found bones by now. I think people saw dinosaur fossils and just imagined the rest. My dad and I once played a trick on my little brother and pretended there was a little dragon that lived at the end of our garden. I made tiny dragon footprints with a piece of wood I'd cut in the shape of a dragon's foot. Then my brother found the wooden dragon's foot in my room and that gave the game away!

Hi, I'm Mark. I think dragons existed in the past, but that they became extinct, like dinosaurs. I mean, they must have been real because they appear in legends from all over the world. There wouldn't have been so many stories written about dragons if they hadn't existed. I think our ancestors have already spilled the beans. We just have to keep our minds open.

Track 1.49 **Unit 5, page 53, exercise 3**

See previous track

Track 2.1 **Unit 6, page 54, exercise 2**

Auguste Dupin is a detective created by the writer Edgar Allan Poe. A famous story featuring Dupin, from 1844, is about a lady's letter. The letter contains some very important information and it has been stolen. The main suspect is a government official, Minister D —, who is the lady's political enemy. The police look for the letter in every corner of the minister's office, but they can't find out what has happened to it; after three days they finally give up. This is when the Chief of Police decides to ask the famous detective Auguste Dupin to look into the case. He tells the detective there is a big reward for the return of the letter and Dupin agrees to investigate.

A few days later, Dupin calls the Chief of Police to his apartment and asks for the reward. The Chief of Police is amazed when Dupin then gives him the missing letter. He wants to know how Dupin was able to figure out where the letter was, when the police had looked behind every painting, in every drawer and under the carpets. Dupin explains that the best way to hide something is not to hide it, but to leave it in plain sight where nobody would think of looking. He explains that this was how he found the letter very easily. He visited Minister D—'s office and saw a pile of letters and cards on the table. He distracted the minister, found the missing letter in the pile and left a fake letter in its place.

Track 2.2 **Unit 6, page 55, exercise 5**

First, they found Alex, sitting in the local café, doing his homework.

'Hi Alex,' said Max. 'We missed watching you play in the last football game.'

'Yeah, that was frustrating for sure,' Alex said. 'But I guess the coach didn't have any choice. Rules are rules.'

Nina and Max asked Alex where he'd been since eight o'clock.

'I've been right here,' he replied. 'You can ask the waitress. I helped her carry a box into the café when she arrived at eight PM'

The waitress confirmed his story.

So, Nina and Max left to go and find their second suspect, Sam. He was watching TV, but he turned it off quickly when he let them in. They told him about Coach Thornton's roses, and he seemed to be shocked. They asked Sam where he had been since 8 o'clock.

'I've been here all evening, watching TV,' said Sam.
'I watched that programme on UFOs that you guys recommended. I liked the bit about Roswell.'

'Did you like the interview at the end with the guy who said he'd been abducted by blue aliens?' asked Nina.

Max looked at Nina quickly, in surprise, but Nina paid no attention to him.

'Yeah, of course,' said Sam. 'The interview was cool, wasn't it?'

Nina and Max thanked Sam and left.

Sam had suggested that Mike was probably at the gym, so they went there next.

Mike was running on the treadmill when they arrived. The timer said he had been running for 30 minutes. He stopped when he saw them, and they told him about the roses. 'It wasn't me,' he said. 'I've been here all evening. Go and check at reception.'

The receptionist said Mike was telling the truth. He had signed in to the gym at 7:30 PM.

As they left the gym, Nina turned to Max: 'So, we now know who ruined the roses, don't we?' She said, grinning.

Track 2.3 Unit 6, page 56, exercise 4

Samantha started asking her classmates and friends about the mysterious boy who had bought food for all his friends. It wasn't long before she found out that it was a new boy called Jerry. She finally tracked him down in the school library and asked him to come outside into the hallway to talk to her. She calmly told him the facts that she had discovered and boldly asked him if he was, in fact, the thief. Jerry looked at his shoes for a long time and then quietly said yes, he had stolen the money.

'But, why?!' Asked Samantha. Jerry told her that he had moved to the area recently and it had been really hard for him to make friends. He had seen the wallet in the window and come up with a desperate plan. He had taken the 30 euros from the wallet and used it to buy snacks for a group of his classmates. He just wanted them to like him and think that he was cool. He said that he had never done anything like this before and he felt really bad, but he had been so lonely.

Samantha and Jerry talked for a while. 'I have an idea,' Samantha said suddenly, 'why don't we be friends? You can help me solve crimes, but you have to promise you'll never steal anything again.' A smile slowly appeared on Jerry's face. 'That would be great,' he said.

Track 2.4 Unit 6, page 57, exercise 5

Lawyer: Veronica Moor. You were the secretary of the Bluewater Tennis Club, weren't you?

Suspect: Yes, I was.

Lawyer: A witness says that on the night of 20th February, he saw you carrying boxes and a big black bag out of the tennis club office. You haven't returned to the club since that day, have you?

Suspect: No, I haven't. I quit because I hated the job. I was taking the things from my desk and my tennis rackets to my car.

Lawyer: But that wasn't all you took, was it? You were hiding money in the tennis bag, weren't you?

Suspect: I wasn't hiding anything. The manager of the tennis club often let me borrow money. I always gave it back.

Lawyer: Yes, but this time you had taken a very large amount, hadn't you? And you Threatened my witness, didn't you?

Suspect: Err, you can't prove anything though, can you?

Lawyer: I'm afraid we can. What you didn't notice is that our witness swapped your bag with his. So actually, we're looking at all the evidence we need, aren't we?

Track 2.5 Unit 6, page 57, exercise 7

Listen and repeat.

Asking a question

1

You're coming to the party, aren't you?

2

He didn't steal the money, did he?

Confirming:

3

You've been to England, haven't you?

4

That film isn't very good, is it?

Track 2.6 Unit 6, page 58, exercise 1

A suspicious mystery

The headline caught Detective David Hunter's attention – Airplane carrying priceless antiques goes missing in the Bermuda Triangle.

He had always been interested in disappearances in the Bermuda Triangle and suspected that some of them were cover-ups for crimes. He had a hunch that there was something strange about this story. Among the passengers on the plane was a wealthy businesswoman who had just acquired the precious cargo, and an amateur anthropologist.

'Hmm – a suspect! The anthropologist would probably know how much those treasures are worth,' Hunter thought, and he decided to contact the journalist who had written the story.

The journalist opened the door, and the detective introduced himself: 'David Hunter, private detective.' 'Dab Pike,' the journalist replied, 'what can I do for you?'

'In your Bermuda Triangle story, you mentioned that there was an anthropologist on board.' 'Yes, Ignatius Wittington. Interesting man. It's a shame he's disappeared, really.'

'Ah, so you've met him?' asked Hunter.

'Well, the acquisition of the antiques was a story in itself,' said Pike. 'I was there before the flight to interview Philomena Stock, the woman who had just acquired the collection. Wittington was there and I spoke to him briefly too.'

'Did he seem to know anything about the collection?' Hunter asked.

'Yes, Ignatius knew all about it.' The journalist paused. A light seemed to go on in his head. 'You think Ignatius Wittington might have... what... hijacked the plane to steal the antiques?!'

'I'm a detective, Mr Pike. We have to look into all the possibilities,' said Hunter. Pike gave Hunter a look that suggested the detective was wasting his time.

'I think you'll find it's just another mysterious Bermuda Triangle disappearance. Now, if you'll excuse me, I have a flight to catch'.

Upon returning to his office, Hunter looked up the coordinates for the plane's last known location and saw that there was a small island nearby. Following his hunch, he decided to go there immediately. As he approached the island by boat, he heard cries for help coming from inside a cave. He ran in and found a huge pile of Egyptian antiques, Ignatius Wittington

and Philomena Stock tied up, and guarding over them, Dab Pike.

'Mr Pike. I thought I might find you here. Which is why I brought a few friends with me,' said Hunter, pointing at the three police officers behind him. Pike looked shocked, so Hunter explained. 'I began to suspect you when you said you knew about the antiques before

the flight. Later, you tried to convince me to stick to the Bermuda Triangle theory. Finally, I noticed a golden statue of a pharaoh in your office... much like that one there!' The detective pointed to an identical golden statue on top of the pile of antiques.
And so, the mystery was solved. Dab Pike was sent to prison and Hunter returned to his office in New York, happy in the knowledge of a job well done.

Track 2.7 Unit 6, page 61, exercise 1
Agatha Christie is one of the most important authors in the history of detective fiction. She wrote a series of books featuring two well-known detective characters, Miss Marple and Hercule Poirot.
Miss Marple first appeared in a short story by Agatha Christie in 1927. She is a kind, elderly English lady who acts as an amateur detective. She's very intelligent and always puts two and two together very quickly. Her appearance often causes other characters to trust her before the penny drops and they realise their mistake. In total, Christie wrote 12 novels and 20 short stories which feature her.
Hercule Poirot is a Belgian detective who appears in over 30 novels and nearly 60 short stories by Christie. He is a short, neat man with a military moustache. Like Miss Marple, he uses his accent and appearance to make people underestimate or trust him. However, he's extremely clever and always hits the nail on the head. He is a logical, clue-based detective and he never jumps to conclusions. The first book about him appeared in 1920, when he arrives in England as a refugee in World War I.

Track 2.8 Unit 6, page 61, exercise 2
See previous track

Track 2.9 Unit 7, page 64, exercise 3

Mobile phones: then and now
Mobile phone technology has been developed at an incredible pace. Nowadays, mobile phones are not only used for communication, they are also used as an address book, alarm clock, camera, GPS, music player, television and more! Because of them, new generations of children are becoming computer literate at a younger and younger age.
But where and when did the first mobile phones appear? Well, the first mobile phone call was made by Martin Cooper, a senior engineer at Motorola, in early 1973. The phone weighed over a 1kg and could only be used for 30 minutes before it had to be charged again!
The price, size and features of mobile phones have changed incredibly since 1973. We now have thousands of different kinds of apps. They allow us to play games with complete strangers and make real-time video calls to friends around the world. The question is, what will mobile phones look like in the future? Will virtual reality become a common feature on our phones one day?

Track 2.10 Unit 7, page 65, exercise 4
An email is an electronic note that is stored in a file the recipient can open at any time. The first email was sent from one computer to another by Ray Tomlinson at MIT in 1971. It was an accidental discovery while something else was being researched by his department. But it quickly become popular and by the 1990s, over 10 million email accounts had been opened. Tomlinson is remembered now mainly for the @ symbol he chose to indicate the destination of a message. It is how emails have been addressed ever since.

Track 2.11 Unit 7, page 65, exercise 5
1 Millions of emails are sent every second.
2 Over 4.6 billion email accounts have been opened worldwide since the 1970s.
3 Hotmail was bought by Microsoft in 1997.
4 Some companies are introducing 'email-free Fridays' because too much time is being wasted on checking emails.
5 The attachment function was not invented until 1992.

Track 2.12 Unit 7, page 66, exercise 4
Boy 1: Welcome to our presentation about how technology helps students. We live in an age dominated by communications technology, so we think schools have a responsibility to teach students how to use the many learning tools available to us.
Girl 1: There are several e-learning tools we think are really useful. In class, we have an interactive whiteboard, which we use for highlighting information in texts, connecting to useful websites and playing video content. We also have a computer room which we can use in and outside of class time. We believe that these tools should be used more for these 5 reasons:
Boy 2: One. Technology is central to how our world works, and our teachers can help us learn to use it properly.
Girl 2: Two. It helps make classes more interesting. Maybe in the future, virtual reality could be used more in the classroom too.
Boy 1: Three. It makes learning easier for students with different abilities. Reading texts can be enlarged to a bigger font size for students with difficulty reading, and videos can have subtitles for students with hearing problems.
Girl 1: Four. Outside the classroom, students can learn at their own pace. Everyone can access the information as many times as they need.
Boy 2: Five. Technology encourages critical thinking skills. We learn how to analyse and evaluate the information we find. These skills must be developed for us to become successful members of society.
Girl 2: In conclusion, we think all schools should have the same level of access to technology. Unfortunately, that is not the case. All students should be taught to make more effective use of technology, not only to improve how we learn, but to prepare us for the real world.

Track 2.13 Unit 7, page 66, exercise 5
See previous track

Track 2.14 Unit 7, page 67, exercise 9

Listen and repeat.
/eɪ/ may, they, pay, safe, space, straight

Track 2.15 Unit 7, page 67, exercise 10

1 chat	**3** cake	**5** day	**7** break
2 train	**4** eight	**6** teach	**8** can

Track 2.16 Unit 7, page 68, exercise 2

Cheating in the age of the Internet

For as long as there have been tests and other forms of assessment, people have found ways to cheat. Some are obvious, like looking over a classmate's shoulder to copy their answers. Other ways are more inventive, like writing notes on crisps with food colouring ink and then eating them. Sometimes, students will go to incredible lengths to pass a test. However, whether obvious or inventive, cheating is never a good idea.

The internet has made cheating a lot easier. Most schools won't allow students to use electronic devices during tests, but it's still difficult to stop people accessing the internet to 'e-cheat'. The most common way to e-cheat is to copy content from a website and pretend it's your own work. This is called 'plagiarism', and students can get expelled from school or university for doing it.

So, why do people cheat? Many students think, 'Everyone else is doing it, so why shouldn't I?' Then there's pressure – students may have a lot of assignments and they need to pass them all. Anxiety can also lead students to cheat. If a student feels that what they write isn't good enough to pass, they might be more likely to look for the content elsewhere. Of course, there's also the cheat's belief that if they can get away with it, why not?

One reason not to cheat is technology. Many universities use a service called Turnitin, which compares students' work with a massive database to check for plagiarism. Teachers who don't have access to technology like Turnitin can always copy a suspicious sentence from an assignment into a standard search engine to see if it's been copied from the internet. For online tests, there is also software that can be installed on computers to check for suspicious behaviour.

But there are better reasons not to cheat. Firstly, when a student cheats, they are being dishonest with themselves and with the people around them. And secondly, testing is designed to help a student learn. If they cheat, they are not really learning.

So, what can we do to combat cheating? Teachers can:

- give interesting assignments that inspire great work from their students.
- support students throughout the exam process.
- encourage students to talk to them if they are feeling stressed or anxious.

Students can:

- begin preparing for assessments well in advance.
- ask for help when they need it.
- understand the value of honest academic work and do their best.

Finally, remember that assignments aren't made just to fill your time. They are created so that you can learn! Also, your teacher is probably better at catching cheats than you think. So, instead of cheating, just make sure you understand what you need to do and try your best.

Track 2.17 Unit 7, page 71, exercise 1

Boy 1: Hey, Kelly! You OK?
Girl 1: Hi Hiran, not really. I spoke to the new girl from school in a chatroom and we
Really got off on the wrong foot.
Boy 1: Oh no! What happened?
Girl 1: Well, I thought we were on the same wavelength about the Geography teacher, so I started listing all the reasons I don't like him.
Boy 1: What's the problem with that? Mr Davies is always yelling at someone!
Girl 1: Well, check out her message…
Girl 2: Kelly, I'll get straight to the point. Mr Davies is my dad. I think I need to show
him what you said.
Boy 1: That's so unlucky! Well, let me know what happens next, yeah? Keep me in the loop.

Track 2.18 Unit 8, page 72, exercise 2

Is technology a problem in modern society?

Aditi: Technology has made our lives easier. In the past, people had to waste so much time doing tasks that were dangerous, difficult or repetitive. Think about how much time a robot in a factory saves! When it's used correctly, technology gives us more time to do the things we enjoy. On the other hand, I think it's sad that most people communicate online now and don't write proper letters to each other any more.

Jackson: In my opinion, technology brings people together. Thanks to the internet you can keep in touch with people who live on the other side of the world. Also, information bouncing off satellites in space means that keeping up on current events is so easy. Free online translation services mean that you can communicate with anyone in any language! It's incredible that half of the people in the world are now online.

Tina: Life is so much busier and more complex than it used to be. People take so many photos of their lives, their food or their pets, that they're not really present in the moment. I'm always doing a lot of stuff at the same time. There are always a million tabs open on my screen and I often look at my tablet while I talk on my phone. I know it's rude to check messages while I'm in front of a friend, but I hear that 'ping' and I have to look!

Track 2.19 Unit 8, page 73, exercise 5

Advice: Are you one of the people who is becoming increasingly dependent on new technology in the last few years? Here are ten tips to prevent digital addiction.
Skills: Multitasking has become a counterproductive activity which causes stress and lack of concentration.
Style: We talk to people who believe that their appearance is more important than their personality and values.
News: 'Digital solitude' is a new mental health issue which is leading to greater social isolation every day; we are experiencing a loneliness epidemic.

Track 2.20 Unit 8, page 73, exercise 7

Listen and repeat.

/ɔː/ cause, talk, more, saw
/ɔɪ/ toy, join, boy, voice

Track 2.21 Unit 8, Page 73, exercise 8

1 board
2 noise
3 ball
4 point
5 oil
6 door
7 taught
8 walk

Track 2.22 Unit 8, page 74, exercise 1

What is publicity?
Publicity is information that is used to raise awareness or to influence an audience. It might take the form of bus stop posters that try to convince people to recycle, or television adverts which try to persuade people to vote a certain way. The writer uses language which is attention-grabbing and appeals to the reader's emotions. Often, the writer wants to promote something, so they usually don't present all of the facts objectively.

Track 2.23 Unit 8, page 75, exercise 7

Dave: Hey, what's going on today? There are a lot of students giving out flyers.
Valerie: Today's is International Technology Day, so Mrs Barnett's class, which your friend Rob is in, decided to create a campaign to promote proper use of technology.
Dave: Ah, that explains the banners in the dinner hall and the stickers everyone's wearing.
Valerie: Yes! Anyway, my friend Jenny, who is holding the placard over there, just gave a speech about technology and the environment. It was really interesting.
Dave: Nice! What other topics have been presented?
Valerie: Well, there was a conference about RSI, which means 'repetitive strain injury'. The speaker was Mr Michaels, who is from the IT department.
Dave: Wow! Well, I guess the campaign has been a great success!
Valerie: It has! I can't believe you didn't know about it. They made a massive poster, which Rob designed, and put it all over the school!
Dave: Maybe all that time I'm spending on my mobile is damaging my eyesight!

Track 2.24 Unit 8, page 76, exercise 2

The information and communication revolution:
If you were born after 1995, you belong to a generation that's called Generation Z, which means you don't remember a time without the internet. This means you are a 'digital native'. You may even have had your own phone since you were about 13. You probably chat with your friends more by messaging them than by talking to them in person. Perhaps your parents sometimes ask you to put your phone down.
Your parents are either Generation X (born between the early 1960s and the early 1980s) or Millennials (born between the early 1980s and the mid-1990s) and they do remember a time without the internet. They are 'digital immigrants'. They remember going to the library to look things up in encyclopaedias. They probably stayed in touch with friends by calling them on a landline phone. They would have had to dial the number every time and, because of this, your parents might still remember some of their friends' telephone numbers. (Go on – ask them!)
There have been more developments in information and communication technology in the last few decades than ever before. These developments have fundamentally changed the way we behave. Information is more instantly available, and we have become better at finding the information we want. Generation Zers, in particular, have become skilled multitaskers. Having the internet in our pockets means we can access cultural content from all over the world. As a result, young people are becoming more global and more tolerant. In one survey of adults over the age of 35, the majority of them said they felt teenagers today have more in common with teenagers from countries than with adults from their own country.
Not all changes are so positive. Surveys have found that 40% of Generation Zers describe themselves as digital addicts. Using digital devices a lot is not a problem in itself. It becomes an issue when we use them so much that they we no longer interact with the people and places around us. Some experts say Generation Z are at a greater risk of loneliness than previous generations.
So, what does the future hold and how should we approach it? New generations of workers will have to keep up to date with technological advances and be able to change careers, when necessary. We must be aware that internet platforms can be used to manipulate, and we should learn to analyse and question the information we receive via online media.
Most importantly, we should enjoy the many benefits that the information and communication revolution has brought to our lives, while continuing to form strong social relationships in the world around us. Meeting people face-to-face, having conversations and developing relationships can be challenging, but they are also some of the most rewarding human experiences.

Track 2.25 Unit 8, page 79, exercise 1

Teacher: So, Selena, can you explain what your project for this class is and how it all went? How did your group work together?
Selena: Really well, I think. It was a great team to work in. We're all a bit different, but we all brought our own useful skills to the project. I think I'm quite good at brainstorming, Mark knows a lot about robotics and Rachel's a good organiser. We worked like a well-oiled machine! So, here's our project: a robot vacuum cleaner. Tadah!
Teacher: It looks great! Can you tell us how it works?
Selena: Yes! It's quite simple, really, not too different from other robotic vacuum cleaners, but we've added a few bells and whistles. So, for example, if something's too big for it to vacuum it's got a little brush that will push it to a corner of the house. Everything will be collected there for you to pick up later; it won't be in the way. It has a function that makes it change direction when it hits something, and it's got a remote control so you can direct it to specific places if you want to.
Teacher: Wow! That sounds really complicated.
Selena: Well – I thought so too in the beginning. I didn't think we'd be able to make it work in time. At one point I started to hit the panic button and I had to be calmed down by Rachel. Thankfully we've got Mark, who's a programming star.
Teacher: So, Mark, are you the brains behind this?
Mark: Well, I helped with the calculations, but we all worked together. I was just another cog in the machine, really.
Rachel: Mark's being a bit modest there. He is a bit of a genius. But it's true we all worked together well.

Track 2.26 Unit 9, page 82, exercise 1

Narrator 1: The Ford Model T was first produced in 1908. It's considered the most influential car of the 20th century because it was the first car to be made on a moving

assembly line. This made production very efficient, so the cars became cheaper and a lot of people could afford one.
Narrator 2: Wilbur and Orville Wright believed that human flight was possible. So, after a lot of investment of money and time, they invented the aeroplane in 1903. This machine was a major turning point in the 20th century because it meant the conquest of the air.
Narrator 1: The United States and Russia were the leaders of the space race. It began in 1955, when both nations announced they were going to launch satellites into space. Although it started as a competition between Cold War enemies, it ended up bringing some universal benefits, including GPS, accurate weather predictions and satellite internet access.
Narrator 2: Although it's difficult to give a precise date for the invention of the personal computer, or PC, many people say it dates back to the 1970s. The first computer to be called a 'personal computer' was the Altair 8800, which came out in 1975. It's hard to remember or imagine computers without the internet now, but they were used for word processing, databases, spreadsheets and, of course, games.
Narrator 1: The internet started as early as the 1960s, mainly as a US plan to set up communication between academic and military computer networks. But it really began to boom when English scientist Tim Berners-Lee invented the World Wide Web in 1989. The internet is a milestone in media and communications because it gave us all easy and widespread access to information and contact with other users.

Track 2.27 Unit 9, page 82, exercise 3

1 work
2 journey
3 personal
4 turning
5 bird
6 entrepreneur
7 first
8 earth

Track 2.28 Unit 9, page 83, exercise 5

Jenny: This article about the most important events of the 20th century is so interesting. I didn't realise cars were such an important invention.
Tom: What's so amazing about cars?
Jenny: Well, they gave people greater access to remote areas.
Tom: That's such an obvious benefit…
Jenny: Yes, it is. But did you know that cars were so influential that cities began to adapt their architecture to traffic?
Tom: How interesting! Anything else?
Jenny: Well, it won't be so long before petrol and diesel cars are gone…
Tom: Then people will drive electric cars. That will make such a difference to air pollution in cities.

Track 2.29 Unit 9, page 84, exercise 2

Causes and consequences
The 20th century was a turning point in history. The world went through so many transformations that it entered a new era. The first half of the 20th century was marked by the two world wars. The First World War caused so much suffering that people promised never to let it happen again. But after the war, the economic situation in Europe was so bad, there were so few jobs and there was so little hope that extreme political ideas took hold, and they led to the Second World War. The two wars caused so much loss of life and so many casualties that world leaders decided they needed to encourage greater cooperation between nations, and they created the United Nations and drew up the Universal Declaration of Human Rights.

Track 2.30 Unit 9, page 85, exercise 4

George: Wow, I'm glad we watched that programme.
Cathy: So am I. I really liked the bit about Gandhi.
George: So did I! I didn't know much about him before.
Cathy: Neither did I. I can't believe that he was assassinated.
George: Neither can I. It was interesting that he was 78 years old when he died, just like Simone de Beauvoir.
Cathy: Yes! I was amazed that she didn't call herself a philosopher.
George: So was I! I love finding out facts about real people.
Cathy: So do I. Let's watch another documentary later.
George: OK!

Track 2.31 Unit 9, page 86, exercise 2

The price of progress
It is estimated that air pollution probably killed as many as 40 million people in the 20th century. That's far more than were killed in the First World War, and nearly as many as were killed in the Second World War. But pollution is just one of many environmental disasters that we have inflicted on ourselves and our environment. Although the 20th century brought great technological, political and social progress, it came at a cost. The fact is that it also saw a huge increase in man-made threats to the environment. Depletion of natural resources, species extinction, deforestation and global warming are just some of the problems that we continue to cause the planet we live on.
Many of the great technological advances of the last century had a negative impact on the environment. The most obvious example is the car. By the end of the century, there were roughly 800 million cars on the world's roads. This has led to massive pollution of our cities and serious health problems. In addition, heavy industry has used fossil fuels to provide the increasing number of goods we demand, and this adds significantly to the pollution of the air we breathe. As a result of this contamination, we are now also witnessing unprecedented global warming.
However, a lot of the environmental damage comes simply from our increased presence on Earth. The last century saw the world population rise by 400%, and our exploitation of natural resources also increased dramatically. We endangered animal species, mined the Earth and cleared large areas of forest for farming and timber. For instance, at the end of the last century, deforestation in Brazil had reduced the Atlantic coastal forest to 8% of its original size. Furthermore, clean drinking water is becoming more and more scare, because of overuse, pollution and climate change.
There are now so many environmental problems that for many people the progress we made in the 20th century has come at too high a price. Throughout the 20th century we demanded more technology, more consumer goods and

more resources. And there were far more of us to demand them. Consequently, we have record levels of pollution and we are rapidly depleting our natural resources.

So, what can we do about it? We can join environmental organisations, recycle our waste and practise responsible buying. We must remember that we only have one Earth, and it is everyone's responsibility to look after it. The problem is that many people don't believe that small actions can make a difference. However, it's the little changes that add up and affect the world around you, whether you're a teenager or a politician. If we all act a bit more responsibly, we might be able to save this beautiful planet we call home.

Track 2.32 Unit 9, page 89, exercise 1

The 20th century saw some of the worst violence in human history. The First World War ended with Europe in ruins. The victorious powers made Germany, who lost the war, pay a huge amount of money to repair the damage done. This made matters worse. It led to a rise in German nationalism and the Second World War. When the Second World War ended with the USA using the nuclear bomb to destroy the Japanese cities of Hiroshima and Nagasaki in 1945, world leaders saw the need for a change, and the United Nations, or UN, was created that same year in San Francisco, although its headquarters are now in New York. The UN was essentially started from scratch, as no other organisation until that time had ever been set up with such ambitious goals.

As well as keeping peace, the UN was very influential in developing human rights and equality. And there were many other developments in these fields in the 20th century. For example, women in most countries couldn't vote until the early 20th century. In the UK, women weren't given the full right to vote until 1928. Interestingly, it was the wars that helped women gain independence, as more women were needed to do the jobs that men had done. Although the other effects of the war were horrific, this was one change for the better.

Another area where there were some positive changes was in race relations, especially in the USA. Until the 1950s, African Americans were segregated; they couldn't use the same rooms, toilets or seats as white people. They had to use the spaces labelled 'for colored people'. They had a separate section on the bus, but even these seats had to be given up if a white person wanted them. Many brave African Americans stood up against this injustice. Then in 1955, a woman called Rosa Parks was asked to give up her seat for a white person. She refused and went to jail for it, but her case shook things up in society and segregation in transportation was later declared unconstitutional.

The world has changed a lot since then. The UK had its first female prime minister in 1975, and the USA its first African American president in 2009. Although there is still a long way to go, since the 20th century humanity has made great advances in human rights, equality and tolerance of diversity.

Track 2.33 Unit 2 Review, page 91, exercise 1

Adam Horwitz is an American entrepreneur who was born in 1991. He's a very successful YouTube vlogger who has gained massive popularity for his Wolves travel channel. However, he hasn't always been a successful vlogger. Between the ages of 15 and 18 he started 30 different websites but none of them made him very much money. These failures didn't put him off and didn't stop him starting an online company called Mobile Monopoly, which he sold for a huge profit, making him a millionaire by the age of 18. As he says, 'The hardest part about being an entrepreneur is that you'll fail ten times for every success.'

He then started a website called Urban Stomp, which gave the location of parties. The site made him lots more money, but it had to be closed down because of its own success. Over 800 people arrived at a party one night, which caused quite a bit of chaos.

Starting a business when you are young has lots of advantages. Adam often used his age as a marketing advantage. He was able to target younger people and, as he tells other young people who want to become entrepreneurs, when you're young you don't really have anything to lose. You're still living at home and you only need money for pizza and to have fun with your friends. If it all fails, you can still finish school, get your degree and then get a normal job.

Track 2.34 Unit 3 Review, page 92, exercise 1

Hi guys, it's Yaz here. Last week we talked about ghost stories – I love a ghost story – and this week I'd like to discuss another favourite subject of mine: mythology. Myths were originally used to explain why the world is the way it is. These days we have a greater understanding of the world based on modern science, but we still enjoy a good story. Here are a couple of my personal favourites.

There are many stories about the city of Atlantis, but did you know that it is not the only mythical lost city? Near-identical stories crop up all over the world. For example, Iram, in the deserts of modern Saudi Arabia, is said to have been wiped out in a single night under a flood of sand. Then you have Ys off the coast of France, which was supposedly flooded around the 5th century by a mythical warrior king. And also, the Hindu myth of Tripura, which the gods destroyed in a rain of fire.

Were these real tragedies based on true events, like Pompeii, or just good stories? I'll leave it to you to decide.

I don't know about you, but I love mythological creatures, especially unicorns and dragons. Now, dragons appear on every continent; medicines were supposedly made with their bones in China and they appear in Norse, Christian and Greek mythologies. In South America the Mayans worshipped a dragon-like snake. British scientists were still insisting as late as 1886 that dragons had once existed. It was only with the discovery of dinosaur bones that people saw the probable link between ancient fossils and dragon myths. It's easy to see how a bit of fact and a large bone can turn into a great story.

Track 2.35 Unit 4 Review, page 93, exercise 1

1

I've been reading about the discovery of our solar system. When ancient astronomers were studying the stars, the telescope hadn't been invented yet. Even so, they managed to spot Mercury, Venus, Mars, Jupiter and Saturn. They also knew about the Sun, Moon and Earth. When Neptune was discovered in 1846, Uranus had already been located by Herschel. Pluto was found in 1930 and was considered a planet until its status was changed earlier this century.

2
Hello and welcome to the planetarium's world record holder's gallery.
Peggy Whitson was 57 during her last flight and she spent an incredible 289 days aboard the International Space Station. During her various spaceflights she totalled an amazing 665 days in space. Russian cosmonaut Gennady Padalka has made five spaceflights and has spent almost two and a half years zipping around the Earth at over 28,000 km/h. US Senator John Glenn flew on the space shuttle in 1998 becoming the oldest person to go into space. In 1962 he was the first American to orbit Earth. This means he had waited 36 years between space flights.

3
Man: Hi, everyone! I'm here with local astronaut Becky Johnson. So, Becky, how do you feel about joining the NASA astronaut programme?
Woman: I'm on top of the world! It's my life ambition.
Man: So, what would be your ideal destination?
Woman: Well humans have only ever been to the Moon, although there are various programmes looking at getting people to Mars at the moment. That would be an exciting mission, but I'm not sure it's for me because it takes nearly a year to get there. To tell you the truth, I'd be over the moon with the moon!

4
Woman: Tim, if you could travel through time just once where would you go?
Man: I'd love to see the dinosaurs, but if I could only go once, I'm not sure I'd go to the past.
Woman 2: Really?
Man 2: I think it'd be interesting to see life about 500 years into the future. I'd love to know if humans have conquered Mars.
Woman 2: So, into the future then?
Man 2: Hmm, well I'd love to see how they built the pyramids, but we do have quite a lot of information about that already. I think I'd rather see what's coming for humanity.

Track 2.36 Unit 6 Review, page 95, exercise 1

1
Boy: Have you any idea why Tom's ignoring me?
Girl: He isn't ignoring you, is he?
Boy: Well I passed him in the corridor and he didn't say hello or even look at me. I thought it was really strange.
Girl: He's got his piano exam today, hasn't he? So maybe he's just nervous about that and focusing on trying to pass. He's not the type of person to deliberately ignore someone, is he?
Boy: Aha, the penny drops! You're right, I'd forgotten about his exam. Fingers crossed he does well.

2
Ana: Hi Mel. I think I'm going to be in trouble with my sister.
Boy: Why? What's happened?
Ana: Do you remember that new hat I wore for the school photos last week? Well it wasn't really mine. I kind of borrowed it from my sister.
Boy: Oh no, and you lost it, didn't you?
Ana: No, but I didn't ask if I could borrow it. Once my mum borrowed something of hers and accidentally broke it. She's been very particular with her things since then. And now she's just seen the photos and she's going to put two and two together. She's going to be so angry!

3
Man: Did you watch Crime 101 last night?
Woman: Yes, I did. It was a good one, wasn't it?
Man: It was! It took me ages to work out who the thief was. I thought it was the Australian football player at first.
Woman: Me too! Then I thought it was the Swedish man who needed the money for his wife's operation.
Man: He was a likely suspect. But who could have imagined it would be the police officer?
Woman: Yes. He wanted the money for his retirement, didn't he?
Man: Exactly. It really kept me guessing to the very end.

4
Woman: Do you fancy going to the cinema tonight?
Man: Yeah, that'd be good. What's on?
Woman: Let me look. There's a new musical comedy out, but it's got terrible reviews, so not that. There's an alien war thing but it looks rubbish too. There's a new Hercule Poirot out… Oh but you hate detective films!
Man: Don't jump to conclusions. I don't like many of them, but is that the one with Kenneth Branagh in it?
Woman: Err, Kenneth Branagh. Yes, it is.
Man: I like him. Shall we see that one then? What time is it on?
Woman: It starts in an hour, so we'd better start moving!

Track 2.37 Unit 8 Review, page 97, exercise 1

I'm Gina. I'm 17 and so I'm a member of Generation Z, which some people call the digital generation. However, I'm not very typical of my generation and some of my friends even think I'm a bit weird because I don't have any social media accounts. I used to have them when I was younger but then I deleted them all.
I realised that I was spending an awful lot of time on various sites just looking at other people - some of whom I didn't even know - and watching their lives. There are people who post about every aspect of their life. It's an addiction. And it's an addiction to keep looking. When I thought about it, I didn't really care about what these people ate, who they dated or which parties they went to. My friends, who I can talk to face to face, are more important to me. My friends are the people I want to spend my time with.
I realised that not only was I spending a lot of time looking at other people's lives, but it was also not good for my wellbeing. It seemed like these people had the most perfect lives, hair, bodies, pets, friends, everything. I started feeling down because their world seemed so wonderful but mine felt so boring. But it's not true; their lives aren't so perfect! Those photos are only showing one moment. Those people don't share the bad times or the just the ordinary moments of everyday life. They spend hours taking hundreds of photos to post the one perfect second. It's all fake! People love to show off and pretend that their life is the best.
Loneliness is afflicting more people than ever before and it affects people from every generation. Researchers are studying the effects of the digital age upon our mental health. So, remember, a lot of what you see on social media sites is just a distorted view of someone else's life –

it's the bit they want you to see. It isn't all true; they want you to be jealous! I feel much happier with my life after cancelling my accounts. I know it isn't for everyone, but it works for me.

Track 2.38 Unit 9 Review, page 98, exercise 1

1
The space race and moon landings in the middle of the 20th century are considered by many to be one of the most amazing milestones of human exploration. In the end, the Americans claimed victory over Russia. However, I say the moon landings never happened. It was all made up so that the Americans could say they had won. In the future, when people really go to the moon, the truth will be discovered!

2
For me, the greatest human achievements of the 20th century were those created by the space race, which improved our ability to explore beyond the Earth. We got people into orbit, onto the Moon and living in the International Space Station. The 21st century will see us go even further and that's why private companies are so important because they have the economic resources to take humans to Mars.

3
I find it so strange that millions of people think that the Americans didn't really go to the Moon. It was such a huge moment in 20th century history that I am amazed that there is any doubt. Twelve people actually walked on the Moon's surface – that is so amazing! We need to go back again soon – that way we can prove it because their footprints must still be there!

4
Space exploration was such a massive achievement during the 20th century but it was also such a massive expense. In fact, it was so expensive that the USA cut the funding for their space programmes and stopped sending people to the Moon. Now there are various private companies owned by prominent billionaires which are in a new space race to take humans around the Moon and even to Mars.

5
The super-rich are trying to shake things up in the new space era. I personally don't believe it should be the job of companies to send people to the Moon or Mars. I think the world's governments should unite in order to create a joint space exploration programme. Rockets are incredibly expensive, so countries should pay for this together rather than allow private companies to take the lead. Surely the goal is to expand our knowledge, not to make a profit?

Track 2.39 Wordlist, page 117, unit 1, Skills and strengths

Skills	active
analytical skills	creative
communication	enthusiastic
creativity	imaginative
empathy	meticulous
negotiation	resourceful
numeracy	sociable
passion	systematic
problem solving	talkative
Strengths	thoughtful

Track 2.40 Wordlist, page 117, unit 1, Business

company	product
earn	run your own business
employee	service
identity	slogan
launch	success
logo	target market

Track 2.41 Wordlist, page 117, unit 1, Jobs

architect	marine biologist
entrepreneur	newspaper editor
firefighter	psychologist
graphic designer	radio DJ

Track 2.42 Wordlist, page 117, unit 2, The entertainment industry

feature film	production
full-length	release
animated	remake
musical	sequel

Track 2.43 Wordlist, page 117, unit 2, Inventions

bubble wrap	invest
copycat	mop
design	perfume
idea	suitcase
insulation	wallpaper

Track 2.44 Wordlist, page 117, unit 2, Success and failure

achievement	motivated
fail	passionate
focused	perseverance
grit	set goals
habits	succeed
lose heart	successful

Track 2.45 Wordlist, page 118, unit 3, Storytelling

biography	introduction
character	novel
climax	play
comic strip	plot
conflict	poem
fairy tale	resolution
fictional	setting
hero	theme

Track 2.46 Wordlist, page 118, unit 3, The natural world

burn	sky
harmony	the Earth
human	the Universe
land	water
light	wood

Track 2.47 Wordlist, page 118, unit 3, Myths

battle
death
evil
fight
giant
gift
god
goddess
Greek
humanity
king
knowledge
Norse

Track 2.48 Wordlist, page 118, unit 4, The Earth

algae
birds
dinosaurs
extinct
fern
homo sapiens
hospitable
life
ocean
oxygen
planet
revolve
swamp

Track 2.49 Wordlist, page 118, unit 4, The Universe

The planets
Mercury
Venus
Earth
Mars
Jupiter
Saturn
Uranus
Neptune

Celestial bodies
asteroid
comet
float
gravity
meteor
meteorite
meteoroid
Moon
orbit
star
Sun

Track 2.50 Wordlist, page 118, unit 4, Space exploration

astronaut
discovery
experiment
ISS (International Space Station)
mission
NASA
remote
research laboratory
satellite
science
Space Age
spaceflight
technology
telescope

Track 2.51 Wordlist, page 119, unit 5, Ancient monuments

archaeologist
build
circular
construction
drawing
Egypt
England
geometric
huge
path
pharaoh
primitive
pyramid
stone
Stonehenge
structure
tomb
tonnes

Track 2.52 Wordlist, page 119, unit 5, UFOs and aliens

alien
being
clue
conspiracy theory
controversy
crash
debris
documentary
fake
footage
military
newspaper reports
spaceship
truth
UFO

Track 2.53 Wordlist, page 119, unit 5, Mysteries

crop circles
evidence
fact
hoax
mysterious
pattern
phenomenon / phenomena
prove
theory

Track 2.54 Wordlist, page 119, unit 6, Phrasal verbs

figure out
find out
give up
look for
look into

Track 2.55 Wordlist, page 119, unit 6, Detective work

alibi
clue
criminal
deduction
evidence
hunch
illegal
lawyer
private detective
red herring
sleuth
steal
suspect
unsolved
witness

Track 2.56 Wordlist, page 119, unit 6, Investigation

analyse
check
conclusion
cover-up
disappearance
discuss
interview
missing
notice
police officer
solve
stick to

Track 2.57 Wordlist, page 120, unit 7, Communication I

app
attachment
computer literate
contact
email account
GPS
junk mail
message
real-time
social media
vlog
mobile phone
email

Track 2.58 Wordlist, page 120, unit 7, The internet

chat room
download
install
online
platform
software
spam
user-friendly
virus
webcam
website

Track 2.59 Wordlist, page 120, unit 7, Academic honesty

assessment
assignment
cheating
e-learning
expel
get away with something
pass a test
plagiarism
punishment

Track 2.60 Wordlist, page 120, unit 8, Communication II

community
globalisation
integration
isolated
keep in touch
multitask
satellite
screen
social media
solitude
tablet
worldwide

Track 2.61 Wordlist, page 120, unit 8, Publicity

advert
blog
brochure
bumper sticker
conference
face-to-face
flyer
get involved
influence
objective
pin badge
placard
poster
privacy
promote
raise awareness
subjective
subscribe

Track 2.62 Wordlist, page 120, unit 8, Technological advances

chat
conversation
device
digital addict
encyclopaedias
generation
internet platform
keep up to date
landline
library
loneliness
Millennial

Track 2.63 Wordlist, page 120, unit 9, Human achievements

aeroplane
AI (Artificial Intelligence)
boom
driverless cars
the internet
milestone
the personal computer
the Space Race
turning point

Track 2.64 Wordlist, page 120, unit 9, The 20th century

Issues
democracy
empire
feminist
freedom
human rights
hunger
living conditions
manufacture
opportunity
oppression
peace
peaceful
political ideas
poor
poverty
protest
religious groups
Events
the Cold War
civil rights movements
the First World War
the Second World War
the United Nations
the Universal Declaration of Human Rights

Track 2.65 Wordlist, page 120, unit 9, The environment

climate change
damage
deforestation
ecological
environmental disaster
fossil fuel
global warming
health
heavy industry
man-made threat
pollution
population growth
recycle
resources
timber
waste

Get started!

Page 6

1 *Student's own answers*

2
1 personal growth
2 volunteer
3 ago
4 skills
5 drive

3
1 affected
2 interested
3 equality
4 commitments
5 prioritise

4
1 to be
2 studying
3 to go
4 preparing
5 to learn

5 *Student's own answers*

6 *Student's own answers*

Page 7

1
1 and
2 volunteered
3 learned
4 met
5 have overcome
6 challenged
7 have achieved

2
1 achieve
2 confidence
3 overcome
4 determination
5 strategy
6 target

3 *Student's own answers*

4
1 Last
2 This
3 in
4 for
5 ago
6 since

5
1 How long have you known your best friend? Student's own answers
2 What did you learn last summer? Student's own answers
3 Have you gone to the cinema this week? Student's own answers
4 When was the last time you met someone new? Student's own answers
5 Who did you talk to on the phone yesterday? Student's own answers
6 Did you go on a trip in 2019? Student's own answers

6 *Student's own answers*

Page 8

1
1 fundraising campaign
2 issue
3 awareness
4 involved
5 management
6 prioritise

2
1 in
2 by
3 in
4 by
5 at

3 *Student's own answers*

4
1 applied
2 were
3 took
4 raining
5 listened

5
1 Holly wishes she had remembered her friend's birthday
2 Holly wishes she had gone to France in the summer.
3 Holly wishes she hadn't started guitar lessons.
4 Holly wishes she had visited her grandparents.
5 Holly wishes she had asked her teacher for help.

6 *Student's own answers*

Page 9

1
1 hope
2 degree
3 suggested
4 make
5 at
6 getting

2 *Student's own answers*

3 *Student's own answers*

4
1 Peter enjoys reading science magazines.
2 Peter wants to go to university in a few years.
3 Peter started learning about astronomy when he was 12 years old.
4 Peter celebrated passing all his exams in August.
5 Peter has recently learned to be patient with his sister.

5
1 Do you know what time it is?
2 Could you tell me what your favourite subject is?
3 Do you know which job you would like to do?
4 Could you tell me what your goals are?
5 Do you know if you would like to get a degree?

6 *Student's own answers*

Unit 1

Page 10

1 **1** d **2** a **3** c **4** e **5** b

2 *Student's own answers*

3
1 Human resources officer
2 Set up a social programme to improve staff relations
3 Made sure all the financial records are accurate and up to date
4 Helped save over ten thousand pounds in unnecessary expenses
5 Christina Brent
6 Web designer
7 Won two awards for the design of the web Page

4 *Suggested answers:*
active: energetic
creative: artistic/imaginative
enthusiastic: interested/passionate
meticulous: perfectionist/careful
resourceful: capable/intelligent
sociable: friendly/good-natured
systematic: organised/analytical
talkative: communicative
thoughtful: attentive/careful

Page 11

5

1 **a** planned **b** wrote **c** made **d** painted

2 **a** prefer **b** go **c** organise **d** draw

3 **a** have thought **b** have persuaded **c** have solved **d** have designed

6 *Student's own answers*

7 *Student's own answers*

Page 12

1 *Student's own answers*

2
1 does; do; Bill Gates runs a charity focused on healthcare, education and ending poverty.
2 has; had; he has had it for 20 years. He started it in the year 2000.
3 did; change; Chanel's designs changed fashion by making women's clothes more practical and comfortable.
4 does; represent; the slogan represents the 'can do' attitude of the company.
5 Has; created; yes, he has created lots more.

3
1 made
2 have loved
3 was
4 wrote
5 got
6 need
7 come
8 realised
9 saw
10 started
11 has grown
12 have worked
13 work
14 have earned

Page 13

4 *Suggested answers:*
1 It must meet some need in the market.
2 It must be simple and original.
3 You should bear in mind that you have only a couple of seconds to catch your audience's attention.

5
1 a charity that provides students with books and food
2 'Together we're better'
3 computer repair business
4 made a list of the most common problems computers have
5 paid friends who know about computers to work for her
6 'There's no party better'
7 helped his friends to plan their parties
8 hired friends and family to host parties

6
1 a logo
2 a slogan
3 a slogan
4 a logo
5 both

7 *Student's own answers*

8 note, open, most, hello, also

9 *Student's own answers*

Page 14

1 *Answers given at bottom of Student's Book Page 15*

2
1 verbal-linguistic and visual-spatial
2 logical-mathematical
3 visual-spatial

3 *Student's own answers*

4
1 True
2 False. We strengthen and abandon nerve connections from when we are born until we're in our 20s.
3 True
4 False. He has identified eight intelligences.
5 True

Page 15

5
1 normal or typical
2 nerve cells
3 the ability of our brains to adapt
4 area
5 the ability to understand yourself

6 *Suggested answers:*
1 It means you should make the most of your strengths and also try to improve any areas of weakness.
2 drawing up mind maps – visual-spatial; listening to music while you study – musical; listening to a friend explain the topic – interpersonal, verbal-linguistic
3 architect: visual-spatial; firefighter: bodily-kinaesthetic; marine biologist: naturalistic; newspaper editor: verbal-linguistic; radio DJ: musical

7 *Student's own answers*

8 *Student's own answers*

Page 16

1
1 PC
2 penicillin
3 jeans
4 cocoa
5 electric cars

2 *Student's own answers*

3
Paragraph 1 c
Paragraph 2 b
Paragraph 3 d
Paragraph 4 a

4 *Student's own answers*

5 *Student's own answers*

6 *Student's own answers*

Page 17

1 c, d, b, a

1 To study for a career she thinks she'll love in forestry or for something more serious like law, which is what her mother wants her to do.
2 If he does what he would like to do and changes groups to work on the charity project, he thinks his teammates will be annoyed.
3 If they write the truth in their blog about who sprayed the graffiti, they might get into trouble for speaking out.
4 She can't decide whether or not to tell the teacher that her classmates aren't doing their share of the work because they might get angry.

3 *Student's own answers*

4
1 went
2 decide
3 had
4 choose
5 was
6 tell

5 1 a 2 d 3 c 4 b

6 *Student's own answers*

Unit 2

Page 18

1 *Student's own answers*

2
1 business
2 empire
3 successful
4 fired
5 imaginative
6 bankrupt
7 achievements
8 amusement

Page 19

3 1 b 2 d 3 e 4 a 5 f 6 c

4
1 he had been successful in film and television;
2 he had had many failures; he had started Laugh-O-Gram Studio and it had gone bankrupt
3 he had created a multimillion-dollar business empire.
4 he had been fired from his job on a Kansas newspaper.

5 *Student's own answers*

Page 20

1 1 a 2 b 3 a 4 b 5 b 6 b

2
1 False. She was named the most powerful celebrity.
2 True.
3 False. He is 1.98 metres tall.
4 True.

3 *Student's own answers*

4 what, job, on, problem

5 *Student's own answers*

Page 21

6
1 created
2 had designed
3 tried
4 had been
5 decided
6 had become

7
1 He had designed the product before he presented it on television.
2 He became successful, so it was clear the investors had made a mistake.
3 By 2016 he was rich because he had sold a lot of Trunkis.
4 He found out that a company had copied his idea.

8 *Student's own answers*

Page 22

1 *Student's own answers*

2 *Student's own answers*

3 **1** The self-help generation
2 Successful people set goals
3 Failure and perseverance
4 Stay focused

4 **1** They usually focus on money.
2 People who write down their goals and a plan of how to achieve them earn more money.
3 They get distracted or lose heart.
4 Perseverance and passion for long-term goals.
5 Develop good habits, remind yourself of your goals regularly and stay focused.

5

Verb	Noun	Adjective(s)
achieve	achievement	achievable
distract	distraction	distracted
fail	failure	failed, failing
focus	focus	focused
	intelligence	intelligent
motivate	motivation	motivated
	passion	passionate
persevere	perseverance	persevering
succeed	success	successful

Page 23

6 *Student's own answers*

7 *Student's own answers*

8 *Student's own answers*

Page 24

1 **1** focused; goals
2 achieve
3 plan
4 effective
5 Failure, improvement

2 **Email 1:** to ask all students to email Mr Harrison with their goals for the year and a plan to achieve them.
Email 2: a student outlining her goals for the year and how she plans to achieve them.

3 **Paragraph 1:** Set her goals
Paragraph 2: Outline her strategies
Paragraph 3: Close the email and say goodbye

4 **1** Regards,
2 Dear Mr Harrison,
3 as you requested.
4 I look forward to hearing your feedback.

5 *Student's own answers*

6 *Student's own answers*

7 *Student's own answers*

Page 25

1 **1** fallen at the first hurdle.
2 passed with flying colours.
3 it in the bag.
4 gone to the dogs.

2 **1** b **2** a **3** c **4** b

3 **1** d **2** c **3** a **4** b

4 *Student's own answers*

Unit 3

Page 28

1 *Student's own answers*

2 **1** language
2 novels
3 traditional
4 fictional
5 facts
6 creation
7 myth
8 legend
9 themes
10 evil

3 **a** plot **b** character **c** setting

4 **Legend:** William Tell
See table below

Page 29

5 **1** was reading
2 forgot
3 happened
4 were fighting
5 took
6 began
7 went
8 won
9 lasted
10 killed
11 defeated
12 were talking
13 rang
14 were sailing
15 were hiding

6 b, c, a

Setting	Characters	Plot
Small town in Switzerland	William Tell Gessler (the tyrannical ruler of the town) William Tell's son	A tyrannical ruler called Gessler makes everyone in the town bow down to him. Tell and his son refuse. Gessler tells them he will kill them both unless Tell can shoot an apple off his son's head with his bow and arrow. Tell does this and saves their lives. Then he kills Gessler and sets the town people free.

7 The Trojan War
See table 1 below

8 *Student's own answers*

Page 30

1 **carve:** to make something out of wood by cutting it.
clay: a material that comes from the earth.
dissolve: mix with a liquid and disappear.
good-hearted: kind and generous.
mindless: without intelligence.
mould: change the shape of something.
nutritious: healthy.
souls: where our feelings or emotions come from.

2 *Student's own answers*

3 **1** decided
2 have made
3 are dissolving
4 was walking
5 carve
6 are
7 were

4 *Student's own answers*

Page 31

5 **1** Mother Earth
2 Every day, a different brother travels through the sky in a chariot to bring light to the humans on Earth.
3 Because he misses his brothers.

6 **1** 'One of us travels through the sky.'
2 'Please leave!'
3 'They aren't listening to me.'
4 'I miss my brothers.'

7 **1** they needed to
2 what they did
3 they played
4 were burning

Page 32

1 *Student's own answers*

2 *Student's own answers*

3 **1** battle
2 goddess
3 look for
4 nervous
5 releasing
6 pain

4 *See table 2 below*

5 *Student's own answers*

6 **1** Thursday
2 Wednesday
3 Friday
4 Sunday
5 Tuesday
6 Saturday
7 Monday

1

Introduction	Conflict	Climax	Resolution
A woman called Helen was the wife of the King of Sparta. The gods made Helen fall in love with Paris, the Prince of Troy. Paris took her to live with him in Troy.	The King of Sparta went to Troy to rescue her. Paris killed the Greek warrior Achilles by shooting him in his only weak spot: his heel.	Greek soldiers entered Troy hidden inside a wooden horse they had pretended to give the people of Sparta as a peace offering.	The Greeks defeated the Trojans.

2

Myth	Thor and the stolen hammer	Pandora's box
Setting	The Norse world	Ancient Greece
Introduction	Gods were created when the land of fire and land of ice collided.	Zeus tells two Titans to create humans and animals on earth.
Main characters	Odin, Frigg, Thor, Freyja, Loki, Thrym	Zeus, Prometheus, Epimetheus, Pandora
Conflict	Thrym the king of the giants steals Thor's powerful hammer. Thor sends his friend Loki to look for it. Thrym says he will only return the hammer if Freyja, the beautiful goddess of love, marries him.	Prometheus steals fire from Zeus to give humans. Zeus is angry and punishes them. He chains Prometheus to a mountain and punishes Epimetheus by creating a beautiful curious woman called Pandora. Epimetheus falls in love with her and they get married. Zeus gives them a box as a wedding present and tells them not to open it.
Climax	Thor dresses up as Freyja and Loki suggests that Thrym should bring the hammer to the ceremony. Thor removes his veil.	Pandora opens the box.
Resolution	Thor takes back his hammer.	Evil, pain and disease escape from the box. The only thing that doesn't escape is hope.

Page 33

7 *Student's own answers*

Page 34

1 **1** lived; had drunk
2 sank; hadn't respected
3 have been; were wasting
4 was sitting; realised; had burnt

2 *Student's own answers*

3 *Student's own answers*

4 **1** Sherwood Forest (England)
2 Robin Hood and the Merry Men
3 King John and the sheriff
4 A group of people can unite to fight against a tyrant and defeat them

5 **1** Once upon a time
2 To introduce the story, present the conflict, the climax and resolution
3 It increases the suspense because we don't know who the two men are
4 It makes the action more immediate and dramatic

6 *Student's own answers*

7 *Student's own answers*

8 *Student's own answers*

Page 35

1 **1** A legendary king of England who may not have existed.
2 It was a magical sword stuck in a stone that only the 'true King of England' could pull out.
3 Merlin was a wizard who helped King Arthur throughout his life and Guinevere was King Arthur's wife.
4 It showed that there was equality between all of King Arthur's knights.

2 *See table below*

3 **1** c
2 d
3 a
4 b

4 **1** the Midas touch
2 a round-table discussion
3 Achilles heel
4 Pandora's box

5 *Student's own answers*

Unit 4

Page 36

1 **1** astronomy
2 the Universe
3 galaxy
4 stars
5 Sun
6 Solar System
7 Moon
8 planets
9 asteroid belt
10 comets

2 **1** The Moon
2 Stars
3 a galaxy
4 a planet
5 a comet
6 the asteroid belt

3 *Student's own answers*

Page 37

4 **1** A meteorite hit the Earth.
2 The Earth began to solidify.
3 Algae formed in the oceans.
4 Primitive forms of life began to develop.
5 Dinosaurs appeared.

5 *Student's own answers*

Page 38

1 **a** Meteorite
b Asteroid
c Meteoroid
d Meteor

2 **1** True
2 False. If a meteoroid enters the Earth's atmosphere it is called a meteor.
3 True
4 False. 90% are made of rock, but some are made of metal.

	Setting	Plot
Pandora	Mount Olympus and Greece	Zeus gave her a box and told her not to open it. She did, and all the evil in the world flew out, leaving only hope inside the box.
Midas	A place that is now modern- day Turkey	King Midas was rewarded by the god Dionysus with the ability to turn things into gold by touching them. One day he forgot and touched his daughter and her into gold too.
Achilles	(Ancient) Greece	His mother dipped his body into a magical river, but his heel didn't touch the water… The god Apollo knew about this weakness and used it to defeat him in battle.

3 *Student's own answers*

4 *Student's own answers*

5 *See table below*

6 *Student's own answers*

Page 39

7 **1** If you weigh 60 kg on Earth, you weigh 10 kg on the Moon.
2 If you use a telescope, you can see planets and stars.
3 You have to eat special food if you live in space.
4 If you look at the Moon, you can see craters.
6 When astronauts live on a space station, they do research.

8 **1** will be; finds
2 send; will have
3 will damage; look
4 won't; don't
5 don't; won't

9 **1** would think; came
2 had; would live
3 would weigh; lived
4 were; would burn.
5 would be; went

10 *Student's own answers*

Page 40

1 *Student's own answers*

2 To protect national security; To co-operate in international projects; To conduct experiments that have led to many scientific breakthroughs such as water-processing technology, remote-guidance techniques for medical procedures in remote areas and the monitoring of natural disasters; To investigate the possibility of colonising other planets; To gain a sense of perspective about our responsibilities to each other and to our planet.

3 **1** b **2** a **3** a **4** c **5** b

4 **1** the Cold War
2 a research laboratory
3 scientific breakthroughs
4 water purification
5 natural disasters

5 *Student's own answers*

6 **Arrogance:** arrogant; opposite, negative
Assertiveness: assertive; opposite; positive
Confidence: confident; opposite; positive
Modesty: modest, positive; neutral
Shyness: shy; synonym, negative or neutral

7 **1** shyness **2** assertiveness **3** arrogance

8 *Student's own answers*

Page 42

1 **1** space exploration
2 technological advances
3 medical technology
4 effective solution
5 significant benefits

2 **1** Do the benefits of space exploration justify the costs?
2 No

3 **Paragraph 1:** *introduce the topic and question*
Paragraph 2: arguments for
Paragraph 3: arguments against
Paragraph 4: conclusion

4 **1** also, in addition
2 However
3 apart from
4 In conclusion
5 in my opinion

5 *Student's own answers*

6 *Student's own answers*

7 *Student's own answers*

Page 43

1 **Name:** Martha Bennet
Nationality: British
Number of trainees on her programme: 19

Name: Vladimir Popov
Nationality: Russian
Greatest ambition: To walk on Mars

Name: David Feld
Nationality: Israeli
Where he works now: the (Kennedy) Space Center in Florida

Planet name	Roman mythology	Scientific facts
Venus	Goddess of love and beauty	It's the brightest. It has almost the same gravity as Earth
Mercury	Messenger of the gods	It's the fastest. It's the smallest
Mars	God of war	It's red. It has thousands of craters

2 **1** d; iii
2 c; i
3 a; Iv
4 b; II

3 *Student's own answers*

Unit 5

Page 46

1 *Student's own answers*

2 **Picture 1:** b, d, e
Picture 2: a, c, f

3 **1** in the South of England
2 large stones standing upright
3 weigh as much as 26 tonnes each
4 in Egypt
5 must have been created as tombs
6 slaves may have made them

4

	Stonehenge	Egyptian pyramids
Noun	evidence	theories belief
Verb	uncover	believe
Adjective	enigmatic unusual	misunderstood mysterious

Page 47

5 **1** mysterious
2 evidence
3 believe
4 enigmatic
5 theories

6 *Student's own answers*

7 **1** may/might/could have existed
2 must have lived
3 might/may/could have been
4 must have believed
5 couldn't have been

8 *Student's own answers*

9 *Student's own answers*

Page 48

1 *Suggested answers:*
debris: rubbish
controversy: disagreement
fake: false, imitation
truth: reality, fact
hoax: practical joke, trick

2 *Student's own answers.*

3 **1** They say
2 I don't believe that
3 Personally, I think
4 I mean
5 I agree
6 I don't think so

Page 49

4 **1** Eric went to a friend's house, but he wasn't there. He went to look for him and saw him with two tall creatures, walking towards a bright light. Eric followed them and they both woke up in their homes three days later.
2 He spends hours on the internet trying to find out what happened to them.
3 Neeti was walking her dog when she heard a humming sound. She felt herself being lifted into the air and heard a voice asking her if she wanted to travel in a spaceship. Then there was a loud bang and she woke up on the ground.
4 She walks her dog every day hoping to see them again and can't stop thinking what it would have been like if she'd gone with them.

5 **1** b
2 c
3 d
4 a

6 **1** had built; would have left
2 wouldn't have gone; had visited
3 wouldn't have been; hadn't found
4 had made; wouldn't have drawn

7 *Student's own answers*

Page 50

1 The photos on the right show crop circles. These are patterns of flattened crops in fields, usually cereals like wheat. The photo at the bottom of the Page shows wheat.

2 *Student's own answers*

3 They are created by some sort of higher intelligence
They might be messages from either aliens or time travellers.
They are an elaborate hoax, started by two Englishmen and then copied by others.
They are man-made, some for art and business.

4 **1** Doug Bower and Dave Chorley
2 William Levengood
3 William Levengood
4 Sampath Iyengar
5 Horace Drew

5 **1** fact
2 opinion
3 fact
4 fact
5 opinion
6 opinion

6 some people say; some people argue; they believe that; they might be; some still claim

7 *Student's own answers*

Page 51
8 *Student's own answers*

Page 52
1 **1** theories
2 fake
3 claims/claimed
4 proved
5 evidence

2 *Suggested answers:*
1 the Pyramids, the Nazca lines
2 Roswell
3 Crop circles
4 Atlantis
5 Stonehenge

3 **Positive:** Fans of mysteries, conspiracy theories and the paranormal will love it; People who are just curious will also enjoy it; It's affordable; The exhibits are varied and well presented; It lets you look at the evidence and decide for yourself.
Negative: It might not be for everyone; It's not easy to find; It's quite small.

4 **1** first paragraph
2 third paragraph
3 second paragraph
4 fourth paragraph

5 *Student's own answers*

6 *Student's own answers*

7 *Student's own answers*

Page 53
1 **1** might have come
2 must have been
3 couldn't have existed
4 may have lived

2 **Name:** Jamie
Believes in dragons? No
Main idea: Dragons were large lizards
Proof: They didn't appear in primitive art and no dragon bones have been found

Name: Tom
Believes in dragons? Yes
Main idea: They existed, but were all killed
Proof: There are many stories about dragons

Name: Anna
Believes in dragons? No
Main idea: Probably imagined from dinosaur fossils
Proof: No fossils or bones have been found

Name: Mark
Believes in dragons? Yes
Main idea: They existed but became extinct, like dinosaurs
Proof: They appear in legends and stories from all around the world

3 **1** had lived on Earth; would have found bones by now; Anna
2 hadn't been, wouldn't have survived; Tom
3 had existed, would have appeared; Jamie
4 wouldn't have been; hadn't existed; Mark

4 **1** d **2** b **3** a **4** c

5 *Student's own answers*

Unit 6
Page 54
1 **1** 25%
2 Student's own answers
3 35%

2 **1 a** **2 b** **3 c**

3 **1** out; d **2** up; b **3** into; c **4** out; a

Page 55
4 **1** True **2** False **3** True **4** False

5 **1** The receptionist at the gym says he was there all the time.
2 Alex
3 The waitress at the café confirmed he was there.
4 Sam
5 He says he was at home, watching the TV programme about UFOs.

6 **1** asked; to help
2 noticed; look
3 saw; running

7 *Student's own answers*

Page 56
1 **1** sleuth
2 clues
3 hunch
4 red herring
5 witness
6 alibi

2 **1** sleuth
2 red herring
3 alibi
4 witness
5 clues
6 hunch

3 *Student's own answers*

4 **1** Student's own answers
2 He stole the money to buy snacks for a group of his classmates because he wanted them to like him.
3 30 euros
4 Student's own answers

Page 57

5 **1** weren't you
2 have you
3 was it
4 weren't you
5 hadn't you
6 didn't you
7 can you
8 aren't we

6 *Suggested answers:*
1 Veronica Moore
2 The bag of money that the criminal was going to steal
3 The witness had swapped the suspect's bag
4 She stole the money because she hated the job and she often borrowed money from the manager of the tennis club.

7 **1** up
2 up
3 down
4 down

8 **1** didn't
2 couldn't
3 wasn't
4 have
5 weren't

Page 58

1 *Suggested answers:*
1 He had always been interested in disappearances in the Bermuda Triangle.
2 His first hunch is that there is something strange about the story and that the anthropologist on the plane is a possible suspect. His suspicion that there is something strange about the story is confirmed. His suspicion that the anthropologist is the criminal is not confirmed.
3 To find out more about his suspect – the anthropologist.
4 He finds out that the anthropologist was called Ignatius Wittington and that the woman who had acquired the treasures was called Philomena Stock. He also finds out that the journalist had spoken to both of them before the flight and that Wittington knew all about the collection.
5 The journalist told the detective he knew about the antiques before the flight, then tried to convince him to stick to the Bermuda Triangle theory. The detective also noticed a golden statue on the journalist's bookshelf.
6 *Student's own answers*

2 **1** wealthy
2 sticks to
3 cover-up
4 shame
5 pile

3 **1** hunch
2 antique
3 anthropologist
4 hijack
5 cave
6 statue

4 *Student's own answers*

5 *Student's own answers*

6 **1** Notice
2 Analyse
3 Check
4 Think
5 Discuss

Page 60

1 **1** to help
2 to believe
3 going off
4 leaving
5 be

2 **1** A portrait has been stolen.
2 The owner of an advertising company, his secretary and a designer.
3 The designer committed the crime. His face goes pale when he hears that the painting was a fake and he looks at his umbrella, where he has hidden the painting.

3 **1** The writer says it is a sunny day, which means the designer doesn't need an umbrella.
2 The company is losing money.
3 Student's own answers

4 **1** They're inside inverted commas.
2 Before.
3 The subject comes before the verb if it's a pronoun and afterwards if not.

5 *Student's own answers*

6 *Student's own answers*

7 *Student's own answers*

Page 61

1 **1** She was one of the most important authors in the history of detective fiction.
2 They were two detectives that featured in her novels.
3 Student's own answers

2 **1** 1927
2 English
3 12 novels (and 20 short stories)
4 1920
5 Belgian
6 30 novels (and nearly 60 short stories)

3 **1** d **2** c **3** a **4** b

4 **1** jump to conclusions
2 put two and two together
3 the penny dropped
4 hit the nail on the head

Unit 7

Page 64

1 *Suggested answers:*
apps: computer programmes we use on a mobile phone
communication: exchanging information
computer literate: the ability to use computers with skill and knowledge
engineer: someone who designs or develops computer systems
feature: characteristic
real-time: instantaneous
virtual reality: a simulated environment produced by a computer

2 **1** e **2** b **3** d **4** f **5** a **6** c

3 **1** communication
2 computer literate
3 engineer
4 apps
5 real-time
6 virtual reality
7 feature

Page 65

4 **1** is stored
2 was sent
3 was being researched
4 had been opened
5 is remembered
6 have been addressed

5 **1** Millions of emails are sent every second.
2 Over 4.6 billion email accounts have been opened worldwide since the 1970s.
3 Hotmail was bought by Microsoft in 1997.
4 Some companies are introducing 'email-free Fridays' because too much time is being wasted on checking emails.
5 The attachment function was not invented until 1992.

6 **1** are
2 were
3 have been
4 are
5 are

7 *Student's own answers*

Page 66

1 **1** platforms
2 files
3 dragging
4 desktop
5 hardware
6 connection
7 install
8 click

2 *Student's own answers*

3 *Student's own answers*

4 *Student's own answers*

5 **1** True
2 False
3 True
4 True
5 False

6 *Student's own answers*

Page 67

7 **1** might
2 must
3 should
4 can
5 should
6 may

8 **1** can / may be discussed
2 could / can be introduced
3 could / might / can be improved
4 should be taken
5 must / should be taught
6 must / should be supervised
7 should be established
8 could / can be decided

9 *Student's own answers*

10 train, cake, eight, day, break

11 *Student's own answers*

Page 68

1 *Student's own answers*

2 **1** Cheating and assessment go hand in hand
2 E-cheating
3 Why students cheat
4 Using technology to catch cheaters
5 Cheating doesn't help you learn
6 How to combat cheating

3 **1** a **2** b **3** c **4** b

4 **1** False **2** False **3** True

Page 69

5 *Suggested answers:*
1 assessment: evaluation
2 to cheat: to behave dishonestly for some gain
3 to e-cheat: to use technology to cheat
4 an assignment: a task
5 plagiarism: to use someone else's work or words and pretend it's your own
6 expelled: ordered to leave (the room, the school)

6 *Student's own answers*

7 *Student's own answers*

Page 70

1 **1** were sold; mobile phones
2 was invented; are connected; the internet
3 are located; be hacked; webcams
4 have been created; were downloaded; phone apps
5 was launched; be typed; tablet

2 2, 3, 1

3 **1** second paragraph
2 third paragraph
3 first paragraph

4 **1** Instant messaging, IM for short
2 your device (the 'client') and IM's central computer (the 'server')
3 'encrypted', which means it is converted into code to keep it private

5 *Student's own answers*

6 *Student's own answers*

7 *Student's own answers*

Page 71

1 **1** foot **2** wavelength **3** point **4** loop

2 **1** The Geography teacher
2 She told the new girl from school that she didn't like Geography teacher and then she found out the teacher was the new girl's dad.
3 Student's own answers

3 **1** c **2** d **3** b **4** a

4 *Student's own answers*

Unit 8

Page 72

1 **1** repetitive **2** robot **3** online **4** keep in touch **5** satellites **6** translation **7** complex **8** tabs **9** rude

2 *Student's own answers*

3 *Student's own answers*

Page 73

4 **1** b; Tina **2** c; Jackson **3** a; Aditi

5 **1** who is becoming **2** which causes **3** who believe **4** which is leading to

6 **a** Style **b** Skills **c** News **d** Advice

7 *Student's own answers*

8 *Student's own answers*

Page 74

1 **1** influence **2** posters **3** adverts **4** attention-grabbing **5** emotions **6** promote **7** objectively

2 **1** raise awareness **2** hack **3** promote **4** influence **5** get involved

3 **a** Click on a link.
b Subscribe to a blog.
c Attend an event.

4 *Student's own answers*

Page 75

5 **1** b; Flyers are paper advertisements that which are handed out to people in the street.
2 a; Posters are large pieces of paper that/which are displayed on walls.
3 e; Bumper stickers are labels that/which are stuck on to the back of your car.
4 c; Placards are pieces of cardboard that/which are held up on sticks by people at protests.
5 d; Pin badges are pieces of metal that/which are attached to your clothes.

6 *Student's own answers*

7 **1** e **2** a **3** b **4** c **5** d

Pages 76

1 **1** The printing press; 1440s; Student's own answers
2 The world wide web; 1980s; Student's own answers
3 The telephone; 1870s; Student's own answers
4 The smartphone; 1990s; Student's own answers

2 *Suggested answers:*
People now chat to their friends more by messaging than talking in person or using a landline phone.
People can look things up on the internet instead of going to the library.
Information is more instantly available and we have become more efficient at finding things out.
Young people have become skilled multitaskers.
We can access cultural content from all over the world.
Young people are becoming more global and tolerant.
Many young people have become digital addicts.
Generation Z are at greater risk of loneliness than previous generations.

3 1 True.
2 False. They used different technologies in the past.
3 True.
4 False. Surveys say that 40% of Generation Z describe themselves as digital addicts.
5 True.

4 *Student's own answers*

5 *Student's own answers*

Page 78

1 1 d 2 c 3 e 4 a 5 b

2 1 4a 2 3e 3 1d 4 2c 5 5b

3 *Student's own answers*

4 1 inform and inspire
2 look the other person in the eye and give them your full attention
3 listen
5 if you don't understand something

5 *Student's own answers*

6 *Student's own answers*

7 *Student's own answers*

Page 79

1 1 a 2 b 3 b 4 c

2 1 a vacuum cleaner
2 Selena - brainstorming, Mark – knowledge about robotics, Rachel – organisational skills
3 *Student's own answers*

3 1 c; iii 2 d; ii 3 a; iv 4 b; i

Unit 9

Page 82

1 1 1903
2 meant the conquest of the air
3 1955
4 brought universal benefits, including GPS, accurate weather predictions and satellite internet access
5 the 1970s
6 word processing, databases, spreadsheets and games
7 the 1960s
8 gave us easy and widespread access to information and contact with other users

2 1 turning point
2 invention
3 imagine
4 milestone
5 boom

3 1 work
2 journey
3 personal
4 turning
5 bird
6 entrepreneur
7 first
8 earth

4 *Student's own answers*

Page 83

5 1 so
2 such
3 so
4 such
5 so
6 so
7 such

6 1 so long
2 such a frightening
3 such an exciting
4 so quickly
5 such an important
6 so expensive

Page 84

1 1 c 2 d 3 a 4 b

2 1 so many
2 so much
3 so few
4 so little
5 so much
6 so many

3 1 There was so little food in Europe during the war that many countries introduced food rationing.
2 There were so many cities that weren't safe that many children were sent to the countryside
3 The war lasted so many years that people moved to different countries and never went home.
4 The two superpowers had so many economic and political differences that they started the Cold War.

Page 85

4 1 So am I
2 So did I
3 Neither did I
4 Neither can I
5 So was I
6 So do I

5 1 spiritual
2 religious
3 peaceful
4 philosopher
5 oppression
6 stereotypes

6 *Student's own answers*

Page 86

1 *Student's own answers*

2 Statement 1

3 *Suggested answers:*
1 In the 20th century it is estimated that 40 million people died because of air pollution.
2 At the end of the last century there were roughly 800 million cars in the world.
3 In the last century the population rose by 400%
4 By the end of the last century, the Atlantic coastal forest of Brazil had been reduced to 8% of its original size.

4 **1** 2 **2** 4 **3** 3 **4** 1

5 *Suggested answers:*
1 The number of cars on the road has led to massive air pollution.
2 Heavy industry has added significantly to pollution and global warming.
3 The rise in the world's population means our exploitation of natural resources has increased.
5 Animal species have become endangered.
6 The Earth has been over-mined.
7 Clearing large areas for farming and timber has led to deforestation in Brazil.
8 Clean drinking water is becoming scarce because of overuse, pollution and climate change.

6 **1** In addition, also, furthermore
2 As a result of, because of
3 Although, however
4 For instance
5 The fact is that

Page 87

7 **1** 5
2 6, 7, 8
3 9, 10
4 11

8 *Suggested answers:*
1 overpopulation; threat (we use more resources and pollute the environment).
2 electric cars; solution (solves the fossil fuel problem, although the electricity has to come from renewable sources).
3 deforestation; threat (it leads to the extinction of species and more polluted air).
4 recycling; solution (reuses waste, although we should also try to produce less non-organic rubbish

9 *Suggested answers:*
1 We will either learn to take care of the environment or we'll have no future.
2 We need to know our history, origin and culture in order to survive and evolve.
3 Travel makes us smarter, wiser and happier.
4 We should consider the impact our actions have all over the world and start by taking small steps to improve the world in our local communities.

Page 88

1 **1** c **2** d **3** a **4** b

2 **1** People who don't recycle and the 80% of Americans who drive to work alone.
2 It can help by replacing plastic with other materials that are less damaging to the environment.
3 Electric cars are becoming more popular.
4 Solar and wind.

3 **1** The fact is that
2 Surely
3 Moreover
4 To sum up

4 *Student's own answers*

5 *Student's own answers*

6 *Student's own answers*

Page 89

1 **1** a **2** c **3** b **4** b

2 **1** c **2** a **3** d **4** b

3 **1** start from scratch
2 shake things up
3 made matters worse
4 changed for the better

4 *Student's own answers*

Unit reviews

Unit 1

1 **1** b
2 a
3 e

2 *Student's own answers*

3 *Student's own answers*

Unit 2

Page 90

1 **1** b **2** a **3** b **4** a

2 **1** c
2 b
3 c
4 a
5 c
6 b

3 *Student's own answers*

Unit 3

Page 92

1 **1** ghost stories
2 modern science,
3 a flood of sand
4 5th
5 unicorns
6 1886

2 **1** b **2** d **3** c **4** a **5** e

3 *Student's own answers*

Unit 4

Page 93

1 **1** a **2** b **3** b **4** a

2 **1** if
2 System
3 It
4 was
5 in
6 had
7 ago
8 our

3 *Student's own answers*

Unit 5
Page 94
1 **1** a **2** b **3** c **4** b

2 *Student's own answers*

3 *Student's own answers*

Unit 6
Page 95
1 **1** a **2** a **3** c **4** c

2 **1** c **2** b **3** b

3 *Student's own answers*

Unit 7
Page 96
1 **1** advertised
2 feeling
3 automatically
4 really
5 conversation
6 activate
7 being
8 frightened
9 agencies

2 *Student's own answers*

3 *Student's own answers*

Unit 8
Page 97
1 **1** digital generation
2 deleted
3 an addiction
4 her friends
5 down
6 mental health

2 **1** have a brother who
2 if you don't
3 You should look
4 are being added to the
5 people had to

3 *Student's own answers*

Unit 9
Page 98
1 **a** Speaker 4
b Speaker 5
c Speaker 1
d Speaker 3
e Speaker 2

2 **1** a **2** d **3** a **4** d **5** b **6** c

Track 1

Unit 1, page 4, exercise 3

Presenter: Hello and welcome to Use Your Head. I'm your host, Nick, and today we're talking about jobs and how to find the right one for you! Nowadays, deciding on a career is more difficult than ever before, so we're talking to psychologists Lara Fox, Simon Davis and Maggie West to find ways to help you decide. Hello, everyone.

Lara, Simon and Maggie: Hi / Hello / Good Morning

Presenter: Lara, what's your top tip for deciding on a future job?

Lara: Well, I always say the most important thing is to know yourself. Write a list of the things that you do and don't like. For example, what subjects do you like best at school? What subjects do you do well in? What are your soft skills?

Presenter: Sorry, soft skills?

Lara: Soft skills are qualities and abilities that you don't learn through education or formal training. They're linked to personality or attitude. For example, if you are empathetic, you may be suited for a career in psychology.

Presenter: And you, Simon? What's your top tip?

Simon: I would suggest you do lots of online research into the professions you are interested in. There are some great career advice resources on the internet with information on salary, levels of job satisfaction and work-life balance. For example, if you are creative, you could decide to be a photographer. In that case, you could check out work done by professional photographers on their online portfolios.

P: Fantastic. OK, Maggie, what's your top tip?

M: I suggest doing some work experience if you can. Seeing what people really do all day can help you to decide if a job is right for you. When you do work experience, you should observe how the professionals work and take lots of notes. My daughter has been working at a fashion magazine on Saturdays. She thought she wanted to be an accountant, but now she says she wants to be a fashion designer!

P: Well, thanks for the great advice, everyone! Unfortunately, that's all we have time for today…

Track 2

Unit 1, page 4, exercise 4

See previous track

Track 3

Unit 1, page 6, exercise 4

Narrator: Good afternoon. Earlier today I talked to three people about their jobs and their achievements, and I asked them each four questions:

1 What job do you do?

2 How long have you done it?

3 What was it like when you started?

4 What have you achieved that you're proud of?

Track 4

Unit 1, page 6, exercise 4

Chris: I'm Chris, I'm a nurse. I've worked as a nurse for eight years and I love it. It was difficult at first because I had to stay calm and focus on helping the patients at the same time as I was learning. I think I've always been able to keep calm in an emergency, but now I've learnt how to solve problems more efficiently and without getting stressed.

Norah: I'm Norah, I'm a computer programmer. I've had this job for 5 years, although I started to learn basic programming before that. I think I found it quite easy at first because my first job was very basic, but then it quickly became more interesting and challenging. Well, recently I became team leader for a project, so I have five people working for me.

Dan: I'm Dan. I'm an architect. I've only just started this company, but I've worked as an architect for ten years. When I started working as an architect, I was quite nervous. Suddenly, after studying for so long at university, I was responsible for making real buildings! Well, I've always wanted to have my own company, and after nine years of working towards it, I finally did it.

Track 5

Unit 1, page 8, exercise 2

Exploring Einstein's Brain

When we talk about brain power, the first name that comes to most people's minds is Albert Einstein. But what was his brain like? Could he do anything he wanted?

Einstein started school when he was five and he was one of the best students in his primary school. He showed a particular talent for mathematics and by thirteen he could solve complex mathematical problems. Einstein's intelligence was very advanced for his age. At seventeen, he started a four-year mathematics and physics course at Zürich Polytechnic and he got his doctoral degree a few years later. Throughout his career he made many important discoveries, and in 1921 he won the Nobel Prize in Physics.

Not only is Einstein considered the most influential physicist of the twentieth century, but he also demonstrated musical intelligence. As a teenager, he developed a love of the violin, and music was a very important part of his life.

Einstein was creative, meticulous and curious, and he showed great intelligence in many areas. However, it is also true that he had some difficulties. He started speaking later than other children and did not form complete sentences easily until he was nine years old. Later, he learnt at least five languages, but he admitted he was never very good at speaking them. Einstein also disliked social situations and found it difficult to communicate well with others.

When Einstein died on April 18, 1955, Dr Thomas Harvey decided to organise studies of his brain to find out more about intelligence. In one study, Dr Marian Diamond suggested Einstein's brain had more glial cells than normal. Glial cells bring nutrients to our neurons and help our brains to make faster connections. She thought that could be the reason for Einstein's intelligence: he could process information faster than normal.

However, in another study in 1999, researchers discovered something else unusual. he areas of the brain related to logical-mathematical and visual-spatial intelligence were 15% bigger in Einstein's brain than in most other people. It seems that more neurons in this region made connections among each other and they worked together effectively. The rest of Einstein's brain was a normal size and weight. The scientists who conducted this study say this may explain why Einstein was so successful in solving mathematical and scientific problems.

Einstein himself believed that his success was due to the support of his parents, thinking creatively and working hard. What do you think?

Track 6

Unit 2, page 12, exercise 2

Speaker 1 - Tom

People often look at famous actors and think, 'Wow, that looks easy.' And maybe for some big stars it is. If you are charismatic or have a certain look, filmmakers might want you just to be you. Or if you're already a celebrity, a filmmaker might even create a film specifically with you in mind. But most of us have to take lots of different roles and do whatever work we can get until people start to know our names. I'd been in thirty TV shows before I got my first big part in a feature film.

Speaker 2 - Tina

There's a lot of competition in the music industry. Many people have their favourite singers or groups and buy every record they release, and nothing else. I won a TV talent show, so I became famous quite quickly. That was good in one way, but then I wanted to write my own songs and I found it hard, I'd never written songs before. I started by copying the styles of the songs I'd sung in the talent show, but people didn't really want to hear my songs – they wanted the ones I'd become famous for. Now I'm starting to find my own musical personality and I've got my first album coming out next week. I hope people like it!

Speaker 3 - Beth

I knew I wanted to work in art from a very young age. I'd always loved drawing and at school it was the only thing that I was really good at. So, when I was 16, I got a job as an assistant to a famous painter. I learnt a lot and I knew that I wanted to work in something creative. I realised that painting wasn't for me, but I started writing and drawing my own comics, just as a hobby. I showed them to some friends and they suggested that I get them published - and I did! They're starting to become so popular that a TV producer has even asked me if I'd like to make them into a TV show.

Track 7

Unit 2, page 12, exercise 3

See previous track

Track 8

Unit 2, page 14, exercise 1

Presenter: Good evening and welcome to Think Tank, the gameshow where you present your products and inventions and we decide if they are good enough to launch. The lucky winner will get 50,000 pounds, as well as help from our experts to develop and produce their product. All ideas should be original, no copycat ideas and nothing already invented! First up we have Lorenzo. Lorenzo, tell us about your product.

Lorenzo: Well, I'm a painter, you see. I decorate apartments and houses. I love my job, but there is so much waste. For example, just last week I decorated a huge house and when I finished there were so many things that I just had to throw away. That's when I had my brilliant idea!

Presenter: And that was…?

Lorenzo: Reusable wallpaper!

Presenter: Reusable wallpaper? I'm not sure I understand.

Lorenzo: Well, wallpaper is what I use to decorate walls; it comes in all types of colours and designs…

Presenter: Lorenzo, I know what wallpaper is! But I'm not sure how you can reuse it. Are you talking about recycling the paper?

Lorenzo: No! My wallpaper is… edible! You can eat it! You use it to decorate your house and when you don't want it anymore, you can eat it! I plan to create lots of different flavours, chocolate, strawberry…

Presenter: Err, I'm still not sure. Thanks, Lorenzo. Next, we have Will. Will, tell us about your idea.

Will: Well, my idea came to me while I was mopping the kitchen floor. I'd dropped a bottle of fizzy drink and I had to clean it up.

Presenter: Ohhh, I hate mopping.

Will: Yes, so do I, and it was taking a while. Suddenly my neighbour put on some really loud music, and I started dancing. That's when my idea came to me.

Presenter: What was the idea?

Will: A musical mop! It has a small media player attached to the handle so you can dance through the house as you clean the floors!

Presenter: But why can't you just carry your phone with you and listen to music on that?

Will: I suppose you could. But this would be cooler. Don't you think?

Presenter: Not really. Sorry, Will. Next!

Track 9

Unit 2, page 14, exercise 2

See previous track

Track 10

Unit 2, page 16, exercise 2

Olympic Success

Can you guess which country holds the record for winning the most Olympic medals? Perhaps unsurprisingly, it's the United States of America, with over 1,000 gold medals in both Summer and Winter Games. They have also held the most Olympic Games competitions – eight. But the Olympics didn't start there. The first Olympic Games were held in Greece in around the 9th century BC, as part of a religious festival to celebrate the father of the Gods, Zeus. They were cancelled in the 4th century AD by the Roman emperor Theodosius I. But then in 1896, Pierre de Coubertin decided to organise the games again. He chose Athens for the re-opening of the Olympic Games because of its tradition and history.

Pierre de Coubertin's idea was for an event that would bring different countries together to celebrate the value of athletic competition. He saw the most important thing as not necessarily to win but to do your best. Just getting the chance to compete is a huge achievement. Dimitrios Loundras found this to be true when he won a bronze medal in 1896. He was only ten.

Successful sportsmen and sportswomen know that nobody has ever succeeded without some obstacles and failures along the way. In 2009, Usain Bolt became known as 'the fastest man alive' when he ran the men's 100-metre race in 9.58 seconds, a new Olympic record. This success did not come easily, however, as Bolt had had a lot of problems with his back early in his career, which made running and training difficult. But Bolt didn't lose heart and stayed focused on his goal. Achieving Olympic success is a challenge that requires lots of hard work and perseverance. The Olympics also teaches us that with passion and motivation we can achieve things people thought were impossible. One example of this is the story of the swimmer Michael Phelps. Another gold medal swimmer, Ian Thorpe, had said he was sure that Phelps would not reach the record of winning eight gold medals in the same competition. Phelps trained hard to prove Thorpe's prediction wrong. He finished his career with 23 gold medals and is today considered the best swimmer of all time. Another example is the gymnast Nadia Comaneci, who achieved the unthinkable – a perfect score of 10, in Montreal in 1976. She went on to win another eight perfect 10s and a total of five gold medals.

Track 11

Unit 3, page 22, exercise 3

Presenter: Today we are discussing myths and legends from around the world. On our panel of experts we have historian Jill Smith, author Ryan Trent and archaeologist Antonia Corelli.

Presenter: Let's start with you, Jill. Are all myths from around the world similar?

Jill: Well, things like characters and settings are different from country to country, but all cultures share the tradition of telling myths and legends, and the stories have a lot of things in common. Firstly, the characters are fictional. They often represent the values of a society, or perhaps things we're frightened of. And myths are set in ancient times and have a conflict and a resolution. Most of them have a hero, but not all.

Presenter: Interesting. Ryan, can you tell us a bit about what we can learn from myths?

Ryan: Sure. Myths generally teach us about the nature of the world and how we should behave.

Jill: Sorry, I have to interrupt here.

Presenter: Yes, Jill.

Jill: Well, there are lots of myths that show characters behaving quite badly. So they're not all about morality and how we should behave.

Ryan: I disagree. I think we can learn about how to behave from examples of bad behaviour, too.

Presenter: Interesting. OK, let's move on. Antonia can you tell us more about the differences between myths and legends from different cultures?

Antonia: Oh, that's a tough question. I suppose one of the main things would be the characters, as Jill mentioned. For example, Odin, the head of all the Norse gods, was the god of knowledge, battle and death.

Presenter: Oh yes, he had a hammer!

Antonia: No, that was his son, Thor. However, Greek mythology talks about Zeus as the head of their gods. But he was the god of the sky and thunder, and he was responsible for the weather.

Presenter: Fascinating. I suppose, as you say, even with different characters and settings, essentially myths help us to see how other people from a different cultures view things.

Antonia: Exactly!

Presenter: Great! OK, let's take some questions from the audience…

Track 12

Unit 3, page 22, exercise 4

See previous track

Track 13

Unit 3, page 25, exercise 4

Teacher: OK class. Today I'm going to tell you about a special competition the head teacher is organising.

Jamie: Oh no, I hope it's not another Maths competition. I don't like those.

Teacher: No, it's not, Jamie. This is something everybody will enjoy.

Bella: Oh, please let it be an art competition! I'm so good at drawing and painting.

Teacher: This isn't an art competition, but you may include pictures if you like. For this competition, you must create and write your own legend or myth.

Jamie: What did she say?

Bella: She said that we have to create our own legend or myth.

Jamie: Oh, I'm not sure about that either!

Teacher: Quiet please you two! Now, take notes of the details. The final day to enter the competition is Friday 30th April. You don't have very long to work on your idea, as that's three weeks from now. Your entry can be in the form of a comic strip or story and, as I said, you can include pictures, if you like. Entries should be at least 200 words long.

Jamie: What do we win, Miss?

Teacher: Good question Jamie. The prizes are very special. The winner will get £500.

Jamie and Bella: What? How much?!

Teacher: Sorry, I mean £50 and a copy of a novel by Stevie Jones.

Bella: He's my favourite author! I'm definitely going to enter!

Teacher: The student who wins second prize will not receive any money, but their story will be published in the local newspaper.

Jamie: Cool! I could be famous!

Teacher: OK, now remember that your myth or legend should contain certain things. It's important that each story contains a moral or purpose. You don't have to include a hero or a villain in your stories, but it might help to make it more interesting. There should also be a conflict and a resolution.

Jamie: Right, that's it. I'm definitely going to try.

Teacher: Don't forget class, that the final day…

Track 14

Unit 3, page 25, exercise 5

See previous track

Track 15

Unit 3, page 26, exercise 2

Myths from around the world

Each week we ask you to get in touch and tell us about your culture and traditions. This week, we're looking at myths, legends and fairy tales from around the world. Here are some of your top posts on our website.

This is a story about the creation of life. In the beginning, there was only darkness everywhere. Suddenly, a yellow circle appeared and in it there was an old man with a long beard. He was a god called The Creator. When the Creator opened his eyes, there was light. Then he put his hands together and a girl appeared. He called her the first goddess. As the days passed, he created more gods by rubbing his hands together. Then the Creator told the other gods: 'Let's make the Earth. Put your hands in mine.' When all the gods put their hands together, a ball fell from the Creator's fingers and the Earth was finally created.
Maya, USA

There are many myths about fairies in the UK. One of the common themes of these stories is the tricks fairies like to play on humans. In some of the tales these tricks are simple jokes, but in others they bring real harm to humans. This is the case of the changeling, where a fairy would go into the mortal world and take a human baby, leaving behind a different baby in its place. While it looked like a human baby, the changeling didn't cry or experience emotion or eat human food. The changeling was only content when there were terrible things like suffering or disease in the house. William Shakespeare even wrote about a changeling baby in one of his most well-known plays, A Midsummer Night's Dream.
Ray, England

Fionn mac Cumhaill was the leader a fearless group of mythical warriors in Ireland called the Fianna. When he was a young boy, he was sent to live with a very wise man named Finnegas. For years, Finnegas had tried to catch the Salmon of Knowledge. It was said that the person who ate this fish would become very wise and know more about the secrets of the natural world than any other person in Ireland. One day, Finnegas and Fionn caught the fish. Finnegas couldn't believe his luck and ordered Fionn to cook it for him immediately. But while he was cooking, Fionn burned his finger and he put it in his mouth to help with the pain. Immediately Finnegas knew that Fionn was now the wisest person in Ireland and he was very sad.
Breda, Ireland

Track 16

Unit 4, page 30, exercise 3

Presenter: Holidays - we look forward to them all year! But we often go to the same places again and again. A new survey has shown that the average person from the UK will visit seven other countries in their lifetime, with France being the most popular destination. However, is this all about to change? Advances in technology mean that there are greater opportunities to travel than ever before. One day we might even be able to go on holiday in space! On today's show we'll be talking about the topic of space tourism. I'm going out on the street to ask some people what they think about it.
Presenter: Excuse me! I'm from Good Morning! Radio. Can I ask you a few questions?
Erika: Sure!
Presenter: Thank you. What's your name?
Erika: I'm Erika.
Presenter: What do you think about space tourism, Erika?
Erika: Oh, that's something I'd love to try! I mean, imagine having the chance to explore Mars and hike up the volcano, Olympic Mons. Did you know that it's over 15 miles high? If I could, I'd go right now! Although…
Presenter: Yes?
Erika: I guess you'd have to do some special training before you go.
Presenter: Right…
Erika: That would probably be hard. I'd still love to go, though!
Presenter: Me too! Thanks for talking to me Erika. Excuse me, can I stop you for a minute? What's your name?
Ken: Ken.
Presenter: Hi Ken, I'm from Good Morning! Radio. Can I ask you, what do you think about space tourism?
Ken: I think it's a bad idea. I mean, I actually studied astronomy at university, so I'm really interested in space, but not space tourism.
Presenter: So why are you against the idea?
Ken: Firstly, there's the cost. The tickets would be half a million pounds. Normal people would never be able to afford it. Then, there's the fact that it would be really dangerous. And wherever there's tourism, there's an environmental impact.
Presenter: Well, that's definitely given me something to think about! Maybe I wouldn't want to go, after all. Thanks, Ken!

Track 17

Unit 4, page 30, exercise 4

See previous track

Track 18

Unit 4, page 32, exercise 1

Leo: Hey Cara, have you seen Nathan? The meeting is about to start.
Cara: Hi Leo. Umm, I think he's running late.
Leo: Right, well, we have to get started. I've called this meeting to talk about what we should do to celebrate Science Day. As you know, this year we're focusing on space exploration and I'd like to organise something interesting for our students.
Nathan: Oh, hello! Sorry I'm late.
Leo: Come in, Nathan. Don't worry, we've only just started.
Cara: Well, I think we should invite an expert to come and talk to the students about planets in the Solar System.
Nathan: Hmm… I'm not sure the students will want to listen to another expert giving
them information. It could be boring.
Cara: I don't agree, we could learn a lot!
Nathan: Yes, but what about grabbing the students' attention? The problems with
teenagers these days is that they get bored so quickly.
Cara: So, what's your great idea then?
Nathan: A visit to the planetarium! There's a new show and it sounds amazing.
Leo: Isn't that going to be a bit expensive, Nathan? How much is it?
Nathan: If we go as a group, it's only 15 pounds each.
Cara: And what does the trip include?
Nathan: There's a simulated journey through the Milky Way. You visit all the planets and look at them close up.

You see Saturn's rings and Jupiter's moons. By the way, did you know that Jupiter has 79 moons?! They also project images of asteroids and meteorites as they fly across the sky. You even watch a meteoroid entering the Earth's atmosphere.

Cara: It sounds good, but 15 pounds is quite expensive. I don't think many students will want to pay that much.

Leo: Yes, I like the sound of it, but it isn't cheap. I think we should ask the students and their parents.

Nathan: Sure, let's see.

Track 19

Unit 4, page 32, exercise 2

See previous track

Track 20

Unit 4, page 34, exercise 2

A day in the life of an astronaut

Have you ever wondered what life is like on the International Space Station? Or how it would feel to look down on our planet from space? As part of our career series A Day in the Life of… , we asked astronaut Bill Weider to document his day. Now we know what it's really like to work and live in the final frontier – space. Bill has a Masters degree in Science and Engineering. He worked as a pilot before joining the Johnson Space Center in Houston. He has currently been on the ISS for three months.

Morning routine

There are no beds on the station, so we have to tie ourselves to the wall at night, because there is no gravity. If we didn't do that, we would float around. When we wake up, we do exercise. It's necessary to hit the gym for at least two hours every day to prevent bone and muscle loss. Then, we 'shower'. It's really a sponge bath. Breakfast is pretty much the same as on Earth. I usually have eggs and toast. Cooking can be interesting, however. We usually just inject the food with hot water!

A day on the job

It's obviously not a typical day at the office! The commute is very different to down on Earth. We have to take a rocket to get to our 'office' and it takes about six hours, so that's why we stay here for at least a month. The station itself is very long and about the size of a five bedroomed house. It's a chaotic network of rooms so you have to know your way around. If we have to go outside, we have to wear a spacesuit. This takes about 45 minutes to put on, and weighs about 140 kilos. That's about the same size as an adult gorilla! One of the best things about my job is, undoubtedly, the scientific breakthroughs. Over the years, experiments on board have helped us find out more about climate change, disease and even medicine. Another great thing is the opportunities to learn and practise languages. It's essential to be able to communicate with our international colleagues. I'm fluent in Spanish and I'm currently learning Russian.

Days off

We work six days a week, 12 hours a day, so we don't get a lot of time off. When I have some time, I read or just look out of the windows. The views of our Solar System are out of this world as the station orbits the Earth! The record number of days that people have spent in space is 1,000! If I were here for that long, I don't know how I would feel. I think I'd miss my family and my dog too much.

Track 21

Unit 5, page 40, exercise 3

Receptionist: Hello, this is the Museum of Mystery. Could I have your name, please?

Danny: Yes, it's Danny Smith.

Receptionist: How can I help you, Danny?

Danny: I'd like some information about the Egyptian Enigmas exhibition, please.

Receptionist: OK, hold on… So, the exhibition includes evidence of how the Egyptians made mummies. Oh, and the most interesting room is about a mysterious animal called Black Foot!

Danny: Black Foot?!

Receptionist: Oh, sorry! I was getting confused with the Black Foot exhibition.

Danny: I see. Is there anything else?

Receptionist: Yes, there are some very unusual artefacts made by the Romans.

Danny: The Romans?

Receptionist: Oh, no sorry. That's the Remembering Rome exhibition.

Danny: Hmm. Well, I'd like to buy six tickets for Saturday. For the Egyptian Enigmas exhibition.

Receptionist: We don't have any tickets left for Saturday, I'm afraid.

Danny: Oh… err… well, what about Sunday then?

Receptionist: Let me see. Yes, that's fine. You'll like the tour very much, although honestly, a lot of people think it's too expensive.

Danny: Err right. So, about the tickets…

Receptionist: Oh yes, so that's seven tickets for the Egyptian Enigmas exhibition on Sunday.

Danny: Six tickets!

Receptionist: Right. Is that six adult tickets?

Danny: No. Four adults and two children.

Receptionist: OK, so adult tickets are £20 each and children enter for free. So that's £90. Do you want to pay by card?

Danny: Wait, shouldn't that be £80 for four adults?

Receptionist: Oh, silly me! Would you like to pay now by credit card, or book online?

Danny: I'll pay by card now, thanks.

Receptionist: Great. What's the number?

Danny: 2305 67…

Receptionist: Hold on. I need to turn on my card machine. It's my first day today, you see. Right, that was £180 for seven adults.

Danny: £80 pounds for four adults! Actually, I think I'd rather pay in cash on the door. I'd also like to speak to your manager. Hello? Hello?

Track 22

Unit 5, page 40, exercise 4

See previous track

Track 23

Unit 5, page 42, exercise 1

Teacher: OK, today's the day for your presentations. Freya and Lucas, you're first. What topic did you choose?

Freya: We chose unsolved mysteries…

Teacher: Excellent. Go ahead!

Freya: Our first mystery is the famous case of the Mary Celeste, a ghost ship found at sea.

Lucas: On 7th November 1872, Captain Benjamin Briggs and the crew of the Mary Celeste left New York for Italy. The captain's wife and two-year old daughter were also on board. However, on 4th December 1872, the Mary Celeste was found by a Canadian sailing ship, the Dei Gratia. It was in perfect condition and nothing was missing…

Freya: Except all of the people! The captain, his family and the crew had completely vanished. A lot of theories were suggested. Some people thought that the ship could have been attacked by a huge sea monster. But if it had been a monster, the ship would have been damaged. Others thought that it must have been pirates, but if it had been pirates, they would have taken everything of value. The real reason behind this mystery remains unknown.

Teacher: Interesting. What other mystery do you want to tell us about today?

Lucas: The second mystery is the case of the Voynich Manuscript.

Teacher: What's that?

Lucas: It's a book that was found in a library in Prague in 1912. It's written in a language that nobody can understand. The paper it is written on is from the 1400s, but nobody knows where it came from or who wrote it.

Freya: The most interesting thing is that it contains pictures of unknown and unusual plants that don't exist!

Lucas: There are lot of theories of course. Some people believe that it was written by the man who found it and that it could have been a hoax. But, if it had been written by somebody in 1912, it wouldn't have been written on paper from the 1400s! What's the truth? Nobody knows!

Teacher: How mysterious. Thank you, Freya and Lucas.

Track 24

Unit 5, page 42, exercise 2

See previous track

Track 25

Unit 5, page 44, exercise 3

Case closed!

Many mysterious things happen in our world that are difficult to explain, and today thousands of mysteries still remain unsolved. However, scientists have sometimes found proof to explain these phenomena and solve the enigmas. While the explanations for many of these mysteries may be more logical than the original theories, it doesn't make them any less interesting!

The Bermuda Triangle is an imaginary area located between Florida, Puerto Rico and Bermuda. It only became famous when American journalists started to write articles about the strange disappearances of ships and planes there. People then started theorising about what could have caused these disappearances. Hypotheses included aliens, sea monsters or even the inhabitants of Atlantis as being responsible. However, writer Lawrence Kusher came to the conclusion that some of the disappearances had never actually happened. In his book The Bermuda Triangle Mystery: Solved, Kusher also claims that the total number of disappearances isn't significantly greater than in any other part of the ocean. This view was confirmed by the United States Coast Guard in 1992 who provided the statistics to prove it. Far from being one of the greatest unsolved mysteries, the Bermuda Triangle is little more than the result of imaginative journalists who want to sell papers.

Since ancient times there have been reports of frogs and fish falling from the sky. The first case was recorded in the first century, and the latest in Ethiopia in 2016. Some people believe that this unusual rain might be caused by aliens or angry gods. Scientific evidence suggests however that they are caused by completely natural phenomena such as tornadoes or strong winds. The animals must have been picked up over the sea, or a lake, and later dropped on land. Not so unusual after all!

When Piltdown Man was found in a village in the UK in 1912, people believed that the bones belonged to an unknown early human and that the link between apes and humans had been uncovered. As well as a skull and jawbone, primitive tools were found at the site. At first, people believed that the body was 500,000 years old. The mystery became a controversy when some experts claimed that it was in fact a fake. Scientists finally proved it was a hoax in 1953, when they demonstrated that the bones came from different animals

Track 26

Unit 6, page 48, exercise 1

Story 1

Good evening. This is Robert Gibson with the nine o'clock news. A painting worth over 2 million pounds was stolen last night from Alton Art Museum when thieves entered the building through a back window. Police say the robbery was well planned, as the thieves had figured out how to turn off the museum's security alarm. Witnesses say that they saw four men escaping in a large white van at around midnight. They were unable to describe the men however, as they had large red scarves covering their faces. Last month criminals wearing red scarves robbed a bank on the high street. Police are looking into the connection between the two robberies.

Story 2

Scientists are examining a three-eyed snake found last week by farmer John Williams of Perth, Australia. Williams saw the snake moving through the grass when he went outside to feed his pigs. Williams's wife heard him shout and quickly helped him to capture the unusual animal. First reports suggest the extra eye was not caused by environmental factors. Experts say mutations like this can occur naturally. When asked about the snake, however, Mr Williams said he would give up farming if he found any other three-eyed animals on his farm.

Story 3

There has been an unusual development in the case of the missing garden gnome in Knightsbridge. When her garden gnome was stolen last month, Susie Dent asked police to find out who was responsible. But Mrs Dent told reporters last night that she has since received several postcards from all over the world, signed 'Gnome'. 'The first postcard was from Sydney, Australia,' she said. 'It said he was having a fantastic time and that the weather was better than in Knightsbridge. Since then I've had postcards from India and Brazil. I feel bad because at first I thought my neighbour had taken the gnome. But she definitely has an alibi because she hasn't been out of the country!' Mrs Dent said she no longer wants police to investigate.

Track 27

Unit 6, page 48, exercise 2

See previous track

Track 28

Unit 6, page 50, exercise 2

Detective Bryon: Excuse me, this is Westport Village, isn't it?

Mrs Mills: Yes, yes it is. Welcome to our wonderful, sleepy village. Well, actually it's not so quiet. There was an unpleasant incident last week. Somebody broke a window and stole £10,000 from Mr Brown's supermarket.

Detective Bryon: That's terrible.

Mrs Mills: It is, isn't it? There were no witnesses unfortunately, but I have a hunch it was his business partner, Mike Hicks. I saw the two of them arguing in the park last week.

Detective Bryon: Really? What about?

Mrs Mills: I think it was about money. Mike Hicks looked very angry. Of course, we can't forget about the other main suspect, can we?

Detective Bryon: Who's that?

Mrs Mills: Why, Mr Brown's son Tom, of course. He went to prison last year for stealing a car.

Detective Bryon: Really? Is he still in prison?

Mrs Mills: No, he came out two weeks ago and I saw him acting very suspiciously last week. He doesn't have an alibi for that night, either.

Detective Bryon: How do you know all this? You aren't a policewoman, are you?

Mrs Mills: No, I'm the cashier at the supermarket. And I know Tom doesn't have an alibi because I asked him. The detective still hasn't come from London, so somebody needs to start solving this case.

Detective Bryon: Hmm…

Mrs Mills: Well, that's just my opinion of course. I'm just gathering evidence to help them. Speaking of evidence, there was a red hat found at the scene of the crime. I think I know where it came from.

Detective Bryon: Where?

Mrs Mills: Well, the only person in the village with a red hat is the new woman, Anna Seymour.

Detective Bryon: And do you think it was her hat?

Mrs Mills: Well, no. I think it's a red herring, actually.

Detective Bryon: So, who put it there?

Mrs Mills: Why, one of the two suspects I mentioned, of course… errr… sorry, I didn't introduce myself. I'm Mrs Mills.

Detective Bryon: And I'm Detective Inspector James Bryon, Madam. Thank you very much for all of your help. Now, can you tell me what your alibi was for that night?

Track 29

Unit 6, page 50, exercise 3

See previous track

Track 30

Unit 6, page 52, exercise 2

The curious case of the yellow man

In Richburg, no crime remained unsolved. Puzzle Hughes, the ten-year-old daughter of Chief Detective Hughes, was a genius at figuring out difficult cases quickly, like the one of the Yellow Man. The police often asked her to go to the police station to help them. Puzzle's real name was Lara and she had always had a lot of curiosity and amazing skills of deduction.

One evening, Puzzle heard her father telling Mrs Hughes, 'The Yellow Man has stolen from another shop. That makes six shops this month. And we can never find him. He's very good at disappearing.'

'What shop, Dad?' Puzzle asked.

'The antique shop owned by Mr Gates and Mr Smith,' answered Detective Hughes.

'Are you sure the robber was the Yellow Man?' asked Puzzle.

'Yes. Mr Smith himself said it was the Yellow Man. Listen to his statement.'

Detective Hughes started to read: I was alone when I heard someone coming into the shop. It was the Yellow Man. I recognised him because he was wearing a yellow coat with a black square on the back, just like they said in the Daily News. He told me to close my eyes. I opened them after he had gone and I saw he had taken all the money. Oh, and he also took my phone. That's why I didn't call the police for three hours.

'Can I see the photo of the Yellow Man?' asked Puzzle.

'No, the police don't have one. However, many witnesses say that he always wears a yellow coat with a black square on the back,' replied Detective Hughes. Puzzle closed her eyes to think. She had a hunch. She went to her room to investigate and quickly found a list of local telephone numbers by searching on the internet.

An hour later, Puzzle found her father and said, 'The case is solved. There is no mystery – it was a cover-up. Mr Smith wasn't robbed. He has lied all this time. Mr Smith was only repeating what he read in the newspapers. If Mr Smith had his eyes closed when the Yellow Man was leaving the shop, he wouldn't have seen the black square on his back! Also, I have proof that his phone wasn't stolen. I just called his number and he answered!'

'That's incredible!' exclaimed Detective Hughes. Mrs Hughes, however, didn't seem convinced.

'I still don't think he is the criminal. Why would he lie?' she asked.

'Simple, I think he may have spent all the money from the shop. He invented the story so that his business partner Mr Gates wouldn't get angry,' said Puzzle.

'I see,' said Mrs Hughes.

'I have to catch him,' shouted Detective Hughes.

'Well, I have a hunch that you will find him at the airport. Get there quickly before he decides to hijack a plane.' Replied Puzzle. She smiled. Another case solved.

Track 31

Unit 7, page 58, exercise 3

Presenter: Good morning and welcome to today's programme. With me in the studio today is local comedian Patrick Boothe to talk about his new book, Spam!

Patrick: Hi, Joel.

Presenter: OK, so tell us about the name of your book.

Patrick: Well, as you know, 'spam' is just another name for junk mail. Last year, after my tour of Scotland, I wrote a play for a theatre company in London, so I had to spend a lot of time communicating with the director by email. But every time I looked at my email, I found ten or fifteen messages from people I didn't know. And I started thinking about the number of people that are sent junk mail every day. So, I decided to do something about it.

Presenter: What did you do?

Patrick: Well, I started sending them junk mail and wasting their time!

Presenter: What do you mean?

Patrick: I replied to them all! The first email was sent from somebody who said he was a prince. He said he wanted to give me a million pounds. All I had to do was send him 1,000 pounds first so he could transfer the money. I received another one telling me I had won 100,000 pounds on the lottery, even though I hadn't bought a lottery ticket. That one had an attachment with a form to complete my bank details. And there was one from somebody pretending to be my lost cousin Pete, asking to borrow a 1,000 pounds. In the end, I was communicating with several of these people every day. A lot of their replies were very funny, so I decided to publish them in a book. I didn't even have to do any research for the book - I had all the information I needed there in my email account!

Presenter: Brilliant! So, where can we buy it?

Patrick: It is being sold in local bookshops, or you can go to my website to order a copy.

Presenter: Well, thanks for joining us today Patrick. I can't wait to read it.

Track 32

Unit 7, page 58, exercise 4

See previous track

Track 33

Unit 7, page 60, exercise 2

Presenter: Hello and welcome to our quiz show, Secondary School Challenge. I'm your host Gary Maddow. Our contestants today are Sammy Stephens, representing Hill Secondary School in Edinburgh, Harriet Wells from Doncaster High in Dublin and Matt Vickers from Brentwood Academy in Essex. And what a coincidence – that's right next door to Brentwood studios, where we're filming today!

Harriet: Hi everyone!

Sammy: Hello!

Matt: Hey there!

Presenter: So, this week's special subject is one that I think you'll know all about. No, don't worry - it's not History or Maths, it's digital communication. So, let's get started! Press your buzzer when you know the answer. First question: what is the name of an area on the internet where particular topics are talked about in real time?

Harriet: A website!

Presenter: I'm afraid not, Harriet.

Sammy: A chatroom!

Presenter: Correct, Sammy! One point for Hill Secondary School. Second question: what is the collective name for the physical parts of a computer?

Matt: I think I know! Is it hardware?

Presenter: Correct! One point for Brentwood Academy! Well done, Matt! Third question of four, so think carefully… What do we call a malicious program that can infect our computer?

Harriet: A virus!

Presenter: Correct, Harriet! One point for Doncaster High! So, last question. It's a draw at the moment, so whoever answers this one correctly will be the winner. What do we call a large interactive screen connected to a computer and projector?

Matt: I know! It's a platform!

Presenter: Incorrect, Matt!

Sammy: An interactive whiteboard?

Presenter: Correct! Let's have a round of applause for Sammy, because our winner is Hill Secondary School in Edinburgh! And I think you are going to like the prize. Your school will get not one great piece of hardware, but two! Two new printers! Don't forget to tune in to next week's show. The subject will be… Business Studies!

Track 34

Unit 7, page 60, exercise 3

See previous track

Track 35

Unit 7, page 62, exercise 2

Technology in the 21st century classroom

We live in the information era. Technology is a part of our everyday lives, in the way we do business, communicate and even spend our free time. And its importance in society continues to grow. Advances in technology have also had a huge impact on education. The learning environment, the role of the teacher and the manner in which students are taught has changed a lot in recent years. But what are the most popular methods of using technology in the classroom? We looked at classrooms all over Europe, and this is what we found out.

E-books

An e-book, or 'electronic book', is the digital version of a book. It can be read on a computer, e-book reader, mobile phone or tablet. At the beginning, e-books were not very easy to use and they only covered specialised topics. However, a variety of new formats and topics were later developed and so the popularity of e-books started to grow. Today, around 180 million e-books are sold every year, and many of them are used in classrooms. Both teachers and students like the interactive elements of e-books, which make learning engaging and fun. An added bonus is that students don't have to carry heavy books to school every day.

Interactive whiteboards

Although the technology has existed for several decades, using interactive whiteboards in the classroom is a relatively new development. There are many benefits to using this technology, but for teachers, the possibility of recording the lesson is one of the most important. This allows students to review the lesson at home to fully understand the topic and easily pass tests. Another feature loved by both students and teachers is the fact that teachers can include text, audio and videos in presentations.

Flipped learning

This method has recently become more popular, especially at universities. Students can watch the lesson or lecture online at home and then research the topic. Time in class is then used for discussion and questions. In this way, the traditional learning environment is inverted, or 'flipped'; students come to class with knowledge of the subject and do the assignments traditionally set for homework, in class. Students are mainly positive about this approach as it allows them to ask questions and understand the subject better. Evaluation of the learning process is also progressive, so students can be given help as soon as they need it.

Track 36

Unit 8, page 66, exercise 3

Presenter: Welcome to Discussion Time. I'm Eve Stewart and today we're talking about technology, do we depend on it too much? On our panel we have sixteen-year-old Rio. Hi, Rio.

Rio: Hey there.

Presenter: And Dr Jane Robson, a specialist in how technology affects teen and adult health. Welcome, Dr Robson.

Dr Robson: Hi Eve, a pleasure to be here.

Presenter: OK, firstly, do we use our phones and tablets too much? And secondly, is it bad for us? Dr Robson, can you answer those questions for us?

Dr Robson: Well, the answer to both questions is yes. We do depend on technology far too much and this has a negative impact on our physical and mental health. For example, if you look at your phone just before you go to bed, it affects the quality of your sleep. And sleep is very important for our health. Poor sleep affects our concentration, mood and immune systems.

Presenter: Wow, that's quite worrying.

Rio: Can I say something here? I do agree with Dr Robson that technology can negatively affect our health, but it can also improve our health. Think about the advances in medical technology that have saved millions of lives. Artificial organs, digital scanners…

Presenter: That's a very good point, Rio. There are also digital X-rays now, so doctors can share information easily.

Dr Robson: But it doesn't change the fact that nowadays we are spending more time on our phones and less time talking to people face-to-face, and that leads to digital solitude.

Rio: That's true. But it's easy to establish some rules. Don't use your phone at the dinner table or after 8pm. Or don't check your email after you finish school or work. It's that simple. Also, for teenagers, technology is an important part of our future. Over 76% of jobs use technology these days.

Presenter: Wow, that is a lot! And I imagine that will be 100% in the future! Well, that's all we have time for, but I think you both made some good points. Join us next week for…

Track 37

Unit 8, page 66, exercise 4

See previous track

Track 38

Unit 8, page 68, exercise 3

Harry: OK, so let's get started on the round-table discussion about our clean-up campaign. Tonight, we'll be focusing on how to raise awareness, starting with the local community.

Anna: I think the first thing we need is an attention-grabbing slogan, Harry.

Harry: Good point. Any ideas?

Colin: How about 'Go green, help clean'?

Harry: Hmm… I'm not sure, Colin. It's a bit impersonal.

Anna: 'Save Lanark, save ourselves'?

Harry: Not a bad idea, Anna. Using the name of the town is better. What does everyone else think?

Emma: Yes, it's OK… but wait. How about simply, 'Love Lanark'?

Harry: Yes! Brilliant, Emma. Is everyone else OK with that?

Colin: Yes, I like it.

Anna: Me too, let's use that.

Harry: So, let's think about how we are going to raise awareness.

Emma: We could make flyers and hand them out near the school when students come out in the afternoon.

Harry: The problem is that flyers aren't environmentally friendly.

Anna: We could print them on recycled paper.

Harry: But they still get thrown away, and sometimes left on the ground.

Colin: How about we organise a demonstration? We could make placards, with photos of all the rubbish in the river.

Anna: Yes, that sounds like something that will attract people's attention.

Emma: I suppose we don't have enough money to pay for a TV advert? Something that explains why the situation in the town is getting critical.

Harry: Well, at the moment, we don't. But it's a shame because TV adverts attract a large audience.

Anna: What about sending out emails?

Harry: Yes, we could send out emails to the people who have subscribed to our blog. We should all use our social media accounts to promote the campaign, too.

Colin: Hey, I've had an idea. You can create your own bumper stickers online nowadays and they're not expensive. Why don't we order some 'Love Lanark' bumper stickers and give them to people who want to put them on their cars?

Anna and Emma: Great!

Harry: I agree! That's decided, then. OK, let's all meet again next Tuesday to talk about…

Track 39

Unit 8, page 68, exercise 4

See previous track

Track 40

Unit 8, page 70, exercise 2

Are you dependent on technology?

Yesterday I wanted to call my mum to wish her a happy birthday, but her phone number was in my phone, which I had lost. So, I couldn't call her because I couldn't remember her number. Later, I wanted to check how much I had spent in the supermarket, but I couldn't work it out, so I had to use my calculator. These two situations made me realise I am totally dependent on technology. I can't survive without it. Anyone else feel the same? Leave your replies below.

Technological advances have made our lives easier and more comfortable, but when we use them constantly, this has a negative impact on our creativity. In other words, we don't use our brain as often as we should. For example, how often do you use a search engine to find out information you should know, but you've forgotten? I do it all the time. And I used to buy a newspaper every day, but I read online news now. I think I'm probably a digital addict, in fact.

Fran, New York

Well, I'm a maths teacher and I've noticed kids can't do even the most basic sums in their heads anymore, because they are so dependent on technology. I mean, I think the internet can be an excellent educational tool, but kids don't

go to the library to consult an encyclopaedia these days. And the English teacher at school says that pupils don't read a whole book now – they read a summary of it on the internet. So, I think we should control how much time children spend using technology.
Barry, Dublin

In our modern workplaces, people use all kinds of electronic devices to do their jobs more productively. But people shouldn't send messages by email or phone each other when they are sitting in the next office. A face-to-face conversation with a colleague is quicker and more efficient. Also, I worry that robots will soon do all our jobs – or simplify them. I think it's time to hit the panic button and say enough! People are happier when life is simpler.
Carmen, Barcelona

We should certainly spend less time on social media and apps – in my house at least. Just the other day my son sent me a message from his bedroom telling me what he wanted for dinner!!! Spending time with family always seems to involve electronic devices, and that's not good for conversation. So we've made a rule now that when we are eating, the kids have to leave their phones in their rooms.
Aled, Cardiff

We shouldn't depend 100% on machines, in my opinion. I mean, I work in the tech industry, but when I have kids, I will restrict the amount of time they spend using technology. Did you know that Millennials are worse at remembering what day of the week it is than people in their fifties and sixties? Technology gives us a huge amount of information, but it's literally changing the structure of our brains – for the worse.
Kyungsun, Seoul

Track 41

Unit 9, page 76, exercise 1

Mum: It's time for dinner, Beatrice.
Beatrice: Can I eat it later, Mum? I have to watch a documentary.
Mum: Watch TV instead of eating dinner? Absolutely not. Watching TV is something you do to relax and you have History homework to do after dinner! Turn off Channel Six right now and come to the kitchen.
Beatrice: But Mum, this is homework. It's part of a project we're doing for social studies on important events in the 20th century!
Mum: Well, OK. But no more than twenty minutes.
Beatrice: Thanks, Mum.
Documentary Presenter: Welcome to another episode of Turning Points. Today, we're looking at milestones in the 20th century. It was a time of many scientific breakthroughs, such as the discovery of penicillin by Alexander Fleming in 1928. This discovery saved the lives of millions of people, as it revolutionised the treatment of infectious diseases. We can't forget about the television, either. Without this invention, you wouldn't be watching this documentary today! Now, let's take a look at other milestones in the field of technology and science that are less well known. For example, Hubert Booth invented the vacuum cleaner in 1901. This device is used to clean houses all over the world today. And what about the invention of tea bags in 1904, by Thomas Sullivan? This led to a boom in sales of tea and it is one of the most popular drinks in the world. But a real turning point in the field of nutrition was the invention of frozen fish by Clarence Birdseye in 1923. This helped people by making fish cheaper. People everywhere suddenly had access to this important source of protein. Another important invention was…
Mum: Beatrice! Beatrice! It's time to eat now. You can finish watching that documentary after dinner.
Beatrice: Yes, OK. I'm hungry anyway. That was a lot of information, but it's an interesting topic. The 20th century certainly wasn't boring. Mum, did you know…

Track 42

Unit 9, page 76, exercise 2

See previous track

Track 43

Unit 9, page 78, exercise 3

Norma: Oh, this is so difficult!
Dad: What's wrong, Norma?
Norma: We have to do an assignment for History class and I don't know what to write about.
Dad: What's the topic?
Norma: That's the problem. We have to write about somebody from our family who did something important in the 20th century. I mean, our family is so boring. Nobody did anything special.
Dad: There are such a lot of people in our family that did amazing things, Norma!
Norma: Like who?
Dad: Take your great-aunt Sally. She moved to the United States when she was a young girl in the 1930s…no, the 1940s. She worked as a waitress. Her living conditions were terrible at first, but she worked very hard and later became an important figure in the fight against racial oppression. Look, here's a picture of her with Rosa Parks.
Norma: Wow! I didn't know that! Who's the other person in the photo?
Dad: That's her brother, your great-uncle Albert. He was a very successful writer and philosopher. He wrote a lot of books about human rights and democracy. Look, we have copies of his books on the shelf!
Norma: That's so amazing.
Dad: And then there's your mother's cousin, Louise Collins. She was a young feminist in the 1970s. She organised a lot of peaceful protests in London.
Norma: Really? That's so cool.
Dad: Yes, it's thanks to people like her that there are now greater freedoms and opportunities for women.
Norma: Where is she now?
Dad: She went to India. She runs a factory that provides job opportunities to women living in poverty.
Norma: She sounds amazing. Is that why there's a painting of the Taj Mahal in the living room?
Dad: No, that's there because Grandad painted it.
Norma: Grandad? But wasn't he a chef?
Dad: Yes, he was, but he was also a very good artist. He went to fight in the Second World War when he was 18.
Norma: That's so brave! can't believe I didn't know this.
Dad: Well you'll be able to do your assignment now. Your only problem is deciding which family member to choose!

Track 44
Unit 9, page 78, exercise 4
See previous track

Track 45
Unit 9, page 80, exercise 2
You can help too
The planet's temperature is rising, and so is air pollution. Environmental disasters, such as fires and floods, are increasing. Over a million seabirds and mammals are killed by pollution every year, and one billion trees are cut down to supply paper to one country alone – the United States. There is also an area of rubbish called The Great Pacific Garbage Patch floating in the water that environmentalists say is the same size as Texas. The fact is that we are destroying our planet. But what can we do to make a difference?
First of all, people need to understand that environmental problems are a serious matter. A lot of people simply don't realise that, in the future, problems such as a lack of drinking water may cause revolution or war. But, if we educate people to take action on a daily basis, we can help solve this serious problem. One way of raising awareness is by designing posters or flyers with pictures that show how human actions have had devastating consequences on the Earth. You could show the shocking effects of global warming, deforestation and pollution.
Another important way of helping is to start a social media campaign. Teenagers and young adults get a lot of their information online nowadays, so why not present the facts in digital form? Furthermore, it is environmentally friendly. Simply writing a social media post or a blog entry can have an impact and encourage people to do more. So, why not start today?
Your ideas should be practical: Explain some simple actions that people can integrate into their daily lives. According to the UN, we can solve more than 40% of the present environmental problems by simply recycling. Carsharing, where friends or neighbours use one car to go to work instead of each person using their own car, is also easy to organise. This would result in an important reduction in the levels of air pollution. In fact, using fewer cars and more public transport is another action that can be adopted by most people. Lastly, encourage people to consume less. When people consume too much, they waste natural resources and this harms the environment, too. Educating people to implement these ideas will reduce global warming.
To sum up, if we don't learn to protect our environment, we won't be able to save our planet. There is still time to make a difference. Now the question we need to answer is: What are WE doing to help planet Earth? If we do not care about the planet, it might stop caring about us.

Track 46
Wordlist, page 98, unit 1, Skills and strengths
See Student's Book transcript, Track 2.39

Track 47
Wordlist, page 98, unit 1, Business
See Student's Book transcript, Track 2.40

Track 48
Wordlist, page 98, unit 1, Jobs
See Student's Book transcript, Track 2.41

Track 49
Wordlist, page 98, unit 2, The entertainment industry
See Student's Book transcript, Track 2.42

Track 50
Wordlist, page 98, unit 2, Inventions
See Student's Book transcript, Track 2.43

Track 51
Wordlist, page 98, unit 2, Success and failure
See Student's Book transcript, Track 2.44

Track 52
Wordlist, page 99, unit 3, Storytelling
See Student's Book transcript, Track 2.45

Track 53
Wordlist, page 99, unit 3, The natural world
See Student's Book transcript, Track 2.46

Track 54
Wordlist, page 99, unit 3, Myths
See Student's Book transcript, Track 2.47

Track 55
Wordlist, page 99, unit 4, The Earth
See Student's Book transcript, Track 2.48

Track 56
Wordlist, page 99, unit 4, The Universe
See Student's Book transcript, Track 2.49

Track 57
Wordlist, page 99, unit 4, Space exploration
See Student's Book transcript, Track 2.50

Track 58
Wordlist, page 100, unit 5, Ancient monuments
See Student's Book transcript, Track 2.51

Track 59
Wordlist, page 100, unit 5, UFOs and aliens
See Student's Book transcript, Track 2.52

Track 60
Wordlist, page 100, unit 5, Mysteries
See Student's Book transcript, Track 2.53

Track 61
Wordlist, page 100, unit 6, Phrasal verbs
See Student's Book transcript, Track 2.54

Track 62
Wordlist, page 100, unit 6, Detective work
See Student's Book transcript, Track 2.55

Track 63

Wordlist, page 100, unit 6, Investigation

See Student's Book transcript, Track 2.56

Track 64

Wordlist, page 101, unit 7, Communication I

See Student's Book transcript, Track 2.57

Track 65

Wordlist, page 101, unit 7, The internet

See Student's Book transcript, Track 2.58

Track 66

Wordlist, page 101, unit 7, Academic honesty

See Student's Book transcript, Track 2.59

Track 67

Wordlist, page 101, unit 8, Communication II

See Student's Book transcript, Track 2.60

Track 68

Wordlist, page 101, unit 8, Publicity

See Student's Book transcript, Track 2.61

Track 69

Wordlist, page 101, unit 8, Technological advances

See Student's Book transcript, Track 2.62

Track 70

Wordlist, page 101, unit 9, Human achievements

See Student's Book transcript, Track 2.63

Track 71

Wordlist, page 101, unit 9, The 20th century

See Student's Book transcript, Track 2.64

Track 72

Wordlist, page 101, unit 9, The environment

See Student's Book transcript, Track 2.65

Unit 1

Page 4

1 **1** finance **2** numeracy **3** information technology **4** problem solving **5** customer service **6** communication

2 **1** active **2** resourceful **3** talkative **4** enthusiastic **5** thoughtful **6** systematic

3 **a** 3 **b** 1 **c** 2

4 **1** education **2** empathic **3** internet **4** creative **5** right **6** fashion designer

Page 5

5 **1** have wanted **2** left **3** flew **4** get **5** love **6** have won

6 **a** love **b** get **c** left, flew **d** have won **e** have wanted

7 **1** has **2** don't **3** seems **4** didn't increase **5** have worked

8 **1** wrote **2** look **3** complete **4** have started **5** have improved **6** haven't learnt **7** haven't decided

9 *Student's own answers*

Page 6

1 **1** Did **2** has **3** was **4** think **5** grown

2 **1** designed **2** has run **3** wasn't; was **4** writes **5** has created

3 **1** do you **2** have you **3** was **4** have you

4 **1** Nurse
2 helping (the)
3 solve problems
4 5 years
5 challenging
6 team leader
7 Architect
8 nervous
9 own company

Page 7

5 **1** slogan
2 entrepreneur
3 logo
4 identity
5 Consumers
6 success

6 **1** do; like
2 does; need
3 are
4 have created
5 have designed
6 did; launch
7 did; have
8 did; realise

7 *Student's own answers*

Page 8

1 **1** Bodily-kinaesthetic
2 Intrapersonal
3 Visual-spatial
4 Verbal-linguistic
5 Interpersonal

2 **1** e **2** d **3** a **4** f **5** b **6** c

3 **1** a **2** a **3** a **4** b **5** b **6** a

4 3

5 **1** curious
2 solve
3 meticulous
4 creative
5 neurons

Page 10

1 *Student's own answers*

2 *Student's own answers*

3 *Student's own answers*

Page 11

1 **1** sleep on it
2 The jury is out.
3 I am in two minds
4 on the fence

2 **1** sleep on it
2 the jury is out
3 in two minds
4 on the fence

Unit 2

Page 12

1

Across
2 achievement
3 business
5 empire

Down
1 amusement
3 bankrupt
4 success

2 **1** b; c **2** a; c **3** a; c

3 **1** F. He says that people think it looks easy.
2 F. He had been in 30 TV shows.
3 T
4 F. She became famous quickly.
5 T
6 F. She writes and draws her own comics.

Page 13

4 **1** a **2** c **3** b **4** c **5** c

5 **1** had started
2 had; earnt
3 had been
4 had organised
5 had had

6 **1** directed three films.
2 directed two Star Wars films together.
3 won two Oscars for Best Director.
4 earnt over 3.7 billion dollars.

7 *Student's own answers*

Page 14

1 **1** b **2** c **3** c

2 **1** They will get £50,000.
2 He decorated a huge house.
3 It's wallpaper you can eat when you don't want it anymore.
4 He has designed lots of flavours.
5 It came to him while he was mopping the kitchen floor.
6 It plays music while you mop the floor.
7 She suggests you could just carry your phone with you.

3 **1** b **2** b **3** a **4** b **5** b **6** a

Page 15

4 **1** used
2 had produced
3 had started
4 hadn't published
5 had tried
6 invented

5 **1** came
2 invented
3 improved
4 had developed
5 worked
6 was
7 created
8 had imagined

6 **1** Karina had completed her degree before she designed her first product in 2009.
2 She had made some prototypes before she launched the SqueeziTube.
3 She had launched the SqueeziTube before she presented it on television.
4 By 2016 she was rich because she had sold a lot of SqueeziTubes.
5 She had become very rich by the time she developed the SqueeziTube 2.0.

Page 16

1 **1** achieved; a
2 set; goals; b
3 succeed; c
4 perseverance; c

2 *Student's own answers*

3 **a** 3 **b** 4 **c** 1 **d** 2

4 **1** To celebrate the father of the Gods, Zeus.
2 Because of its tradition and history.
3 He had problems with his back.
4 You need to work hard and persevere.
5 He won eight gold medals in one competition.
6 She got a perfect score of 10 in gymnastics.

5 **1** c **2** f **3** a **4** d **5** b **6** e

Page 18

1 *Student's own answers*

2 *Student's own answers*

3 *Student's own answers*

Page 19

1 **1** fall at the first hurdle
2 has gone to the dogs
3 is in the bag
4 pass with flying colours

2 **1** fall at the first hurdle
2 is in the bag
3 pass/passed with flying colours
4 has gone to the dogs

Unit 3

Page 22

1 **1** f **2** e **3** d **4** c **5** a **6** b

2 **1** languages
2 fictional
3 myth
4 themes
5 evil
6 novels

3 **Expert 1:** b
Expert 2: a
Expert 3: c

4 **1** b **2** b **3** a **4** b **5** b **6** a

Page 2 3

5 **1** were listening
2 didn't like
3 was crying
4 was fighting
5 escaped
6 killed

6 **1** T
2 F. It is Perseus.
3 T
4 F. It's their marriage.

7 **1** climax
2 introduction
3 theme
4 hero

8 **1** called
2 was finishing
3 was
4 attacked
5 were sleeping
6 won

9 *Student's own answer*

Page 24

1 **1** Earth
2 wood
3 harmony
4 good-hearted
5 water
6 nutritious

2 **1** The goddess of spring lives in a magic garden.
2 I am dying.
3 Fight the enemy!
4 We (have) carved the people from wood.
5 Where are you going?
6 Why don't you live in a castle?

Page 25

3 **1** wanted some water
2 was an evil goddess
3 the Moon had taken Rona
5 had done it to punish her
6 to pour her water on the Earth (when she felt sad)

4 **1** b
2 c

5 **1** Friday 30th April
2 three weeks
3 comic strip
4 200 words (long)
5 £50; a novel
6 moral
7 a villain
8 conflict; resolution

6 *Student's own answers*

Page 26

1
1 conflict
2 resolution
3 climax
4 introduction
5 main character
6 hero

2
a 2
b 1
c 3

3 1 b 2 a 3 b 4 c 5 c 6 b

4
1 the yellow circle
2 the fairies
3 a changeling
4 Fionn

5
1 Content
2 Disease
3 Well-known
4 Fearless
5 Wise
6 Luck

Page 28

1 *Student's own answers*

2 *Student's own answers*

3 *Student's own answers*

Page 29

1 1 a 2 a 3 a 4 b

2
1 Achilles heel
2 Pandora's box
3 a round-table discussion
4 the Midas touch

Unit 4

Page 30

1 1 c 2 a 3 b 4 c 5 b 6 a

2
1 planet
2 Moon
3 astronauts
4 space

3 1 a 2 c 3 b

4
1 France
2 space tourism
3 (over) 15
4 bad idea
5 astronomy
6 half a million pounds

Page 31

5
1 extinct
2 homo sapiens
3 hospitable
4 birds
5 oxygen
6 life

6
1 had you eaten
2 had killed
3 had been
4 had you done

7
1 had
2 died
3 had
4 analysed

8 *Student's own answers*

Page 32

1 1 c 2 b 3 a 4 d 5 e

2
1 Science Day.
2 Planets in the Solar System.
3 It could be boring.
4 They get bored quickly.
5 1 5 pounds
6 79
7 A meteoroid.

3
1 meteorite
2 Mercury
3 asteroids
4 Venus

4
1 Universe
2 celestial bodies
3 planets
4 Sun
5 orbit
6 Moon

5
1 A; suggested answer: Craters.
2 B; suggested answer: Because there is no gravity.
3 A; suggested answer: They die.
4 B; suggested answer: It melts.
5 A; suggested answer: You damage your eyes.

6 1 b 2 d 3 a 4 c

7
1 were; would be
2 didn't have; wouldn't know
3 hadn't come; wouldn't have learnt
4 got; wouldn't survive
5 won; would be

8 *Student's own answers*

Page 34

1 **1** telescope
2 mission
3 research
4 natural disasters
5 Space Age
6 satellite

2 5

3 **1** e **2** a **3** c **4** f **5** b

4 **1** F. Sleeping on the ISS is not the same as sleeping on Earth.
2 F. Food is cooked by injecting the food with hot water.
3 F. The journey to the ISS from Earth is difficult and long.
4 T
5 T
6 F. Bill doesn't have a lot of free time.
7 T

5 **1** gravity
2 inject
3 commute
4 breakthroughs
5 colleagues
6 orbit

Page 36

1 *Student's own answers*

2 *Student's own answers*

3 *Student's own answers*

Page 37

1 **1** move heaven and earth
2 written in the stars
3 on top of the world
4 thank your lucky stars

2 **1** written in the stars
2 on top of the world
3 heaven and earth
4 thank my lucky stars

Unit 5

Page 40

1 **1** mysterious
2 evidence
3 geometric
4 belief
5 theory
6 uncover

2 **1** mysterious
2 geometric
3 theory
4 evidence
5 belief
6 uncover

3 **1** b **2** a

4 **1** Egyptian Enigmas
2 mummies
3 artefacts
4 (too) expensive
5 free
6 £80
7 first

Page 41

5 **1** might have carved
2 could have made
3 may have created
4 couldn't have formed
6 must have drawn
7 might have been

6 **1** must have left
2 might have fallen
3 can't have been
4 may have been
5 could have found
6 must have put

7 **1** could have been
2 must have felt
3 may have visited
4 might have run
5 might have seen

Page 42

1 a, b, d, e

2 **1** M 1
2 B
3 M1
4 M1
5 M2
6 M2
7 B

3 **1** claims
2 controversy
3 truth
4 fake
5 hoax
6 prove

4 **1** b **2** c **3** d **4** a **5** f **6** e

Page 43

5 **1** been; told
2 have gone; invited
3 had; would
4 have; seen
5 investigated; have
6 filmed; could

6 **1** If you had been here earlier, you would have seen the UFO.
2 We would have found debris by now if there had been a crash.
3 He wouldn't have come if I hadn't invited him.
4 If scientists had discovered evidence of aliens, we would have heard about it.
5 If we had solved the mystery, what would the police have said?

7 1 If Margaret hadn't woken up late, she wouldn't have forgotten her bag.
2 Margaret wouldn't have missed the train if she hadn't answered her phone.
3 If Margaret had arrived at the office on time, she would have been involved in the new project.
4 If Margaret hadn't got home late, she would have watched her favourite TV programme.

8 *Student's own answers*

Page 44

1 1 Archaeologists
2 hoax
3 figure
4 fake
5 facts

2 *Student's own answers*

3 1, 2, 3, 5

4 **a** 2 **b** 3 **c** 4 **d** 1

5 1 (American) journalists.
2 Aliens, sea monsters or inhabitants of Atlantis.
3 The United States Coast Guard.
4 To sell newspapers.
5 Natural phenomena.
6 They showed that the bones came from different animals.

6 1 logical
2 uncovered
3 primitive
4 phenomena
5 proof

Page 46

1 *Student's own answers*

2 *Student's own answers*

3 *Student's own answers*

Page 47

1 1 give the game away
2 keep me in the dark.
3 covering his tracks.
4 spills the beans.

2 **Rule 1:** keep; dark
Rule 2: cover; tracks
Rule 3: give; game
Rule 4: spill; beans
Now you! Workbook 4 Answer key

Unit 6

Page 48

1 Story 1; c
Story 2; a
Story 3; b

2 1 painting
2 window
3 (security) alarm
4 farmer
5 environmental
6 naturally
7 garden
8 postcards
9 alibi

3 1 up
2 out
3 out
4 into

4 1 gives up
2 look into
3 figured out
4 find out

Page 49

5 1 b 2 b 3 a 4 a 5 a 6 a

6 1 standing
2 find
3 return
4 to help
5 to find out
6 to go
7 drinking

7 1 notices
2 watching
3 asks
4 to find out
5 don't want
6 to know
7 hears
8 screaming/scream
9 tells
10 to leave

Page 50

1 1 clues
2 hunch
3 red herring
4 witness
5 alibi
6 suspect

2 1 f 2 e 3 b 4 d 5 a 6 c

3 1 £10,000.
2 There were no witnesses.
3 She saw Mr Brown and Mike Hicks arguing.
4 He stole a car.
5 She suspects Tom Brown and Mike Hicks.
6 A red hat.
7 She thinks that it is a red herring.

Page 51

4 **1** unsolved
2 deduction
3 witness
4 lawyer
5 suspect

5 **1** c **2** e **3** f **4** a **5** b **6** d

6 *Student's own answers*

7 **1** am I
2 didn't you
3 was it
4 weren't you
5 is it
6 could you
7 have you
8 can't I

Page 52

1 **1** stick to
2 cover-up
3 wealthy
4 disappearance
5 notice

2 **1** c **2** b

3

Lara Hughes	**1** The ten-year-old daughter of Chief Detective Hughes
Detective Hughes	**2** Lara's father, the chief detective of Richburg
Mrs Hughes	**3** Lara's mother, the chief detective's wife
Mr Smith	**4** One of the owners of the antique shop
Mr Gates	**5** Mr Smith's business partner
The Yellow Man	**6** The thief who has stolen from five shops this month

4 **1** The Yellow Man
2 Puzzle/Lara Hughes
3 Detective Hughes
4 Mr Smith
5 Mrs Hughes
6 Mr Gates

5 **1** a **2** a **3** b **4** b

Page 54

1 *Student's own answers*

2 *Student's own answers*

3 *Student's own answers*

Page 55

1 **1** on
2 jump
3 penny
4 two

2 **1** put two and two together
2 The penny dropped
3 jump to conclusions
4 hit the nail on the head

Unit 7

Page 58

1 **1** communication
2 computer literate
3 apps
4 features
5 real-time
6 virtual reality

2 **1** Virtual reality
2 mobile phone
3 apps
4 messages
5 social media
6 computer literate

3 **1** c **2** b

4 **1** junk mail
2 communicating
3 messages
4 replies
5 research

Page 59

5 **1** Millions of emails are sent every day.
2 Too much time is wasted on social media platforms.
3 A new virtual reality app has been developed (by engineers).
4 How many email accounts have been opened since 1971?
5 A lot of time is spent deleting junk mail.
6 The first electronic note was sent (by someone) in the USA.

6 **1** is being used / is used
2 was developed
3 are being sold / are sold
4 have been created / are being created
5 hadn't been used / wasn't used
6 are being followed / are followed

7 **1** stolen
2 were
3 have
4 developed
5 are
6 hadn't

8 *Student's own answers*

Page 60

1 **1** connection
2 click
3 link
4 download
5 virus
6 install
7 webcam
8 chatrooms

2 **1** c **2** a

3 **1** Dublin
2 communication
3 buzzer
4 Harriet
5 point
6 hardware
7 Matt
8 printers

Page 61

4 **1** must be taught
2 can be planned
3 can/may be used
4 must be done
5 should be installed

5 **1** Internet use should be restricted by parents.
2 Online bullying should be reported to an adult.
3 Robot teachers may be used in the future.
4 One day, all classes could be taught online.
5 Photos we post online can be seen by anyone.

6 **1** can be developed
2 can be found
3 can be improved
4 should/must not be shared
5 should/must be followed
6 should/must not be forgotten
7 can be used

Page 62

1 **1** search engine
2 Click
3 assessment
4 pass
5 cheat
6 assignment
7 plagiarism

2 3

3 **1** T
2 DS
3 F. The technology has existed for several decades.
4 F. Students come to class with knowledge of the subject.
5 F. Students are mainly positive about it.

4 **1** They were difficult to use and specialised.
2 New formats and topics were developed.
3 The possibility of recording the lesson.
4 They can include text, audio and videos.
5 At universities.
6 Because evaluation is progressive.

5 **1** communicate
2 pass
3 online
4 inverted
5 assignments

Page 64

1 *Student's own answers*

2 *Student's own answers*

3 *Student's own answers*

Page 65

1 **1** got off on the wrong foot
2 are on the same wavelength
3 get straight to the point
4 keep him in the loop

2 **1** keep me in the loop
2 got straight to the point
3 are on the same wavelength
4 get off on the wrong foot

Unit 8

Page 66

1 **1** c; satellite
2 b; multitask
3 d; solitude
4 c; keep in touch

2 **1** translation
2 complex
3 robots
4 repetitive
5 rude
6 social media

3 **1** a **2** c **3** b

4 **1** c **2** a **3** b **4** c

Page 67

5 **1** multitasking
2 counterproductive
3 globalisation
4 worldwide
5 simplification
6 repetitive

6 **1** c **2** b **3** a **4** d

7 **1** that leads to
2 which allows
3 who spend
4 which is
5 who uses
6 who has

8 **1** There are satellites in space that send information back to Earth.
2 This is the new computer that/which has a webcam.
3 This is my friend Ruby who is good at multitasking.
4 I have a phone that/which has a broken screen.
5 There are robots that/which do the work humans used to do.
6 I've bought a new tablet that/which has a lot of memory.

Page 68

1 **1** promote
2 objective; subjective
3 advert
4 influence
5 attention-grabbing
6 flyer

2 **1** poster
2 TV
3 language
4 emotions
5 promote
6 facts

3 **1** c **2** b **3** a

4 1 How to raise awareness of the clean-up campaign.
2 It's a bit impersonal.
3 Near the school.
4 Photos of the rubbish (in the river).
5 To the people who have subscribed (to their blog).
6 Social media.
7 Bumper stickers.

Page 69

5 1 d 2 b 3 a 4 e 5 f 6 c

6 1 World Information Society Day, which is very special, was first celebrated in 1969.
2 This special day, which is celebrated every year, aims to promote communication technologies.
3 The speakers, who are all experts, will talk about digital opportunities.
4 Worldwide access to the internet, which is not possible nowadays, is the theme this year.

7 *Student's own answer*

Page 70

1 1 phone
2 online
3 social media
4 screen
5 tabs

2 b, e

3 1 F. He used to, but now he doesn't.
2 F. He says it is an excellent educational tool.
3 T.
4 T.
5 F. She will restrict their use of it.

4 1 b 2 a 3 a 4 a 5 a 6 b

Page 72

1 *Student's own answers*

2 *Student's own answers*

3 *Student's own answers*

Page 73

1 1 bells and whistles
2 hit the panic button
3 like a well-oiled machine
4 a cog in the machine

2 1 like a well-oiled machine
2 bells and whistles
3 a cog in the machine
4 hit the panic button

Unit 9

Page 76

1 1 b 2 a

2 1 Turning Points
2 1928
3 diseases
4 1901
5 tea bags
6 frozen fish
7 1923

3 1 boom
2 aeroplane
3 Driverless
4 computer
5 space race

4 1 a 2 c 3 b 4 e 5 d

Page 77

5 1 f; benefit
2 d; mobile
3 c; turning point
4 e; internet
5 b; milestone
6 a; artificial intelligence

6 1 such
2 such
3 so
4 so
5 such
6 such

7 1 so
2 so
3 such
4 so
5 such
6 such
7 so
8 so
9 so
10 such

8 *Student's own answers*

Page 78

1 1 so much
2 so little
3 so many
4 so much
5 so few
6 so much

2 1 There was so much interest in entertainment that silent movies were released.
2 There were so many people killed in the First World War that politicians promised never to go to war again.
3 There were so few jobs that people were starving during the Great Depression.
4 There was so much death and destruction in the Second World War that the United Nations was formed.
5 There was so little support for communism in Eastern Europe that it fell very quickly.

3 1 d 2 b 3 c 4 a

4 1 living conditions
2 oppression
3 human rights
4 feminist
5 protests
6 poverty
7 War

Page 79

5 **1** So am I
2 Neither did I
3 So did I
4 Neither can I
5 So was I
6 So do I

6 **1** feminist
2 peaceful
3 living conditions
4 war
5 oppression
6 consequences

7 *Student's own answers*

Page 80

1 **Problems:** burning fossil fuels, climate change, deforestation, endangered species, global warming
Solutions: clean energies, consume less, recycling, reduce waste, use public transport

2 3

3 **1** DS
2 T
3 F. They get most of it online.
4 F. It can have an impact and encourage people to do more.
5 F. It would solve 40% of the present environmental problems.

4 2

6 **1** The fact is that
2 First of all
3 Another important way
4 Furthermore, it
5 To sum up,

Page 82

1 *Student's own answers*

2 *Student's own answers*

3 *Student's own answers*

Page 83

1 **1** shake things up
2 make matters worse
3 change for the better
4 start from scratch.

2 **1** started from scratch
2 change for the better
3 To make matters worse
4 shake things up

Grammar practice

Unit 1

1 **1** Does she work in the Marketing department now?
2 Did you enjoy the film about Coco Chanel last night?
3 What do you usually do in Art class?
4 Do you go on holiday every summer?
5 When did Bill Gates create Microsoft?
6 Have you read this autobiography yet?

2 **2** a **6** b **4** c **3** d **1** e **5** f

Unit 2

1 **1** He had built the empire before he died.
2 By 2015 he was very rich because he had opened a successful business.
3 He had invented many things before he invented electricity.
4 She became famous because she had played the leading role in a lot of films.
5 He had worked in theatre before he did a feature film.
6 She had been in a band before she became a solo artist.

Unit 3

1 **1** saw
2 was driving
3 was reading
4 was
5 were doing
6 was living

2 **1** Dad said it was only a legend.
2 Susie said she believed many legends were about true events.
3 The actor said he had to leave because it wasn't safe.
4 Helen said she was feeling ill so she was going to the doctor.
5 The teacher told the class to stop talking.

Unit 4

1 **1** had lived
2 had arrived
3 hadn't read
4 started
5 was

2 **1** c **2** e **3** f **4** g **5** a **6** b **7** d

3 *Student's own answers*

Unit 5

1 **1** a **2** a **3** b **4** c **5** a

2 **1** If he hadn't gone with them, he wouldn't have disappeared.
2 If it hadn't rained, they wouldn't have crashed the car
3 If I had slept well, I would have gone to the party.
4 If they hadn't visited the tombs, they wouldn't have found a gold crown.
5 If I hadn't seen the documentary, I wouldn't have known about the controversy.
6 If we hadn't gone to the museum, we wouldn't have learnt about the pharaohs.

Unit 6

1 **1** The police didn't let the criminal go.
2 The police officer asked us to tell them what happened.
3 The neighbours heard the suspect enter/entering the house.
4 The people on the train saw the robber steal/stealing the bag.
5 The witness helped the police (to) solve the crime.
6 We wanted the inspector to look into the disappearance of our cat.

2 1 could she
2 have you
3 wasn't she
4 hadn't they
5 didn't he
6 have you

Unit 7

1 1 is spent
2 is being used
3 was created
4 are being invented
5 have been sent

2 1 can
2 should
3 might
4 could
5 should
6 must

Unit 8

1 1 who/that
2 who/that
3 that/which
4 that/which
5 who/that
6 that/which

2 1 e; My friend Tom, who spends all day online, is a digital addict.
2 d; My new tablet, which has a lot of memory, is my favourite device.
3 c; Young professionals, who often work and live abroad, use the internet to speak to their families.
4 b; Digital loneliness, which is a modern-day problem, mostly affects the young.
6 a; The car, which travels up to 200km per hour, was made in Germany.

Unit 9

1 1 so
2 such
3 such
4 so
5 so

2 1 so little
2 so much
3 so few
4 so many
6 so little

3 1 So did I.
2 Neither did I.
3 So do I.
4 So am I.
5 Neither do I.

Wordlist Exercises

Unit 1

1 1 enthusiastic; target market
2 Graphic designers; creative; imaginative
3 radio DJ; communication; talkative
4 psychologist; analytical; empathy
5 entrepreneur; negotiation; problem solving
6 run; own business; success
7 company; logo; slogan
8 Architects; earn

Unit 2

1 1 succeed; focused
2 perseverance; failure
3 passionate; achieve
4 sets goals; loses heart
5 animated; musical
6 remake; produced
7 invest; design
8 perfume; copycat

Unit 3

1 1 e
2 j
3 d
4 a
5 b
6 i
7 h
8 g
9 f
10 c

Unit 4

1 1 hospitable
2 Moon
3 satellite
4 asteroids
5 gravity
6 oxygen
7 revolve
8 Mars

Unit 5

1 1 hoax; i
2 footage; e
3 evidence; h
4 theory; a
5 Documentary; b
6 Military; f
7 construction; j
8 Debris; c
9 stone structure; d
10 Egyptian pharaoh; g

Unit 6

1 1 for/into; Student's own answers
2 out; Student's own answers
3 up; Student's own answers
4 out; Student's own answers

2 1 Potato – because the others are all fruit.
2 Criminal – the others are jobs related to the law.
3 Illegal – the others are verbs.
4 Unsolved – the others are nouns.
5 Disappearance – the others are adjectives.
6 Alibi – the others are people.
7 Steal – the others are steps in investigating crime.

Unit 7

1 1 cheating
2 install
3 junk mail
4 attachment
5 social media
6 virus
7 punishment
8 message

Unit 8

1 1 placards
2 keep in touch
3 raise awareness
4 subjective
5 conversation
6 influence
7 conference
8 privacy

Unit 9

1 1 h
2 a
3 g
4 f
5 d
6 b
7 e
8 c

2 1 air pollution
2 man-made threat
3 climate change
4 fossil fuels
5 living conditions
6 religious groups
7 human rights
8 driverless cars

Richmond ®
58 St Aldates
Oxford OX1 1ST
United Kingdom

Publishing Director: María Lera
Managing Editor: Catherine Richards
Development Editor: Ben Pincus
Editorial Team: Joanne Fairgrieve, Natalie Krol, Jayne Marshall, Siobhàn O'Connor, Nicola Strutt

Video: MTJ Media
Audio: EFS Television Production Ltd. Motivation Sound Studios

Art Director: José Crespo
Art Coordination: Rosa Marín, Javier Tejeda
Cover: EMC Design Ltd.
Design and layout: ColART Design

Technical Director: Jorge Mira Fernández
Technical Coordination: Rocío Lominchar Romero
Photo Researcher: Amparo Rodríguez

Photos:
ARCHIVO SANTILLANA

Printed in Brazil
ISBN: 978-84-668-3411-7

The editors would like to thank all those teachers and consultants who provided invaluable help and insight with their participation in this book.